T0265693

ENGAGING
—*the*—
CIVIL WAR

Chris Mackowski and Brian Matthew Jordan, Series Editors

A Public-History Initiative of Emerging Civil War
and Southern Illinois University Press

THE LEAD MINE MEN
THE ENDURING 45TH ILLINOIS VOLUNTEER INFANTRY

Thomas B. Mack

Southern Illinois University Press
Carbondale

Southern Illinois University Press
www.siupress.com

First printing July 2024.

Cover illustration: "Explosion of the mine beneath Fort Hill, Vicksburg. . . ." *House Divided: The Civil War Research Engine at Dickinson College.*

Library of Congress Cataloging-in-Publication Data
Names: Mack, Thomas B., - author.
Title: The Lead Mine men : the enduring 45th Illinois Volunteer Infantry
/ Thomas B. Mack.
Identifiers: LCCN 2022058084 (print) | LCCN 2022058085 (ebook) |
ISBN 9780809339143 (paperback) | ISBN 9780809339150 (ebook)
Subjects: LCSH: United States. Army. Illinois Infantry Regiment, 45th
(1861-1865)—History. | Illinois—History—Civil War, 1861-1865—Regimental
histories. | United States—History—Civil War, 1861-1865—Regimental
histories.
Classification: LCC E505.5 45th .M34 2024 (print) | LCC E505.5 45th (ebook) |
DDC 973.7/473—dc23/eng/20240419
LC record available at https://lccn.loc.gov/2022058084
LC ebook record available at https://lccn.loc.gov/2022058085

SIU
Southern Illinois University System

Contents

Contents

Tables and Illustrations

Tables

Maps

Figures
Gallery following page 110

Capt. John M. Adair

Republican congressman Elihu B. Washburne

Initial command staff of the 45th Illinois

Brig. Gen. John O. Duer

Capt. Luther Cowan and 1st Lt. Nesbitt Baugher

1st Sgt. Wilbur F. Crummer

1st Sgt. Nathan A. Corbin

Bivouac of the 45th near the Shirley House, Vicksburg, Mississippi

Attack of the 45th at Fort Hill crater, Vicksburg

"Explosion of the mine beneath Fort Hill"

Preface

The origins of this work go back to my childhood, when my love of history began. Encouraged by my history teachers, I devoured history books throughout my school years. Although I majored in business in college and graduate school, I continued to study history into my thirties. Soul-searching after a first-time layoff led me to pursue and gain entrance into the history doctoral program at the University of North Texas.

Initially, I planned for my dissertation to be an expansion of a thesis paper, but after some thought, and with my love of Civil War history—formed while growing up in Springfield, Illinois, home to Abraham Lincoln—I decided to make this era the focus of my research. After learning that just 20 percent of Civil War units had works devoted to them, and wanting to concentrate on the conflict's soldiers, its key participants, I began a search for Illinois infantry units that had compelling stories, had participated in the war's key battles, had been commended for their performance in battle, and had served throughout the conflict. During this research, I reviewed Frederick Dyer's three-volume work, *A Compendium of the War of the Rebellion*. Here I found Dyer's brief history of the 45th Illinois Volunteer Infantry, in which he included after the regiment's name "(Washburn Lead Mine Regiment)." Intrigued by this name, and as the 45th had fought in some of the key battles and campaigns in the war's western theater and served on the Savannah and Carolinas Campaigns, I began to search for sources on the regiment.

A key early source was Wilbur Crummer's history of his service in the regiment during the war's first two years. Here I found Crummer's account of the unit's service during the Vicksburg Campaign and, notably, its bloody fighting in the crater rent by the explosion of the mine the men had helped dig under the 3rd Louisiana Redan. Crummer's stirring description of this fighting, and of the honor the 45th received after Vicksburg's surrender, led me to find other sources, which I used to write three seminar papers on the regiment.

With my study complete, I received my doctorate in December 2015. Life and other responsibilities delayed further work on my manuscript until 2018, when I journeyed to the National Archives in Washington, D.C., and secured medical, service, and pension records for the 45th. I completed my research at the archives during a second trip in January 2020, and in February I submitted the first draft of my manuscript to Southern Illinois University Press. Further revisions followed three reviewers' suggestions for improvement. Finally, in 2022 I incorporated the suggestions for improvement from the press's Engaging the Civil War series editor and submitted the final revision of my manuscript. When the press then extended a contract for publishing, the long and rewarding journey had reached a successful conclusion.

Acknowledgments

First and foremost, this work would not have been possible without my parents, Sheila and Thomas, who nurtured and instilled in me a love of history, intellectual curiosity, and a desire for lifelong learning. In high school I had two excellent history teachers, Tom Lavin and George Trotter. At the University of North Texas, I gained entrance into the History Department's doctoral program through the help of professors Alfred Hurley and Adrian Lewis. While I was in the program, history professors Randolph B. Campbell, Harland Hagler, and Geoffrey Wawro provided expert tutelage, advice, and learned instruction. Most of all, Dr. Richard Lowe, my major advisor, helped identify the 45th Illinois as the subject of my regimental study and guided my work, with critical feedback, to its conclusion.

Along the journey to this work's completion, many have helped me find primary sources: historian Steven Woodworth at Texas Christian University; the librarians at the Abraham Lincoln Presidential Library, Jan Perone, Debbie Ross, Cheryl Schnirring, and Gwenith Podesch; National Military Park historians Terrence Winschel and David Slay at Vicksburg and Charlie Spearman at Shiloh; Col. H. Scott Wolfe, USV (ret.) of the Galena (Illinois) Public Library's Alfred Mueller Historical Collections Room; and William Shawn Scott of McAlester, Oklahoma, onetime resident of Galena, who generously shared his personal collection of files on the regiment. The staff at the University of North Texas Willis Library, specifically those in the Interlibrary Loan and Microfilm Department, obtained many books and newspaper microfilm reels for my research. The National Archives staff in Washington, D.C., helped locate the 45th's medical files, service records, and pension files. At Southern Illinois University Press, several anonymous readers and the Engaging the Civil War series editors, Brian Matthew Jordan and Chris Mackowski, read my manuscript and offered suggestions that helped improve this book. Sylvia Frank Rodrigue, the executive editor at the press, provided invaluable assistance, with the aid of acquisitions assistant Sarah Jilek. And Joyce Bond's excellent editing brought this manuscript to completion.

Hal Jespersen provided permission to use several of his Civil War maps, as did the American Battlefield Trust for its Vicksburg Campaign map. I also obtained permission from the state of Michigan to use its picture of Capt. John Adair and the Galena–Jo Daviess County (Illinois) Historical Society for its photos of the regiment's benefactor and several of its members. Other sources of pictures and engravings were Dickinson College, the Library of Congress, the Smithsonian American Art Museum, and Wikimedia Commons.

Many thanks to Elka Ortiz, whose wise counsel, advice, and understanding helped me through a very hectic 2015. Finally, to my children, Brendan and Lauren, thank you for your understanding and support throughout the many years of my studies, most especially during the many stressful times while I was working on this manuscript. I could not have completed this book without your love. Love you always, Dad!

The Lead Mine Men

ENGAGING
—*the*—
CIVIL WAR

For additional content that will let you engage this material further, scan the QR code on this page. It will take you to exclusive online material and related blog posts at www.emergingcivilwar.com.

Point your smartphone's camera at the QR code or use a QR scanner, which is readily available for download through the app store on your digital device.

✳ Introduction

Capt. John M. Adair wrote the first history of the 45th Illinois Volunteer Infantry Regiment and delivered his account in 1869 at the unit's second postwar reunion. The captain singled out the regiment for its fighting on June 25–26, 1863, during the siege of Vicksburg, noting that in being the first to attack after the mine explosion under the 3rd Louisiana Redan, the 45th experienced such horrific savagery in the fighting that it made the rest of the unit's service in the American Civil War seem like "mere boy's play in comparison." The fighting on those two days earned the regiment a place of honor eight days later, as well as lasting renown.[1]

After Confederate lieutenant general John C. Pemberton surrendered the Confederate citadel of Vicksburg, Mississippi, at 10 A.M. on July 4, 1863, Maj. Gen. Ulysses S. Grant led members of the Union's Army of the Tennessee into the captured city. Following Grant, his staff, and the corps commanders marched the 45th Illinois, given this honor because of its service during Grant's eight-month-long campaign to take Vicksburg and because it had volunteered to lead the June 25 attack. The regiment suffered a 33 percent casualty rate during the campaign, and in the assault on the Confederate bastion, it experienced severe losses, with the unit's entire command staff either killed in action or mortally or severely wounded.[2]

Adair's remembrance of the regiment's fighting on those two days in June 1863 in contrast with the rest of its experience in uniform should not detract from the stoic service the men of the 45th provided to their country throughout the war, from Camp Douglas in Chicago in 1861 to their mustering out of service in Louisville, Kentucky, in 1865. Although not all its members served honorably, the 45th Illinois as a unit never broke and ran during combat.

The 45th, called by its men the Lead Mine Regiment to honor the history of iron ore mining in Galena, Illinois, was organized in the latter half of 1861 and compiled an impressive record during the Civil War. In addition to the Vicksburg Campaign, the unit served in Grant's 1862 Tennessee Campaign, Maj. Gen. William T. Sherman's Meridian raid, and Sherman's Atlanta,

Savannah, and Carolinas Campaigns before marching in the postwar cele-bratory Grand Review in Washington, D.C., on May 24, 1865. The first phase of the regiment's service encompassed its inception, raising, and extended training period from July 1861 to January 31, 1862. During the second phase, from early February 1862 to early July 1863, the 45th's soldiers first experienced Civil War combat, fought in five major battles and minor skirmishes and actions, and served in the war's first major siege, suffering catastrophic losses from disease, sickness, and battle. These pragmatic soldiers embraced their leaders' new war goal, emancipation, and widening of the war's destruction, regardless of the impact on them or the Confederacy's citizenry. The men of the Lead Mine Regiment completed their service by reenlisting to become a veteran unit and then displayed their self-reliance, hardiness, and commitment to their republic by walking nearly 2,000 miles in implementing the Union's hard war on the Confederacy from July 1863 to July 1865. Historian Mark Grimsley stated that the Union leadership's final policy toward the Confed-eracy and its people, its hard war policy, included the use of Federal armies to go beyond the destruction of private property and taking of civilian foodstuffs to destroy Southern public property and ruin the Confederacy's economy by obliterating its industry and transportation network.[3]

While defending their republic, the Lead Mine men built an outstanding record. The regiment earned honors before entering the field and later at a corps inspection and received commendations for its fighting at Fort Donelson and Shiloh, during the Vicksburg Campaign, and later on General Sherman's Meridian raid. Some in the regiment deserted, others suffered punishments for various transgressions, and still others shirked their responsibilities during battle. Overall, however, the regiment's record is impressive. Yet despite this honored service, a study of the 45th Illinois does not exist.

In a 2008 article titled "Battling Stereotypes: A Taxonomy of Common Soldiers in Civil War History," historian Jason Phillips called for more unit studies to "retrieve some of the individuality" that the war had quashed. He pushed for these studies to counter stereotypes, especially that the "Civil War soldiers were God-fearing, independent, hard-working, family men." Accord-ing to Phillips, the studies should show these soldiers' various backgrounds, social statuses, and incomes as citizens and that they were "not angels yet not brutes," but men of their era, flawed yet fighting for their nations. Moreover, Phillips advocated for more works on the "crack regiments" of men who be-came outstanding soldiers and "merit more attention because of their excep-tional influence" on "individual soldiers or groups." Phillips argued that unit studies, unlike monographs, would "transcend historiographic debates that pigeonhole soldiers" and tell a story about "how men experienced the war" and "soldiering in the nineteenth century," as well as how to write history today. Historian Peter Carmichael, in his 2018 work on Civil War soldiers, also called for more studies of these men so as to "fully recover the life of the rank and file as it was lived." To Gary Gallagher, the Union armies "composed of citizen-soldiers occupied a central position in the grand drama," yet another reason for more unit studies.[4]

This work answers Phillips's and Carmichael's calls in part, as it shows the soldiers of the "crack" 45th Illinois as they were, men of their time, who eventually accepted President Abraham Lincoln's expansion of the Union's war goals to include the emancipation of the Confederacy's enslaved people. They knew the policy hurt their enemy's ability to wage war, and they had empathy for the enslaved after seeing the brutal realities of chattel slavery. There is no evidence, however, that the regiment's members favored emancipation for ideological reasons.

This is not to say all were patriotic Christian saints fighting for their republic. As men of their time, most likely did not see Black Americans as their equal; yet these everyday men became enthusiastic emancipators, knowing their service would aid in bringing an end to the institution of slavery. The 45th initially had a dim view of Lincoln's decision to create Black regiments, but in time these sensible men saw that the president's plan benefited them in several ways, notably by working to end the war sooner. The regiment's views of the antiwar Northern Democrat Copperheads, however, never strayed from virulent hate and desire for retribution. From their first days in the field, the 45th enthusiastically joined in the pillaging that came with the Union's increasingly hard war on the Confederacy and its citizenry, out of opportunism to gain personally, knowing that this would help shorten the war, and because they had seen the horrors of slavery. Of note, the Lead Mine men's and their comrades' pillaging happened much earlier than what several historians have contended. While some men operated as Sherman's bummers out of personal gain in implementing this hard war, the majority accepted their leaders' policy change even though it caused them severe hunger at times and increased the possibility that they could be captured and die in an enemy prisoner-of-war camp.

Over 80 percent of the Lead Mine men came from eleven northern Illinois counties dominated by Republicans but with concentrations of pro-Union Democrats when war came. That the 45th's members shared the same fervent patriotism is evident in the regiment's battle record, its reenlistment in 1864, and the fact that the Copperheads' treasonous antiwar work did not result in the unit's demoralization or the high numbers of desertions that occurred in other Union units. Compared with the Union army as a whole, the regiment suffered far fewer desertions (2.7 percent versus 8.6–14.3 percent), despite suffering greater losses as a percentage of the unit (6.7 versus 4.7 percent). A benefit to the Lead Mine men was their relationship with influential Republican congressman Elihu B. Washburne, who secured for the unit first-rate weapons and equipment, which few Illinois regiments had in 1861. Ulysses S. Grant also benefited from his relationship with Washburne.

Several of the regiment's officers and enlisted men had what was probably a unique prewar relationship with Grant, which continued during the war's first two years. This perhaps gave its members a certain level of prestige during their service and almost certainly helped the 45th achieve its honored position on July 4, 1863. The regiment's unblemished war record and many commendations and awards likely contributed to its members' esprit de corps, with many performing nobly throughout the unit's service. In a few cases, Confederate soldiers believed the unit to be regular army because of its performance, discipline, and appearance. Moreover, throughout its history, general officers consistently chose the 45th to lead attacks. That the regiment was an exceptional performing unit in the field and in combat was a result of several factors: the officers' excellent work in learning their craft and drilling their men, the culture they developed, the men's respect for their officers, the excellent character of both officers and men, and the unit's integrity.[5]

The 45th's extensive training also helped bolster the soldiers' indomitable character throughout the trials and sacrifices they experienced during their service. Unlike other Union regiments, such as the 16th Connecticut, which received scant training before entering the maelstrom of Civil War combat, the Lead Mine men had six months of training before entering battle. Besides the quality of the training provided by the unit's excellent officers, the soldiers' patriotism, fortitude, and stamina served them well as they became proficient in the art of war, even when lower-ranked officers replaced those lost to combat casualties, promotions, and resignations.

Factors playing a part in the Lead Mine men's general stamina and hardiness may have been that the unit's enlistees were generally younger than those in the Union army and that a much higher percentage had been involved in agriculture than in the army as a whole. The older average age of the unit's officers, who had more life experience and thus perhaps greater wisdom, also made possible the regiment's excellent service in its initial battles, especially in the chaos during the Battle of Shiloh. While not overly religious, the Lead Mine men used their faith in Providence to explain the war's events, a faith that was shared by civilians on both sides and soldiers in both armies and helped sustain the men throughout the conflict. All these factors, plus the regiment's untarnished combat record to date, are presumably what gave the Lead Mine men the courage to accept the mission to lead the attack on June 25, 1863, as well as to maintain their honor throughout the war.[6]

Over the last fifty-plus years, historians have gone beyond the military and political aspects of the American Civil War to include its social, cultural, and economic aspects and beyond the study of the "great white men" to include the perspective from all its actors, including enslaved and free Black Americans and the soldiers' families. The story from the perspective of the key participant in the war—the soldier—is incomplete, however. By 1980 works existed for only 20 percent of all Union and Confederate infantry, cavalry, and artillery units.

In recent years, historians have attempted to address this historiographic void. Mark Dunkelman told the story of a New York regiment that had a strong esprit de corps, fought in the eastern and western theaters, and served in Sherman's final three campaigns. Lesley Gordon focused on an eastern Union regiment that was far from exceptional and, because of its scant training, had a disastrous experience in the war. Douglas Egerton examined the creation, war experience, and impact on the Union of three Black regiments, while Kelly Mezurek looked at one Black regiment and its members' experiences during Reconstruction. Susannah Ural spotlighted a famous Confederate brigade whose commitment stood strong throughout the war, despite suffering horrendous losses, as well as the soldiers' families. David Mellott and Mark Snell considered an eastern calvary unit that kept its commitment to the Union despite suffering severe losses. Finally, Christopher Rein concentrated on a Union regiment that fought in a lightly focused theater far beyond the Mississippi River. Notably absent is a work on a unit of resilient midwesterners in the famed Army of the Tennessee. This undefeated army won at Shiloh, captured Vicksburg, aided in rescuing Chattanooga, was General Sherman's force on his Meridian raid, helped capture Atlanta, and constituted half of the general's army on his Savannah and Carolinas Campaigns, while instigating with their comrades the Union's hard war on the Confederacy. *The Lead Mine Men* fills this historiographic void.[7]

This book is a comprehensive modern unit study of the 45th Illinois Volunteer Infantry Regiment's service in the war, including the members' postwar lives. Of prime importance are the soldiers' experiences in camp, on the march, and in combat. Included is an analysis of the soldiers from demographic, social, political, and military perspectives, along with their views on slavery, emancipation, the arming of Black men, the South, Southerners, and key individuals in the war. By showing the men as they were, their good qualities as well as their human frailties and faults, this work on the Lead Mine men adds to our understanding of the Civil War soldiers, who by enlisting successfully saved their republic and ended slavery within its borders, and whose positive impact on their country lasts to this day.

The 45th's creation in mid-1861 and its members' transformation into soldiers are detailed in chapter 1, followed by a demographic study of the men and a political study of their home counties in chapter 2. Chapters 3–9 provide a chronological narrative, from the regiment's baptism into Civil War combat at Fort Donelson to its mustering out after the war's end. Chapter 10 concludes by exploring how the surviving members went back to their civilian lives after the war and fought a war of words to secure their unit's legacy.

1. ❧ From Citizen to Soldier

A huge crowd gathered for the send-off on April 25, 1861, in Galena, the seat of Jo Daviess County, in the far northwestern corner of Illinois. Included in the throng were Galena's mayor, city council, and civic societies. Following two marching bands down Main Street came the Jo Daviess Guards, a company of men recruited from Galena and neighboring areas who had answered President Abraham Lincoln's April 15 call for 75,000 soldiers to put down the rebellion. Jasper A. Maltby, a Mexican-American War veteran and future colonel of the 45th Illinois Volunteer Infantry Regiment, served as the procession's chief marshal. Just thirteen days earlier, Confederates had fired on Fort Sumter, sparking the beginning of the American Civil War. Many of Galena's notable residents had given speeches and worked to help fill the Guards' ranks, including Republican congressman Elihu B. Washburne, Ulysses S. Grant, and County Treasurer John E. Smith, a jewelry store owner, friend of Grant's, future colonel of the 45th, and later major general in the Union army. Two other friends of Grant's also helped recruit: John A. Rawlins, the lawyer for the Grant tannery, future major in the 45th, and later Grant's chief of staff and major general in the army; and William R. Rowley, Galena's clerk of the circuit court, future lieutenant in the 45th, and eventual member of Grant's staff. Galena's citizens had made the recruits' uniforms, and Grant had drilled the Guards.[1]

The soldiers left by train for Springfield to join one of six Illinois regiments formed to meet Lincoln's call. In these heady days following Fort Sumter, towns throughout the Union and Confederacy held events similar to Galena's. Most everyone, including Lincoln, the recruits, and the civilians who cheered them on, expected the war to be over quickly. The men who answered Lincoln's first call were but a small percentage of the millions who eventually donned uniforms on both sides before the war ended in April 1865, with hundreds of thousands making the ultimate sacrifice for their causes. The men of the 45th Illinois were just some of those who answered the call after the initial pomp and circumstance had died out.

Nearly one-third of the 45th's members hailed from Jo Daviess County, which was known for its lead ore mining. Native Americans first mined the ore, but the arrival of U.S. citizens in 1819 greatly increased lead ore production in the county, from 425,000 pounds in 1823 to a peak of 54.5 million pounds in 1845—83 percent of the 65 million pounds of ore mined in the United States that year. Galena's prodigious lead-mining industry made it the wealthiest city in Illinois in the 1840s and early 1850s. By 1861, however, the city had lost its preeminent position for several reasons: miners had left for the California gold rush, railroads bypassed Galena because its leaders had rejected the initial offer to build a rail line to the city, foreign lead ore production created competition, and the Galena River became unnavigable. While Galena did not prosper during the Civil War, it did provide more generals than any other city in the Union—a total of nine, including Grant, Rawlins, Smith, Maltby, Rowley, and John O. Duer, the final commander of the 45th.[2]

The 45th Illinois's informal beginning in Galena came soon after the Jo Daviess Guards left for Springfield. On April 30, 1861, a group of local men formed a unit called the Galena Greys and elected the unit's officers; the Greys eventually became Company D of the 45th. The preamble of the unit's constitution noted that its ranks consisted of patriots who stood ready to preserve the "soil and institutions" of their country against the rebellion. The state's quota had already been met, however, so the assistant adjutant general of Illinois rejected the company's offered services on May 8. Undaunted, the men continued to meet throughout May.[3]

The impetus for the regiment's official formation came on June 1 when Congressman Washburne made a formal tender to Secretary of War Simon Cameron for an independent rifle regiment from his district. Washburne, an early Republican and longtime friend of President Lincoln's, had great influence in Washington and later did much for Grant's fortunes during the war. Washburne requested that Col. John E. Smith, a prewar acquaintance, command this unit. Smith was forming up new regiments in Springfield at the time. John M. Adair, the eventual captain of the 45th's Company G and the regiment's first historian, boasted that Washburne had made the request because of the congressman's obedience to the patriotism of the people in his district and their desire to quickly organize a regiment. Not yet aware of the war's eventual scale and the number of soldiers that would be needed to win it, the War Department refused Washburne's tender.[4]

Despite this setback, men from Galena and across the district continued to sign up to fight. Peter Bellingall, a sixteen-year-old clerk at a store frequented by Grant, Rawlins, Smith, Rowley, and Washburne, obtained the hard-won written consent of his reluctant mother to enlist on June 3. The War Department required his mother's consent because he was not yet eighteen. Bellingall wrote later that on seeing the Guards and Grant leave for Springfield, "I got the fever to go into the army." A week later the private and other volunteers began training at the nearby Jo Daviess County fairgrounds.[5]

After the Union's defeat at the First Battle of Bull Run on July 21, 1861, the thought of a short war vanished for many in the Union from common citizens to President Lincoln. Within four days after the battle, the president signed two bills that authorized the enlistment of 1 million additional soldiers, which led to the War Department authorizing the raising of regiments across the Union, including the 45th Illinois. In a July 23 telegram to Colonel Smith, Washburne stated that Secretary Cameron had accepted the regiment if it could be ready to move out in fifteen days. The headlines the next day in the *Galena Daily Advertiser* read, "WAR! WAR! WAR!" The paper printed the War Department's order and called all men who believed the country had a "Government worth sustaining and perpetuating" to come to its aid and volunteer. The patriotic yet naive editor thought that with Colonel Smith, Maltby, and Rawlins in command, the regiment would have no problem meeting the deadline. Although Smith lacked military experience, the editor was certain that the colonel had the military aptitude and constitution to withstand fatigue and described him as "cool, prompt, and unflinching in the hour of danger." The editor also noted Maltby's experience as a lieutenant in the Mexican-American War, the serious wound he had suffered at the Battle of Chapultepec, and the honors he had received.[6]

Throughout July and August men enlisted in Galena and across northern Illinois, and newspapers commended the volunteers for their patriotism. Meanwhile, Melancthon Smith, a Republican Party member, former lawyer, and postmaster of Rockford, Illinois (in Winnebago County, two counties east of Jo Daviess), received permission to leave his postmaster position to raise a company for the unit. Soon a local newspaper said Melancthon Smith's company contained "some of the most sterling and wealthy men" in the county. Despite the recruiting efforts, Col. John Smith notified Washburne that he would not have the regiment ready, and the War Department extended the deadline to September 10.[7]

Early in August the soldiers nicknamed the 45th the Lead Mine Regiment to honor the county's history of lead mining. The War Department assigned as mustering officer Lt. W. F. Goodwin, who most impressed the men. Captain

Adair called him the "greatest hero of the age." Work continued to fill the regiment's ranks, with full companies sent to the fairgrounds in Galena for training. The *Warren Independent* confidently predicted a full regiment with the requisite ten companies once the men had completed the harvest and noted the current $100 enlistment bonus. On August 22 Captain Smith advertised in the *Rockford Republican* for men to fill out his company, now called the Rockford Rifles, noting he wanted "*brave substantial Men*" to serve their country from the "highest motives of patriotism." Later, the *Republican* confidently predicted that the Rifles would be at full strength in short order because of Smith's military knowledge, his known "energy of character, and his patriotic enthusiasm." On August 26 the *Galena Daily Advertiser* expressed confidence in the "crack" Galena Greys and Corcoran Guards of the city. After a parade by the Guards, the paper exclaimed, "We can safely say that no finer body of men have been seen in the streets of Galena." South of Jo Daviess, in Carroll County, the enlistees in the Mount Carroll Independent Rifles took their oaths of enlistment on August 29 and arrived in Galena after a forty-two-mile journey on wagons provided by the county's farmers.[8]

As companies formed up, they held elections to determine their officers. On August 20 Warren's Union Rifles elected Luther H. Cowan as captain and Nesbitt Baugher as first lieutenant. The *Warren Independent* noted that Cowan, the surveyor for Jo Daviess County, had a "well-known coolness in times of danger," which would make him a good officer. Cowan's diary and letters extensively documented his service and the history of the regiment up to May 1863. The paper said that Baugher would make a good officer because of his "well-known firmness and masterly ability." Here as elsewhere in the Union, by electing their company officers, the 45th's men exercised their republican citizen liberties. According to historian Andrew Bledsoe, this satisfied the Union's citizen-soldier ethos, built trust between the enlisted men and their officers, and strengthened the enlistees' devotion to the cause. When the Union Rifles moved off for Galena on August 30, the *Independent* reported that this was the "finest looking and hardiest of any set of men" seen to date and that all in the company were in "good spirits" and eager to leave. As did other mothers across the Union, Pvt. John Houlihan's mother found the parting difficult, crying and begging her son not to leave. "Mother," Houlihan responded, "no use crying. Woman's tears cannot save the Union." Despite the comfort given by onlookers, the inconsolable mother believed she would never see her son again. Sadly, her premonition proved correct, as Houlihan, wounded at the Battle of Shiloh, later died of scarlet fever in Vicksburg, Mississippi.[9]

As August ended, Galena's city leaders renamed the county fairgrounds Camp Washburne in honor of the congressman's work to create the regiment. On September 2 Washburne persuaded the War Department to extend the deadline for raising the unit to October 1, and he communicated instructions for the regiment's transportation, how to order its equipment, and how to get the soldiers' uniforms made. The congressman's most significant act, however, was his acquisition of 1,000 new Enfield rifles. With the promise of the rifles from the chief of ordnance, Brig. Gen. James W. Ripley, Washburne wrote to Colonel Smith, "I believe I have done all that can be done and I hope your regiment will now go right ahead." He had indeed provided much for the men: instead of outdated smoothbore muskets or inferior rifled weapons, they received modern rifles, weapons given to only five other Illinois regiments in 1861.[10]

Captain Adair considered the starting point of the 45th's history to be Colonel Smith's naming of 1st Lt. William T. Frohock of Company A to command the camp on September 5, 1861. Some recruits complained about the harsher life of a soldier and called their lodging and food "barbarous," but Adair later wrote, "Had we known what we had to endure before our terms had expired, how contentedly we would have adapted ourselves to the circumstances." As the men began their squad, company, and battalion drilling, they had to endure unseasonably cold weather for early September. Later in the month, some soldiers caused a brawl in Galena in which a thrown rock severely injured one civilian, while other, less rowdy men stole watermelons from a local farmer as he negotiated terms of sale with some officers. Apparently, some Lead Mine men, like new recruits across the Union, chafed under the military discipline in camp. Adair recalled that in a short time, the men felt confident they knew more about drilling than any book could teach them and thought themselves ready for war. Perhaps it was the brawling or mischief with the watermelons that caused Colonel Smith to name Capt. Melancthon Smith of Company F as drill instructor in late September. Under the captain's tutelage, the men realized they were not ready. According to Luther Cowan, Captain Smith subjected the men "to rigid discipline and drill," and they made "rapid progress in the knowledge of the tactics and drill." Smith and other officers and their men likely studied Winfield Scott's 1835 manual and William J. Hardee's 1855 manual. The seriousness with which Captain Smith and the men of the regiment approached their training would hold them well in the fighting to come in 1862.[11]

In early September, however, Captain Smith had only sixty men recruited and worked hard in Rockford to fill out his company. A paper boasted of the captain's patriotism and that the current enlistees were "moral, sober, intelligent, and patriotic," the best in Illinois, men who had resolved to "vindicate the Nation's honor on the field of blood," would protect the Union's "free institutions," and would defeat the "minions and myrmidons of the slave power." Historian Chandra Manning echoed what the editor found—that in going to war, the soldiers in both armies, as well as the civilians on both sides, believed the institution of slavery had caused the war. During September, Colonel Smith traveled to Waukegan, Illinois, 150 miles east of Galena in Lake County, to add men to the regiment. The trip produced few recruits, despite a newspaper publishing the colonel's recruitment letter and his requisition for the regiment's Enfields.[12]

During September the people of Jo Daviess County worked to help the soldiers. Local tailors in Galena made the unit's uniforms, and civilians from the area brought "roast chickens, turkeys, cakes, [and] pies." On September 18 some 4,000 civilians and four sister companies met Captain Smith and the Rockford Rifles when their train arrived in Galena. The Lead Mine men listened to a patriotic speech, which was followed by a generous dinner at a local house. An impressed observer of the Rifles said, "*There is morality enough in that Company to save any Regiment from becoming demoralized.*" Shortly thereafter, Colonel Smith promoted the Rifles' captain, Melancthon Smith, to major; the promotion was necessary because Brig. Gen. Ulysses S. Grant, with Congressman Washburne's orchestration, named Major Rawlins to his staff in August. On September 20 the *Galena Daily Advertiser* published the words to the "Lead Mines Rally" and called for men to enlist to protect their country, their government, free institutions, and their flag, exhorting them not to give up until "each traitor in death is laid low!" The paper also commended Anderson Chapman of Hanover, in Jo Daviess County, and his four sons for enlisting. Sadly, the war wound up taking a severe toll on the Chapman family: disabilities forced Anderson to transfer to the Veteran Reserve Corps, son John died of fever in May 1862, and his brother Thomas, wounded in the jaw at Shiloh, died in September 1863 of chronic diarrhea.[13]

By the end of September, seven companies drilled at Camp Washburne. The 45th Illinois ended the month with a somber duty and a lesson on the impermanence of life in uniform. The Lead Mine men had to transport several dead Galena soldiers from another regiment from the train station to a cemetery and bury them after the services. The soldiers had died in Indiana when the bridge their train was crossing collapsed into a river. After burying the fallen men, the 45th returned to camp and enjoyed a huge picnic hosted by people from nearby towns. One report noted the "bountiful feast, infinite in variety"—an assortment and amount of food the men would surely miss when subsisting on standard army fare. The event included patriotic speeches by two preachers and music from several bands and left the Lead Mine men full of "glad hearts." Receiving food and encouragement from local civilians was a common experience shared by army comrades elsewhere in the Union.[14]

The 45th still lacked the requisite ten companies and recruiting continued in October. The local newspapers repeatedly touted the regiment and called for volunteers. On October 8 one paper announced that the first shipment of Enfield rifles would soon arrive in Galena. The *Freeport Bulletin* boasted that the 45th would become a "crack" regiment, in part because of Colonel Maltby's service in the Mexican-American War. The colder-than-normal October weather, the lack of adequate clothing, and the camp's leaky barracks caused many in the unit to suffer greatly. Despite their suffering, Captain Cowan heard little grumbling from his men and considered them "true patriots" for admirably tolerating the situation with patience and determination. Soldiers across the Union shared these same hardships. This month also saw the first men leave the regiment: on October 11 Colonel Smith drummed out Pvt. William H. Frasier for stealing, and on October 28 Pvt. Jonathan Bonney deserted.[15]

The men continued to drill throughout October as they waited for their uniforms and rifles. Visitors commented on the camp's cleanliness and the men's robust health from the wholesome food supplied to them. Meanwhile, Congressman Washburne worked to expedite the regiment's rifles. After seeing the Enfields in an arsenal, he wrote to Maltby, "Our boys will be delighted" with the superb weapons. The uniforms secured by Colonel Smith arrived in Galena on Friday, October 25, bringing shouts of joy from the men and enabling the entire regiment to be fully uniformed. The next day Major Smith took the fully uniformed Company F into Galena for "military evolutions" in front of the town's civilians, and local papers expressed hope that the uniforms would entice men to enlist.[16]

As November began, the uniformed men still did not have rifles, but more than half had overcoats. The regiment's leadership was formalized, with Colonel Smith, Lieutenant Colonel Maltby, and Major Smith in command;

Lieutenant Frohock as adjutant; and Dr. Edward D. Kittoe as head surgeon. On November 5 the colonel received an order to have his companies ready to leave Camp Washburne by the fifteenth. The men cleaned their quarters and prepared to move to Camp Douglas in Chicago. From November 9 to 16 the unit's Enfield rifles arrived, which the soldiers "proudly . . . shouldered." The much-impressed editor of the *Galena Daily Advertiser* wrote that the Enfield was "one of the neatest imaginable" weapons, "armed with the Sabre bayonet." News of the unit's new rifles reached the *Chicago Tribune*, which lauded the congressman's unflagging efforts to secure them: "Well done, Mr. Washburne."[17]

Five days later the entire regiment marched to Galena and received two stands of colors "of the most beautiful design and texture," which brought enthusiastic cheers from the soldiers. Colonel Smith thanked the ladies who had sewn the American flag and regimental banner and the townspeople who had donated money for their creation. Like other Union commanders who received flags from local citizens, Smith promised that the colors would never "be tainted with dishonor." Adair asserted that this promise had been kept, stating that the men never deserted nor disgraced the flags.[18]

The next week was momentous, as the regiment was to leave Galena for Chicago by train. Although the unit did not yet have its full complement of ten companies, it was equipped with everything it needed to go to war, including cartridges and balls, boxes of packing ammunition, infantry accoutrements, cartridge boxes, caps, pouches, gun slings, belts, and sheaths. Major Smith received an outstanding horse from the people of Galena and his former company, whose men expressed their love for Smith and said they were "proud to hail him as their Major," which brought tears to the officer's eyes. Friends in Galena and nearby Scales Mound gave Dr. Kittoe a saddle and "one of the finest horses." The doctor expressed his "warm and heartfelt acknowledgements" for the generous gifts, though he believed them unwarranted, and noted that despite his English birth, he had always been treated as a "friend and a brother."[19]

Before leaving for Chicago, the officers voted to change the name of the unit to the Washburne Lead Mine Regiment, 45th Illinois Volunteers, in honor of the congressman's "untiring and successful efforts" to outfit the regiment with the best equipment and weapons. Washburne thanked Colonel Smith and said he had only done what he owed the unit's patriotic men, who had enlisted to put down the "existing wicked and causeless rebellion." The congressman confidently predicted that the Lead Mine men would "vindicate the honor of the National Flag and give additional luster to the glory" of the state he loved. In humbly accepting the tribute, Washburne said he believed it a great honor to be associated with the unit but feared it was undeserved.[20]

Having broken up Camp Washburne the day before, at midafternoon on November 23 the seven companies marched to the train depot fully uniformed, their fixed bayonets "flashing . . . like a line of light," and boarded a train bound for Camp Douglas, about 171 miles to the east (see Map 1.1). Before leaving, F. A. Hope of Galena presented the unit with its own music, titled the "Lead Mine Regiment Quickstep." Escorted by Galena's fire department and brass band, the 45th marched, according to one observer, with greater discipline than on previous occasions. Some soldiers had mixed emotions about parting with their friends and family; nonetheless, the men boarded the train's twelve cars amid "shouts and hearty salutations" and expressions of goodwill from thousands of people. Such great fanfare and patriotic farewells were a common occurrence across the Union and Confederacy as regiments departed for war.[21]

Accompanied by Washburne, the regiment arrived in Chicago early on Monday, November 25. At one of the train's stops, the Lead Mine men were

Map 1.1. Key counties supplying men to the 45th Illinois and route from Galena to Chicago, November 23–25, 1861. *Sources: Office of the Illinois Secretary of State, Muster and Descriptive Rolls; map of Illinois counties created by David Benbennick on February 2, 2007, https://commons.wikimedia.org/wiki/File:Map_of_Illinois_counties.svg* (changes made to the original).

pleased when a large group of people met them and cheered, said goodbye, threw kisses, hurrahed, and cried. Other than this stop, to one soldier the trip was "unimportant: rainy, sleepy, somewhat thoughtful, somewhat sad, otherwise joyous." Situated four miles south of Chicago's courthouse, Camp Douglas covered forty-two acres of land donated by the estate of the late senator Stephen Douglas. The famous Wigwam, where Abraham Lincoln had won the Republican nomination for president eighteen months earlier, was three miles north of the camp and became the enlisted men's first home, while the officers lived in a nearby house. During the winter of 1861–62, 25,000 soldiers from thirty-one units trained at Camp Douglas. Later in 1862 the camp housed captured Confederates.[22]

The men suffered greatly during their four days in the Wigwam. The building provided little protection from the cold, and the close quarters facilitated the spread of several diseases. It was a "villainous place" to Captain Adair. The sickness experienced by the men in the Wigwam, in Camp Douglas, and later in Cairo, Illinois, was similar to the experience of other Civil War units. Overcrowding and unsanitary conditions caused diseases to easily spread among the soldiers, and most regiments lost considerable numbers before entering battle for the first time.[23]

After the soldiers had moved three miles south into their Camp Douglas barracks, one reported that the regiment's health was good, with a normal number of colds and "minor complaints," but another said the number of sick men in the unit increased with an outbreak of scarlet fever. Pvt. William Tebbetts told his parents that the men were as comfortable as possible and had enough to eat, but that their conditions were very rough. As with other camps during the war, one cause of sickness and death in Camp Douglas was the lack of a sewer line. The camp's commandant requested one, which would have cost $7,000, but the Illinois legislature declined his request.[24]

In early December Dr. Kittoe worked urgently to improve the men's health. Kittoe reported that the weather that had replaced the bitter cold was as "bad as possible, warm, wet and foggy," and had made the entire camp a knee-deep "perfect mudhole." The doctor noted that in general, the men were in good condition, but that he had seen 100 cases of measles. The day before, the doctor had returned another 100 men to duty. Thus the unit had over 20 percent of its members sick at one time. On December 6 Kittoe found Major Smith sick with cholera. Luckily, the major's health greatly improved over the next few days. Captain Cowan described the barracks as providing little protection from the cold and said that this and the insufficient number of stoves in the barracks were causes of the sickness in camp. The soldiers' housing was built with poor-quality green lumber, resulting in cracks in the walls; these were so big that Colonel Smith joked that the men used the cracks to see out rather than the windows. Measles caused the most Lead Mine men to fall sick; others fell ill with diarrhea, fever, rheumatism, bronchitis, typhoid fever, or mumps.[25]

During the four days the Wigwam housed the enlisted men, Company I joined the regiment. The company hailed mostly from Lake County, the northeasternmost in Illinois, and from the western counties of Mercer, Henry, and Rock Island (see Map 1.1). In short order, the company elected Oliver A. Bridgford as captain, and the original captain from Lake County, James Balfour, agreed to be first lieutenant. In early December two companies of the Rock Island Regiment became Companies H and K in the 45th, giving the unit the requisite ten companies. These men also hailed from Rock Island, Mercer, and Henry Counties, as well as nearby Knox County. Meanwhile, Lt. William R. Rowley of Company D returned to Galena to recruit men so that the company could reach the 100-man quota. A Galena paper petitioned for men to sign up, boasting about the unit's officers, predicting the war would be over in short order, and advertising the enlistment bounty of $100 in gold.[26]

A soldier's letter printed in a Galena newspaper provides a glimpse of life in camp. Despite the sickness there, most men thought it was a "good omen" for the men defending the country to stay in the "great National Wigwam" where a "President was made." The man reported on the bitterly cold weather, "prairie winds," and snow covering the ground. The soldier also noted that before entering Camp Douglas, the regiment had paraded through the streets of Chicago for three miles, and as they entered the camp, they "stepped with a more lively motion and grasped their arms with commendable energy" as they marched to their barracks. Soldiers and spectators lined their route, and another member reported that the regiment's Enfield rifles impressed onlookers. In another parade two days later, the unit's "martial bearing and excellent appearance" impressed onlookers.[27]

The daily routine for the Lead Mine men, as well as their 5,000 comrades in camp, consisted of reveille at sunrise, many drills and roll calls, and lights out bugled at 9:30 P.M., ending each day. Some in camp used their free time to attend prayer meetings on Thursday and Sunday evenings, and most soldiers besieged the camp's post office daily for papers and letters. The 45th had traded "hair mattresses and turkey dinners" in Galena for a "pine board and coffee without cream." They had little leisure time and could visit Chicago only with a pass signed by several officers. A high fence surrounded Camp Douglas, and one-story, company-size barracks lined the camp, with the space in between used for drill. The enlisted men slept in one great room, with three men to each flat wooden bed, while the officers and first sergeant slept in a separate room. All ate in "cook houses" attached to the back of each barracks.[28]

Back home, the newspapers boasted about the regiment. The *Waukegan Weekly Gazette* proclaimed that Illinois had no better unit and that the men in the "crack" Company I had the "vigor of manhood" to withstand the work and privations they would soon face. The *Gazette* and the *Chicago Daily Tribune* pointed out that the 45th was the only Illinois regiment that had all its weapons and equipment before leaving for war. Both papers lauded the extraordinary effort made by Washburne in obtaining the Enfield rifles and the fact that every man had the same weapon, whereas most regiments had a mixture of arms. The *Tribune* went farther, saying, "This regiment is completely armed and equipped in a manner equal if not superior to any regiment in the field from the state" and that the men were "well drilled." The *Gazette* noted that Company I, like other organizations across the West, faced stiff recruiting competition from other units. Indeed, forty-three infantry, cavalry, and artillery units recruited for men in the eleven counties that contributed the bulk of men to the unit.[29]

On December 7 the men received their first two months' pay, $26, which caused scores of sutlers to descend on them "like vultures to the dead," attempting to sell the soldiers tobacco, fruit, stationery, pastry, and all manner of trinkets and luxury items. While soldiers of other units bought eagerly, a man from the 45th bragged that many in his unit sent most of their money home for "safe keeping," while others still had an unbroken $20 bill. The Lead Mine men marveled at Chicago, a "greater Babel" of a city in late 1861. Some soldiers visited the house and grave of the late senator Stephen Douglas, about 1,300 feet from the camp, and reflected on why they were in a camp named after him. For some in the 45th, the routine of camp life paled in comparison to Chicago. On Monday, December 23, when a few members slipped out of camp without a signed pass to drink alcohol at a nearby bar, the unit's officers tasked others with finding their comrades and returning them to camp. In January the 45th's Pvt. John Stone nearly died from exposure before his fellow soldiers found him almost frozen to death in the city.[30]

As many of the men were away from their families for the first time, they worried about how their loved ones were making out in their absence. Captain Cowan, in a letter to his wife on December 9, sent home a piece of fine cloth he had bought for a cheap price, saying he hoped his wife could make clothes for his children. Cowan regretted that he could not send any money because of the cost of his two sets of uniforms and his officer's sword; the captain had to borrow money to buy a new set of uniforms, as his first was not up to Colonel Smith's expectations. Owing money and thus not being able to send much home was a common misfortune among Union enlisted men and officers. Cowan thanked his wife and his daughters for their letters, complimented his daughter on her adultlike writing, and promised to send pictures of himself in his new uniform.[31]

Life in camp to one member of the regiment meant "some drill, considerable pomp and circumstance, and very much mud." The "pomp and circumstance" included escorting, with the rest of the camp, another regiment as it marched to the railway station for their trip to St. Louis. The march was an "imposing affair," with Lake Michigan on the horizon and the "great city" to their front and right. On the march, the men had to "avoid the innumerable Michigans of mud," and as the tired soldiers trudged back to camp, they reached their barracks only after a "ragged" battalion drill.[32]

By December 20 the newness of Camp Douglas had worn off for the men of the regiment, with life in camp becoming a tedious and unchanging routine of drill and other repetitive duties. One member, however, bragged in a letter home that the regiment's prowess at drill gave it an "entirely honorable and creditable" reputation "not often attained by Volunteer Regts." Chicago newspapers, though, misreported that the "Lead Mine Fence Climbers" had rioted. In actuality, it was the 56th Illinois Infantry, the "Mechanic Fusileers," who had built the camp and rioted after receiving lower wages than they had expected. The Fusileers tore down part of the camp's fence behind the 45th's barracks, escaped the guard, and attacked and partially destroyed a sutler's store. Under orders, two of the 45th's companies suppressed the revolt. The next night the Fusileers rioted again, tearing down even more of the camp's fence. The officer of the guard then called out the entire Lead Mine Regiment, whose men, with bayonets fixed, quelled the uprising and returned the rioters back to camp. Major Smith protested about the newspapers' error to the camp's commandant and to the *Chicago Times*. Smith defended the regiment's honor and pointed out that in fact, the 45th had quelled the riots, and for its service, it had received three cheers from the other men in camp. One member reported that some soldiers in camp had lied to the papers because they were a "little jealous" of the 45th's Enfield rifles and proficiency in drill.[33]

In mid-December Colonel Smith, Lieutenant Colonel Maltby, and Lieutenant Rowley petitioned their prewar acquaintance Brig. Gen. Ulysses S.

Grant to order the unit to his headquarters in Cairo. Grant sent a request to the assistant adjutant general for the Department of Missouri for the regiment's transfer, noting that the unit came with "improved arms for 1,000 men and clothing for the same" and that its members were anxious to get to Cairo. It took eight days for the order to move south to arrive.[34]

On December 25, 1861, Christmas Day, 920 Lead Mine men took their oaths and mustered into service for three years. Of those who had enlisted, 18 were no longer among their numbers. Diseases had caused 2 deaths, and 4 soldiers were discharged because of disability and other reasons. Colonel Smith drummed 1 man out of the regiment for stealing, another 3 transferred to other units, 2 officers resigned their commissions, and 6 men deserted.[35]

In late 1861, as they prepared to enter the war, the men of the 45th, like their countrymen in northern Illinois, held firm to their belief in Providence, that God "the Almighty ruled over affairs large and small." In this they joined the rest of the Civil War generation, civilian and soldier, Confederate and Unionist, and those of all faiths, as demonstrated by historian George Rable in his religious history of the war. Rable showed how faith in Providence helped provide consolation after a military defeat or losing a loved one in the conflict, explained victories, and "undoubtably helped sustain morale and lengthen the war." The editor of the *Warren Independent* wished "God-speed" when the regiment left for Chicago and again when the men left for Cairo and declared that God would enable the regiment's success. The *Freeport Bulletin* reported that the people cheered and said "God Bless You" to the men when they left Chicago. The regiment's members relied on their faith in Providence to explain events throughout the war. In Chicago, Private Tebbetts, in expressing sorrow for being away from his family, urged them to "trust in God and all will be well," pronouncing, "There is a brighter day coming." An unnamed comrade wrote home that "Providence permitting," the regiment would perform well in its first battle.[36]

Most members of the 45th likely enlisted for patriotic reasons, urged by their governor, Richard Yates, to "rally once again for the old flag, for our country, Union and liberty." Patriotism as discussed here is defined as devotion to and vigorous support of one's country. The men enlisted, as did the majority of those in northern Illinois, to save the Union. Pvt. John Houlihan declared that patriotism was why he had enlisted—to save the Union—and Pvt. Peter Bellingall enlisted because he felt the patriotic "fever to go into the army." Private Tebbetts noted that although peer pressure, the desire not to look "like cowards," was one reason why he and his brothers had enlisted, patriotism was their main reason—to sustain the "best government that ever was" and not let the "rebels tear down and destroy" the country for which their "forefathers fought, bled, and died." Here Tebbetts echoes what Gary Gallagher finds as the motivation for most Union soldiers to enlist: to save the Union that the Revolutionary War generation had created from the evil slavery aristocracy that was bent on destroying said republic. Tebbetts volunteered despite having a wife, five young children, and a promising position as a high school principal. Sadly for his family, the private paid the ultimate sacrifice, being killed during the Battle of Shiloh on April 6, 1862. Years later, in his service memoirs, Wilbur Crummer echoed Tebbetts's sentiments. Captain Cowan wrote to his wife that he had enlisted "to change the course of [his] life" and to prove his manhood so that his wife would "never be ashamed," and that he would rather die than to be reported a coward back home. Cowan epitomized historian Peter Carmichael's practical Union soldier in noting that he would "take things as they come." Perhaps it was because of the unit's patriotic citizen-soldiers, who, like the majority of their Union comrades, served to sustain their republic, their guarantor of liberty, equality, and self-government, that most in the unit were able to keep their resolve and commitment to their country during the war.[37]

Although not his primary reason for volunteering, ending slavery was a secondary reason for Sgt. John P. Jones. After the war, he stated that slavery was the "great overwhelming cause" of the war and said that if he had "not believed that the war would extinguish slavery, [he] would not have volunteered in defense of the Government." Jones thought this was the "dominating motive of thousands" to enlist. He expanded on why he had enlisted: "It was not excessive bravery. It was not for pay. It was not for glory or adventure, but simply to aid in 'preserving the Union,'" and in so doing, "it meant the death knell of slavery." Historians Peter Carmichael, Gary Gallagher, and Zachery Fry found other Union soldiers who, like Jones, believed that to save the Union, slavery had to be extinguished.[38]

Historians have studied extensively why the Civil War soldiers volunteered. The consensus is that most Union soldiers enlisted for patriotic reasons—to preserve the best government in the world and protect their liberties against the threat posed by the rebellion of slaveholders and "traitors." Other reasons the men mentioned included "the prevailing excitement, the lure of far places and the desire for change," "war fever," and peer pressure from friends and family members who were enlisting. Additionally, historian Bell I. Wiley found that the recession during the war's early years prompted some to enlist for the consistent $13 monthly salary of an enlisted man. While most Union soldiers enlisted for multiple reasons, Wiley reported that only 10 percent joined primarily to free the enslaved. This is a small percentage, but according to historians, many Union soldiers enlisted to fight against the slaveholders. Historians Gary Gallagher, James McPherson, and Zachery Fry discovered soldiers who noted they had enlisted to defeat "slave power." In defeating these aristocrats, or "oligarchs," who were threatening to destroy the Union, the soldiers would save their country and secure free labor and the soldiers' freedoms as guaranteed by the Constitution. Other soldiers enlisted to protect their manhood or honor, or their family's honor, by showing courage in battle, which also displayed a man's faith in God.[39]

At the end of 1861, just six weeks away from entering battle, the Lead Mine men, like many of their comrades, were filled with great anticipation of fighting patriotically to restore their Union. The pragmatic 45th had proven their mettle in putting down the Fusileers' riots and had drilled diligently under the dutiful attention of their officers during their lengthy training. Their excellence and commitment to learning the art of war would soon be demonstrated in combat.[40]

2. ❄ The Men of the 45th

From a demographic perspective, Leonard A. Stearnes perhaps epitomized the Lead Mine men. He enlisted in 1861 at the age of 18, joining other young enlistees who were single, lived in Illinois before the war, and were born in the United States. Like nearly two-thirds of the 45th, Stearnes was a farmer. It is probable that the young age and agricultural background of many of the unit's members gave them the stamina to withstand the long walks and travails encountered during their service. Stearnes survived wounds in the unit's two most terrible experiences: the Battle of Shiloh and the June 25, 1863, attack in the 3rd Louisiana crater during the Vicksburg siege. The private lived in the fervently pro-Union and Republican Winnebago County, which likely imbued in him a strong love of his country that led him to enlist.[1]

A total of 938 officers and enlisted men joined the Washburne Lead Mine Regiment during 1861. Besides the 10 companies, the headquarters staff consisted of 9 officers and enlisted men, and 15 musicians formed the unit's band. In addition to the initial 938 soldiers, another 551 men joined the unit after 1861, with most doing so in 1864. Of these new enlistees, 220 never reported for duty. This left 331 men to refill the ranks during the conflict, a number that fell woefully short of replacing those lost during the war as a result of sickness, disease, disabilities, desertions, accidents, wounds, and deaths in battle.[2] (See Table 2.1.)

On average, the enlisted men of the 45th were younger than their comrades in the Union army, while the unit's officers were older. Pvt. Charles W. Post, just 13 years old, was only four feet, eight inches tall—the same height as an Enfield rifle and one of the 157 Illinois enlistees who stood five feet, one inch or shorter. Three other Illinois men enlisted at this young age, while Pvt. Solomon Brunor enlisted at 64. Post and Brunor represented the youngest and oldest of the 1,269 men who served in the unit. (See Table 2.1.) The unit's men averaged 25.1 years, very near the average in the army. The 45th's enlisted men averaged 24.9 years of age at the time of enlistment, nearly 11 months younger than the average of 25.8 found by Benjamin Gould in his study of

Table 2.1. Men mustered into service in the 45th, 1861–65

Year	Total # of enlistees	%	# of enlistees who served	%
1861	938	63.0	938	73.9
1862	69	4.6	64	5.0
1863	34	2.3	34	2.7
1864	418	28.1	204	16.1
1865	28	1.9	28	2.2
N/A	2	0.1	1	0.1
Total	1,489		1,269	

Source: Office of the Illinois Secretary of State, Muster and Descriptive Rolls.

1,012,273 enlisted Union soldiers. The largest group of enlisted men in both the regiment and Gould's study was 18-year-olds, while the second-largest was 19-year-olds in the 45th but 21-year-olds in the army as a whole. This means that 29.2 percent of the enlisted Lead Mine men were under age 20 when they enlisted, while only 20.2 of Illinois soldiers and 23.1 of all Union soldiers were under 20.[3] (See Appendix Tables B.1 and B.2.)

The regiment's officers averaged 31.6 years of age, 22 months older than the 29.9-year average age of the 37,184 officers in Gould's study. The older age of the 45th's officers may have given them greater wisdom and experience, allowing for better decision-making in the heat of battle, all of which would have contributed to the unit's excellent performance in Civil War combat.[4] (See Appendix Table B.1.)

Historians Bell I. Wiley and Kathleen Shaw both found that many younger Union men lied about their age to circumvent the army regulation requiring men to be 18 to enlist without a parent's consent. The 1860 U.S. Census points to at least three young Lead Mine men who lied about their age. James Houlihan and Archibald Mathison likely both were only 17 but stated they were 19 when they enlisted in 1861, and Pvt. Michael O'Conner enlisted at a stated age of 18 in early March 1865 but was probably only 16. Despite their young age, Mathison and Houlihan reenlisted and survived the war. Private O'Conner, however, died in a New York hospital of typhoid fever on March 29, 1865, presumably without having served in the field. Older members, who may have been rejected had they stated their actual age, also lied. Private Brunor stated he was 43 in 1861, but his discharge papers in 1862 put him at

64, and Pvt. James Wild, who died of pneumonia in early 1862, stated that he was 44 years old when he volunteered, but medical records showed him to be 52. With nearly four times more men 19 or younger than those 40 and older, the Lead Mine men likely averaged younger than 25.1.[5]

Historian William Marvel challenged James McPherson's thesis that the Civil War was not a "rich man's war and poor man's fight," as well as McPherson's and other historians' contention that a majority of Union soldiers at the start of the war enlisted out of patriotism. Marvel conceded that Union soldiers enlisted for a variety of reasons, but his research demonstrates that the median wealth of 94 Union companies all fell below their states' median wealth. Because of this and the ongoing economic recession in 1861, Marvel concluded that "economic influences" caused many soldiers to enlist in the Union army for the consistent army pay.[6]

Applying Marvel's methodology shows that the men of the 45th Illinois averaged $1,904 of wealth compared with $528 for Illinois. The median wealth of the regiment, though, came to just $400 compared with $815 for the state. The young age of many in the unit is probably why 263 members had no wealth in 1860. A review of the wealth of just a few of the regiment's members demonstrates how reliance on raw numbers to determine motivations for enlisting is problematic. For instance, Quartermaster Evans Blake, a banker, reported $4,000 in wealth in the 1860 census ($117,180 in today's dollars), so it is unlikely Blake enlisted for the $25-a-month quartermaster wage. Dr. Edward Kittoe chose to serve despite having $11,000 in wealth in 1860. And Pvt. John A. Rollins, given his father's substantial wealth of $65,000, likely did not enlist for the $13-a-month private's salary. Two members commented on pay not being a motivation for enlisting. Sgt. John P. Jones stated he had not enlisted for the pay, and in July 1862 Capt. Luther Cowan wrote to his wife that he had enlisted knowing that at home he could earn more in a month than he could make in a year as an officer. Later, Cowan, in writing about the suffering by the soldiers, stated that "anyone who has formed the opinion that the thirteen dollars per month is what the soldiers are soldiers for, is very much mistaken in his conclusion." These examples do not align with Marvel's thesis, nor does the fact that the regiment's average wealth was twice that of the state's average.[7]

The Lead Mine men's ability to withstand their tribulations while in uniform may have stemmed from the fact that nearly two out of three, or 65.4 percent, had worked in the labor-intensive field of farming before the war. This percentage is higher than in all but two of the units and populations others have studied. A total of 834 members of the 45th had worked in agriculture. In contrast, only 51 percent of the adult males in Illinois and 43 percent of a sample of Union males listed farmer or farm hand as their occupation in the census. Just 49 percent in Gould's sample and 48 percent in Wiley's sample of Union veterans worked in agriculture. Only Gould's sample of Illinois veterans, with 66.6 percent, and the Confederate Walker's Texas Division, with 78.1 percent, had a higher percentage of farmers than the 45th. Most notably, the unit had a higher percentage of farmers than in Wiley's sample of 9,057 Confederate soldiers and his sample of white males in seven Confederate states. (See Appendix Tables B.3 and B.4.) Given the dominance of agriculture in the Southern economy, this is a significant aspect of the 45th Illinois. In total, the members had held eighty-four different occupations before the conflict.[8]

According to the regiment's muster rolls, Pvt. William Bryson from Jo Daviess County and 103 of his comrades in the regiment were Irish-born. These members made up 8.3 percent of the unit—its largest group of foreign-born men. German-born members were the next largest, at 6.9 percent. The regiment's compiled nativity from the muster rolls contradicts Ella Lonn's sources, which indicated that the 45th Illinois was half German. Gould's and Wiley's studies both found that German-born soldiers outnumbered Irish-born in the Union army as a whole. Non-native-born men made up 26.2 percent of the 45th, slightly more than the 24.5 percent in Gould's study and nearly equal to the percentage of foreign-born in Wiley's sample of 14,330 Federal troops. This percentage was greater than the 22 percent of foreign-born Union soldiers from Illinois, the 20 percent of foreign-born Illinoisans in 1860, and the 15 percent of foreigners in the United States at the time. The westward movement of Americans during the nineteenth century is likely why 227 New York–born members made up the largest contingent of native-born men in the regiment—more than the 212 men born in Illinois. Overall, the men were born in forty-three different states and countries.[9] (See Appendix Table B.5.)

Sgt. Wilbur F. Crummer, the eventual author of a history of the regiment, lived in Illinois before his enlistment, as did 1,143 other men, 90 percent of the unit. All told, men came from forty-two different Illinois counties and twelve other states to enlist in the 45th. Of the 1,143 Illinois men, 1,058, or 83.4 percent of the 45th, hailed from eleven counties. (See Map 1.1 in chapter 1 and Appendix Table B.6.) Nearly one-third of all members, 393 enlistees, or 31 percent, resided in Jo Daviess County.[10]

With the number of young men in the regiment, it is not surprising that the 45th Illinois included only a small minority of married men and an even smaller number of fathers. Just one in five members, 21.4 percent, were married when they joined up. Even fewer, 189 men, or 14.9 percent of the unit, were fathers. Of those married, two out of three were fathers. Of the unit's forty-five officers, 42.2 percent were both married and fathers, or over three times the percentage of enlisted soldiers who were married fathers. (See Appendix Table B.7.) The low number of married members may have been one factor in the reenlistment of more than 75 percent of the regiment in early 1864.[11]

Nearly 40 percent of the 551 men who enlisted in the 45th Illinois after 1861, a total of 220, never reported for duty. There were a few notable differences between these men and those who served in the unit. They likely received a substantial bonus for enlisting or for agreeing to be a substitute for another man, but their failure to report hurt the strength of the 45th in the war. Eugene Murdock found that once President Lincoln instituted the draft in 1862, bounties increased as communities, counties, and states added to the Federal bounty to meet their quotas and avoid the negative stigma of resorting to a draft. Some enlistees received more than $1,000. Ella Lonn noted that as bounties increased, more men failed to report. The army considered these men deserters; the public labeled them bounty jumpers. Given the $289 average yearly income in 1860, bounty jumping was financially lucrative, especially for those who repeated the practice in several communities. The first draft in September 1862 included bounties to entice volunteers, and perhaps not coincidentally, the five men who enlisted in the 45th that month, substitutes all, failed to report. In 1864, out of 214 deserters, 211 were substitutes, and all but one enlisted in the fall draft—the draft that Murdock concluded had the highest bounties paid out during the war and the highest percentage of deserters.[12]

All 220 bounty jumpers were enlisted men and averaged five months younger, 24.4 years of age, than the enlisted men who served. Over 50 percent of the deserters were foreign-born, which concurs with Lonn's finding that Union bounty jumpers were more likely foreign-born than those who served. More of the bounty jumpers lived in Cook County, the home of Chicago, than the men who served, which matches Lonn's finding that bounty jumpers were more likely to come from urban areas than were the men who honored their enlistments. The bounty jumpers' average wealth, $353, was less than one-fifth the average wealth of those who honored their enlistments—one possible reason these men took the bounty money with no intention to serve.[13]

An analysis of the election results and political speech in the newspapers in the eleven counties that provided 83 percent of the 45th's members—Jo Daviess, Winnebago, Carroll, Rock Island, Knox, Mercer, Cook, Lake, Stephenson, Boone, and Henry—provides additional insight into the men of the regiment. With Whigs and then Republicans controlling the northern half of Illinois in the last years of the antebellum period and during the war, it is not surprising that Republicans and pro-Republican speech dominated from 1856 to 1865. The Republican presidential candidate in 1856, John C. Frémont, won the eleven counties with more than two-thirds of the vote. Republican William H. Bissell won the gubernatorial race but in a much closer election. Republicans won the congressional elections for the eleven counties by a greater margin than Frémont, with Congressmen Elihu B. Washburne gaining over 72 percent of all votes in the 1st Congressional District. Only in Galena did the congressman's margin of victory narrow, a result of the city's large concentration of transplanted upper South Democrats. The 1858 congressional elections again resulted in a Republican sweep.[14]

In the landmark election of 1860, Abraham Lincoln won the state of Illinois, winning the eleven counties with nearly the same percentage as Frémont's in 1856. Southern Illinois Democrats, though, caused Lincoln to win the state with a 3.5 percent margin of victory. Republican Richard Yates's victory margin in the governorship nearly equaled Bissell's. In the eleven counties, Republicans again easily won the three congressional districts. In 1862 the Union's lack of success in the war, the thousands of Union dead and wounded, and President Lincoln's pending Emancipation Proclamation resulted in Democrat electoral victories. Illinois Democrats won control of the legislature, while Republicans again won the eleven counties, albeit with a lower average margin of victory than in the three previous elections.[15]

Historians have contended that three Union army victories in the summer and fall of 1864—Gen. William Tecumseh Sherman's capture of Atlanta, Adm. David G. Farragut's capture of Mobile Bay, and Gen. Philip H. Sheridan's defeat of the Confederate forces in the Shenandoah Valley of Virginia—contributed to Lincoln's victory in November. Historians Gary Gallagher, Jonathan White, and Zachery Fry all found that the Democrats' peace platform and the Copperheads' antiwar actions also contributed to Lincoln's reelection, driving many Union men to vote for the president over the Democratic nominee, former Union general George McClellan.[16]

Thus most of the 45th Illinois came from counties politically dominated by Republicans. Republican newspaper editors also dominated the political speech in the counties, and their antislavery, free labor, free soil commentary and, notably, their opposition to the extension of slavery into the territories correlate with what historians have found to explain why Republicans came into power.[17]

The weight of political opinion in the counties during 1856 was against Sen. Stephen Douglas's 1854 Kansas-Nebraska Act, believing it was an atrocity that opened the territories to slavery and had caused the violence in Kansas. Pro-Republican papers were generally outraged over the proslavery attack on Lawrence, Kansas. The beating of Republican senator Charles Sumner by Southern Democratic congressman Preston Brooks also elicited their fury. Regarding the 1856 presidential election, most articles favored Republican John Frémont, but the Republican editors had little comment on James Buchanan's victory, which the Democratic newspapers cheered. The Supreme Court's decision in the Dred Scott case on March 6, 1857, produced much negative commentary—the decision enabled slavery's extension into the territories and possibly into Illinois. The Lecompton Constitution, passed by the proslavery faction in Kansas, brought condemnation from editors of both parties.

Unified opposition to the Lecompton Constitution continued in 1858, while the constitution's defeat in Congress brought united approval. Political speech that year centered on the Illinois senatorial contest and heavily favored Abraham Lincoln over incumbent senator Stephen Douglas. While Democratic newspapers cheered Douglas's victory, Republican editors predicted success for Lincoln in the 1860 presidential election. John Brown's insurrection at Harpers Ferry, Virginia, dominated political commentary in late 1859. Republican papers condemned Brown's raid, considered him a religious fanatic, and defended Republican leaders against charges that they had funded the attack. Democratic editors accused Republicans of funding Brown's raid and calling for a general slave insurrection in the South.[18]

Not surprisingly, the particularly partisan political speech in 1860 focused on the year's presidential election. Republican editors touted the party platform's key plank—the prevention of slavery's expansion into the territories—and their favorite in the race, Lincoln. Democratic papers pushed Senator Douglas as the only candidate who could preserve the Union and predicted that Lincoln's election would mean disunion. Republican editors cheered when proslavery Democrats walked out of the party's convention in Charleston, South Carolina, on April 30, while Democratic editors remained confident in Douglas's chances. Republican editors were overjoyed with Lincoln's victory on November 6, with one headline reading, "GREAT REPUBLICAN VICTORY."

Democratic and Republican editors then joined in defending Lincoln against charges by Southern politicians that he was an abolitionist and a threat to slavery. South Carolina's secession brough unified condemnation.[19]

In 1861 pro-Union speech was pervasive in all the counties' papers, and all opposed secession. Democratic editors criticized Lincoln's inactivity, lack of comment between his election and inauguration, and unwillingness to compromise, and they thought his inauguration speech hinted at coercion. Not surprisingly, Republican editors approved of Lincoln's speech and believed he would uphold the Constitution. When Confederates fired on Fort Sumter, some papers blamed Lincoln for not evacuating the fort, but all were confident that the Union would put down the rebellion and preserve the country. Unified patriotism abounded after Lincoln's call for 75,000 volunteers, but some Democratic editors insisted the war should not be a crusade against slavery.[20]

With Republican political control in the eleven counties, and pro-Republican, pro-Union, and antislavery content dominating the counties' newspapers, it is likely that patriotism was what motivated most men of the 45th to enlist—to save their country and restore it. Indeed, several members noted patriotism as the reason for their enlistment. Their hometowns' patriotism, via sent letters and newspapers, also likely sustained the men during the hard marches and tough conditions. No matter their demographics or politics, the Lead Mine men in Camp Douglas, at the end of December 1861, prepared to go to war. They were six weeks away from serving in the field and entering combat for the first time. Both experiences would change them significantly.

3. ❄ Down among the Secesh

The 45th Illinois saw their first combat on February 13–15, 1862, in the Battle of Fort Donelson. The majority served honorably while exhibiting the calmness and composure normally seen in veteran soldiers; this was a result of their general character, their extensive training, and their officers' leadership. But what hardened the men of the 45th and prepared them for more horrific fighting was their experience in combat and caring for the wounded afterward. They were no longer civilians nor eager for battle.

During the first two weeks of January 1862, the soldiers busily prepared for their move to Cairo, Illinois. The year started with a parade by all units at Camp Douglas, which brought abundant praise from newspapers and the crowds in downtown Chicago. Activity increased when orders came for the regiment to be ready to leave camp. Some, like Capt. Luther Cowan, wrote home to let their loved ones know of their impending move. The captain told his wife that he likely would not be home until summer and would be "among the Secesh" the next time he wrote. Happily, the men received back wages, and many sent money with their letters to their loved ones. Some bought items they thought necessary on their trip south, such as pens, paper, ink, postage stamps, pocketknives, pistols, pipes, and tobacco, and some had photographs and daguerreotypes taken for their families. Cowan could only send $50 to his wife, for he had to pay off loans and purchase a pistol, trunk, and blanket. The impending move may have prompted him to spend $20 on a $1,000 life insurance policy. Cowan promised to return to his wife, but if not, he knew the money would help. He concluded by saying that if the 45th got into a battle, "*I intend to fight* live or die."[1]

Pvt. William Tebbetts also wrote home. The private, despite his pay, asked his parents for a loan to help his wife and five children. In asking for money, Tebbetts reminded his parents that he and his comrades were enduring hardships in uniform that those back home were not and that half of those in his company had left their wives and children to "defend the rights of their country." The private added that he and the others were pleased to be in the 45th,

31

for it contained the most "splendid set of men as you ever saw." He boasted that all were "snorting for a battle" and that his parents would soon hear of the regiment's heroic fighting.[2]

According to the *Supplement to the Official Records of the Union and Confederate Armies*, the Washburne Lead Mine Regiment left Chicago and Camp Douglas on January 15, 1862, via the Illinois Central Railroad, bound for Cairo (see Map 3.1). The regiment marched out of Camp Douglas at 2 P.M., and Capt. John Adair wrote that it left with the reputation of being the finest-drilled unit in camp. The *Chicago Tribune* noted the regiment's superior weapons and equipment and the men's discipline, saying they were "fully prepared to take the field." Escorted by their campmates, the Lead Mine men marched to the "enthusiastic congratulations" of throngs of people who "bade the men God speed upon their patriotic errand." The regiment boarded the train at 4 P.M., and as the train departed, the men happily left Camp Douglas's snow and cutting winds behind.[3]

Because of sickness and disease, many in the regiment did not leave Chicago on January 15. Most of those who stayed behind suffered with measles, including Sgt. John P. Jones of Company F. After he had spent a few weeks in the hospital, his comrades moved him back to the barracks. The sergeant believed that had they not rescued him, the hospital's crude care would have killed him. Soldiers in both armies shared Jones's loathing of hospitals. Before the unit's departure, Assistant Surgeon Francis Weaver inspected Jones and reported him "fit for duty," even though he could not walk across the barracks. Capt. Alfred Johnson, Jones's commander, incensed by the surgeon's conclusion, reported it to Lt. Col. Jasper A. Maltby, who informed Dr. Edward Kittoe. The unit's chief doctor, after hearing of Weaver's report, said, "The d——d fool, why he'd die before we get to Cairo," and ordered Jones kept in the camp's hospital. Later, the army sent Jones home to recuperate.[4]

The 45th Illinois arrived in Cairo at about 8 P.M. on January 16. As much as the men had disliked Camp Douglas, they considered Cairo worse. Luckily, their stay lasted a mere three weeks. The soldiers marched to their barracks, which were just under a levee, and went to bed hungry, having had only coffee on their trip. Historian Donald Miller called Cairo a "torpid, mosquito-ridden mudflat." Captain Cowan wrote that Cairo contained "dirt, filth, mud, mean houses and accommodations, and meaner men" and was "a place for rascals and rascality." The poorly built barracks had not housed soldiers for a month and looked as though large animals had recently vacated them, with the doors knocked down, holes in the floors, and no stoves for the men to warm

Map 3.1. Travels of the 45th Illinois during 1862. *Source: US map—rivers and lakes, created by U.S. Department of Interior on July 27, 2009, https://commons.wikimedia .org/wiki/File:US_map_-_rivers _and_lakes3.jpg* (changes made to the original).

themselves from the cold. To Pvt. William C. Taylor, their new accommodations nearly matched those in Chicago. The camp's deep mud brought the most ire from the Lead Mine men and their comrades. Luther Cowan wrote to his daughter Molly about the ankle-deep, and in some places knee-deep, muck: "Mud—Mud—You never saw such mud, enough to plaster all the rest of the Union." The men joked that they did not need the land grant from the state of Illinois that came with their enlistment, for they had the equivalent of 160 acres clinging to their boots. Taylor wrote to his father, "The mud is so bad here that it takes the boys about half of their time to keep themselves and their barracks clean," and some wished they were back in frozen Chicago. The mud was due to Cairo's damp weather and the fact that the camp sat mostly below the waterline of the Mississippi and Ohio Rivers, behind leaky levees. Details of men, including the 45th, constantly worked to repair the levees. Sarcastically, Colonel Smith told his wife that if the rivers flooded the camp, at least the water would drown the bold rats that ran over the men as they slept.[5]

The Federal troops spent most of their time in camp drilling. According to Captain Adair, the soldiers knew that they were in the "enemy's country" and that this required greater discipline. This discipline included the shooting of a "poor calf" that tried to pass the guards on duty without giving the countersign. Pvt. Wilbur F. Crummer remembered it as being one of the "darkest and rainiest days" of his service, when the sentries had to walk in some of the "deepest and blackest mud" he had ever seen. With the arduous guard duty and drilling, the Lead Mine men soon longed to leave Cairo. Until then, officers kept the soldiers busy with reveille at 6 A.M., followed by squad, company, and battalion drills, numerous roll calls and dress parades. The day ended at 9:30 P.M. In what little free time they had, some men studied the manual of arms, but most focused on cleaning their bunks and guns—work made difficult by their environs. Private Taylor wrote of the two-mile round-trip walk in knee-deep mud to get water from the Mississippi River. Despite the mud, one Sunday Taylor bathed in the icy "grand old Mississippi" and warm and balmy air. Soon Capt. Benjamin Holcomb Jr. and Lt. John Gray joined him, and the three then practiced their marksmanship for thirty minutes at forty paces—marksmanship they boasted would not bring dishonor in battle.[6]

The war was indeed close. On the day the Lead Mine men reached Cairo, they heard of General Grant's recent 10,000-man reconnaissance expedition toward the Confederate stronghold at Columbus, Kentucky, and thus they expected this to be their destination. To Colonel Smith, Columbus did indeed appear to be Grant's first objective. On January 18 Smith and Lt. William Rowley visited Grant, their Galena neighbor, and his family before crossing the Ohio River on a ship. Later, they rode horses to meet Grant at Blandville, Kentucky, fifteen miles to the south. The group reconnoitered to within ten miles of Columbus, but the muddy roads soon became "impassable" for an army and prevented an attack on Columbus. The next day, though, orders arrived for the men to prepare five days' rations and be ready to leave on Monday, January 20. With raised spirits Colonel Smith believed the men soldiered in greater earnest.[7]

Smith spent most of his final days in Chicago and Cairo hearing his men's wants and complaints and punishing offenders, including some for drunkenness. A few in the company spread false rumors about Captain Cowan that the army would soon cashier him and kick him out. With Smith's full confidence, Cowan handed down punishments to the men responsible. Lt. James Balfour of Company I dealt with a greater connivance when 2nd Lt. Henry Boyce led an effort to get rid of him and the company's commander, Capt. Oliver A. Bridgford. Balfour described Boyce as an ambitious man who considered second lieutenant "too small a place" and would only be satisfied when he commanded the company. Boyce and two sergeants, James Jamieson and Samuel Allen, induced sixty men to sign a petition to remove Balfour and Bridgford saying they were "afraid to entrust their lives" in battle to the two officers. Bridgford and Balfour reported the incident to Colonel Smith, who questioned the company and found that Boyce and the two sergeants had forged most of the signatures. The colonel arrested the threesome in front of the entire company. Despite a court-martial, the court did not drum them out of service; instead, the three spent time in the camp's jail. Their temporary release on February 1 called them to act with soldierly bearing, and if they did so, Colonel Smith would "release them permanently from arrest." Boyce's horrendous wounds from Shiloh and Vicksburg eventually led to his resignation on December 27, 1864; Jamieson's wounds at Shiloh and later at Mendon Station forced his discharge on March 10, 1863; and kidney disease likely caused Allen's discharge on June 10, 1862. It is unknown whether their status in society as a teacher, farmer, and lawyer, respectively, helped them escape harsher punishment, as historian Lorien Foote found for other Union officers during the war.[8]

As in Chicago, sickness spread through the camp and the regiment at Cairo. The damp, wet conditions likely contributed to the number sick, though Cowan believed his sick comrades had been "careless of their health." Lieutenant Balfour called the camp an unhealthy mess and, sarcastically, "*beautiful.*" As the men prepared for their departure, they occasionally saw a "secession prisoner" brought into camp. One member, on seeing his first rebel, believed the enemy to be a "mean, contemptible looking set of villains," an assessment he shared with many in the Union army. As they prepared to leave, the Lead Mine men felt confident in their skill and vigor and were unworried about how they would perform in battle. By late January the men knew their departure was imminent, as several members were tasked with loading transport ships with "ammunition, commissary stores, and all needed accessories for an army."[9]

On February 1 orders placed the regiment in Col. W. H. L. Wallace's 2nd Brigade of Brig. Gen. John A. McClernand's 1st Division. That day Wallace received orders for his brigade to move out the next morning by steamboat. Grant planned to move first up the Ohio River and then the Tennessee to capture the Confederate forts Henry and Donelson. Fort Henry was on the east bank of the Tennessee River, while Donelson sat on the west bank of the Cumberland River. The goal was to pierce the Confederate defensive line across Tennessee and Kentucky, enabling the capture of Tennessee's capital, Nashville, and forcing the Confederates out of Kentucky, which would permit Union troops to move down the Mississippi River. Despite Grant and others petitioning Gen. Henry Halleck to use the rivers as an invasion route, Halleck issued orders for the campaign only after Lincoln's General Order No. 1 called for "a general movement of the land and naval [forces] of the United States" against Confederates forces by February 22, 1862. With their orders, the Lead Mine men prepared their rations and baggage. They, with Grant's army, were to be the first Federal troops on Tennessee soil. That night Lieutenant Colonel Maltby addressed the regiment: "Soldiers and officers: We are about to leave for the land of Dixie. Every soldier and officer must trust in God and keep his powder dry, and do his duty. When on the field keep cool, take good aim, and down comes a secesh." Maltby told the men to trust in Providence when battle came. Captain Bridgford hoped Providence would be favorable to his family as he prepared to leave Cairo and later as the regiment prepared for battle at Donelson.[10]

That night the regiment boarded the transport ship *City of Memphis*. Each soldier carried forty rounds of ammunition and three days' rations, and to Captain Cowan, all were "fixed for a fight." Cowan boasted to his wife that the next time she heard about the unit would be when they had defeated the Confederates. He promised her she would never be ashamed of the way he fought and that he intended, with God's help, to kill "at least one Secesh." The regiment's January 31 Consolidated Morning Report showed that 746 officers and soldiers reported for duty, with 120 members sick, 49 absent for various reasons, and 4 under arrest. On February 3, however, Colonel Wallace reported only 702 men of the 45th on board the *City of Memphis*—35 officers and 667 enlisted soldiers. Sickness likely caused the absence of the additional 44. With 702 men, the Lead Mine Regiment went to war with 76 percent of its original strength—a far higher percentage than many Civil War units, which lost upward of 50 percent before entering their first battle, evidence perhaps of the regiment's hardiness.[11]

Most of those in the unit who did not head south on the *City of Memphis* lay in hospitals. Held back to take care of the sick in Cairo were Assistant

Surgeon Francis Weaver and 2nd Lt. Edwin Lawrence of Company F. Sources show that for 35 of the members not on the expedition, 11 soldiers had been discharged, 10 had deserted, another 10 had died, and 4 had transferred to other units. Among those discharged were Pvt. George L. Royce, who had pneumonia, and Pvt. Samuel Mason for an unspecified disease on November 18. Typhoid fever killed 3 men, including Pvt. Daniel Bowden on January 28, and 2 others died from measles. The case of Pvt. Charles W. Post, a drummer, is one of the saddest. The youngest and shortest man to enlist, at age thirteen and four feet, eight inches tall, he died of an unspecified disease at Camp Douglas on January 17, 1862. Perhaps a poor inspection of Post or an ill-advised parental consent resulted in his enlistment. And Pvt. James Wild, age fifty-two, who stated he was forty-four when he enlisted, died of pneumonia complicated with pleurisy on February 27, 1862, after entering the main hospital at Cairo on January 17.[12]

The 45th Illinois left Cairo on the *City of Memphis* on February 2, along with twenty-two other transports, four ironclad warships, and three gunboats. The Lead Mine men went to war well trained, unlike some regiments, such as the unfortunate 16th Connecticut, which fought at Antietam after only three weeks of training. To reach Pine Bluff, Tennessee, the destination of General McClernand's division, the ships headed up the Ohio and then up the Tennessee River, to Pine Bluff, which lay on the east bank, just south of the Kentucky state line and about 4 miles north of Fort Henry and 140 miles from Cairo (see Maps 3.1 and 3.2). The men of the regiment were eager for battle, and Captain Cowan wrote to his wife that he intended to fight and die honorably if he must.[13]

The Union soldiers enjoyed pleasant weather on their trip upriver. With the Lead Mine men packed on their ship "like a box of sardines," many chose to sleep on deck in the cool night air. The next day the *City of Memphis* put ashore before reaching Pine Bluff, likely in Kentucky, to get more wood for fuel. The officers allowed the men to leave the ship to stretch their legs. The owner of a nearby warehouse secured some troops from the Union officers to guard his many barrels of whiskey outside the building. A few ingenious men, however, managed to secure some of the "fiery stuff": one soldier crawled under the deck on which the barrels were sitting, bored a hole through the deck and one of the barrels, and filled many canteens with whiskey. On seeing several drunken men, officers accused the guards of dereliction of duty until the pilfered barrel fell over empty. With their deed exposed, the men were arrested and punished, likely in accordance with General Grant's order not

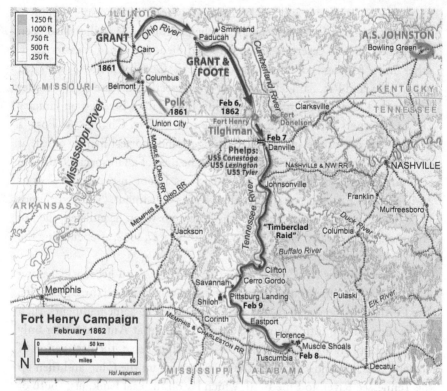

Map 3.2. Gen. Ulysses S. Grant's Tennessee Campaign, February–April 1862. *Source: Map created by Hal Jespersen on January 19, 2023, https://www.cwmaps.com* (changes made to the original).

to forage or destroy Confederate citizenries' property, although these soldiers had not yet entered the Confederacy. Grant had issued his order in adherence with the Union government's conciliatory policy, which forbade theft and destruction of the Confederate citizenry's property in the hope that it would bring them back into the Union. Despite Grant's order, his officers clearly could not prevent all pillaging.[14]

General McClernand's 1st Division landed at Pine Bluff on February 4. Capt. Oliver Bridgford of Company I negatively described the land near the unit's camp as "very poorly improved" and with "very thin soil," but he said that the nearby "swollen streams," which ran among heavily timbered and high rolling hills, contained good water. Bridgford felt that the 45th had the "post of Honor," placed east of the division as its picket force along with the 11th Illinois and a battery of artillery. There the men could see the Confederate flag flying over Fort Henry four miles upriver. A rainstorm that night drenched the soldiers and leveled many of their tents. The next day the Lead Mine men saw for the first time dead soldiers, men from both armies killed in a nearby brief skirmish. Close to the unit's location lay a civilian's farm, and Colonel Smith ordered Private Crummer and others to guard it in adherence to Grant's order. The men soon grew disgusted that their service meant guarding "a lot of dirty pigs that were not half as good" as those back home. During the storm that night, the men heard squawking from the civilian's farm, and in the morning, the farmer accused them of stealing his goose. Officers searched the tents, including Crummer's, where a sleeping man back from guard duty went undisturbed, but they found no goose. After the farmer left, Crummer and his tentmates had a breakfast of "mighty good" tasting "Dixie" goose—the stolen bird had been hidden in the sleeping man's pillow. The soldier who stole the goose may have simply been opportunistic, like those who had stolen the whiskey, or he may have taken the bird because of being frustrated with the Union's conciliatory policy, as were other Union soldiers as they entered the Confederacy. Or perhaps cases like the stolen goose, the whiskey, and the watermelons back at Galena represented the soldiers' testing of the army's discipline, as they were citizens first before donning their uniforms.[15]

Despite rain again on February 5, the 45th went to sleep in good spirits, in part because of Maltby's stirring speech in which he had told the men that he expected each to "do his whole duty," and that with God's help and the men's "good guns," they would be victorious in battle. On hearing that they would enter battle the next day, the men roundly cheered; soldiers in both armies looked forward to their first action. The Lead Mine men then began to prepare two days' rations, a task made difficult given the rain that night and the green wood they had to use. At 11 A.M. on February 6 McClernand's division marched out for Fort Henry with orders to take a position on the road between Forts Henry and Donelson, attack Henry if necessary, and prevent reinforcements from reaching the fort and the defenders from escaping. The overnight rains made the roads very muddy and streams swollen, making the march difficult. The soldiers had to build temporary bridges and use their shoulders to help get artillery unstuck. According to one Lead Mine man, Maltby's confident intensity and vigor "inspired new energy into the men" during the march.[16]

While the soldiers trudged south, the Union gunboats under command of Flag Officer Andrew H. Foote opened fire on Fort Henry, which quickened the pace of the Federals. The 45th thought the naval battle was portentous and boasted of hoping to get to the fort and "class ourselves with our forefathers."

They considered the gunboats' fight with the fort "most thrilling" and said that "the whizzing of fragments of bursting shells; the deafening roar of the guns in the fort; the black sides of five gunboats belching fires at every port hole was something to be remembered a lifetime." John Adair recalled the odd inexpressible exhilaration he and his comrades felt when they heard the cannons firing. Captain Cowan noted in his diary that the battle "lifted every soul and swelled every muscle," as he and his men moved off at a quicker pace and sang "Yankee Doodle" loudly, eager to enter combat. News that the Confederates had evacuated the fort after the two-hour battle resulted in cheers from some in the regiment, silence from others, and dejection in many for not getting a chance to fight. Private Crummer wrote in retrospect, "How foolish we were then" in regretting missing the battle. As the Union column's rear guard, the 45th finished their tiring eight-hour, eleven-mile march at 8 P.M.[17]

The Lead Mine men did not bring tents or any kind of shelter with them on their march to Fort Henry, and if not for their fires, the bitterly cold night of February 6 would have been unbearable. Adding to the men's rude awakening to the life of a soldier, many had foolishly left their overcoats and blankets back at Pine Bluff and regretted "their folly" that night. The next day they toured the fort. While General McClernand had believed the fort would be difficult to capture, some in the 45th thought the Confederates insane for situating the fort on very low ground, surrounded by a swamp. The hungry Union men gratefully ate the food left by their enemy, including biscuits in the ovens. The fort contained several dead and mangled Confederates, the men killed by Union shells and those slain when the rebels' rifled 24-pounder cannon exploded. The explosion tore several men to pieces, leaving "masses of human flesh" stuck to the broken gun carriages. Many soldiers took the images of the mutilated dead to their graves.[18]

Rain, sleet, and snow two days later postponed Grant's plans to move his army to Fort Donelson, as it was "entirely impracticable" to move artillery and wagons over the impassable roads. The delay gave the officers more time to prepare for the movement, and despite the bad weather, the 45th's strength was bolstered during the wait. From February 9 to 11 the unit's sick list decreased from 51 to 12 soldiers, and the next day 734 officers and enlisted men were able to report; the additional 32 men likely had recuperated sufficiently from sickness to rejoin their comrades.[19]

As he prepared for his army's move to Fort Donelson, General Grant continued to implement the Union's policy of conciliation by issuing a field order that called for the immediate punishment of those caught destroying, pillaging, or harming civilian property and any officer who failed to punish offenders. On February 10 the Jessie Scouts, an irregular Union scouting unit, and their commander went north under arrest, the first men punished for violating Grant's order. That same day General Grant issued instructions for the pending move, which forbade the carrying of tents or baggage and allowed for only the men's cartridge boxes with forty rounds and haversacks with two days' rations. The wagons carried an additional three days' rations. Grant set February 12 as the date for his army's departure for Fort Donelson to the east (see Map 3.3).[20]

With their longer route, McClernand's division left at 4 P.M. on February 11. The troops' muddy march lasted four miles before they stopped for nightfall. Those who had not discarded their overcoats and blankets during the warm day benefited from their foresight on the clear but very cold night, while those without coats, like many in Grant's army, suffered greatly. The men renewed their march at daybreak, and again the 45th constituted McClernand's rear guard. The division's artillery train once more slowed their movement, and they did not arrive near Fort Donelson until after 3 P.M., over three hours late. When still two miles from the fort, they passed General Grant and Colonel Wallace, who ordered them to drop their knapsacks—an order they soon loathed. The Lead Mine men then rejoined their brigade on the reverse side of a hill, 400 yards from the fort's breastworks, just as both the gun battle between the Union gunboats and the bastion and the sharp skirmishing between the opposing pickets ended. That night McClernand moved his men south to better guard the southern route out of the fort. Forbidden to leave the lines to retrieve their knapsacks or blankets, the soldiers went to sleep in their lines in the "dangerous neighborhood" near the fort, cold, hungry, and wet from the night's rain. Wilbur Crummer and his comrades realized what a "cruel thing a soldier's life was," and after their frigid experience near Donelson, they never again traveled without their blankets.[21]

Confederate artillery fire shattered the cold morning of February 13. The rebel cannoneers aimed at McClernand's division, on the far right of the Union line. Colonel Wallace's 2nd Brigade, in the middle of the division, faced the center of Fort Donelson (see Map 3.4). Under orders from General Grant to "avoid everything calculated to bring on a general engagement," McClernand did not immediately tell his men to return fire. But as enemy sharpshooters joined in to cause casualties, and so that his lines would stay in order and hold their ground, he ordered his batteries to return fire. McClernand naturally boasted in reporting that his artillery had silenced the Confederate guns and

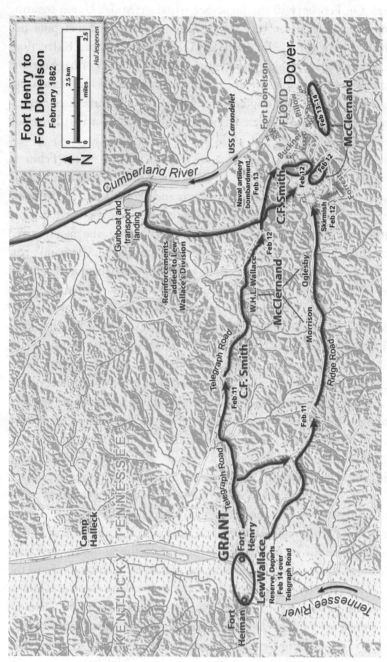

Map 3.3. Fort Henry to Fort Donelson, February 1862. *Source: Map created by Hal Jespersen on January 22, 2023,* https://www.cwmaps.com.

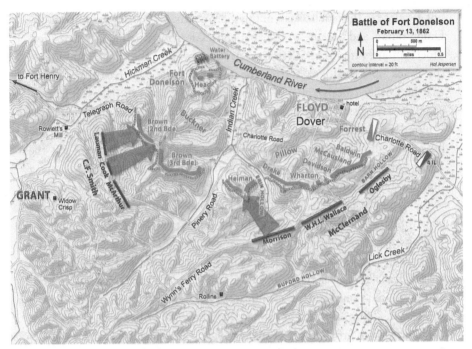

Map 3.4. Battle of Fort Donelson, February 13, 1862. *Source: Map created by Hal Jespersen on January 16, 2023, https://www.cwmaps.com.*

caused confusion in the fort. Colonel Smith later wrote that the enemy shells exploded "every few minutes so near us that it was very unpleasant" and helped familiarize his men with the noise of battle.[22]

Perhaps because of Brig. Gen. Charles F. Smith's earlier attack with units in his 2nd Division, General McClernand believed it was promising to take the fort's Redan No. 2, and thus at noon he ordered three regiments to attack. The Union soldiers went forward and marched up a steep, 150-foot hill to the redan, which the Confederates had protected with an "impenetrable abatis" of felled trees with "sharpened ends." When heavy enemy artillery and rifle fire caused the assault to slacken and men to fall back, at 2 P.M. McClernand ordered the 45th Illinois to move forward to the right of the line, strengthen it, and cover the entire front of the redan. The Lead Mine men gave "three hearty cheers," and according to Colonel Wallace, they advanced in "beautiful order" 600 yards down the hill, across the low ground, and up the steep embankment, where Colonel Smith ordered the men to fix bayonets. Soon the unit received heavy fire from the Confederates in the fort, which the men withstood, and as McClernand reported, they "gallantly" attacked but could not get close to the fort because of the sharp abatis. Casualties mounted in the Union ranks, and because of the abatis, McClernand ordered a retreat some ninety minutes after the 45th first received enemy fire. The general considered the attack "most brilliant" during the four-day battle. He boastfully claimed that had other troops and the Union gunboats joined in his assault, they could have successfully taken the redan. McClernand, the leading Democratic congressman in Illinois after Sen. Stephen Douglas died in June 1861, earned his generalship for his work to raise troops that year. The general left the Army of the Tennessee later in 1862 to raise troops in the Midwest. During the Vicksburg Campaign, General Grant relieved McClernand of command of the corps the latter had raised after he violated army regulations with his boastful, falsehood-filled account of the campaign.[23]

Regarding the regiment's baptism of fire, Private Crummer remembered the attack as the men's first chance to honor their promise to fight "gallantly for the dear old flag" as they climbed up the hill with the "*zip, ping, ping*" of bullets around their heads, the "murderous fire of musketry," and the "grape and canister" from the rebel cannons. Another soldier believed it a wonder the Confederate fire did not cut them all down. The men learned from Confederate prisoners after the fort's capture that the unit's discipline in not firing until close to the redan caused the rebels to mistake the 45th for U.S. Army regulars. The prisoners said they scarcely risked firing after the Lead Mine men's first volley, for as soon as a man raised his head, "he would fall back with an Enfield ball through it." One captured man said that the 45th's first volley killed twenty men, and a "secesh officer" noted that the regiment's initial volleys resulted in so many casualties that he could not make his men stand up. One member believed the 45th acted like veterans in waiting to fire. Sgt. Henry H. Taylor remembered Colonel Smith as "*brave*" and in "*firm command*" in ordering the men to load and fire their rifles. Captain Adair could not fathom how he and his raw, untried comrades had withstood their "first shock of battle" with "cool, almost reckless bravery." Before entering the battle, Crummer recalled, "my heart was in my mouth." But after the enemy began shooting at him, his "fear had been displaced by a savage instinct to inflict injury on the enemy." Like many of their peers in both armies, the Lead Mine men bragged of their bravery after their first battle. Colonel Smith, seemingly indifferent to the minié balls shrieking around him, worked to keep the regiment in position, while one enemy artillery shell, he said, "whistled so close that I thought I felt the wind."[24]

The 45th and other Union soldiers exchanged fire with the enemy as they marched backward to the Union lines. Adair remembered the calmness of the men as they retreated, and Colonel Smith wrote in his official battle report that despite their "severe ordeal" under fire, his soldiers never broke ranks. In exercising self-restraint under the stress of battle, the Lead Mine men had exhibited the gentlemanly nature so valued by their army and society. They opened fire when only fifty yards from the fort, and when Smith found that he was unsupported, instead of retreating, he pulled his men into a ravine and had them keep up their fire. Captain Cowan believed that the unit suffered only two dead and nine wounded because the Confederates, firing downhill, sent most of their bullets over the heads of the Union men. Colonel Wallace felt that "the 45th did bravely." Col. Isham N. Haynie of the 48th Illinois, who commanded the attack, reported that Smith and his soldiers had acted in a very respectable and "gallant manner" during the assault. Smith credited his soldiers' "determined bravery" for why they did not flinch or retreat when fired on.[25]

That night the Lead Mine men and their comrades again suffered without tents to protect them against the rain, snow, and severe wind. The cold and hungry soldiers generously shared their scant hard bread and coffee. After Donelson, the men always packed extra hardtack. Making matters worse, the hungry men learned that their enemy in Donelson had ample food. Still worse, their officers forbade the building of fires to avoid drawing enemy fire, and the men got little sleep when Grant ordered trenches dug and breastworks built for the Union artillery. While February 14 was a respite from battle, the cold weather continued, and some men died from exposure. For two Lead Mine men, Pvt. Solomon Brunor and Pvt. Hugh Owen, the cold resulted in their later discharge for exhaustion and exposure, and Pvt. Benjamin Coates contracted typhoid fever at Fort Donelson and died two months later.[26]

The battle on Saturday, February 15, made the fighting two days earlier seem like a mere skirmish (see Map 3.5). The Confederates surprised General Grant: at 5:45 A.M. they moved 10,000 men out of the south end of the fort and savagely attacked the Union general's right flank. Fearful of the contracting Union lines around their fort, the Confederate generals had ordered the attack to enable an escape south. Despite their cold night, McClernand's men stood ready for battle that morning. The enemy hit the general's right flank hard with infantry and field artillery. Facing this onslaught, McClernand had on his far right the 1st Brigade of Brig. Gen. C. F. Smith's 2nd Division, moved

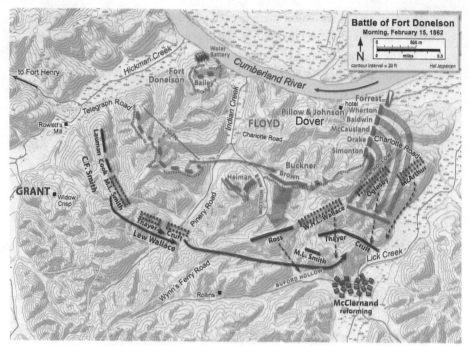

Map 3.5. Battle of Fort Donelson, morning of February 15, 1862. *Source: Map created by Hal Jespersen on January 16, 2023, https://www.cwmaps.com.*

to support McClernand, then his 1st, 2nd, and 3rd Brigades from right to left. The 45th Illinois was positioned on the far left of the 2nd Brigade, where the unit suffered far fewer casualties than those on the far right.[27]

By 7 A.M., with the two rightmost Union brigades heavily engaged, Colonel Wallace ordered his regiments and artillery to occupy a hill to the right of his brigade. This wheeling maneuver turned the colonel's men ninety degrees to the right to face the "strong masses" of onrushing enemy, which Wallace said "gave way before the steady, well-directed, and continued fire" of his soldiers, also forcing the retreat of a second wave of rebel troops. To the 45th's Private Tebbetts, the second wave of enemy soldiers, likely attacking in column formation, appeared "ten-times as strong" as the first. By 8 A.M. General McClernand's two rightmost brigades, low on ammunition, retreated from the "pressure of overpowering numbers" of Confederates. Now the Lead Mine men and their brigade mates constituted the right flank of Grant's army. Confederate artillery in the fort soon bombarded the Union soldiers' left flank with "grape and cannister and bom[b] shell," while the attacking enemy soldiers fired at them from their front. Thankfully, the fire from three Union batteries reduced the fire from the fort. McClernand told Wallace to rely on his own judgment but to maintain his position against all dangers until reinforcements arrived from Brig. Gen. Lew Wallace's division, which soon came up and protected the 2nd Brigade's right flank. When the 20th Illinois charged after some retreating Confederates, this left McAllister's battery "closely pressed" by the enemy, causing its gunners to abandon their cannons. Seeing this, Colonel Smith ordered his men forward, and they drove the Confederates back and rescued the Union guns. Colonel Wallace's brigade held its position for two hours; all the while, a "thick rain of rifle balls" fell around them, whistling through the trees and around their ears "very unpleasantly." With his right flank and rear endangered, and his men and ammunition nearly exhausted, Wallace moved his brigade back and right 400 yards as part of McClernand's retreat of his entire division (see Map 3.5). During this maneuver, Smith kept the left wing of the regiment firing at the enemy while having his right retreat, after which the left wing retired.[28]

Those not carrying rifles also experienced the dangers of the battlefield. Grant's medical director, John H. Brinton, watched the 45th's chaplain, George Woodward, courageously save wounded men by riding onto the battlefield, dismounting, lifting a hurt man onto his horse, and leading it back to a field hospital. Woodward survived the battle unharmed, and Brinton reported his admiration for the chaplain's courage and "the sincerity of his religion."[29]

While McClernand's soldiers rested and replenished their ammunition, General Grant attacked. He believed that to attack, the Confederates had stripped men from their right flank and had failed to take advantage of the confusion in the Union ranks, and he assumed equal confusion reigned in the enemy units. Thus Grant sent General Smith's 2nd Division to attack the northern end of the fort. After Smith's men successfully took possession of part of the bastion's entrenchments, Grant ordered McClernand and Brig. Gen. Lew Wallace to attack. The Lead Mine men and their comrades, despite the "hours of exposure to a heavy fire" they had already withstood—bravely, according to Grant—attacked and recovered the lost ground from the morning. February 15 ended with the fort fully invested by Grant's army and escape routes closed to the Confederates. The battle had lasted for over nine hours, with both sides fighting in "dead earnest" and General McClernand's division taking the brunt of the Confederate attack. The exhausted Lead Mine men and their comrades worked to find what wounded they could in the dark and got them to the doctors, and then they went to sleep hungry, having eaten only one meal in two days.[30]

According to Captain Adair, "a brighter and more beautiful morning never dawned" as that on Sunday, February 16. It was the only day of pleasant weather experienced by the Union men while near Donelson. Confederate brigadier general Simon B. Buckner made the morning even brighter for the Federals when he surrendered Fort Donelson to Grant, which brought cries of "Hip! Hip! Hurrah!" and celebration from Grant's men. The 45th joined in, and Sergeant Crummer asked years later, "Did we shout?" "Well if we didn't use our lungs then we never did."[31]

Victory accolades followed Fort Donelson's capture. The army promoted Ulysses S. Grant, C. F. Smith, McClernand, and Lew Wallace to major general. McClernand trumpeted the work of his subordinates: "The battle was won by the Second Brigade," who thwarted the Confederates' attempts to turn the Union's right flank. Col. W. H. L. Wallace also commended his officers, including Lieutenant Colonel Maltby of the 45th, whom he praised for being brave and efficient during the battle and for "encouraging and animating his men" even after he suffered a severe wound to his thigh. Colonel Wallace wrote that Colonel Smith and Maj. Melancthon Smith of the 45th "distinguished themselves by their bravery and contributed by their example to the attainment of the brilliant result." The colonel praised his brigade's surgeons and singled out the 45th's Dr. Kittoe for the "valuable assistance" he rendered after the battle. Major Smith lauded the ailing Lead Mine men who, despite their condition, had picked up their rifles and joined their comrades. Newspapers back home touted the "gallant conduct" of the regiment, who "did all that could be expected of brave men to do on the bloody field." The officers were "cool and collected in the midst of greatest danger," while the enlisted men obeyed "every order . . . without confusion."[32]

For the 45th Illinois, taking the remaining wounded of both armies to the doctors and burying the dead were worse than the battle. One Lead Mine man wrote that the battlefield contained many "awful, horrid, unnatural and fiendish sights," while another described it as "awful, death staring you in the face in every shape." Adair remembered how the sun's brilliance "played upon the upturned features of hundreds of our brave boys in death's embrace on the field where they fell." One member, on finding his dead brother on the battlefield, simply turned away silently. Captain Cowan wrote that for days afterward, they found dead Confederates "piled up in the woods, old houses, and thrown into holes." Writing to a friend, Colonel Smith noted of his men, "They were more eager than they ever will be again to get into a fight. The Boys were constantly wishing they could have a fight. You do not hear any such wishes now." Clearly, because of the human carnage of their first battle, the men of the 45th, like other soldiers in both armies, no longer saw glory in war.[33]

Several members of the Lead Mine Regiment were fortunate to survive the battle. A spent cannonball struck Cpl. Julius Esping in the chest but only caused soreness. After a bullet struck a comrade of Esping's in the chest, the man calmly walked back and sat against a tree. The bullet had zigzagged across his chest and left an "ugly looking flesh wound." A stray bullet struck and knocked down another member while he drank coffee early on February 15; the flattened bullet lay just under his scalp, and for the rest of the war his comrades called him "Old bullet-proof skull" and "Old hard head." A "nearly spent" bullet knocked down William Tebbetts but merely bruised the lucky private, who praised God in a letter to his sister; he believed Providence had saved him because God had more work for the private to do in defending his liberties. Tebbetts promised to fight until the last enemy soldier put down his gun. He longed for home but was not sorry for enlisting, despite the suffering he had endured.[34]

Pvt. Henry Winters survived a serious wound. On March 4, from a bed in the Jewish Hospital of Cincinnati, he wrote to his brothers of his experience in the battle. Even though as a musician he was exempt from fighting, Winters had picked up a rifle and joined the February 13 attack. During the battle, a bullet hit him above his right eye and knocked him over like "a shot hog." The private, unconscious for an unknown length of time, awoke to find blood flowing down his face and "bullets whistling" around him "like a hail storm." The private realized he was not dying and found the strength to crawl the 200 yards back to the Union lines. Although Winters had lost a great deal of blood, because of the large number of wounded, doctors did not remove the bullet until the next day. Sent to a hospital in Mound City, Illinois, Winters contracted erysipelas, a bacterial skin infection, which the private said "nearly finished" him. Winters believed he was lucky that doctors moved him to Cincinnati, where he received excellent care and "plenty of good wholesome victuals." The private's positive experience was atypical of most soldiers' experiences in Civil War hospitals. Besides the wound to his head, as a result of the battle Winters was nearly completely deaf in his right ear and partially paralyzed on his right side, with no strength in his right arm and leg. Eventually Winters healed sufficiently to rejoin the regiment, but the lingering effects of his head wound forced his transfer on May 1, 1864, to the Veteran Reserve Corps.[35]

A comrade of Winters's was not so lucky. According to Captain Cowan, an unnamed member had suffered a mortal wound to his stomach. On the night of February 15 the captain visited the man, who handed Cowan a letter from his girl. The doctor then gave the soldier a shot of morphine and left him to die. The man passed away just after uttering, "I am afraid"; his last moments haunted Cowan for months.[36]

Other musicians also fought in the battle. One, Isaac Bridgford, picked up a rifle and "fought manfully" until a bullet hit and broke his left arm. Sent to a hospital in Mound City, Bridgford died on March 21, 1862, likely from an infection caused by the wound. Peter Bellingall, the sixteen-year-old drummer of Company D, although tasked to carry the wounded to the doctors, initially ran from the sounds of battle but eventually chose to fight. On February 13 Bellingall, told that his comrades were being "killed like sheep," took off running like a "frightened rabbit" from the flying bullets and crashing of artillery shells. He was joined by a fellow drummer, and the young men ran until exhausted. Fearing capture, they returned to the Union lines on February 14. Unable to find the 45th, they grabbed the rifles and cartridge boxes of two dead men and served with the 49th Illinois. Early on February 15 they found the 45th. When Bellingall told his story to Capt. Thomas Conner of Company D, the captain replied, "Well, Billy, you are a hero, although you are so small, you can shoot and take a man's place." The private and his comrade, despite their fear, stayed in the line and fought throughout the day. Three weeks later Colonel Smith called the two drummers "noble young heroes" in front of the entire regiment. Because they had "acted so heroically," Smith gave them the choice to stay drummers or take a rifle and join the other soldiers; both men chose the latter option.[37]

The 45th Illinois sustained 30 casualties in the battle, with 2 men killed in action, 6 later dying from mortal wounds, and 3 dying from infections from their gunshot wounds. Not included in those who died from their wounds is Cpl. William Philpot, who received a slight wound in the battle, only to die at home of typhoid fever while on furlough. An infection likely killed Pvt. John Eckart, who suffered a severe wound to his arm; he never reached home, dying of fever on March 15, 1862, while in a Paducah, Kentucky, hospital. Lieutenant Colonel Maltby and two other officers were wounded. Maltby endured a serious wound from a bullet passing through his thigh, which required three months to heal. The regiment had the fewest losses in the 2nd Brigade, however. The 11th Illinois, also in the 2nd, had 329 casualties, 56 percent more than the next highest total in Grant's army. In his official report,

Colonel Smith wrote of the 45th, "It will be perceived that the mortality of the regiment was slight," which he attributed to his soldiers never losing their wits in the battle. He shared the belief with other officers in the army that losses could be lessened if a unit kept together. One member wrote that the men kept an orderly line of battle and never balked when fired on. Another man attributed the few casualties to the men's long-range rifles, which did "terrible execution" with "secesh scattered round with heads shattered by Enfield rifle balls."[38]

The men's deaths were major news in the papers back in Illinois. The regiment's commissary sergeant, John Travis of Rockford, died as he discharged his duties removing the wounded from the battlefield. The *Rockford Republican* said that Travis was "universally respected for his many sterling qualities." Israel Sovereign of Rockford retrieved his friend's body after the battle and took it home, where a massive crowd at Travis's funeral "attested how deeply the death of a patriot soldier and good citizen touches the popular heart." The sergeant left behind a wife and three children.[39]

The 45th Illinois and most of General Grant's army stayed near Fort Donelson for the next two weeks. In their letters home, the men speculated on the war and their opponents. Capt. Alfred Johnson and 1st Lt. James Balfour joined Grant in predicting the war would end in a few months. Grant believed the Union army could now take the southwest "without much resistance." The battle also lowered Captain Cowan's and some comrades' estimation of the Confederates. Cowan's opinion stemmed from the fight on February 15, when the 2nd Brigade held back, in the captain's assessment, an enemy force that was five times larger for three hours.[40]

The regiment also dealt with the boredom of camp life, the rainy weather, and their muddy camp, which caused many to want to leave the area. Captain Bridgford worried about his family, reminding his wife to make sure their kids went to school and to teach them to obey their parents and God's laws. He also mentioned how he and his comrades lived "like princes," eating the captured Confederates' crackers, rice, beans, hominy, molasses, sugar, rice, coffee, and butter while protected from the rain by "Cesesh" tents. A grateful comrade wrote that he no longer had to sleep on a "pile of brush." Colonel Smith had his tent and blankets stolen, as well as his pocketbook out of his coat; perhaps worse, he read a false newspaper report that said the 45th Illinois had "ingloriously fled" during the battle. To a friend, Smith conveyed that he would "rather have been shot than have seen" the article and noted that the official report of his brigade commander, Colonel Wallace, told of the regiment's honorable fighting during the battle. The rain and continued exposure to the elements, with poor water and sanitation, caused many in Grant's army to fall sick. For the 45th, Lieutenant Balfour estimated that sickness left barely "350 sound men." Captains Cowan and Bridgford both believed that Providence had kept them healthy, while Private Crummer and another member thought their faith in Providence had seen the men through battle.[41]

In the weeks after his capture of Fort Donelson, General Grant issued orders to prevent his soldiers from pillaging the local civilians' property, but Captain Bridgford saw firsthand how other soldiers had plundered the houses' furniture for firewood. Such acts lent support to Confederate propaganda, which said that Union soldiers would plunder civilians' houses, steal slaves, and kill women and children. Bridgford boasted that none in the 45th had committed such evil. Regarding the enslaved people used by the Confederates on the fortifications, General Grant acted under the First Confiscation Act and prevented their return to their enslavers, although historians have shown that Grant kept them because he needed laborers to repair Forts Donelson and Henry.[42]

Before leaving the area around Donelson, Grant ordered Lt. William R. Rowley of the 45th, a friend of the general's from Galena, to become his aide-de-camp. Again with Washburne's arrangements, Grant had taken a Galena friend from the regiment for his staff. The *Galena Daily Advertiser* considered Rowley worthy of the honor because he was a "brave soldier and a clear headed and thorough business man."[43]

On March 1 the 45th gratefully received orders to leave Donelson and move south. They prepared to go knowing they had, in their first test, fulfilled their promise to the people of Galena to fight honorably and not tarnish their colors. The Lead Mine men had lost their innocence at Donelson, but the experience readied them for their next, much more difficult challenge in uniform. The next day the men cooked three days' rations and loaded their cartridge boxes with ammunition. As Pvt. Matthew Miller prepared to leave, he anticipated that as Grant's army moved south, he might see some of his former Yale classmates who were now "secesh" and had left the university to fight for the Confederacy.[44]

4. ❧ Bloodied yet Unbroken

The men of the 45th next participated in the Battle of Shiloh, a watershed event for the unit. The regiment's stalwart fighting helped the Union win but at a terrible price—in terms of those wounded and killed, the unit suffered some of the highest losses in General Grant's Army of the Tennessee. The regiment's strength never recovered from these losses.

On March 4–5, 1862, Grant's soldiers marched from Fort Donelson to the Tennessee River. Enduring freezing cold and heavy snow and rain, the men marched in mud up to their ankles. The treacherous footing caused some to fall into freezing swamps. While doctors had held those too sick to travel at Fort Donelson, five Lead Mine men dropped out of the march. Like many Union officers during the war, who interpreted the inability of their men to endure the hard conditions to be "evidence of poor character and clear violations of military law," Captain Cowan harshly considered the men lazy. But though Cowan could be harsh at times, he showed his commitment to his soldiers' well-being, a trait necessary to being a good officer, and gave his coat to one soldier to stop his complaining. The men slept without tents in the windy, wintry conditions, which on March 6 caused the quarter-mile march to the transports to take most of the day; Captain Bridgford considered it the most disagreeable day of his life.[1]

Given the late departure on March 6, the Union flotilla made it only two miles upriver before stopping so the men could cook their dinners and sleep for the night. Bridgford wrote that it took the soldiers only thirty minutes to completely dismantle a nice house, outbuilding, and large warehouse to fuel their fires, and the men supplemented their army fare with the civilian's chickens, pigs, and vegetables. When the ships shoved off the next morning, the Federals had laid waste to the area, leaving it barren. After the transports had traveled about a dozen miles, they edged to the shore, where they were tied up so the men could disembark for lunch. The soldiers used nearby fences for their fires and ate another civilian's chickens, pigs, and turnips from a large patch. Like other Union officers who witnessed similar behavior, Captain

Bridgford of the 45th believed the plundering was wrong and did "injury to the union cause." But despite the Union's conciliatory policy and orders against pillaging, the officers had failed to prevent their soldiers' actions. As before with the whiskey and goose, no reason was noted for their looting. Not having experienced any hatred or acts of resistance against them by Confederate citizens, as had Union soldiers elsewhere, these Federals may have simply been resourceful or opportunistic. Or perhaps, after having suffered from hunger and cold at Donelson and seeing their comrades killed and wounded, they were, like Sergeant Crummer of the 45th and other Union soldiers, disgusted that their service meant protecting Southern civilians' property.[2]

All these examples of the 45th's destruction and pillaging are evidence that the early presence of Union soldiers in the Confederacy brought hardship to its citizens—and much earlier than some historians have asserted. Historian Joan Cashin found that from the start of the war, both Union and Confederate soldiers caused the rebel nation's citizens to suffer by taking their food for sustenance, their dwellings for shelter or use as hospitals, and wood from their forests and fences for fires. The officers of both armies failed to control their men and adhere to their government's articles of war; the primal needs of the soldiers won out over army policy, the norms of civilian society, and the values of the soldiers' antebellum culture. In his work on the Union's changing policy toward Confederate civilians, historian Mark Grimsley contended that the Union's leadership changed from its initial conciliatory policy to a pragmatic policy during General Grant's Mississippi Central Campaign in the late fall of 1862, when General Grant ordered his men to forage for food from civilian supplies and destroy Confederate war-making facilities to enable operational success. While historians have debated the start of this phase, the pillaging by the Lead Mine men and their comrades, from the days leading up to Donelson to these instances in March 1862, happened more than nine months before Grant's Vicksburg Campaign. Grimsley conceded that Union soldiers acted in ways during the conciliatory phase that became the norm in the pragmatic phase and the later hard war phase.[3]

The Union transports set off upriver after the soldiers' lunch. Three days later, on March 11, they reached Savannah, Tennessee, on the east bank of the Tennessee River, eight to ten miles northeast of Pittsburg Landing and the Shiloh church and less than twenty miles north of the Mississippi state line (see Map 3.2 in chapter 3). As the 45th waited to go ashore, the Union armada grew to seventy ships. With information that the Confederates were amassing a large army to the south, many rumors spread as to Grant's destination after he arrived at Savannah on March 17. Captain Bridgford, despite the many rumors, correctly placed the Confederates thirty-five miles to the southeast, in Corinth, Mississippi. In a letter to his wife, Cowan reiterated his hope that his insurance policy would help her if he died, but he remained confident that the Union men would easily "whip the Secesh" and said that Providence had enabled him to withstand the cold weather and hunger at Donelson.[4]

As they waited to go ashore, the soldiers enjoyed warm, "beautiful nights" on the transports but had mixed impressions of the area and its inhabitants. The well-developed countryside impressed one Lead Mine man, but he did not think much of the "poor, miserable hamlets" he saw on the trip south, and he said of the local civilians, "A meaner looking, more contemptible set, ignorant, villainous, never encroached on God's footstool. If these are the Southern chivalry, God deliver us from such a country and such a people." The soldier preferred Illinois's cold winters and "honest, intelligent, free, en- lightened, industrious, patriotic noble" people. Captain Bridgford though enjoyed the pleasant May-like weather and sent home peach blossoms to his wife, telling her that the area around Savannah contained many wealthy men with numerous enslaved people, yet also many Unionists. He believed a "Live Yankee" could do well there after the war. Many Union men across the Confederacy held the enlisted man's low opinion of the citizenry, while others shared Bridgford's view of a Union man's future chances in the South.[5]

As the regiment moved into camp, Col. John E. Smith lamented some aspects of life in uniform in a letter to his wife. He described the theft of his property and the food she sent him, saying it was impossible to get any items past the "pack of thieves" who handled items sent to the soldiers. The colonel enjoyed soldiering but warned that if their son Ben wanted to enlist, he had to make up his mind to work hard, his father could not favor him over the other soldiers, and it was preferable that his son obtain a hospital steward position. At Savannah, General McClernand worried about camp security and nearby Confederate cavalry units; thus he gave strict orders on the issuance of passes to visit Savannah and limited the passage of civilians through the camp. Like other Union commanders there, McClernand sent out men to find the enemy. On March 18 the 45th left camp with other units to search for Confederate horsemen. After a three-day, fifty-mile march, during which it rained and the men had to sleep without tents, they returned without having found the rebel calvary.[6]

Although they had been in the field for just shy of seven weeks, at Savan- nah the regiment's officers requisitioned new pants, shoes, and socks because their uniforms had already worn out, as had those of their comrades in Mc-Clernand's division. Dr. Kittoe, the unit's head surgeon, had more pressing matters—the health of his men. On March 14 he reported to the division's chief surgeon that the regiment did not have enough vegetables, many suffered from dysentery and diarrhea, and scurvy had recently afflicted others. The doctor noted that 118 men were unfit for duty and wrote of the deleterious effect coffee had on those afflicted with dysentery. Kittoe noted his failed attempt to obtain tea from the commissary and stressed the absolute need for more fresh vegetables and meat. Like their comrades throughout the Union army, the men of the 45th got sick because of their poor army food, poor sanitation, and drinking water in camp, and many were removed from their ranks.[7]

The Pin Hook raid was the most notable action during the regiment's time at Savannah. On March 24 Grant ordered the 45th's Maj. Melancthon Smith to lead an expedition to capture a massive store of Confederate bacon. Smith, along with the 150 men from Companies B, C, and G and a company from the 4th Illinois Cavalry, embarked on the steamer *John Rains* and left Savannah the next day. The general ordered the expedition after a local Unionist informed him of a considerable store of pork at a Confederate warehouse near Nicholas Landing, up the Tennessee River forty to sixty miles south of Savannah, likely into Alabama. Grant ordered Smith not to harm the property of the largely Unionist people in the area and to avoid fights with Confederate cavalry. With information from a slave, the Union column found the warehouse shortly after reaching the landing. Using wagons from the warehouse and others supplied by local Unionists, the soldiers carried upward of 60,000 pounds of bacon back to the ship.[8]

As the men returned to the transport, they took an additional 30,000 pounds of bacon found on nearby plantation. The slaveholder offered to go with his enslaved workers to take the meat back to the ship because he did not want them to be unsupervised near the Union soldiers. Two of the enslaved people ran onto the *John Rains*, but Major Smith, adhering to Grant's orders and the First Confiscation Act, which permitted the taking of the enslaved if they were used to help the Confederate war effort, allowed the slaveholder to come aboard the ship to retrieve his bondsmen. The force sustained no casualties during the raid, but one of the Lead Mine men, Pvt. Levi Blanchard, began to feel sick after the mission's fifteen-mile round-trip march and died of typhoid fever shortly after returning to Savannah. Blanchard's captain, Oliver Bridgford, told the private's parents, "I have lost a brave soldier, always prompt and ready for duty, and well beloved by not only myself but all his brother soldiers. I hereby tender you my heartfelt sympathy in this your hour of affliction and sad bereavement."⁹

In ordering this mission five months before the Union's official change in its policy toward the Confederacy and its citizenry, the opportunistic Grant ordered the capture of the Confederate bacon to both hurt his enemy's war effort and feed his soldiers. Equally opportunistic, the pragmatic Major Smith captured the slaveholder's bacon and thereby hurt those dependent on the food. Grant's soldiers, suffering from the inadequate Union supply system, enjoyed the captured meat, and their camps soon smelled of cooked bacon. Unlike Grant's and Smith's opportunism, some Union commanders elsewhere at this time, including Maj. Gen. Ormsby Mitchel in northern Alabama, ordered their men to pillage out of retribution and to eliminate resistance and stem acts of violence against their men by Confederate citizens.¹⁰

The day the Pin Hook force left Savannah, on March 25, the rest of the 45th Illinois boarded a transport and moved upriver eight miles to Pittsburg Landing on the west bank of the Tennessee River. Maj. Gen. William Tecumseh Sherman had selected the landing as the embarkation point for Grant's drive on Corinth because its high ground protected the army from the rising river. The regiment bivouacked on the high ground that night, and the next day the men marched two miles inland to their camp, where the three Pin Hook companies arrived two days later. McClernand's division camped from 600 yards to, at most, three-quarters of a mile east and northeast of General Sherman's division and the Shiloh Church. While McClernand's troops partially overlapped Sherman's, the 45th's and their brigade mates' camps were situated in Woolf Field, in a northeasterly direction from Sherman's units (see Map 4.1).¹¹

By most accounts, the move to Pittsburg Landing had a positive impact on the health of the regiment and for some in Grant's growing army. Unlike the cold they had endured at Fort Donelson and the rain at Savannah, here they enjoyed sunny weather, as warm as Illinois in June. Cowan believed the good weather rapidly improved his soldiers' health, although many remained sick. Wounded in the shoulder at Fort Donelson, 1st Lt. James Balfour appreciated the good weather and dry land at Pittsburg Landing. A doctor had applied a poultice to reduce the inflammation and boils on his wounded shoulder, and although weak, it had completely healed. Captain Bridgford wrote to his wife that he had recently attended church, the first mention of men going to church since entering the field. The captain also believed the food his men

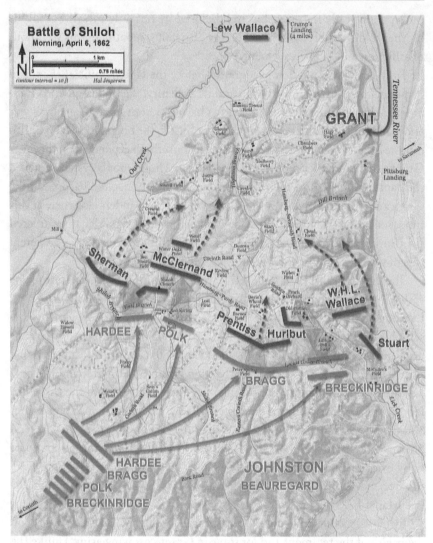

Map 4.1. Battle of Shiloh, morning of April 6, 1862. *Source: Map created by Hal Jespersen on January 22, 2021, https://www.cwmaps.com.*

had bought from the nearby enslaved people had improved their well-being. The Lead Mine men's first experience with the bondsmen was positive, as they ate lavishly on the purchased chickens, eggs, corn bread, milk, and other items. Their Union comrades throughout the South similarly supplemented their diets with food sold to them by the enslaved. At this point in the war, though, and not having seen the horrors of slavery yet, the 45th at Savannah, on the Pin Hook expedition, or at Pittsburg Landing were not yet the aggressive slave emancipators their comrades elsewhere in the Confederacy had already become. Despite the good health of many in the regiment, disease continued to reduce the rolls; on March 29 Assistant Surgeon Francis Weaver died of an unspecified disease, and four days later Pvt. Francis Reed died of typhoid pneumonia. One account suggested that Reed's death was due to exposure during the March 18–20 expedition, reported that the private had distinguished himself with his fighting at Fort Donelson, and noted that because he was the first in Company D to die, his sudden death caused much sadness in the company.[12]

With the regiment reunited, the soldiers resumed battalion and company drills. Captain Cowan thought it was a "great sight to see the men drilling" and working hard to prepare for the expected "big fight." Captain Bridgford, however, had no love for Major Smith, the unit's drillmaster. He wrote to his wife that although they were expecting a horrific battle, with rampant rumors of 100,000 Confederates nearby, he considered the major an "old *ass*" and hoped to see Smith's usual scowl in the unit's upcoming dress parade. The major did not disappoint, scolding the officers after the parade. The hard drilling by Smith, though, served the men well in the upcoming battle. While not on picket duty or drilling, many men read and answered letters from home. Lieutenant Balfour told his wife and son that while the men did not cower from battle, they no longer eagerly looked forward to it as they had before Fort Donelson—the suffering of their wounded comrades had changed their attitudes on combat. Balfour, like others in the unit, had lost his taste for the army diet of salted pork, coffee, and hardtack, which made him so constipated that he had to take castor oil. Even so, the thrifty Balfour refused to pay the high prices for fresh food from the regiment's sutler.[13]

As the impending battle drew closer, Captain Cowan reflected on his soldiers' performance at Fort Donelson. He bragged about his company's performance but noted the twelve "damn cowards" in the company who, despite coaxing, skulked and did not join the rest of the men on the February 13 attack on the fort; the skulkers' comrades never let them forget their cravenness. Lieutenant Balfour wrote that the men in Company I considered Pvt. Alonzo Pulver "the greatest coward in the company" because he had played "possum all the time" back at Donelson. Hence, like other Union soldiers, these enlisted men enforced, without their officers' help, their society's concepts of honor and manhood, or manliness. On April 3 the 45th's band enhanced the springtime feeling in camp by serenading General McClernand, who afterward thanked the men with a "stirring speech." According to Dr. Frank Reilly, who had just joined the regiment on April 1, the sounds of "Home Sweet Home" soothed one soldier suffering from typhus during his last few moments; the man died shortly thereafter.[14]

The routine of camp life ended abruptly when, at 4 P.M. on Friday, April 4, McClernand ordered the 45th and other units to fall into line and then move out at the "double quick." Two regiments of reconnoitering Confederates, with two sections of artillery and 500 cavalry, had caused the alarm by driving in General Sherman's pickets and killing, wounding, and capturing some Federals. After several hours of no contact with the enemy, officers deployed skirmishers, and the men returned to camp.[15]

Given the events of April 4, Wilbur Crummer wrote later that he could not understand how Grant and his generals had not seen that the attack was imminent or why they had kept wide gaps between their divisions. With the many reports of contact and skirmishes with Confederate troops, and Grant's knowledge of Johnston's work to build up his forces in Corinth some twenty-two miles to the southwest, it is indeed difficult to understand why Grant did not have his army better situated to withstand an attack. Perhaps it was because of the heavy rain that started near midnight on Saturday, April 5, and continued into the early morning hours, which Adj. William Frohock reported made the roads "almost impassable"; the rain and muddy ground had indeed slowed Johnston's march from Corinth. As the battle neared, continued sickness at Pittsburg Landing reduced the rolls in Grant's army, including Company B of the 45th, whose Captain Cowan, sick since the Pin Hook expedition, entered the hospital on April 2.[16]

According to Sergeant Crummer, early Sunday morning, April 6, suggested the beginning of a lovely spring day; likewise, Dr. Reilly thought that a "day more beautiful had never dawned," with its bright sun and chirping birds, which did not forewarn the men of the horrific fighting soon to start. After the battle, Colonel Smith joined with many reporters in writing that his men were "completely surprised" by the Confederate attack, but Dr. Reilly and Sergeant Crummer, along with others, including Capt. John Rawlins, Grant's chief of staff, disagreed. General McClernand and other commanders had pickets thrown out during the night and morning of April 6, and these men had fired on Confederate forces as they attacked that morning. To Crummer, the Lead Mine men were not surprised or caught off guard; rather, Grant simply did not expect a general attack by Johnston, and thus he had no fortifications or earthworks dug and did not have his divisions formed into a single line. Crummer's statements accord with the conclusions of several historians—that Grant and his generals focused their preparations on launching an offensive against Johnston in Corinth, once Maj. Gen. Don Carlos Buell's Army of the Ohio arrived from Nashville, instead of on defending against an attack by Johnston. Before the battle, Grant wrote that his men needed more time drilling and more discipline rather than more "experience with the pick, shovel, and axe."[17]

The first shots of the Battle of Shiloh occurred around 5 A.M. on April 6, but the men of the 45th Illinois did not hear firing until two hours later. Sergeant Crummer had just dressed for breakfast when he heard the "rattle" of musket fire. Some men continued to eat their breakfast, while others discussed what the firing meant. The local topography, with few roads, uneven ground, and many ridges, gullies, and ravines, caused this confusion and the delay in hearing the early fighting. According to one Union man, it was "heavily wooded," shrouded by the forests and undergrowth, and a "perfect wilderness." The few roads and haphazard fields and clearings in the area limited the soldiers' visibility to the next growth of trees; walking the battlefield today, one sees much the same. By 7:15 A.M., with wounded members of Sherman's division hobbling back through their camp and the disturbing sounds of musketry and stray cannonballs landing near them, the men knew the long-awaited battle had begun. Sergeant Crummer wrote that the Lead Mine men's "blood quickened" when the long roll of drums sounded, and although alarmed, they quickly grabbed their rifles and cartridge boxes and fell in line in five minutes' time. Their numbers included many sick members who were in the hospital but picked up their rifles. According to Dr. Reilly, they cared little for their condition and marched out filled with the "glow" of martial spirit. After a thirty-minute wait in the 1st Division's parade grounds, near 8 A.M. McClernand's 1st and 2nd Brigades moved forward at the "double quick" to support General Sherman's division. As the blue ranks moved out to meet the enemy attack, the division's surgeons cleared the hospital for the expected wounded, but when artillery shells and bullets began to hit close, the doctors moved to a ravine behind the camp of the 45th Illinois.[18]

With what remained of Sherman's division, the 45th moved to the left and faced the Review Field with their comrades in the 1st Division, including the 3rd Brigade, who had retreated after battling the Confederates in their advance camp. The men readied for an attack along the Hamburg-Purdy Road, on either side of the Corinth Road, some 500 yards northeast of the Shiloh Church. Meanwhile, the Confederate soldiers who had attacked the 3rd Brigade pillaged the brigade's camps. The 45th then saw the troops of Col. Rufus P.

Neely's 4th Tennessee regiment. Receiving no command to fire to check the charging enemy with their "rebel yell," Crummer and his comrades soon grew "uneasy." For some, the tension was too much, and they fired without orders. An officer, thinking the oncoming soldiers were retreating Federals, screamed at the men to cease fire, to which one Lead Mine man retorted, "The hell they are! You will find out pretty d——d they are not." With no Union volley, Crummer wrote, Neely's men poured a "most destructive volley of musketry" into the regiment, knocking men down like "autumn leaves." The 45th and their comrades quickly returned fire, which initially checked the Confederates' advance, but when other units joined in the attack, regiments on the 45th's right retreated without orders in disarray. To prevent the enemy from flanking his men, at about 11 A.M. General McClernand ordered his division to retreat through their camps 200 yards to the northeast.[19]

After his division's withdrawal, McClernand worked to re-form his lines. He had time because the Confederate soldiers, exhausted from their exertions and battered during the attack, rested while some pillaged the 1st Division's camps; "exulting in a victory," they marched off with the Federals' belongings. Here, like Grant's green troops, Johnston's inexperienced soldiers negatively affected his army's performance in the battle. The chaos and confusion in the Confederate ranks mirrored that of their Union counterparts, but Generals McClernand and Sherman ably rallied their units and steadied their soldiers. Sherman met with General Grant, and then at about noon he ordered the Union soldiers forward with some reinforcements to meet the Confederates, who had renewed their assault. Despite taking fire from an enemy artillery battery situated in the 45th's camp, the men in blue marched on and waited to fire until close to their enemy. Soon the rapid-firing Union soldiers drove the Confederates back through the Federal camps for over 500 yards. Pvt. Peter Bellingall recalled that the two-hour Union attack was "one of the most fiercely contested engagements" for the regiment on April 6. During the assault, Dr. Reilly followed behind the regiment and tended to the wounded of both armies. His dedication resulted in his own wounding, as a bullet passed through his calf and grazed his fibula. He limped painfully for three hours back to the Tennessee River before doctors treated his leg.[20]

The Union troops pushed forward until they reached the ridge beyond McClernand's headquarters, where Confederate resistance stiffened with the addition of artillery units and Col. Robert P. Trabue's 1st Brigade. The gray tide then surged forward, and when the units to the right of the 45th disintegrated and fell back in chaos, the enemy again threatened to flank McClernand's right. Marsh's 2nd Brigade then moved to the left in an advance position that was on low ground, which exposed them to enfilading fire from the enemy. Nevertheless, Adjutant Frohock wrote, the men put up a "determined resistance" and caused many casualties in the gray ranks. Bellingall remembered how Colonel Smith's fiery exhortations to "keep cool, [and] lie low" bolstered the men during the fighting. Marsh's brigade resisted the relentless Confederate fire until its right was "hard pressed," and with ammunition running low, General McClernand ordered a northeasterly retreat to some woods at the edge of Jones Field. On reaching the field, Colonel Marsh ordered the ammunition divided equally among his regiments. During the fight on the low ground, the regiment lost 1st Lt. Nesbitt Baugher of Company B, shot seven times, and Captain Bridgford of Company I, shot twice.[21]

Two Iowa regiments reinforced McClernand's division, after which he ordered another counterattack; he later boasted that this caused "great slaughter" of Confederate troops. Some regiments fell back because of a shortage of ammunition, again endangering the Lead Mine men's right. In his report on the battle, McClernand stated that the 45th was the last to retire and escaped capture only by "boldly cutting their way through the closing circle of the enemy's lines . . . under the daring lead of Colonel and Major Smith." Adjutant Frohock, however, recalled that McClernand had ordered the men of the 45th to remain where they were until he issued further orders. When a "heavy force of the enemy" appeared in the regiment's front and Confederate cavalry passed around them, their capture seemed "inevitable." Colonel Smith recognized the dangerous situation and led the men back toward the river, through a ravine to safety, likely near Cavalry Field. McClernand's attack had lasted just thirty minutes.[22]

The 45th and the rest of the 2nd Brigade finally ran out of ammunition at about 3 P.M. The Federals retreated in search of cartridges. They came upon a line of fresh soldiers and begged for cartridges, but their rifles were of a different caliber—a common occurrence that day. As the Confederates continued to press forward, the situation looked desperate, so much so that Capt. Abraham Polsgrove of Company A exclaimed to Colonel Smith, "My God, Colonel, they are not fifty yards from my company, and we haven't a shot to defend ourselves." Smith admonished Polsgrove to be quiet and keep calm because the Confederates did not know they were out of ammunition and the regiment would "come out all right yet," which they did. As the exhausted men of the 45th Illinois retreated, they met up with the division's ordnance officer, who had several wagons of ammunition. According to Sergeant Crummer, his comrades went after the ammunition more eagerly than a "hungry lot of men" after dinner. With their cartridge boxes replenished, the soldiers quickly filled in with the rest of the division along the Hamburg-Savannah Road; with a small move back at an angle from the road, they now formed part of General Grant's defensive line near the Tennessee River (see Map 4.2). The Lead Mine men finished their "bloody work" that day by detaining stragglers and putting them into the line, while Union cannon fire defeated several "disorganized"

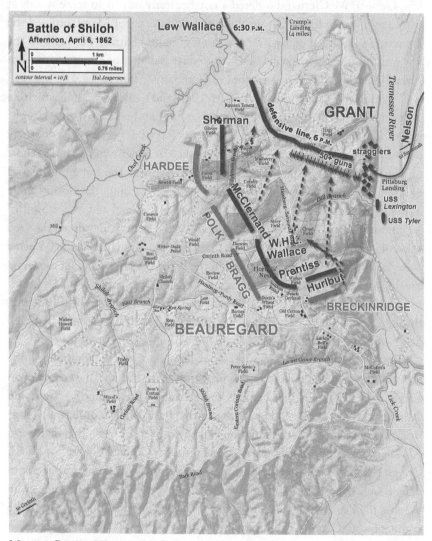

Map 4.2. Battle of Shiloh, afternoon of April 6, 1862. *Source: Map created by Hal Jespersen on January 22, 2021, https://www.cwmaps.com.*

Confederate attacks. As the carnage-filled day ended, Crummer noticed the setting sun was an appropriate blood red.[23]

The weary, exhausted, and hungry Lead Mine men, who had not eaten since breakfast, appreciated their light supper of hardtack and cheese—except perhaps for a German-born comrade who had his front teeth knocked out by a Confederate bullet during the battle. Despite this, he had continued to fire while swearing "like a trooper" in broken English, damning his enemy: "Dey tinks dey vill spile me so I can't eat hard tack, d—— 'em, I'll sow dem!" Details searched for the wounded, a difficult job given the nearby Confederate lines. When these men reached the hospitals with the wounded, they saw a "*horrible*" sight—great piles of amputated limbs next to the makeshift hospitals. The night was terrible for all, Confederate and Union soldiers alike, but worse for the latter's wounded; with much of the Union medical supplies now in enemy hands, they suffered amputations with no anesthetic but a few sips of brandy. During the night, wounded soldiers made it back through the enemy lines, including one very lucky man whom a sentry from the 45th almost shot. While John Adair and some of his exhausted comrades slept soundly, the torrential cold rain that fell that night and the fire of the Union gunboats' eight-inch guns at the Confederate lines prevented many from sleeping. For Sergeant Crummer and others, the terrible cries and groans of the wounded men, some burning to death in the fires, kept them awake, as did the sounds of feral hogs eating the dead. Over fifty years later, Crummer could still hear "those poor fellows crying for water." For the soldiers in both armies, more fighting awaited them the next day.[24]

With the 20,000 men of General Buell's Army of the Ohio on the battlefield early on April 7, and with the greatly delayed arrival of Gen. Lew Wallace's 7,000-man 3rd Division, General Grant decided to launch a counterattack on the morning of April 7 (see Map 4.3). As dawn broke, the Lead Mine men, near the center of Grant's defensive line, had a small breakfast and readied for battle. A Federal artillery barrage heralded the start of the attack, then Colonel Marsh ordered his brigade forward.[25]

Union cannons "briskly answered" Confederate artillery fire, then the regiment moved forward with orders to support an artillery battery. They crossed a field and moved into the woods beyond it, where, according to Captain Adair, they woke up a "hornet's nest of rebels." The Confederates, part of Brig. Gen. Patrick Cleburne's 2nd Brigade of Maj. Gen. William J. Hardee's 3rd Corps, then attacked McClernand's left. This caused two regiments to the 45th's left to "ignominiously" retreat, leaving the unit's left flank exposed.

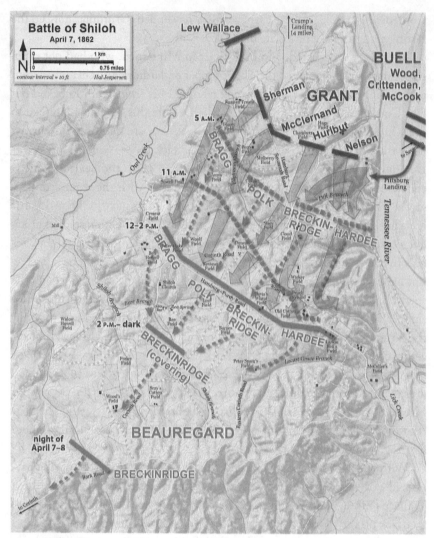

Map 4.3. Battle of Shiloh, April 7, 1862. *Source: Map created by Hal Jespersen on January 22, 2021, https://www.cwmaps.com.*

An ordered retreat, back and to the left, saved the Lead Mine men from being "gobbled up" by the enemy a second time during the two-day battle. The Union troops met Cleburne's attack, and next under orders, they charged forward and began the hardest fighting of the day. For a time, the Confederates obstinately yielded each foot of ground. At noon, however, a general Union charge broke the enemy lines, and despite the forlorn efforts of the 20,000 rebels, including valiant counterattacks, they could not resist the Union attack of 40,000. The 45th and their comrades gradually drove their enemy back, but the Confederates fought hard, making the "sharp awful work" of the battle last the entire day. The battle ended with the Lead Mine men back in the camp they had so hurriedly left the day before. Like the rest of Grant's army, the men of the 45th were too "decimated and exhausted" to pursue the retreating Confederates and bivouacked in their ransacked camp. Few tents remained standing, and these were "torn and riddled by shot and shell."[26]

Before sleeping that night, the Lead Mine men and their comrades first took the wounded men to the doctors, then built fires and cooked a meager meal. As they ate around the fires, the men recounted the acts of bravery performed during the battle and spoke kindly about their "brave comrades who had fallen." Even though he was very sick, Captain Cowan wrote later, he would have given anything to be with the men in battle and could barely listen to them relive their experiences. As with the rest of Grant's troops, the Confederates had stolen much from the 45th's camp. Crummer lost everything, including a Bible from his mother and his most cherished item—his girlfriend's picture. Adjutant Frohock said their camp had seen some of the "most awful carnage," yet the soldiers had no problem sleeping, even though the dead of both armies surrounded their camp, for they now feared only the living. John Adair recalled that the men went to sleep in their "dilapidated and dreary" camp in a somber mood because the terrible battle had removed so many from their ranks that their "hearts wept bitterly." To Sgt. Joshua Vanderwort, the horrors seen at Donelson paled in comparison with those at Shiloh: "The sights I saw were *terrible*. God forbid that I should ever witness the same again." Clearly, the savage combat and terrible loss of men at Shiloh left the remaining members sickened by war.[27]

Sgt. John P. Jones of Company F returned to the unit that night, having recuperated from measles contracted at Camp Douglas, and was appalled to find less than half the number of his comrades who had left Chicago in January. Jones's toughened mates had no problem sleeping in the rain on the wet and muddy ground, but unaccustomed to life in the field, the sergeant slept on an army wagon's tongue that night. His initiation into the war only got worse with his assignment to command the division's hospital commissary department. Here he saw scenes he never wanted to see again: delirious men dying, suffering from "every imaginable kind of wound," and "amputations by the wholesale."[28]

The next day General Grant's depleted ranks set to work burying the dead. Wilbur Crummer vividly remembered the day when the 45th had to bury the dead that lay from their camp to 200 yards west. They first buried the Confederate soldiers in a four-foot-deep, sixty-foot-long trench. The hot weather made this work even more difficult, as the decomposing bodies "poisoned" the air. As some men dug graves, others loaded the dead onto wagons, then brought the wagons to the graves; here men stacked the bodies two deep in the grave, before others covered up the bodies with dirt. The men placed a wooden board as a "monument" over the grave, and Crummer etched on it "125 rebels" with his knife. The Lead Mine men dug separate graves for their deceased regimental mates and interred other Union dead in a grave with a marker stating "35 Union." During the day, officers furnished the men with great quantities of whiskey. The soldiers worked past nightfall, by which time they were half drunk, which Crummer wrote had enabled the completion of the grisly work. More gory work awaited the men the next day, as they had to haul and stack the decomposing horse and mule carcasses, before setting the fallen animals on fire.[29]

The days after Shiloh did not get easier for the Lead Mine men, for they were ordered to build "breastworks of log and dirt." The pickets were also on a much keener watch and were more apt to fire at any unexpected movement. One picket, only fifty yards away, fired at Captain Cowan, who had ridden out to inspect his soldiers. Luckily, the man missed the weakened Cowan, who now commanded a company of just thirty men—one-third the number who had mustered into service in December. The five-foot, nine-inch captain now weighed just 140 pounds, down 30 pounds since falling sick.[30]

Pvt. Erhart Dittmar's story is an interesting one of survival and plundered possessions. On April 6 he received a wound to his left thigh, which broke a bone. His comrades saved him from capture and carried him to an ambulance. When the private reached Dr. Kittoe's makeshift hospital, the doctor bound his swollen leg, which burned with "indescribable" pain as if on fire; later, the private admitted he did not know how he survived it and that at times he wished the doctors had amputated the appendage. He was transported by ship to a hospital at Mound City, Illinois, where a doctor saved Dittmar's leg from amputation by applying water poultices, which reduced the swelling. By April 15, with much of the infection gone, doctors set the leg and "put [it] into a box, splintered, and bound." The private's prolonged suffering at the Pittsburg Landing hospital, the memories of which remained with him for the rest of his days, was typical of the experiences of Union soldiers in hospitals during the war and why most dreaded a trip to one. After he was sent home, a doctor removed the flattened bullet, which allowed Dittmar's leg to fully heal. Later, he returned to the regiment, reenlisted, and served for the rest of the war. During the battle, Confederate soldier H. P. Grier plundered Dittmar's belongings, including his German-language Bible. Grier returned the Bible in 1887 to Dittmar's brother, George; regrettably, Erhart had died in 1883.[31]

After the victory at Shiloh, the generals, officers, and enlisted men in Grant's army received many congratulations. Secretary of War Edwin Stanton lauded Generals Grant and Buell for their victory. Gen. Henry Halleck, commander of the Western theater, praised Grant, Buell, and the rest of army for their "bravery and endurance" in defeating the Confederate army. Later, Halleck partially blamed the "sad casualties" in the battle on the poor conduct of some officers, whom he believed unfit for the ranks they held. General Grant saluted his officers and troops, who, he boasted, had so "gallantly maintained, repulsed, and routed a numerically superior force of the enemy." Grant mourned the dead and wounded but noted they had also "won a nation's gratitude and undying laurels" for their victory. The victory was great indeed, for it enabled the Union's campaign to continue moving south. More important, it made the Confederates' hold on west Tennessee and along the Mississippi River untenable and enabled Federal control of the waterway down to Memphis, which they soon captured.[32]

The 45th's officers received acclaim for their actions at Shiloh. General McClernand reported that Col. John E. Smith and Maj. Melancthon Smith "signally distinguished themselves by their exemplary constancy and indomitable courage." In his official report, Colonel Marsh noted that he was "much indebted" to both men for their leadership during the battle, and though they were no less exposed than their fellow officers, they survived the battle unharmed. Dr. Christopher Goodbrake, Marsh's acting brigade surgeon, mentioned the valuable assistance provided by Dr. Kittoe and Dr. Reilly, who, despite his wounded leg, continued to care for others. The regiment's namesake, Congressman Elihu B. Washburne, wrote to Colonel Smith, "My heart swells with emotions of pride at the glorious deeds of the Lead Mine and yet it bleeds when I think of the dead and wounded." Sergeant Crummer believed the colonel exhibited "courage and skill" during the battle, which merited his promotion to brigadier general afterward. Pvt. Henry H. Taylor remembered the colonel's "unselfishness & bravery" and "cool determined effort." A newspaper back home printed thanks from the commander of Dresser's battery, who praised the admirable work of the 45th and an Iowa unit in preventing the capture of his guns during the later stages of the battle on Sunday. Once again, the convincing, confident, and excellent leadership by Colonel Smith and his officers had served the unit well in the much more chaotic and unpredictable fight at Shiloh. Smith's composure when the unit ran out of ammunition calmed not only his junior officer but likely others in the regiment as well, perhaps a more valuable trait than the courage he displayed.[33]

The bloody two-day battle completed the Lead Mine men's transition from civilian to veteran soldier and left them with dreadful memories they would not forget. Unlike at Fort Donelson, the 45th Illinois suffered terrible casualties. Sadly for the soldiers and their families, the unit's stubborn fighting resulted in the most casualties in General McClernand's 1st Division and the seventh-highest number of casualties in Grant's army, or the sixth-highest when counting only those killed and wounded. In total, the regiment had 23 men killed in action, 187 wounded, and 3 missing. With 2 officers killed in action and another 16 wounded, only one other regiment in Grant's army exceeded the casualty total in the 45th's officer ranks. Another 26 members, 3 officers and 23 enlisted men, suffered mortal wounds or died from infections that set in after the battle. For yet another 45 men, their wounds resulted in their discharge from service, and for 6 more, their wounds caused their transfer to the Veteran Reserve Corps. Thus, of the 213 casualties, 100 did not return to the ranks. With 475 officers and men before the battle, the unit sustained 45 percent casualties, whereas the 1st Division and 2nd Brigade averaged just 25 percent casualties.[34]

A few companies suffered more than others. With Captain Cowan in the hospital, 1st Lt. Nesbitt Baugher led Company B and received seven gunshot wounds. Overall, the company had 50 percent casualties, with 3 men killed and another 25 wounded. With Baugher's wounding, Sgt. Joshua Vanderwort initially commanded the company after the battle and helped bury his fellow sergeant Nelson Blineberry and Pvt. Holoway Wood in a grave of "reasonable depth" with walls of logs built around it. In a letter to his mother, printed in the *Warren Independent*, the sergeant noted that in the two-day battle, he had "avenged" Blineberry's death. Captain Cowan told his daughter that after being wounded in the left breast, Blineberry walked ten steps and "fell dead never uttering a groan." Cowan believed Blineberry to be "as good a soldier as ever left Joe Daviess County and that is saying a good deal for Joe Daviess sent but few bad ones."[35]

The battle also took a toll on the officers of Company I. Already wounded at Fort Donelson, 1st Lt. James Balfour suffered a wound to an arm, which resulted in its amputation. An infection likely set in after the surgery, as Balfour died on May 19. A Confederate bullet wounded Capt. Oliver Bridgford's leg but did not break a bone, and by April 30 the captain was able to get around on crutches. The captain eased his wife's worries, writing to her that he would soon recuperate and to "thank God it is no worse." Bridgford credited the nurses, including the famous "Mother" Mary Ann Bickerdyke, who he believed was the "best woman in the world," outside the wives and mothers of the men. Sergeant Crummer wrote that over and over, the men in the hospitals uttered, "God bless Mother Bickerdike." The sergeant believed it was Providence that had enabled the Union victory at Shiloh and echoed the War Department's congratulatory orders to Grant after the battle, which gave thanks to the "Lord of Hosts" for the victory. Finally, Erhart Dittmar believed his survival was "God's will." Clearly the Lead Mine men's faith in Providence stood strong after their bloodiest battle.[36]

The deaths of the men naturally saddened their families. Shot in the throat, Pvt. John Casey died during the action on April 7. The *Galena Daily Advertiser* lamented that Casey's "poor mother" had lost her only supporter. The paper also mentioned Lt. George Moore, whose "great gallantry" at Fort Donelson resulted in his promotion. Moore's wounds at Shiloh initially appeared slight but later proved fatal, as he died on April 8 at Pittsburg Landing. Two of the unit's officers, Capt. Thomas D. Conner of Company D and Capt. Alfred Johnson of Company F, were killed in action at Shiloh. After an enemy bullet hit Conner in his left breast, he handed his sword and belt to a boy "for preservation" and walked about thirty feet to a "small thicket," where he "laid down and died," all without speaking a word. One man reported that Conner's "common cool and impassible manner never left him in all the excitement." The men of the company found Conner's body the day after the battle, and later his brother-in-law retrieved it and took it back to Galena on April 25. The people of Galena, with a band and four fire companies, "largely" attended the captain's three-hour-long funeral. Many businesses closed for the funeral, with flags flown at half-mast. A paper wrote of Conner, "A brave, true and patriotic soldier, a most useful citizen, a firm friend, and a man of great integrity and worth, sacrificed his life for his country when he died," and said that all who knew him respected him and that he was "greatly beloved" by his company because their welfare had been his constant focus.[37]

No death shook the Lead Mine men and the people of Galena and Warren more than that of Lt. Nesbitt Baugher. Shot seven times on April 6, Baugher wondered later how he survived the battle. The first enemy bullet hit him in the left leg but luckily did not break any bones. Knocked down, Baugher, in trying to crawl off the battlefield, suffered another wound two inches from his rectum. Hobbling again, the lieutenant was hit by a third bullet in his right shoulder. When he turned to confront the enemy and held up his sword, he was wounded in the face and struck by a mostly spent bullet between two fingers. Most of these wounds were not major, but the bullets in his leg and hip were more threatening. Baugher crawled fifty more feet, then fainted behind a fallen tree. He awoke to hear the voices of Confederate soldiers as they marched past him. One enemy soldier saw the lieutenant but ignored him even though Baugher said to him, "Well you have caught me at last." Later, a Union attack placed the lieutenant between the Confederate and Union lines, but when the Federals drove the rebels back, Baugher's comrades were able to carry him to a hospital. By April 21 Baugher was in a hospital in Quincy, Illinois, 200 miles south of Galena on the Mississippi River. One optimistic observer reported that Baugher's "naturally strong constitution" had him doing as well as could be expected, but by late April Baugher was "very weak," and the people of Galena sent for his father, Rev. Henry Baugher, the president of Pennsylvania College in Gettysburg (now Gettysburg College).[38]

The reverend reached Quincy on May 6 and made sure his son received all the attention needed to make him comfortable. The elder Baugher wrote a letter thanking those in Galena who had come to Quincy and provided care, for which his son had "unfeigned gratitude." The reverend added that the unequaled Christian care his son received did his "heart good." Baugher's health was much improved, and with devoted friends caring for him, his father left for Gettysburg. Despite an improvement in his health over several days, on May 14 Baugher developed a severe chill, and his health deteriorated until he died on May 16. One newspaper said in memoriam, "No braver man than Nesbitt Baugher stood for his country on the terrible field of Pittsburg Landing . . . cool and clear of head and warm and courageous of heart, he had the power of attaching men to him strongly. . . . But, after all, he attained the highest honor of the soldier—HE DIED FOR HIS COUNTRY."[39]

The *Warren Independent* announced Baugher's death to its readers: "It is a melancholy task, yet affectionate duty, to record this tribute to the memory and virtues of our departed friend." Regarding Baugher's family, the editor wrote, "May heaven assuage their sorrow, and pious resignation follow this keen bereavement." Because he had put his entire trust and salvation in Jesus

Christ in his final days, "his Christian parents may rejoice in hope of meeting him in heaven." The *Independent* said Baugher was highly intelligent, having graduated with honors from his father's college at the young age of eighteen. He had studied law before he moved to Warren and practiced it for a time until he became an editor at both the *Independent* and the *Galena Daily Advertiser*. Baugher initially volunteered as a private in Company B, but because of his instrumental work in raising the company, the men immediately voted him their first lieutenant. Reverend Baugher had his son's body sent back to Gettysburg and had him laid to rest with military honors in Evergreen Cemetery. Two military units, students at Pennsylvania College, and many Gettysburg residents attended Baugher's funeral. The people of Gettysburg later erected a monument over his grave.[40]

The soldiers of the 45th mourned greatly over the death of Lieutenant Baugher. Captain Cowan wrote that the regiment missed or lamented no man lost at Shiloh more than "our beloved and worthy brother Lt. Baugher," whom every member in the unit respected. The *Warrant Independent* reported that although the war's hardships had hardened the men, when they learned of Baugher's death, "many an eye was wet with tears" and many became silent. Cowan was hit so hard by the news that he could not even express his feelings to his wife on the loss of his close friend.[41]

On April 11 General Halleck arrived from St. Louis and took command of the Union forces at Pittsburg Landing. Because of his concern for the safety of the army, Halleck had Grant issue orders for the use of pickets and cavalry to limit civilian passage through camp and prevent soldiers from leaving camp. Less than two weeks after his arrival, Halleck issued orders for his army to move out and attack Gen. P. G. T. Beauregard's Confederate army at Corinth, Mississippi.[42]

During the movement from Fort Donelson to Pittsburg Landing, the 45th Illinois and others in General Grant's army, without orders, initiated a pragmatic approach to their relations with the Confederate citizenry and their property by taking the civilians' food and using their buildings for their fires. The practical General Grant had set a precedent when he ordered the Pin Hook expedition to capture Confederate bacon to feed his men. For the 45th Illinois, this hardening from the war did not yet include the confiscation of enslaved people, as happened later in 1862. The veteran Lead Mine men, with many of their comrades, stubbornly fought while retreating on April 6, 1862, which helped give General Grant the time to organize a defensive line near the Tennessee River before the Confederates could push the Federals into the river. The 45th's stoic service saw the unit through to the end of the battle on April 7. These patriotic men had again fought honorably to defeat their enemy. In total numbers, however, the regiment never recovered. In the next phase of the war, changing Union policies led the 45th to move beyond the battlefield to defeat the Confederacy by removing its citizens' most valued property—their enslaved. The men eagerly adapted to their republic's hard war on its enemy.[43]

5. ✿ Pragmatic Emancipators

The enslaved girl's screams could be heard for blocks by the Union soldiers stationed at Jackson, Tennessee. Sgt. John P. Jones and other men of the 45th, under orders from their division commander, had returned the girl to her master during the summer of 1862, work that made the men ashamed of their uniform. Soon changes in Union policy ended the return of formerly enslaved people to Confederate slaveholders. By August 1862 the Lead Mine men were pragmatic, willing emancipators, as they loathed slavery, enslavers, and the antiwar Northern Democrats' treasonous work. Late 1862 saw the beginning of an uncontrollable "war of recrimination" between the combatants, as well as severe hunger among the Union soldiers on a bleak retreat. Despite their suffering, the 45th's commitment to their republic remained strong.[1]

On April 24, 1862, the 45th, along with other elements of Gen. Henry Halleck's 100,000-man army, made up of soldiers from the Armies of the Tennessee, Ohio, and Mississippi, set out from Shiloh to take Corinth, Mississippi, twenty miles to the southeast. Halleck's concern for his armies' safety overrode his goal of defeating the enemy, turning what should have been a three-day march into a "slow and tedious" monthlong slog. Though initially glad to leave Shiloh and the stench of the shallowly buried bodies, the Lead Mine men and their comrades despised Halleck's operational management, which meant short marches, the building of so many breastworks that the men denuded several heavily timbered areas, and monotonous days spent behind their parapets. Sergeant Jones wrote, "We had no fighting, would have liked it better if we had," as the men dealt with boredom, poor rations, and a lack of water.[2]

With Colonel Marsh very sick and on leave, Col. John E. Smith of the 45th commanded a "now very small" 2nd Brigade of only 1,000 men fit for duty—the size of a full-strength regiment. Smith reflected on the "demoralizing tendency" that took so many from the ranks because of battlefield casualties, disease, and accidents. Worried about the health of his son Ben, now a hospital steward, Smith sent him home. Captain Cowan reflected that after just three months of fighting, only 24 men were able to report for duty in his company, a loss of 75 percent of its soldiers since the regiment left Chicago. He also told his wife that with southern Tennessee's many fruit groves, he considered it a good place to move following the war. The captain added that the local women at first considered the Union men "awful wicked, ugly beasts" but warmed to their presence after finding out the contrary. Cowan sent home a memento of his close friend Lieutenant Baugher, a piece of rough wood from the log Baugher had laid his head on during the Battle of Shiloh.[3]

The regiment experienced further losses in its officer ranks on May 5, when Capt. Thomas Burns, commander of Company C, resigned his commission after battling long-term health issues. On June 1, 2nd Lt. Luther Hunt resigned his commission, noting in his diary, "I find myself unfit for the life of a soldier." Hunt was the fourteenth junior officer (lieutenant or captain) the regiment lost, the others having died in action, sustained a mortal wound, left because of disability, transferred to another unit, or resigned their commission. Historian Andrew Bledsoe found that junior officers in both armies suffered casualties at an "appalling rate"—the Union regiments in his study had an average of 43.4 percent. The 45th, however, had a much higher casualty rate of 60.3 percent. For the junior officers lost to promotion or unit transfer, the rates were similar: 17.5 percent for the 45th versus 16.7 percent in Bledsoe's Federal regiments. Perhaps it was because of the unit's patriotic devotion or hardiness that only 27 percent of the regiment's junior officers were lost to resignation or discharge from disability (the army did not cashier or dismiss any of the unit's officers), 9 percent less than in the Union regiments in Bledsoe's study. It is a testament to the learned study and capabilities of the 45th's junior officers and the enlisted men who received officer commissions that the performance of the regiment did not diminish after the loss of so many junior officers.[4]

It had taken two weeks for the 45th to move just eight miles south of Shiloh, but by May 18, after driving back Confederate pickets, the Lead Mine men were now just two miles from Gen. P. G. T. Beauregard's Corinth fortifications. On May 28 Halleck finally decided to take Corinth and its critical rail nexus. Brig. Gen. John A. Logan, the new commander of the 45th's division, gave Maj. Melancthon Smith, the 45th's officer of the day, command of the Union skirmishers 300 yards in front of the Union line. Confederate skirmishers met Smith's men, and severe firing soon began. Both sides added men to the fight, but as the day ended, the Federals had held their ground and the enemy retreated. The next day, with additional Lead Mine men added to the skirmishers, a "very severe" fight developed. According to Captain Cowan, the regiment "went into them the old way, and drove them back." He boasted of the veterans' coolness under fire—fire that scarred the ground and trees but caused no casualties. Logan commended his men and considered Major Smith a "brave officer and in every respect worthy of the duty assigned him." The two armies were now just 1,000 yards apart.[5]

The following day, May 30, Beauregard evacuated Corinth, his departure punctuated by the explosions of anything useful to Halleck's armies. The Union general's soldiers entered the town and inspected the departed Confederates' vast and stout fortifications. While many did not know why Beauregard had evacuated, the patriotic Captain Cowan believed the enemy had left Corinth and declined battle because of their unjust cause. Unbeknownst to the Union men, it was the lack of enough good water that had forced Beauregard's evacuation. Sergeant Jones wrote that the men welcomed the "piles of meat, meal, beans etc." left by the retreating Confederates. They also gratefully received their pay for the first time since leaving Cairo, with immediate "cheerful faces." Some men bought overpriced items from the regimental sutler, while others sent money home to their loved ones and friends. Still others were more industrious, like Pvt. Henry Decker, who built ovens in which to bake bread and pies and sold them to his now cash-rich comrades. In one day he made $40, three times his monthly salary.[6]

Corinth's lack of good water meant that Halleck could not pursue the Confederates, who were currently at Tupelo, Mississippi. Given the importance of Corinth as a railroad junction, Halleck expected Beauregard to attack him there, but when the Confederates failed to do so, the Union general broke up his army to guard 360 miles of railroad supply lines and territory in northern Mississippi and southwestern Tennessee. The army sent the 45th and the 3rd Division to secure and repair the Mississippi Central Railroad around Jackson, Tennessee, a depot 120 miles west of Nashville, as the railroad was a critical supply line for an overland attempt to capture Vicksburg. The regiment marched ninety miles over five days in very hot weather, and on June 4 the men camped in a "beautiful grove just east" of Jackson. Captain Cowan much admired the lovely gardens and houses in the town of 12,000, and the men appreciated the nearby "clear, cool, sparkling water" and abundant blackberries and other fruit. The good water and bountiful fruit improved the men's health. Cowan regained his strength lost during his illness at Shiloh, and Sergeant Jones was now fit after having contracted measles at Camp Douglas and suffered from diarrhea on the march to Corinth. Despite orders issued in July against trespassing on civilian property, the Lead Mine men escaped punishment for their foraging. By the end of August, though, orders came instructing the officers to send out foraging teams. Perhaps it was the fluid nature of the army's policy regarding foraging or empathy for their men seeking to supplement the poor army fare that led to the officers' leniency here.[7]

While at Jackson, the 45th first encountered large numbers of fugitives from slavery, which one member described as "thicker than blackberries." The men, like their comrades across the South, enjoyed playing music and watching the formerly enslaved people dance. These individuals were initially hesitant to enter the Union lines, for they believed their enslavers' gruesome lies that Union men would commit atrocities against them. The 45th also saw the brutal realities of slavery for the first time. Sergeant Jones wrote of an incident he witnessed after he and some comrades returned a girl to her enslaver. The man tied her to a tree near General Logan's headquarters and whipped her, and the poor girl's "screams could be heard for three or four blocks." Nevertheless, Logan twice ordered Jones to return fugitives from slavery to their former enslavers. After returning more than fifty formerly enslaved adults and children, both male and female, Jones and his men, who believed this work dishonored their uniforms, were ordered to return freedmen living with a Michigan regiment. The unit's colonel, however, called out his men and said to Jones, "Sergeant, if you want those n——s, take 'em." General Logan agreed with the sergeant's discretion in returning without the freedmen. Later, on August 11, Grant issued an order that stopped the return of formerly enslaved people to their enslavers—an order likely driven by the recently passed Second Confiscation Act, in which Congress authorized the seizure of Confederate civilians' property, including their enslaved people, as well as Halleck's August 2 directive to take Confederate property for army use. Jones wrote to his wife, "I am getting to be more and more of an abolitionist," and said that for there to be peace, "this accursed institution," a stain on the country, must end. Jones was grateful that he no longer had to "wink at such atrocities" and that the men were no longer "used as a slave catcher" or "ashamed of being an American soldier." Slavery's horrific realities had led the Lead Mine men and many of their comrades to be willing emancipators, both for humanitarian reasons and also, pragmatically, to damage the Confederate war effort.[8]

While the men of the regiment liked the fruit and water near Jackson, they were not so fond of its people. Captain Cowan, along with Dr. Kittoe and others, believed the civilians to be the "hottest kind" of secessionists. The women were worse than the men—"the devil himself couldn't be more bitter"—and heaped "all kind of curses" on the Federals, believing the rumors that the former would commit "atrocities" against them and their property. Cowan thought the civilians had inferior intelligence to those in the North. While Union soldiers throughout the Confederacy suffered its citizenry's verbal barbs, the men at Jackson luckily did not experience violence, being shot at, or being wounded and killed by nearby civilians, as Federals elsewhere did at this time.[9]

The 45th's duties allowed the men time to write home. In a lengthy letter to his daughter, Captain Cowan impressed on her and her brothers the importance of getting a good education and of being honest, so as to "insure the blessing of God." He also wrote how the insects, especially the lice and cockroaches, were the soldiers' worst afflictions. Lice pervaded the ranks of both armies; with the close quarters, all suffered from the miserable "graybacks," which attacked the men at night and prevented them from getting much sleep. The insect tormentors tested soldiers' commitment, even that of the stoic Cowan. Capt. Oliver Bridgford of Company I wrote to his wife that his duties allowed him to attend church at another regiment, "a good Old Fashioned Camp meeting." The demands of life in uniform, however, removed Bridgford from the ranks. After recuperating from a leg wound sustained at Shiloh, the captain returned to the unit on June 28. But his leg never fully healed, preventing him from fulfilling all his company commander duties, and he resigned on September 3. In camp, officers had many duties, including completing official forms for the parents and wives of men who had died in service so that they could receive their loved ones' back pay and bounties. Occasionally, officers had to defend their soldiers' reputations. Lt. Col. Jasper Maltby wrote to a Rockford, Illinois, newspaper on July 14 to defend that of Pvt. Silas D. Lasier. The paper had reported that Lasier had been convicted for treason and awaited execution. An indignant Maltby noted that Lasier had not been convicted of treason, but in fact had received citations for bravery at Fort Donelson and Shiloh, and that the private's wounding at Shiloh had "sealed his devotion to his country."[10]

Captain Cowan wrote a letter to a friend in which he conveyed the horrors of battle and bragged about the Union men, who were still committed to their cause despite suffering from the "rain, sleet, snow, wind, and cold" and the loss of so many comrades. The captain attributed the Union victories at Donelson and Shiloh to the "cool stubborn fighting" of the determined Federals. Not all in the unit behaved honorably, though. Although General Halleck honorably discharged the regiment's band on July 17, Pvt. Peter Bellingall recalled that Colonel Smith had castigated the band for their craven actions at Fort Donelson and Shiloh. After Donelson, in front of the entire regiment, Smith called the entire band "a lot of cowards" for their misdeeds, which brought punishment in the form of additional work and greater punishments for the band's leader and drum major.[11]

During June and July 1862 the 45th suffered no casualties from marauding Confederate cavalry and guerilla fighters. Perhaps it was luck or the members' vigilance that prevented the losses incurred by other units at the hands of enemy forces near Jackson and elsewhere. Overall, the men enjoyed restful service during this period. Enslaved people continued to come into the Union lines and typically brought the men food and sometimes their enslavers' horses. One Lead Mine man wrote that they were happy with the Union leaders' change in policy regarding foraging and believed "conciliation is played out." This was a common feeling among Union soldiers. At Jackson, several men wrote home to ask for reinforcements. Cpl. Kingsley Olds informed his father that the soldiers, tired of mere accolades, wanted more men and a harder war on the Confederacy to end the conflict sooner: "We need more troops now, and we need them badly." Olds called for all those back home who felt the Union was worth saving to enlist. On July 12 Colonel Smith sent members home to recruit; they successfully enlisted thirty-seven men in August and September. One of these men, Pvt. Nathan Corbin, never mentioned any hostility from the unit's veterans toward him and the other new recruits, perhaps because none were substitutes or draftees. The still loyal Lead Mine men, like other Union troops, demonstrated the chasm between the soldiers and the civilians back home. They also showed their practicality regarding their country's policies against the Confederacy; questioning the patriotism of those back home and beckoning them to enlist illustrated their rational analysis of the measures necessary for the Union to win the war.[12]

The most significant action for the 45th during their time near Jackson came in late August while guarding rail stations south of Jackson. On August 7 General McClernand dispersed the regiment twelve to twenty-three miles southward, to Medon, Treager's, and Toone's Stations and to several railroad trestleworks (see Map 5.1). Lieutenant Colonel Maltby commanded the soldiers at Toone's Station, while Capt. James Rouse commanded those at Treager's and Capt. James Palmer those at Medon. As at Jackson, fugitives from slavery continued to come into the lines, and Maltby, acting as a practical liberator, put them to work as paid cooks, servants for the men, and teamsters. He wrote in a letter home that the army should go "whole hog"

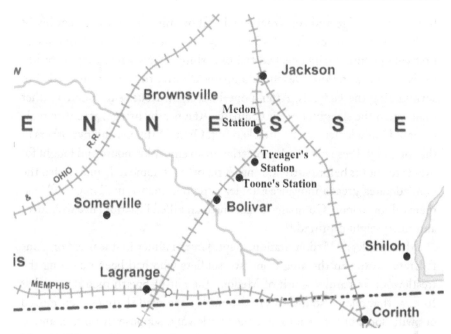

Map 5.1. Western Tennessee, August 1862. *Source: Map created by Hal Jespersen, https:// www.cwmaps.com* (changes made to the original).

in the use of formerly enslaved people to alleviate the "heroes of Donelson and Shiloh" from menial work and that all Union soldiers were abolitionists. Historian Chandra Manning contended that it was the Union soldiers fighting the Confederacy, like Maltby, who "forged the crucial link between slaves and policy makers." Via their letters touting emancipation, the men convinced civilians and politicians back home that it was a worthy war aim. Historians Gary Gallagher and Zachery Fry also noted this link and the influence of the Union soldiers on the question of emancipation.[13]

Initially, this service differed little from the members' earlier railroad guard duty near Jackson, as the soldiers feasted on thousands of bushels of peaches and blackberries. The men stole nearby citizens' chickens and geese to show their commitment for a hard war against the Confederate populace. This uneventful service ended on August 31, when Confederate cavalry drove in the pickets at Toone's Station and captured Pvt. James Harding of Company B, though no attack on the cotton-bale-fortified station occurred. Harding carried dispatches and died while a prisoner of war. At nearly the same time, Col. Richard Alexander Pinson's cavalry attacked Treager's Station. Given warning by a runaway slave, Captain Rouse had his company dig a ditch in front of the bridge and construct a wall out of railroad ties to protect his 38 soldiers against the estimated 400 enemy horsemen. The Lead Mine men's first volley temporarily checked the onrushing rebels when they were 100 yards from the station. Despite Company C's fire, the enemy succeeded in surrounding the Federals. After a one-hour fight, Rouse surrendered rather than watch the slaughter of his company. At a nearby bridge, an entire regiment of Confederate cavalry attacked Sgt. Orrin Williams and five others of the company. These men took protection in an empty log house and fought for over three hours before surrendering. A report sent home to Illinois noted the Confederates' great annoyance after learning that such a small force had held them off for so long. Company C had one man killed in action, five wounded, and thirty-eight captured.[14]

Meanwhile, at Medon Station, Capt. James Palmer first learned of Confederate cavalry in the area from two soldiers who had been guarding the trestlework four miles south of Medon. The out-of-breath men reported at 10 A.M. that enemy soldiers were driving up the road. Palmer then moved out with some of his men to save the trestlework, supposedly on fire, and to determine the force opposing him. After they had gone two miles, a train from Jackson reached Palmer, bound with supplies for Toone's Station and soldiers for the Bolivar, Tennessee, depot. With the trestlework likely on fire, the forty men of the 11th Iowa Volunteer Infantry got off the train, which returned to Jackson. On reaching the trestlework, Palmer's men worked to put out the burning structure, but Confederate cavalry soon fired on them and caused several casualties. Palmer ordered his men back to Medon, which they reached, just escaping capture by the gray horsemen. With an attack looming, Adj. William Frohock had the soldiers and formerly enslaved people fortify the station with a breastwork made of cotton bales. The Union force of 165 men readied for the attack by the estimated 1,500 enemy cavalry of Brig. Gen. Frank C. Armstrong.[15]

The three-hour battle at Medon started at 3 P.M. The Union men held their fire until the enemy were close and then, according to a report sent home, fired a "murderous volley" into the onrushing dismounted cavalry. After repeated attacks, Armstrong's troopers eventually struck from three sides, in a semicircle, using nearby houses, fences, stumps, and trees as cover. Reportedly, the Confederates cheered as they attacked, while the Union troops fired in silence. At about 6 P.M. the train that had brought the Iowans returned to Medon with six companies, 250 men, from the 7th Missouri Volunteer Infantry; soldiers sent by Col. Michael K. Lawler in Jackson on learning of the Confederate assault. The arrival of the Missourians caused the enemy fire to slacken. Seeing the regimental flags of their comrades, the Illinois and Iowa soldiers started "frantic hand shaking all round" and rejoiced. A member of the 45th wrote home that the regiment's "noble little Assistant Surgeon," Dr. Frank Reilly, was on the train and soon treated the wounded with unflagging attention. The Federals then formed into a line and "attacked the enemy vigorously and drove him from the field," ending the fighting. They captured several prisoners and inflicted a large number of casualties in the Confederate ranks.[16]

Of all the men in the 45th Illinois, Pvt. Peter Bellingall likely had the most harrowing day. The private had volunteered to guard the trestlework four miles south of Medon Station with three other soldiers. Bellingall wrote that he had the "privilege of the regiment" that day, which meant he could wear a civilian suit, which resembled a Confederate gray uniform. Had Bellingall been captured, he likely would have been hanged for being a spy. With the presence of enemy cavalry in the area, Captain Palmer had ordered the four soldiers to burn the trestlework if attacked. That morning Bellingall spotted a band of Confederate cavalry, at which his two comrades ran off to warn Palmer; the other had left to look for food. Bellingall walked across the bridge to ascertain whether the calvary was Confederate. When the horsemen fired at him, the private set fire to the trestlework and ran northward toward Medon.[17]

Bellingall ran to the safety of a canebrake, but his repeated attempts to leave the cover and enter the road drew enemy fire. Just before noon he encountered a civilian, who let him pass without sounding the alarm. He soon reached a peach orchard, where the hungry private ate his fill, having had no breakfast that day. Bellingall kept to the canebrake to elude the enemy burning the trestlework and reach Medon, now five miles away. Luckily for the private, he exited the cover just 200 yards from the west side of Medon Station in an area not covered by the enemy. Though afraid his comrades might shoot him because of his gray clothes, Bellingall raced to the Union cotton blockade, where a comrade yelled out, "It's the dead drummer," a reference to Bellingall's old position and the fact that he had been reported killed by the Confederates. The private reached the Federals' blockade with only a slight wound to his hand. The 7th Missouri reached Medon thirty minutes later, just as Bellingall shot and killed an enemy soldier. The private, after his ordeal, still had the energy to want to knock "out of existence" a comrade who stole the dead enemy's stash of half dollars.[18]

Medon was Sgt. John P. Jones's first time under fire, as he had been sick with measles during the Battles of Fort Donelson and Shiloh. He recalled later that he was "perfectly cool," which may have resulted in his promotion to orderly sergeant. With numerically superior Confederate forces still in the area, other, more seasoned men calmed their anxiety over another attack by working to strengthen their fortifications.[19]

The fighting on August 31, 1862, took a severe toll on the 45th. The unit suffered 59 casualties: 3 men killed in action, 13 wounded, and 43 taken prisoner. Of the wounded, 2 sustained mortal wounds and died shortly thereafter. Those taken prisoner, except Private Harding, were later paroled, and several reached Galena by September 29. With 369 members present for duty on August 31, the casualties represented 16 percent of the regiment. Of those paroled, at least 2 deserted and never returned to the unit. Colonel Maltby's report on the day's events noted that the Confederates had 8 soldiers killed and 40 wounded, but that an untold number of wounded had been carried off by their mates. Despite the capture of so many men, the decisive, competent, composed, and empathic leadership of Captains Rouse and Palmer no doubt saved the lives of many more of their soldiers, especially with Palmer's surrender to prevent the annihilation of his men and Rouse's quick decision to retreat. Rouse's competent leadership came after just four months in command of Company C. Their performance was likely a result of their serious study of the art of war, their learned study of their senior officers in the unit's previous battles, and the character of the men they commanded. The men of the 45th were not the only isolated Union troops on railroad guard duty at this time attacked by superior groups of Confederate horsemen.[20]

The Lead Mine men enjoyed a quiet September and happily returned to garrison duty at Jackson on the seventeenth. On October 1 they joined with the rest of soldiers for a night of "singing, playing the violin, dancing, playing cards, talking" and other relaxing activities. The melancholy Captain Cowan, though, dwelled on those who had died or been disabled by wounds, as well as those who would die before the war ended. While the duty in Jackson helped improve the health of the Lead Mine men, they longed to leave the boredom of camp life, especially after hearing of the Union victory at Corinth on October 3–4. They shared this dislike of guard duty with others in Grant's department and anxiously awaited orders that would relieve their tedium. When not building fortifications, some men pitched horseshoes, played cards or checkers, sang, or wrote letters home, while others fretted over how their families would fare the coming winter. Captain Cowan trusted in Providence to provide his family with the necessities. He told his daughter that he had gone to church on October 5, and while he did not think the sermon had "much affect on the boys," the men believed, like others in the army, that Providence would bring a Union victory in the war. As November approached, the weather turned colder, with cold north winds and the first snow of the year. The men welcomed the cold, as it rid them of the tormenting lice.[21]

At 4 A.M. on November 2 the 45th Illinois gratefully left Jackson to join Grant's Mississippi Central Campaign to capture Vicksburg. The Lead Mine men marched as members of the 1st Brigade, 3rd Division, 17th Corps—their home for the rest of the war. Following the Union's pragmatic policy, Grant instructed his men to forage for food from civilians. Although Grant ordered that no harm come to the civilians' other property, his soldiers caused wanton destruction. By November 4 the 45th reached La Grange, Tennessee, some fifty miles southwest of Jackson. Most of the regiment stayed there for three weeks as provost guard as Grant waited for the 20,000 men he had requested from Halleck. Grant's orders called for issuing civilians Union vouchers for confiscated cattle and sheep. The 45th's Lt. J. Warren Miller took six cows from one plantation but doubted "the propriety of giving a voucher" to a farm owned by a man fighting in the Confederate army. Other Federals foraged for all manner of food without issuing vouchers, used fences for firewood, ransacked houses, and burned houses, barns, and other structures. These actions likely caused the "inveterate hatred" of the Union soldiers by La Grange's women, who believed rumors that the Federals would murder and rape them. Some civilians told Cowan they were tired of the war and only wanted the men not to "meddle with their N——s." Under Grant's order not to return formerly enslaved people to their enslavers, men like Dr. Kittoe became practical abolitionists, seeing how the loss of slave property hurt the Confederacy's war effort. In a letter to Washburne, Kittoe favored a hard war: "The iron gauntlet must be used more than the silken glove to crush this serpent."[22]

A mission ordered by General Grant changed Captain Cowan's impressions of his enemy. At La Grange Grant ordered Cowan, with eighteen soldiers, to take 165 Confederate prisoners to Cairo, Illinois, via transport ship. By time he reached Cairo, Cowan now believed most Confederates to be "fine men, both physically and intellectually, and worthy of a better cause than that in which they are engaged." Other Federals likewise held a positive opinion of their enemy after close interaction. After several prisoners told the captain that they "had done their last fighting," Cowan judged that most had lost faith in their cause and wished the war to be over. Again reflective, the captain estimated that there were only "two hundred or three hundred" sunburned faces remaining of the "proud and noble-hearted thousand" who had left Chicago twelve months earlier. Cowan joined others at La Grange in fondly remembering their comrades lost to date in the war.[23]

On November 28 the Lead Mine men and their comrades left La Grange; they reached Holly Springs, Mississippi, twenty-five miles to the south, on November 30 (see Map 5.2). Along the way, amid rich cotton country, they passed great, mostly deserted plantations, with nary a white person on them

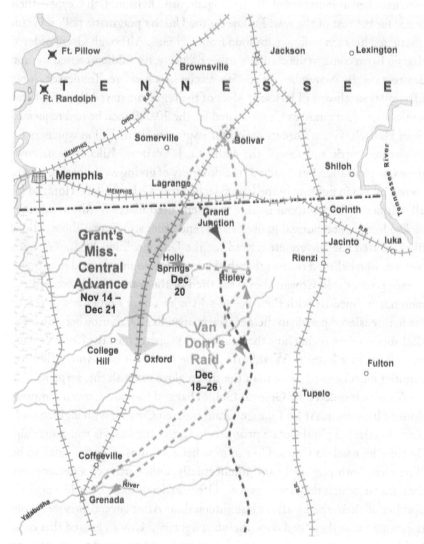

Map 5.2. Gen. Ulysses S. Grant's Mississippi Central Campaign, November 1862–January 1863. *Source: Map created by Hal Jespersen, https://www.cwmaps.com* (changes made to the original).

and most populated by only a few worn-out older enslaved people. The deserted plantations became easy targets for destruction by the men in blue. The areas they passed contained "all Secessionists!" whose women heaped abuses on the Union men. The formerly enslaved flocked to the Union lines, telling the soldiers that their enslavers had moved those of working age south to keep "from getting sight of 'De Yankees.'" They also helped the men find hidden items to pillage. On December 5 the regiment reached Oxford, thirty miles south of Holly Springs. In the rain, sleet, and snow, they foraged for food and "killed plenty of pork." The men also saw much destruction, hastily dug graves, many dead mules and horses, and smashed and burned wagons, evidence of the fighting by Grant's forward units.[24]

While on the campaign, in early December the 45th Illinois lost its commander when the army, after General Grant's repeated requests, promoted Col. John E. Smith to brigadier general. Newspapers back home lauded Smith's service and said his promotion was justly deserved. The regiment's officers petitioned the army to promote Maltby to colonel, to take Smith's place, and Cowan to lieutenant colonel over Maj. Melancthon Smith. The latter request was possibly made because of Major Smith's continued detached service as Memphis's provost marshal. Just days later, on December 16, General Smith addressed his former regiment. He mentioned his debt to his men, saying that he owed his promotion and reputation to the soldiers' bravery in battle and that the regiment's reputation throughout the Army of the Tennessee was simply that "the 45th can be relied on." He called all in the unit his friends and hoped for a postwar reunion. Three days later, the regiment's officers penned a reply, noting their "feelings of mingled pride, pleasure and regret" on hearing of Smith's promotion. They thanked him for his "gallant, manly, officer-like bearing," which they believed had helped the men withstand the Battles of Fort Donelson and Shiloh.[25]

On December 20 progress on General Grant's campaign ended when Maj. Gen. Earl Van Dorn's Confederate cavalry attacked, captured, and destroyed Grant's supply base at Holly Springs and cut all telegraph communications to Memphis. When Confederate brigadier general Nathan Bedford Forrest's calvary destroyed sections of the railroad supplying Grant's army, the Union general's movement south was now untenable, and thus he ordered a retreat to Memphis. In his memoirs, the general stated that during the retreat north, his soldiers' foraging adequately provided food for them. Although several historians have concurred with Grant's recollections, historian Steven Woodworth found that nearly all records by men in the Army of the Tennessee mention the hunger they experienced on the retreat north. The Lead Mine men likewise suffered from hunger on the retreat, their greatest during the war.[26]

The regiment and their brigade mates began their retreat very early on December 22 from Springdale, Mississippi. After a thirteen-mile march, they reached Oxford and went to sleep hungry, with no food to eat or coffee to drink. Captain Cowan wrote of Christmas Day, there was "no snow—no cake—no turkey . . . not even a cup of coffee nor a drop of water nor rot-gut nor a morsel of meat or bread." Cowan left it up to Providence as to when conditions would improve: "God knows when that will be." Sergeant Jones remembered being so hungry that he picked up half of a cracker off the road and "ate it ravenously." While foraging occasionally produced "bacon, sweet potatoes, corn meal, peas, hogs and free beef," the men existed on half rations for much of the retreat; Grant and the Union's hard war policy against the Confederacy meant the men had to rely on the uneven results of foraging, which resulted in little food at times and hunger and suffering for the men in blue. The civilians lost their enslaved people, food, forage, and in some cases their houses and other buildings, while the Lead Mine men ended 1862, their first full year in uniform, hungry and tired.[27]

On New Year's Day 1863, each man in the 45th Illinois "feasted" on three ears of corn, and the men lived for the next week on parched corn as they marched north. By order of General Logan, Capt. Abraham Polsgrove of the 45th, a miller before the war, commanded the operation at four corn mills, which soon yielded 300 bushels a day for the nearly 30,000 Union soldiers. The men joked of their "high lives" as they ate cakes made from coarsely milled corn. They suffered from hunger and cold in their ragged, filthy, flea-infested uniforms, with some men sockless and shoeless, all without being paid in over six months.[28]

Their suffering on the retreat only got worse when the men reached Collierville, near Memphis. The weather turned colder and windier, and by the morning of January 15 six inches of snow covered the ground. Foraging failed to produce sustenance, and thus the men went hungry. The men's foraging on their southward movement had left little to scavenge on the retreat north. To one civilian, Grant's campaign had made northern Mississippi a "blackened waste," and thousands of formerly enslaved people were now under Union protection. Historian Donald Miller contended that Grant's men had gone further by initiating "a social upheaval, the first major threat to the culture of plantation slavery in the cotton empire." Hungry, the Lead Mine men shivered in their tents with no fires, and soon the bitter weather froze their only good water source. On January 17 a train transported 103 sick members, all without shoes, and others in the army to Memphis. The rest of the unit reached the city at 3:30 P.M. on January 21. The long, torturous, failed campaign had finally ended, as had the soldiers' suffering from hunger and the bitter cold.[29]

The army housed Pvt. Nathan Corbin and 1,000 of his sick comrades in the large, six-story Overton Hospital in Memphis. Corbin wrote of the Sisters of Charity's excellent care, yet men died every night in the overcrowded hospital. Each day the private peered down through a window at the "lifeless as clay" bodies on the ground. Corbin left the hospital three months later without a discharge and boarded the first ship south to rejoin the unit, which had left to join Grant's Vicksburg Campaign. Despite the large number of sick soldiers, of the hardy and robust Lead Mine men only Pvt. Benjamin Burleigh died of sickness on the terrible retreat.[30]

The 45th Illinois and the rest of Maj. Gen. James B. McPherson's 17th Army Corps spent the rest of January and almost all of February camped near Memphis because of a lack of space near General Grant's headquarters at Milliken's Bend, Louisiana. While there, the "all gristle" Lead Mine men added to their laurels during an inspection of the 17th Corps. On February 1 Insp. Gen. William E Strong reported that the regiment had "carried off the honors of the Inspection" because no unit could compare to it. The army must have resupplied the regiment because Strong reported that every member had a complete uniform and a full complement of equipment: knapsack, cartridge box, bayonet, haversack, and canteen. Their Enfield rifles, with barrels and stocks that had "hardly a bruise or a scratch," had saber bayonets that "shone like burnished silver." The experienced veterans of the 45th recognized, as most veterans did, that a clean weapon paid dividends during battle. Even though their camp was situated on low ground, its cleanliness met all regulations and stood above other camps in their brigade. Strong concluded that the unit was "finely drilled and under good discipline," and the honor was justly deserved. To Captain Cowan, Strong's words were a "a compliment, for everybody knows that the regular army officers won't say anything favorable of volunteer soldiers if they can avoid it." The results of inspection are evidence that despite the members' travails on the retreat, enduring bitter weather, hunger, and lice, their pride in service to the Union had not diminished.[31]

During late 1862 and early 1863 the Lead Mine men commented on some of the war's larger issues. According to Cowan, some members considered President Lincoln's Emancipation Proclamation unconstitutional, but it did not take long for most to support ending slavery. Cowan called the reports false that stated the Union soldiers opposed the emancipation of the enslaved and would not fight for them. Believing that emancipation removed the Confederacy's workforce, weakened the rebellion, and enabled the perpetuation of the Union, 1st Sgt. Joshua Vanderwort said the regiment was "*for the Union, and being so are for every move and act of the Administration that is designed to perpetuate or defend it.*" Cowan's and Vanderwort's pragmatic views that emancipation and the creation of Black regiments would help preserve the Union mirror Gallagher's and Fry's findings that the majority of Union citizens and soldiers viewed emancipation and the creation of the Black regiments as war measures to help defeat the Confederacy and achieve the main war goal of preserving the Union. The Lead Mine men had not enlisted to free the enslaved and did not consider the Black man to be equal to the white man, but the letters of several members demonstrate that emancipation as a war measure, to hurt the enemy, was viewed favorably, as was the arming of the formerly enslaved men so that they could fight for their freedom. No sources indicate that any of the Lead Mine men favored emancipation on moral grounds, as did a small minority of Union soldiers. Certainly some members were against emancipation and the creation of the Black regiments, but the regiment's letters reveal that those who opposed these measures were in the minority. Cowan believed that the Black soldiers would prove wrong those who thought the "negro could not be made to fight like soldiers" and was sure the Union would not regret the decision to arm the Black men. The captain explained to a friend that Lincoln's moves had strengthened the Lead Mine men's resolve; they were for "war, harder and more of it, till the victory is proclaimed."[32]

The rise of the Copperheads, the Democrat-led antiwar Northerners in the Union, raised the most ire among the Lead Mine men. Sergeant Vanderwort considered them "traitorous villains" and a "strong *secesh* element." Traitorous indeed, as Copperheads wrote to Union soldiers calling them to desert, worked to discourage enlistments, colluded with Confederate spies, attempted to break Confederate soldiers out of Union prisoner-of-war camps, and took up arms against Union soldiers in Illinois, Indiana, and Ohio. Vanderwort believed the "*infernal black-hearted copperheads*" had not discouraged the regiment—the men promised vengeance when they returned home and were emboldened to win the war as quickly as possible, no matter the hardships. Cowan believed the Copperhead Democrats were as bad as the secessionists: "I am afraid our country is in a bad fix now between the Secesh and the Democrats." The 45th's anger likely stemmed from learning that Galena Copperheads had "severely beaten and mauled" Capt. John Rouse of Company C while he was on his parole. The regiment's virulent hate of the Copperheads mirrored what historians found for the Union army. The antiwar movement, orchestrated by men in covert organizations, initially lowered morale in the blue ranks, as many saw it as giving aid to their enemies. Later, the soldiers' hate of the Copperheads strengthened their resolve to end the war sooner, return home, and exact violent revenge.[33]

Regarding emancipation and the creation of Black regiments, the 45th's sentiments matched that of most of their comrades in Grant's army and in the Union army as a whole. Though the unit did not pass resolutions to return to Illinois and drive the now-majority Democrats from the state legislature, as five other Illinois units had, the 45th was in favor of the resolutions against the Democratic "tories" and "infernal lying politicians." Capt. James J. Palmer promised "broken heads" if the politicians had "not changed their tune" before the men came home. Clearly, unlike other units, the 45th saw its morale boosted and not diminished by the Copperheads' antiwar work This is evident in that only three members deserted in late 1862–early 1863, whereas many other Illinois, Ohio, and Indiana regiments had large numbers of desertions. During this time, two of the 45th's officers resigned their commissions, but no reason was recorded, so it is unclear whether these two men resigned over emancipation, the creation of the Black regiments, or disillusionment over the Copperhead campaigns, as historian Jonathan White found with other Union officers.[34]

Historians have generally agreed that a large majority of Union soldiers were initially against Lincoln's Emancipation Proclamation, for they had not enlisted to free the enslaved. Eventually, however, most changed their minds and backed emancipation after seeing the brutality and inhuman nature of slavery and how the Confederates were hurt by losing their enslaved people. They came to see emancipation and ending slavery as a necessary measure to end the war sooner, and some believed it would cause a rebirth of the Union. White concurred that the soldiers who favored emancipation did so because they saw it as a practical war measure. However, he challenged the belief that most Union soldiers favored emancipation, stating that "large numbers of soldiers opposed Lincoln's war policies, especially emancipation." White also demonstrated that Union officers intimidated and punished anti-emancipation soldiers and that these efforts influenced many soldiers to favor Lincoln's war measure. Colonel Maltby's comments written while at Toone's Station and Dr. Kittoe's at La Grange, among others, lend support to the findings of Chandra Manning, Gallagher, and Fry that many Federals believed it was logical to remove enslaved people from their enslavers; the soldiers took all manner of Confederate property, and the Confederates were weakened by the loss of every enslaved person that came into the Union. Others grew to favor emancipation after seeing that the formerly enslaved men made good soldiers.[35]

On the creation of Black regiments, historians have found that most Union soldiers were initially against the move, largely for racist reasons, but as with Cowan, Vanderwort, and others in the 45th, the majority in the army changed their minds. They saw that the Black soldiers fought well at Port Hudson, Fort Wagner, and Milliken's Bend and that in losing many of their comrades, the Black men were willing to die for their freedom. Moreover, the Black soldiers relieved white soldiers from unpleasant fatigue and garrison duties, and by carrying guns, the Black men would eliminate more Confederates and end the war sooner. Finally, Black regiments provided an easier path for enlisted men to become officers than in white units. Though a relatively small number of white soldiers took this path, historians have found that for some, the higher pay—a first sergeant made $20 a month, while a lieutenant earned $105.50— was the reason these men chose to become officers in the Black regiments.[36]

On Wednesday, February 18, the 45th Illinois and their comrades in General Logan's 3rd Division received orders to move south. The joyful Lead Mine men had received two months' pay and would soon leave the Memphis mud. One member wrote of his pragmatic comrades that they knew many more of their brothers would have to fall in battle, as well as to disease and sickness, before defeating the rebellion, yet they went south with somber resolve to fight on despite the "copperhead venom" at home. Two days later the division marched to the city's wharf and boarded forty steamboats, which left Memphis on February 22. The 45th experienced beautiful but cool nights on their pleasant trip and cheered "as lively as a bunch of school boys" as the ships grandly made their 200-mile journey. On February 25 they reached Lake Providence, Louisiana, on the west bank of the Mississippi, joining the rest of General McPherson's 17th Corps. The Lead Mine men would not return north before experiencing additional trials and earning additional laurels because of great sacrifice—sacrifice they made to help save their republic.[37]

6. ❄ On to Vicksburg

On May 19, 1863, the 45th Illinois and the rest of the 1st Brigade reached the Confederates' east-facing fortifications near Vicksburg. These troops' fighting over the previous nineteen days played a critical role in securing three victories in General Grant's successful campaign to reach the Confederate citadel from the east. In this next increment of the Union's hard war on their enemy's citizenry, because of an order from General Grant for his men to live off the land, the Federals experienced much hunger due to the uneven results of their foraging as they marched in choking dust and heated temperatures. Despite the campaign's ordeals, the 45th held true and fought honorably to help bring Grant's army to the doorstep of Vicksburg. In doing so, the Lead Mine men, with their comrades, continued to cause enslaved people to leave their enslavers along their march, while the arrival of Union soldiers led to suffering for nearby civilians.[1]

Federal preoccupation with Vicksburg began early in the war when, on November 15, 1861, President Lincoln identified it as a key target in splitting the Confederacy. Taking the strategically located fortress would cut off food and supplies from the Trans-Mississippi region—Arkansas, Louisiana, and Texas—and thereby help win the war. According to Lincoln, "The war can never be brought to a close until that key is in our pocket." Confederate president Jefferson Davis considered Vicksburg critical to his nation's defense, especially by March 1863, when only Vicksburg and Port Hudson, Louisiana, remained of the Confederacy's river fortresses. The Union's leadership in 1862 became convinced that only a joint army-navy operation could take the citadel, with its tall bluffs and stout defenses. That year General Grant's overland campaign to take the city had failed, as did his Chickasaw Bayou expedition, which attempted to take Vicksburg from the north and east of the Mississippi River. Grant then initiated the Lake Providence project and several others during the spring of 1863 to attack Vicksburg from above and below the city.[2]

At Lake Providence, the 45th disembarked and marched to their camp on the lawn of the Bellagio Plantation, on the banks of the lake four miles west of the Mississippi River. The Union troops worked to cut down the trees in the bayous below the waterline to enable shallow-draft ships to pass through and also cut levees between Lake Providence and the Mississippi and between the lake and Bayou Baxter to the south. If Grant's plan worked, the water levels in the bayous would rise enough to allow his ships to carry his army 220 miles through the lake and bayous, into the Red River, then north up the Mississippi 130 miles to attack Vicksburg from the south. Most in the 45th did not worry about the coming destruction of many fine plantations and other property when the Mississippi River rushed into the lake and bayous. Meanwhile, Union soldiers continued the hard war by tearing down civilians' fences and houses for fires and foraging their livestock, vegetables, and other food—punishing the Confederate civilians for starting the war and forcing the men to fight and die to restore the Union.[3]

The Lead Mine men both enjoyed and lamented their camp at the lake. Captain Adair wrote of the area's "romantic beauty" and believed this camp was their best during the war. The men loved the warm weather but not the torrential rains, which nearly inundated them. When not working, men fished or hunted to supplement their diet and read in their tents. The terrible lice still tormented the soldiers, who also had to deal with new antagonists, including alligators. As in Mississippi and elsewhere in the Confederacy, slaveholders abandoned their "immensely rich" plantations and moved most of their enslaved people to remote areas, leaving only a few very old, fervent Confederates, children, and thousands of acres of unpicked cotton. Thousands of formerly enslaved people now lived in Union camps. Grant employed the men in army jobs and paid the women and children to pick cotton so that the army did not have to provide them with shelter and food.[4]

Despite reports that the area's good water improved the regiment's health, sickness took many from the corps, with pneumonia and smallpox killing the most. The hardy 45th had four members die—from congestive chills, pneumonia, disease, and unspecified causes, respectively—while disease and disability caused two soldiers' discharge. Grant's men in their Milliken's Bend and Young's Point camps, south of Lake Providence, also experienced debilitating sickness in the dank and wet terrain near the Mississippi River.[5]

At the lake, the pragmatic Lead Mine men continued to embrace emancipation, and their diatribes persisted against the treasonous Copperheads. Captain Cowan likened these traitors to Brutus stabbing Julius Caesar and stated that his comrades were for all acts that hurt slavery. An unnamed member believed that God would defeat the Copperheads and said the soldiers were "to a man in favor of the President's war policy.—Emancipation" and any other act that would end the rebellion. He proclaimed that the soldiers hated the Copperheads the most, followed by the "lawless Guerilla, next a regular butternut, and last and least, the devil." The Lead Mine men's loathing of the Copperheads also stemmed from hearing from enslavers that the antiwar Northerners' work emboldened the rebels' war effort. The 45th and their army comrades saw emancipation and the willful taking of civilian property, notably enslaved people, as sensible means of hurting the Confederacy, and the men's hatred of their enemy led to wanton foraging and taking whatever they pleased from the civilians. Historian Donald Miller discovered that some regiments in Grant's army incurred up to fifty desertions because of the Copperhead antiwar and anti-Grant letters; however, the Lead Mine men's commitment to their republic remained unchanged, with only Pvt. Samuel Wait of the 45th deserting while at Lake Providence.[6]

With the levee opened to the bayous on March 15, the 1st Brigade, including the 45th Illinois, and the rest of the 17th Corps marched to the Mississippi River in heavy rain and boarded crowded transports. Two days later, several men completed the final work to cut the levee between Lake Providence and the Mississippi River. As the river flowed into the lake, soldiers from another unit set fire to a church near the river, breaking windows and tearing up the building, which brought shouts and cheers from the thousands of men on the ships. Despite Grant's orders against destruction of nonmilitary buildings, nobody, not even the officers, worked to put out the fire. Captain Cowan wrote that onlooking freedmen took "pleasure, enjoying the sights" of the soldiers destroying the church, but the onlooking white civilians did not see the "fun in the operation." The captain joined other Union soldiers in his dislike of this wanton destruction, yet he still approved of the soldiers' actions because he knew it would end the war sooner. It is unknown whether the Federals' destruction of the church was retaliation for a pro-Confederacy or proslavery sermon by its minister, as happened elsewhere in the Confederacy during the war.[7]

An "immense volume of water" from the Mississippi River now flowed into the lake from a 150-foot-wide opening in the levee. Cowan dispassionately wrote that the "inconceivable force" of the water would destroy the mostly deserted plantations south of the lake. The continued lack of space in General Grant's camps near Vicksburg caused the transports to deliver the 17th Corps north five miles upriver at the Vista Plantation. Thankful to be off the crowded and terribly dirty ships, the Lead Mine men happily camped in an old cornfield and, in the warm weather, swam "like frogs" in the river.[8]

While the antiwar Copperheads in the Union caused the 45th, like other Union men, to distance themselves from the civilians back home, Captain Cowan thanked a civilian and his group of patriotic youths back in Illinois who had provided firewood to the soldiers' families. Cowan wrote that the civilians' efforts encouraged the soldiers to endure "the hardships of war" and save the Union. In a letter to his daughter around the same time, Cowan noted that there was something "grand sublime and fascinating in a battle," but the work to help their comrades suffering from terrible wounds sickened the men, and the agony of the wounded stripped a "great deal of the beauty" from battle.[9]

Two notable events occurred in March for Cowan. On March 2 he received a promotion to major instead of lieutenant colonel. The Illinois governor had ignored the unit's officers' earlier petition for Cowan's promotion to lieutenant colonel despite it containing Grant's and other senior officers' endorsements. This led both Cowan and Colonel Maltby to resign. The army rejected both resignations, and eventually Cowan humbly accepted the promotion. In late March he gratefully went north on a furlough home to take care of his sick wife. After a snowy trip, the major reached Warren, Illinois, on April 3 and spent most of the next eight days caring for his wife, work he lamented prevented him from spending much time with his children. In letters written later that month, he exhorted them to obey their mother, aunts, and teachers and asked his daughter to help her younger brothers. He reminded all three to study hard and to help in the garden and said he hoped to return to them after the war. Cowan rejoined the 45th on April 16. Anxiety over his wife's poor health caused Cowan to get little sleep on the trip, and because of this, he considered it his "hardest campaign."[10]

Just two days after the major's return to the Vista Plantation, General McPherson's corps boarded ships and reached Milliken's Bend, which now had room, as General McClernand's 13th Corps had marched south to New Carthage, Louisiana, in late March. At Milliken's Bend, the 45th welcomed back their former colonel, Brig. Gen. John E. Smith, as their new brigade commander. The unit, however, lost its head surgeon, Dr. Edward Kittoe, to a promotion to General Sherman's staff. Later, General Grant, one of Kittoe's former patients, made the doctor his medical inspector and staff's medical director.[11]

In early April, with a lack of sufficient shallow-draft boats and the proposed route still blocked by too many trees, General Grant canceled the Lake Providence project. He had made four other attempts to get to Vicksburg in early 1863—Grant's Canal, Yazoo Pass, Steele Bayou, and the Duckport

Canal—but these also failed. Thus Grant decided to move his army down the west bank of the Mississippi River to a point south of Vicksburg, cross the river, and then attack from the south. While he waited for the water south of Milliken's Bend to recede, on April 16 Grant sent supply transports, protected by navy gunboats, past Vicksburg's cannons, which sank only one ship. Success here led Grant to schedule a second transport mission (see Map 6.1). The general had three reasons for his eagerness to move southward: to get south of Vicksburg while his many diversions confused Confederate Lieutenant General John C. Pemberton as to Grant's intended route; to enable his soldiers' departure from the damp, unsanitary, disease-ridden camps; and to get his campaign back in motion so that the two observers sent by President Lincoln, Charles Dana and Adj. Gen. Lorenzo Thomas, could send positive reports back to Washington and relieve Grant of the political pressure over his many failures to get at Vicksburg. Historian Timothy Smith called Grant's decisions to move his army down the Louisiana side of the Mississippi River and send transports past Vicksburg's guns the "gamble of gambles," which broke "every rule of warfare in the book."[12]

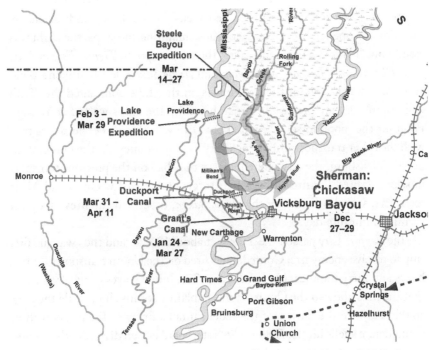

Map 6.1. General Grant's Vicksburg Campaign, December 1862–April 1863. *Source: Map created by Hal Jespersen, https://www.cwmaps.com* (changes made to the original).

For the next sortie to take place, however, Grant needed 150 volunteers to man the ships, as most of the civilian crews had balked at the dangerous mission, which would lack the protection of gunboats from Vicksburg's 172 cannons. On April 22 General Logan and others made speeches, asking for volunteers from the 3rd Division to man the ships. The resulting 750 volunteers much impressed Dana and Thomas. Colonel Maltby spoke plainly of the dangers before asking for volunteers from the 45th, telling them that "in all probability the steamers would be riddled with shot and shell" and many might die. Nevertheless, at least half of the 45th volunteered. Captain Adair called the selection of several of these members to man the ships one of the "memorable events of the war." Lead Mine men manning these ships included Capt. Leander B. Fisk commanding the *Anglo Saxon*, with eight other members constituting one-third of its crew; four more members of the 45th manned other transports.[13]

Before the mission began, the soldiers bulwarked the transports' engines and pilothouses with hay, cotton, and beef barrels; to protect the hulls, they attached ration-filled barges to both sides. So that the ships could drop as noiselessly down the river as possible, the captains had orders not to turn on their engines until they had reached Vicksburg's defenses and the enemy batteries had opened fire. Luckily for those manning the ships, the night was cloudy and "black as a bottomless pit." The six transports, *Tigress, Empire City, J. W. Cheeseman, Horizon, Moderator,* and *Anglo Saxon,* left Milliken's Bend at 9 P.M., and the fate of their comrades on the ships dominated the 45th's discussions as they prepared to march south. The ships waited at Young's Point for the moon to set, then at about 11:15 P.M. the *Tigress* began its trip, with the other transports following every fifteen minutes. As the Union ships neared Vicksburg, the city's defenders, as they had on the previous transport mission, lighted bonfires to see their targets more easily. One Lead Mine man, Pvt. Charles Evans on the *Anglo Saxon,* described the fires as almost turning night into day.[14]

The *Empire City* passed the *Tigress* at about 12 A.M. and thus was the first ship to receive enemy fire; Confederates fired on the Union transports for two hours and forty minutes. On the *Empire City,* John Graves of the 45th wrote that the fires allowed the Confederates to plainly see his ship, while the crew could easily see the flashes of the rebel cannons firing at them. Soon three Confederate shells hit the *Empire City*'s starboard boiler, disabling the engine. The ship, however, successfully made it past the enemy's guns, reaching the western shore of the river south of the city. The badly damaged *Tigress* then came ashore nearby and sank. With the help of other ships, the battered *Empire City* reached its destination, New Carthage, Louisiana, ten miles below Vicksburg, at 9 A.M.[15]

As the *Anglo Saxon* neared the first of Vicksburg's batteries, Captain Fisk ordered the transport to full speed. A shell quickly hit the ship's stern, disabled the rudder, and cut loose the barge nearest to Vicksburg. This caused the ship to steer toward the Louisiana shore, where it struck the bank opposite the fortress. After the crew cut the other barge loose, the transport continued its journey. Soon, however, an enemy shell disabled the starboard engine. The Confederates then sent a huge 124-pounder shot through the pilothouse. It shattered the wheel and knocked the pilot, Private Evans, through the wooden wall of the bridge, stunning him "considerably." Despite the efforts of his shipmates, the *Anglo Saxon* was uncontrollable and completely inoperable, and it floated by the enemy guns at the speed of the current. Amazingly, although severely damaged by some thirty "shell, canister, and musket shots" that struck its stack, office, cookhouse, and cabin, the *Anglo Saxon* managed to stay afloat and was towed to New Carthage by other transports. In his report, Captain Fisk noted his entire crew's "bravery and coolness" under fire.[16]

None of the Lead Mine men sustained any bleeding wounds from the Confederate shelling. Private Evans suffered shock from the impact but reenlisted and served throughout the war; however, the Confederate shell had caused internal injuries, which led to his death just a few years after the war. After the mission, General Grant gave the 45th's Harrison Hines a furlough home, with free transportation, because of his "meritorious conduct." The mission resulted in two Union soldiers killed and six others slightly wounded, with only the *Tigress* sunk, even though the Confederates had fired an estimated 500 shots at the Union ships.[17]

Back at Milliken's Bend, the 45th prepared for their seventy-mile march south to cross the river. To the boastful Major Cowan, the men were in excellent health, ready to take on any hardship. The soldiers discussed only two topics: their commitment to fight until they had defeated the rebellion and the work by Adjutant General Thomas to raise Black units at Milliken's Bend. After Thomas's April 8 speech to McPherson's 17th Corps, several Lead Mine men earned commissions in Black regiments. By war's end, eleven members had done so, including 1st Sgt. James C. Robbins and 1st Sgt. Matthew M. Miller, who accepted captain and second lieutenant commissions, respectively, in the 9th Louisiana Infantry (African Descent). They joined other white Union soldiers in the army who took this opportunity for advancement and greater pay and were not, as Cowan put it, "ashamed or afraid to take command of black soldiers." Historians have shown that this opportunity for advancement and greater pay converted many to Lincoln's program.[18]

Early on April 25, 1863, the 45th and the 17th Corps began their march south, happy to leave the boredom of camp life (see Map 6.2). The "intensely hot" weather during the first two days made the trek difficult, as did the bad water in the area, which caused thousands to fall out with fatigue. The soldiers, as ordered, foraged liberally for food, but in tearing down civilians' fences and houses for their fires and shelters, including some grand cotton plantation homes, and plundering other homes, they ignored Grant's order against "'wanton destruction' or theft of household property." Clearly, once unleashed, the Union's hard war was uncontrollable, and some 2,200 formerly enslaved people were in Union lines by the end of the march.[19]

On the morning of April 27, after "torrents" of rain the previous night, the men marched in near bottomless mud. General McPherson wrote that his men reached their destination that day, over the "almost impassable" roads, only because of his pioneer troops' work to corduroy the roads, his soldiers' "most strenuous exertions," and the "doubling" of teams of horses and mules pulling the artillery and wagons. Snakes and other creatures also tormented the men, but the worst were the mosquitoes, which were abundant in the humid climate, and the lice, which spread easily throughout the army. Despite the men's travails, Major Cowan believed their situation improved on April 28 after Congressman Washburne and Governor Yates informed them on the war's progress, how their families were doing, and what those back home were saying. The two politicians complimented the regiment's service to date and called on the men to sustain their good reputation in the upcoming battles.[20]

When Union warships could not subdue and capture the Confederate batteries at Grand Gulf, Grant chose to cross the Mississippi farther south, at Disharoon's Plantation, after a freedman told him that across from it, at Bruinsburg, Mississippi, a road ran to Port Gibson. On April 30 the 45th Illinois and their mates in the 17th Corps reached Disharoon's Plantation, near Hard Times, Louisiana. With Grant's order to travel light over to Mississippi, the soldiers left their knapsacks and baggage behind and carried only three days' rations and forty rounds of ammunition. The anxious Lead Mine men then crossed the river as one of the lead elements of the 17th Corps.[21]

At 7 A.M. on May 1 the 1st Brigade marched out of Bruinsburg and began a busy and tiring day. The men moved toward the sounds of artillery and rifle fire in the direction of Port Gibson, twelve miles to the northeast, with

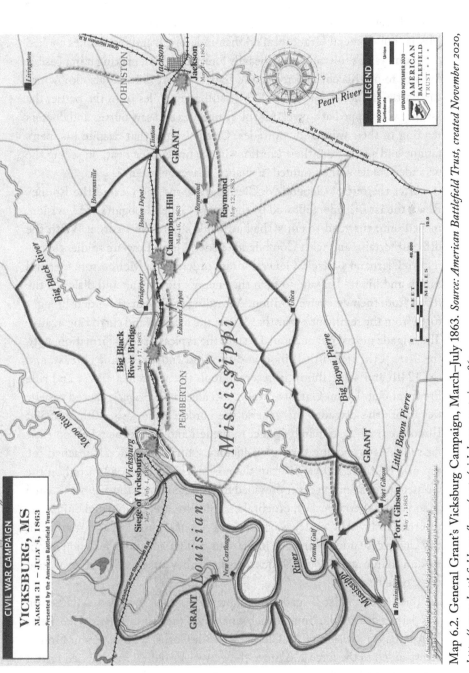

Map 6.2. General Grant's Vicksburg Campaign, March–July 1863. *Source: American Battlefield Trust, created November 2020,* https://www.battlefields.org/learn/maps/vicksburg-campaign-1863.

Vicksburg just thirty miles beyond. Major Cowan wrote that it was a difficult march because of the "steep hills . . . deep ravines and gulches" of western Mississippi. General Grant recalled that underbrush and canebrakes choked the countryside's hills and deep, heavily forested gullies, making it impossible for him to use his entire force in the Battle of Port Gibson (also known as the Battle of Thompson's Hill). While still a few miles from the battle, the 1st Brigade stopped at a creek for thirty minutes and saw nurses and doctors tending to their wounded comrades. Cowan stated that despite his men's fatigue and sweat from their exertions in the unbearable heat, on seeing the wounded soldiers, they wanted "a chance to avenge" them.[22]

After the rest of General McClernand's corps had cleared the Rodney Road, the 1st Brigade, followed by the rest of General Logan's 3rd Division, moved onto the road to enter the battlefield's northwest corner. With the difficult terrain, and with Confederate general John Bowen's soldiers spoiling McClernand's attack, General Grant ordered, via McPherson, General Smith and his 1st Brigade to turn the enemy's right flank and dislodge the rebels from their defensive position. According to Cowan, the orders brought forth from the regiment a roar that "made the heavens and earth ring again." The brigade moved out at about 3 P.M. in the typical Federal formation, with the 31st, 30th, and 20th Illinois and the 23rd Indiana in line abreast, and the 124th and 45th Illinois in reserve. Soon the accurate artillery and rifle fire from Col. Isham Garrott's well-concealed rebel brigade caused casualties in Smith's brigade. The general then ordered the 45th, 20th, and 31st Illinois regiments to march farther to the left and attack the rebels on their far right. After moving through difficult country, the Federals reached the top of a hill, just 100 yards from the enemy's right flank, and fired on the Confederates from the cover provided by a sunken road. The enemy, situated in some blackberry bushes, canebrakes, rifle pits, and dilapidated buildings, returned fire with a "pretty warm response," but the road's cover resulted in few Union casualties, with none in the 45th. After two hours the Union troops made a charge at the double-quick, yelling as they attacked, which dislodged the Confederates.[23]

The rest of the 1st Brigade then joined the attack, which to McPherson was perfect despite the "impracticable nature of the country." Brig. Gen. Peter J. Osterhaus's division of McClernand's 13th Corps, with others in Grant's army, added to the force and drove the gray-clad soldiers in a hurried retreat north toward Port Gibson for about four miles, until nightfall. The rough countryside's ravines prevented the capture of the Confederates, who reached

Port Gibson. Before stopping for the night, Grant, McPherson, Logan, Yates, and Washburne rode by the 45th. The congressman shouted, "I told you, boys, what you would do to-day, and you have done it." Historians have attributed Grant's victory to his diversions—General Sherman's attack at Haynes' Bluff, Col. Benjamin Grierson's famous calvary raid, and the navy's attack at Grand Gulf—which confused Pemberton as to Grant's intentions and resulted in Brigadier General Bowen having only three brigades to oppose McClernand's corps and Logan's division. Major Cowan attributed the victory to the Union soldiers' bravery and the cool command by Grant, McPherson, Logan, and Smith. He also commended Maltby's calm efforts in leading the regiment. Logan boasted of the "gallant" Smith, who led the 1st Brigade, and said that their charge "was executed with a zeal and heroism" and added to their honors earned on "the bloody fields of Belmont, Donelson and Shiloh." After the battle, the brigade cheered the untested 124th Illinois for its gallant performance in its first battle. Both Cowan and his former colonel, General Smith, believed Providence had seen them through the battle unharmed.[24]

Grant's victory at Port Gibson forced Pemberton to evacuate Grand Gulf, eight miles northwest of Port Gibson on the Mississippi River. This gained Grant many artillery pieces, a large number of small arms, and more important, a supply base and bridgehead for his campaign. Grant addressed his army and thanked the men "for adding another victory to the long list of those previously won by [their] valor and endurance," noting that it was one of the most important in the war to date. He also commended them for enduring extraordinary hardships during the tough march without complaint. Bowen had 832 casualties, with 68 killed, 380 wounded, and 384 missing. Grant's casualties totaled 875, with 131 killed, 719 wounded, and 25 missing. The 45th's only casualty was Cpl. John H. Botts of Mount Carroll, Illinois, who went missing during the battle.[25]

The next morning Grant renewed his pursuit of the Confederates, but the gray ranks escaped northward over a bridge spanning the south fork of the "formidable" Bayou Pierre, to which they set fire once across. With this route closed, Grant sent General Smith's brigade east along the bayou. After marching about three and a half miles, they forded a swamp and crossed Big Bayou Pierre on a makeshift bridge built by the retreating enemy. The brigade skirmished with the enemy and captured a few stragglers before bivouacking late that night after a tiring fifteen miles. The choking dust, hot sun, hills, and "gulches, bogs, [and] cane breaks" had made for a difficult march. The lone bright spot that day was the capture of more than 7,000 pounds of bacon found at a farm. Given their limited rations, the 3rd Division soldiers much appreciated the captured meat.[26]

As Pemberton frantically worked to consolidate his forces, Grant moved McPherson's and McClernand's corps east and north of the Big Black River. This move shielded his soldiers from Pemberton's army, forcing the Confederate general to move his forces out of Vicksburg's fortifications and east of the river. Grant aimed east to tear up the Southern Railroad of Mississippi and cut off Pemberton's supply line, after which he planned to turn west to attack Vicksburg. The general traveled to Grand Gulf to assess its usefulness as a supply base and while there made a momentous decision—he would not wait, as ordered, for Maj. Gen. Nathaniel Banks to capture the Confederate bastion at Port Hudson, Louisiana, and then join up with him, but rather, he would keep the initiative gained at Thompson's Hill and move on to take Vicksburg with only his army. Donald Miller called this "one of the pivotal decisions of the Civil War." The general had ammunition, supplies, and three days' rations loaded onto wagons and headed eastward to his men. These were the only rations he provided his men from their landing at Bruinsburg until they reached Vicksburg; he was confident his soldiers' foraging would furnish enough food. On May 4 Grant's troops halted near Rocky Springs, fifteen miles northeast of Port Gibson, for three days to await the supplies, and allow Sherman's 15th Corps time to join the other corps. Having the men forage for their food hurt the local Confederate populace, but as foraging produced uneven results, it also led to much hunger among his men before they got to Vicksburg. According to historian Steven Dossman, Grant's orders for his men to forage "transformed his army into an instrument of economic and psychological warfare that would affect southern civilians and their ability to continue the war," because once unleashed, Grant's officers could not contain their soldiers, who destroyed grand plantations and other property and stole personal items.[27]

The Battle of Raymond took place on May 12, 1863, and as at Port Gibson, the 1st Brigade of the 3rd Division of the 17th Army Corps played an instrumental role in securing victory. Raymond lay about forty-five miles northeast of Port Gibson. The Union troops marched early that morning on the Utica Road toward Raymond, with the goal of capturing food in the town. After having seen vedettes of Confederate cavalry earlier, the members of Logan's 3rd Division, sweating in the heat and humidity, encountered enemy pickets and received fire from Confederate artillery stationed on a hill about two miles west of Raymond. Confederate general John Gregg had shrewdly placed his

5,000 men on either side of his two artillery batteries, on the hills flanking the road, where his cannons could cover the road and the bridge the Union troops had to cross. McPherson then ordered Logan's division to advance and Gen. Marcellus Crocker's division to follow.[28]

When Confederate artillery opened fire on the Union soldiers in earnest, McPherson ordered Logan to deploy his 2nd Brigade to the north of the road and the 1st and 3rd Brigades to the right and south of the road. Orders soon came for the 1st and 3rd Brigades, with the 1st on the far right, to attack the Confederate left flank. To Logan, the battle "became general" across the line when the enemy charged his center. The general then ordered the 1st and 3rd Brigades to move at the quick-step across 400 yards of open ground, which the 1st did with a "tremendous hurrah." The enemy, however, met the charge with "very heavy combined fire of infantry and artillery," and shells landed "pretty thick" among them. Nevertheless, Logan wrote, "every man stepped promptly and majestically forward, and did his duty as a soldier."[29]

The 45th and their comrades soon reached the "banks of a deep gully or hollow" fifty yards from the hill occupied by the Confederates. From the protection of the hollow, they fired on the onrushing enemy soldiers, who hit the Union center the hardest and broke through in several places. Logan reinforced his middle with additional troops, including soldiers from General Crocker's division, who blunted the enemy attack. The Union men then moved by the right flank to clear the forest and cross Fourteen Mile Creek. When back in line, they charged up the steep hill and flanked the enemy's main artillery battery. Not routed yet, a charging Confederate brigade fired on the 45th, on the far right of the Union attack, from the unit's right rear, making its position "untenable." This forced General Smith to order a retreat back to the main Union line. As the men retreated, two accurate volleys from the 31st Illinois, which Smith had held back and fortuitously placed in some woods to protect the brigades' right flank, saved the 45th from being "cut to pieces" and "gobbled up" by the Confederate brigade. Next, two volleys from the entire brigade and from other Federals forced the Confederates to retreat back up the hill. The 3rd Division then hounded the enemy relentlessly through the hills and ravines toward Raymond. After receiving fire from a Confederate battery one mile east of the battlefield, the Union artillery returned fire and the Federals charged the guns, which forced the Confederates to quickly leave the field, ending the fighting.[30]

A Lead Mine man reported to a newspaper back home on the "hotly contested" four-hour battle, calling it the "severest fighting" the regiment had seen, more so than even at Shiloh. Major Cowan likewise noted that it had been "as warm as almost" any battle to date. The Union soldiers buried the dead and brought the wounded to the ambulances before marching into Raymond. General Logan's 3rd Division suffered 99 percent of the 442 Union casualties, losing 438 men, with 53 percent of the total lost being from the 1st Brigade. Because the 20th Illinois and 23rd Indiana regiments withstood the worst of the Confederate charge, they sustained nearly all the casualties in the brigade. The 45th Illinois had 21 casualties, with 16 wounded and 5 captured. One of the captured Lead Mine men, Pvt. Milo Guiles, had a wounded hand that required the amputation of his middle finger. Following his parole, Guiles reenlisted and served throughout the war. Confederate general Gregg had 514 casualties, with 73 killed, 251 wounded, and 190 captured or missing, of which 40 were captured by the 45th. General Logan commended his division for doing their duty "most nobly." Congressman Washburne witnessed the battle and applauded the 45th's fighting, especially Dr. William Lyman for disregarding his own safety and staying with the regiment throughout the battle. General Smith praised his commanders, singling out Colonel Maltby, who, although sick and in an ambulance, mounted his horse and commanded the 45th throughout the battle.[31]

Raymond's civilians quickly grew to dislike the Union soldiers, because the men had a "great time taking bacon, sugar, molasses, and whatever they can get from the old Secesh," including a large feast cooked by the town's ladies in anticipation of a Confederate victory in the battle. The pillaging and plundering here mirrored that at Port Gibson. The Union soldiers at Raymond also deprived nearby slaveholders of their enslaved people. A Lead Mine man reported that "two of Jeff's chosen children . . . delivered themselves into the followers for Father Abraham." Grant's officers put the formerly enslaved people to work as "teamsters, cooks, laborers, and eventually Union soldiers."[32]

After Raymond, General Grant decided to not attack westward and thereby leave Confederate general Joseph E. Johnston, who had amassed troops in the state capital of Jackson, in his rear. Thus he moved to attack Johnston and cut off Pemberton from any relief forces. On May 13 the 45th enthusiastically set out for Jackson, fifteen miles to the east. They enjoyed the afternoon rain, which relieved them from the hot and dusty conditions. Grant boasted that his soldiers "marched in excellent order, without straggling and in the best of spirits." Their foraging provided little food, though, and the Lead Mine men went to sleep that night hungry and muddy from the day's rain.[33]

Early on May 14 the 17th and 15th Corps moved out and converged on Jackson from the west and southwest. The blue columns first encountered General Gregg's pickets five miles from the city and drove them back. With "incomplete and poorly located earthworks" protecting Jackson, General Johnston had ordered Gregg's three brigades to defend the state's capital and delay the Union advance enough to enable the evacuation of war materiel. Sherman's 15th Corps then swiftly defeated one of Gregg's outnumbered brigades near Jackson. Once a storm had passed, McPherson had General Crocker's 7th Division move out with Logan's 3rd Division in support. Crocker's men fought with Gregg's other two brigades until 2 P.M., when the Confederate general pulled his men east of Jackson after all the supply trains had left the city. The worst danger the 45th encountered as the division's reserve was angry bees disturbed by Confederate bullets. The irate bees attacked with "terrible ferocity," causing the soldiers to break formation and re-form away from the irritated insects. Because a smallpox hospital was nearby, the Lead Mine men did not join in the pillaging of Jackson, where a fire soon turned much of the town, including civilians' homes, into cinders; the Federals had gone beyond Sherman's orders to destroy anything of military value.[34]

Grant's forces were now fifty miles east of Vicksburg and stayed near Jackson on May 15. Once again the Lead Mine men went to sleep hungry without rations and wet from the day's rain. Many had no shoes and blankets, which had been lost in battle or discarded on the hard marches. At 2 A.M. Major Cowan reflected on the campaign in his diary and boasted of the indomitable spirit of the general's soldiers despite twenty days of marching in hot weather with inconsistent rations. He thanked Providence that so many had escaped the battles unharmed and believed the men were still committed to their cause. Sergeant Crummer similarly noted that although they were "wet to the skin, hungry, and tired," not "one word of grumbling could be heard" from the men. Cowan went to sleep that night grateful for the fortitude to withstand the hardships to date but wondered whether he was the same "Lute Cowan" who had gone to war or some "new being."[35]

Grant's soldiers slept little that night, as he had them move out toward Vicksburg at 5 A.M. on May 16. With the rest of General McPherson's 17th Corps, the 45th marched fifteen miles northwest along the Jackson Road, through Clinton, and bivouacked east of Baker's Creek. Two railroad men who had passed through General Pemberton's army earlier that morning were responsible for Grant's urgency, for they told him that Johnston had ordered

Pemberton to move out of Vicksburg and attack Grant. In fact, Pemberton had his army at Champion Hill preparing for battle as May 16 dawned. After McPherson received word that General McClernand had found Pemberton's forces, he ordered his 17th Corps along with Gen. Alvin Hovey's 12th Division of McClernand's corps to double-quick three miles to the sounds of battle. When an artillery battery and Hovey's division begun to clash with Pemberton's soldiers two miles from the commanding 140-foot-tall Champion Hill, General Logan formed the 3rd Division into line of battle, and it moved to the right of the Clinton Road.[36]

The entire 17th Corps moved forward at noon, with Crocker's 7th Division and Logan's division arrayed left to right. Grant with McPherson watched this movement. The 1st Brigade then halted before a ravine that was 300 yards from the crest of Champion Hill. Next, General Smith ordered the 45th Illinois and 23rd Indiana forward to support Battery D of the 1st Illinois Light Artillery, posted on the brow of a hill opposite Champion. Before Smith could move up the rest of the brigade, Confederates in a ravine just to the west attacked, in "fine style" according to a man in the 45th, in an attempt to capture the Union guns. The two Union regiments, however, repulsed the assault. The general then moved up the rest of his brigade but soon discovered that enemy infantry had occupied the ravine to his front and the ridge behind it. This brought an order from General Logan for a charge by his 1st and 2nd Brigades, which forced the enemy to retreat to a second ridge. When his men came under enfilading fire from a Confederate battery to their right, Logan's ordered bayonet charge by the 3rd Brigade captured the battery. Now, with his entire division in a line, Logan ordered his men forward, and they attacked up the north to northeast side of Champion Hill and to its right, while Hovey's men attacked from the east. Smith bragged in his report that the Union soldiers "completely routed the enemy," who "fled in greatest disorder," and captured 1,100 enemy prisoners and six artillery pieces. Logan's division then joined Hovey's men to defeat a Confederate charge, the enemy having retaken the crest of Champion's Hill for a time. Pemberton's defeat resulted in the capture of thousands of his men, with "masses of disillusioned Confederates" fleeing back westward to Vicksburg.[37]

The Battle at Champion Hill was the largest fight of General Grant's Vicksburg campaign. Out of Grant's 29,000 soldiers who were on the field of battle, only about 15,380 actively fought—about the same number as had fought in General Pemberton's command. The Union sustained 2,441 casualties. Even with their attack up Champion Hill, General Logan's 3rd Division had just 407 casualties, with the 45th losing only 4 men killed in action, 20 wounded, and 2 captured, despite the unit's bullet-ridden colors. Of those wounded, sadly, Sgt. Isaac Hammond died in agony from his wounds, according to Adjutant Frohock. General Logan commended his soldiers for their performance in the battle; they did not falter although "exposed to a raking fire." Pemberton lost several thousand rifles and 27 artillery pieces and had 3,840 casualties, with 381 killed, 1,018 wounded, and 2,441 missing or captured.[38]

Grant's soldiers had once more been victorious, and one Lead Mine man boasted that they had again driven the "Southern traitor from his chosen position." The tired 45th, with others, brought the wounded of both armies to the Union surgeons and then buried the dead. Sergeant Crummer wrote of the "horrible picture" of the "dead and dying" and the "groans and cries" of the wounded. His comrade, 1st Lt. John Rollins, wrote that those back home knew little of the "heart-sickening horrors of this unnatural war." Union surgeons commandeered nearly every nearby barn and farmhouse for their gory work, including the Champion family's home. Crummer recalled seeing the blood of both armies flowing like "rivulets of crimson" and hearing the screams of wounded soldiers who suffered amputations without any anesthetic, only gritted teeth.[39]

General Grant awarded Cpl. Peter Bellingall of the 45th a meritorious furlough home because of his actions in the battle. Two years earlier, Bellingall, as a sixteen-year-old store clerk, had waited on the general back in Galena. During the battle, the corporal reached one of the rebels' abandoned cannons, "crowed like a rooster," and then led his comrades in turning the weapon around and firing it at its former owners. What he did not know was that Grant had witnessed his actions through field glasses. After the battle, the general summoned Bellingall to his command tent. With "fear and trembling," the corporal reported to two fellow residents from Galena, former members of the 45th who were currently on Grant's staff, Lt. Col. John Rawlins and Capt. William Rowley. On seeing Bellingall, Rawlins exclaimed, "Well, by God; Billy, is it you?" The scared corporal exclaimed, "I didn't do anything," but Rawlins turned to Grant and said, "General, make him a captain." This was too much of a reward for the eighteen-year-old Bellingall, who replied, "I want to go home," which he did after Vicksburg's capture.[40]

Their work cleaning up the Champion Hill battlefield kept the 45th Illinois and the rest of the 3rd Division from fighting in the Battle at Big Black River, about nine miles to the west. The congested roads to Vicksburg caused the division to reach the northeast portion of the Union lines around the besieged city on May 19, just after the attack by Sherman's corps failed to break through Pemberton's northern defenses. Logan's men took up the lines on either side of the Jackson Road, the main road into Vicksburg. The 1st Brigade, after driving off Confederate skirmishers near the Shirley House, also known as the White House, occupied the lines in front and to the north of the dwelling.[41]

On reaching Vicksburg, Logan wrote that despite his soldiers marching an arduous 200 miles and fighting in four battles against an enemy waiting in ambush, there had been "numerous instances of personal valor." McPherson commended his men's service; they had campaigned without shelter from the elements and had to forage for most of their food. The Lead Mine men had again served nobly in battle, emancipated many enslaved people, and suffered from the uneven results of their foraging. More hard service and fighting remained for the 45th Illinois as part of General Grant's campaign to capture Vicksburg—fighting that included a dangerous attack, which earned its members great honors at the campaign's end but took a terrible, bloody toll.[42]

Capt. John M. Adair, first historian of the 45th Illinois.
*RG 2019–13, Archives of Michigan Legacy Digital Collections, ca.
2009–18, Civil War Photographs, digital file 292501322102004
_7014913221020042.*

Republican congressman Elihu
B. Washburne, benefactor of the
45th Illinois. *Courtesy of Library
of Congress, https://www.loc.gov
/pictures/item/2010649393/.*

Initial command staff of the 45th Illinois. *Left to right:* Maj. Melancthon Smith, Lt. Col. Jasper A. Maltby, Col. John E. Smith, and Dr. Edward D. Kittoe. *Courtesy of Galena–Jo Daviess County Historical Society.*

Brig. Gen. John O. Duer, final
commander of the 45th. *Courtesy
of Galena–Jo Daviess County
Historical Society.*

Capt. Luther Cowan (*seated*)
and 1st Lt. Nesbitt Baugher.
*Courtesy of Galena–Jo Daviess
County Historical Society.*

1st Sgt. Wilbur F. Crummer, author of *With Grant at Donelson, Shiloh, and Vicksburg. Courtesy of Galena–Jo Daviess County Historical Society.*

1st Sgt. Nathan A. Corbin. *Courtesy of the Abraham Lincoln Presidential Library and Museum.*

Bivouac of the 45th Illinois near the Shirley House, Vicksburg, Mississippi, 1863. *Courtesy of Library of Congress, https://www.loc.gov/resource/hhh.ms0133.photos/?sp=1.*

"Explosion of the mine beneath Fort Hill, Vicksburg, Mississippi, June 25, 1863, artist's impression." *House Divided: The Civil War Research Engine at Dickinson College, https://hd.housedivided.dickinson.edu/node/40861.*

Attack of the 45th Illinois at the Fort Hill crater. *Courtesy of Library of Congress, https://www.loc.gov/item/2013645286/.*

7. ❀ Sacrifice in the "Death Hole"

As the Lead Mine men trudged past Maj. Gen. John A. Logan with their wounded, the general exclaimed, "My God! They are killing my bravest men in that hole." The regiment, on June 25, 1863, was the first to enter and fight in the crater rent by the explosion of a mine under the 3rd Louisiana Redan, a mine the 45th had been instrumental in digging and in which the men had placed explosives. The savagery of their fighting and the losses they incurred here and during the campaign and siege to take Vicksburg led to the 45th's venerated place nine days later.[1]

Having arrived at the Vicksburg siege lines on May 19, the weary and hungry men of the 45th had three days' rest in their camp, in a ravine on the south side of the Shirley House. On May 21, with a supply line open, the grateful soldiers ate the standard army fare of "hard tack, sow bacon, beans and coffee." Sergeant Crummer said the soldiers welcomed this once-maligned meal because of the "hardships of the last month." The 45th's 1st Lt. John P. Jones believed the food would enable the Union men to "stand it as long as Pemberton." General Grant, who had provided his men with just five days' rations since April 30, wrote in his memoirs that although his first priority at Vicksburg was to open a supply line, his soldiers on the campaign were "abundantly supplied with corn, bacon, beef, and mutton" from their foraging and reached Vicksburg in superb health. Despite Grant's assertion, the Lead Mine men and their fellow soldiers experienced much hunger from the uneven and inadequate results of their foraging. Crummer recalled that his "gnawing" hunger on the campaign led him to remove the dirt from a piece of bacon he found on a road and eat the "great treasure" with a "ravenous appetite." A comrade in the regiment turned down an offer of $5 for his small bit of corn bread, and many in the Vicksburg siege lines greeted Grant with cries of "Hard Tack! Hard Tack!" Historians have concurred that Grant's army arrived at Vicksburg famished because Confederates had removed most of the food between there and Jackson and that his soldiers' hunger was behind Grant's urgency to open up a supply line.[2]

At the Shirley House, the Lead Mine men faced the 3rd Louisiana Redan, or Fort Hill to the Union men. The redan, 550 yards westward, stood on the highest ground in Warren County, down and to the north of the Jackson Road, which ran along a ridge. The Union command considered it the strongest bastion and principal fort of the Confederate lines. Union soldiers saved the house of the pro-Union Shirley family when they killed the Confederate soldier charged with destroying the structure. Adeline Shirley then waved a sheet affixed to a broom, which stopped the Federals from firing on the house. It became the 45th's headquarters as soon as the army moved the family back from the line.[3]

General Grant set 10 A.M. on May 22 for his next attempt to break the Confederate lines with his entire army. General Sherman's 15th Corps manned the lines north of the city, General McPherson's 17th Corps the northeastern section, and General McClernand's 13th Corps the southeastern lines (see Map 7.1). Grant attacked because he wanted to capture Vicksburg before Confederate general Joseph E. Johnston could come to Pemberton's aid and because he thought his soldiers were impatient to capture Vicksburg and had earned the attempt to end the campaign without a siege. Historian Brooks Simpson believed that Grant ordered the attack because he feared sickness would drain the strength of his army during the hot summer. Sergeant Crummer wrote later that many men agreed with Grant that with their recent victories on the campaign, they could "whip any armed force," yet contended that had his general known of the strength of the enemy entrenchments, he would not have attacked. Historians Earl Hess and Timothy Smith found that some of Crummer's comrades shared his optimism, while others dreaded the order and preferred a siege to capture Vicksburg, expecting "some heavy work" in the attack. Western Mississippi's irregular terrain of "steep hills, deep gullies, underbrush, cane and willows" limited the Federal attacks to the narrow roads atop the hills.[4]

On May 22 the Union attack started at about 10 A.M., just after a three-hour Federal bombardment of the Confederate lines. General Smith's 1st Brigade of veterans had orders to attack the menacing 3rd Louisiana Redan. Facing them were Pemberton's "best and freshest" troops, because the general expected the main Union attack there, what with the Jackson Road being the critical main artery into Vicksburg. With General Grant watching, General Smith sent forward the 23rd Indiana along the woods to the north of the road with orders not to fire their rifles until they reached the fort. Despite Smith's and an engineer's reconnaissance, an unseen deep ravine and heavy abatis

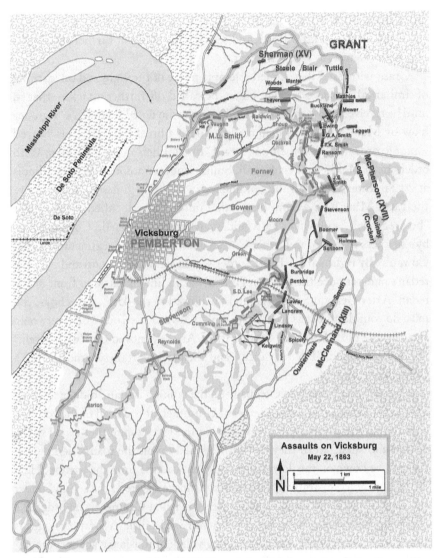

Map 7.1. Union assault on May 22, 1863, and the Vicksburg siege lines. *Source: Map created by Hal Jespersen, https://www.cwmaps.com* (changes made to the original).

prevented the 23rd from reaching the "dead space" under the bastion's right parapet. With no cover from the Confederates' fierce fire, Smith ordered a retreat. He then ordered the 20th Illinois to proceed up the road and gain the parapet on the left side of the bastion. Starting some 200 yards from the fort, after coming out of a protective cut, the unit charged the fort under heavy fire, but with the ditch in front of the bastion, the fort's ramparts were too high. Thus Smith ordered the 20th to seek the protection of the ridge on the south side of the Jackson Road, and seeing the futility of further attacks, he sent no more men to attack the fort.[5]

Grant witnessed these failed attempts to break through, and on learning of similar failures by Sherman's men, he called off further attacks—that is, until he received messages from McClernand, who noted that with a "vigorous blow by McPherson," his men could achieve a breakthrough. This swayed Grant to order an "overwhelming attack" by McPherson and Sherman. With orders from McPherson via Logan, Smith sent forward just the 45th Illinois at 2 P.M. Though he had full confidence in all his regiments, Smith chose the Lead Mine men, whom historian Timothy Smith called the general's "best regiment," knowing they would "go wherever I ordered." Colonel Maltby's sickness meant Maj. Luther Cowan commanded the regiment that day. Cowan's "By right flank, charge" order would send his men up and over the redan's parapet once the entire regiment was in line of battle in front of the redan. After General Smith's adjutant bellowed to the 45th, "Now boys, you must do your duty, just as you always [do]," Cowan called out, "Let every man stand to his post, Forward, Forty-Fifth!" As they moved out "with a yell," the major shouted, "Double quick," and then fell mortally wounded from a Confederate bullet.[6]

Capt. Robert P. Sealy of Company G, the ranking captain, did not know of Cowan's wounding, and thus Sergeant Crummer, at the head of the column, kept the men moving four abreast toward the fort despite the "awful volley of shot and shell," until they had fully formed up on the road. Then he had the men lie down on the downslope of the road across from the bastion. Here the men were "comparatively safe from the musketry fire of the enemy" under the crest of the fort's parapet. Once Sealy reached Crummer, he ordered a charge up the fortress's rampart. The veteran 3rd Louisiana Infantry met this attack with artillery fire and a "sweeping volley of musketry at short range," while the 45th's fire was ineffective against the enemy's breastworks. Even with the Confederate fire, a few men managed to reach the top of the fort's works to plant the regimental colors on the parapet and fight hand to hand with the enemy, before Sealy ordered all in the unit to retire to safety under the redan's brow. With further attacks futile, General Smith kept the 45th and 20th Illinois under the fort until darkness fell, during which time enemy soldiers threw hand grenades and rolled lighted shells at the Union soldiers. It was not until the early morning hours of May 23 that the men could retreat to the Union lines under the relative safety of night.[7]

No Union attack that day achieved a breakthrough, and the outcome was thousands of Union casualties. Hess attributes this to the recent work by Pemberton, his chief engineer Maj. Samuel Lockett, and their men to shore up the neglected fortifications and move up artillery pieces from the river to the entrenchments. Hess and Timothy Smith both blamed the failed attacks on the inability of Grant's corps commanders to take advantage of their numerical advantage and bring "massive weight of numbers to bear on the battlefield." Lt. John P. Jones of the 45th called the attack an "almost mad plan of storming the works." His fellow lieutenant, John Rollins, believed the Confederates held "the strongest natural position I ever saw," calling it the "hottest fire I ever been under before (and I was in Shiloh)." The Union dead and wounded lay in the hot sun in front of the Confederate siege lines for three days. The stench of the bloated and blackened Union dead led Pemberton to ask for a truce, to which Grant agreed on May 25. The Federals then retrieved their wounded brothers and buried the maggot-and-worm-infested bodies, which "burst as they were moved." During the two-hour truce, the men of both armies talked with "perfect courtesy and good feeling . . . and good humored bantering," while others traded items, and Lieutenant Jones joined with others in giving food to the Confederates. Some rebels, despite their officers' efforts, successfully deserted to the Union lines. One Lead Mine man, Pvt. William Williamson, wrote that as the men parted, they smiled, shook hands with well wishes, and lamented how both sides shot at each other in "so barbarous a manner." Nevertheless, when the soldiers reached their trenches, they renewed their deadly work.[8]

The May 22 assault cost Grant 3,199 casualties, the most during his campaign. The 45th had 1 man killed, 19 wounded, and 2 missing, near the average for the units that had attacked the 3rd Louisiana Redan. Maj. Luther Cowan was the lone member killed in action on May 22. The bullet had hit his sword's scabbard, went through his hand, entered his left hip, "glancing upward," and struck a main artery, killing him "almost instantly." The major's brother, 1st Lt. Dan Cowan, sorrowfully wrote to his sister-in-law of her husband's death.[9]

Many mourned the major's passing. Cpl. Kingsley Olds told his father that Cowan was "as brave a man as ever lived," and Cpl. John Graves wrote that the major was much loved by all who knew him because he was "a model soldier and a gentleman." The *Galena Daily Advertiser* lamented the loss of the honorable Cowan, who had the respect of his men. The paper noted that with the major's death, the county had lost "one of our most worthy citizens and our country one of its bravest officers." The *Warren Independent* wrote that

the "esteemed" Cowan was "genial, frank and gallant." Cowan had been Jo
Daviess County's surveyor before the war and was forty years old at the time
of his death. The *Independent* believed Cowan had "exhibited the greatest
skill and courage" during his service and "GAVE HIS LIFE TO HIS COUNTRY."
Cowan's funeral did not occur until March 30, 1864, but despite the bad
weather, his service was "largely attended." The many mourners included
some members of Cowan's old company.[10]

Back at Vicksburg, General Grant reported that his men had "simply failed
to enter the works of the enemy." Later, he recalled that his soldiers' "assault
was gallant in the extreme" but that Pemberton's "position was too strong,"
and he regretted having renewed the attacks after receiving McClernand's optimistic messages. Grant then ordered his army to begin a siege of Vicksburg,
which gave his soldiers a daily routine until July 4: details of men worked as
sharpshooters to keep the heads of the enemy down, while others worked on
digging thirteen saps aimed at the enemy lines. When not tasked with these
duties, the soldiers rested in their camps.[11]

Grant believed his troops worked "diligently and cheerfully" as they settled into this routine. The Lead Mine men used their time in camp to wash
their clothes, something most had not done for two months. Some wore new
clothes courtesy of their enemies, who had left knapsacks on the recent battlefields. Early in the siege, Private Williamson wrote, "I think the rebels
will soon surrender," a widely held belief among the Federals. The Union
artillery constantly bombarded the enemy lines and Vicksburg, while Union
sharpshooters engaged in lethal duels with their Confederate counterparts.
Wilbur Crummer recalled, "Not a man in the trenches on either side could
show his head above the breastworks without being picked off." One day his
comrades tested their enemy's aim by placing a hat on the end of a ramrod and
raising it above the logs at the top of a trench. Confederate snipers quickly
pierced the hat several times. Betting on how many bullets would hit a raised
hat became common practice in Grant's army. With shortages in munitions,
Confederate sharpshooters had to conserve their ammunition while firing
on the Union lines and the Federals digging the Union approaches. For every Confederate sharpshooter, there were ten Union sharpshooters, and the
latter eventually suppressed the rebels' artillery and sharpshooter fire. Given
the 400 to 500 yards that separated their lines, both armies' riflemen likely
learned how to account for their bullets' parabolic flight to make their shots
as deadly as possible.[12]

Capt. Andrew Hickenlooper, chief engineer for the 17th Army Corps, wrote that the 3rd Louisiana Redan became the "main objective of the engineering operations" for General McPherson's corps because of the fort's "strength, commanding position, and heavy armament." Historian Justin Solonick considered it one of the Confederates' "most formidable forts." The lines of General Logan's 3rd Division faced the fort; hence their sap became known as Logan's Approach—the most important Union sap, according to historian Edwin Bearss. Hickenlooper first had the men build sharpshooting trenches parallel to the enemy lines, before beginning work on the approach. During the May 25 truce, the captain had scouted the path of the sap to the redan. As General Smith's 1st Brigade commanded the line around the Shirley House and the Jackson Road, work on the sap fell mostly to his troops. As they began to dig, Hickenlooper's pioneer corps gathered materials from the area and built "sap-rollers, gabions, and fascines" to protect the Union diggers. The men pushed the sap roller, a platform topped by barrels wrapped with willow saplings and filled with earth and cotton, ahead of the diggers to protect them from "enfilading fire" and that from their front. Confederates set the roller, nicknamed the "bullet-stopper" or "Logan's Gunboat," on fire several times during the siege.[13]

The men dug Logan's Approach eight feet wide and seven feet deep so that a four-man-wide column could march through it without being exposed to Confederate fire. Details of up to 150 men worked on the sap day and night. As it progressed toward the fort, the approach zigzagged to give the diggers additional protection, and Captain Hickenlooper placed three batteries of artillery at turns in the approach. These batteries helped render nearby Confederate artillery silent for much of the siege. At each turn, men dug trenches parallel to the Confederate fortifications, which enabled Union riflemen to be moved up for more effective fire at the rebel sharpshooters. Union snipers shot from relative safety through raised "headlogs" and holes bored through squared timbers laid on the top of the trenches. The men made the most progress at night by moonlight; despite the sap roller and Union suppression fire, Confederate fire during the day made work "prohibitively dangerous." As the sap approached the enemy's lines, a good-natured verbal banter developed between the combatants. One day Wilbur Crummer heard a Confederate soldier yell, "Why don't you come and take Vicksburg?" to which a Federal replied, "Oh, we're in no particular hurry; Gen. Grant is not yet ready to transfer you North."[14]

Time in camp was less dangerous than sharpshooter or sap detail, but dangers still existed. The location of the regiment's camps on the side of a ravine generally protected them from Confederate bullets but not artillery shells, especially mortars. The enemy fire caused Federal casualties when the men used cooking fires and when they walked to a nearby spring to get water. Because of inefficiencies in the Union Commissary Service, the men had to fish and forage for fruit to supplement their diet. To resolve these inefficiencies and eliminate the danger from enemy fire, Pvt. Giles Hard received approval to create a "regimental mess" back from the lines, staffed by formerly enslaved and convalescent men. On hearing of Hard's success, General Logan implemented similar messes in his division. As both armies had agreed to spare the Shirley House from artillery fire, the 45th's officers made its basement their quarters. Despite this agreement, one night an enemy shell crashed into a basement wall, prompting the shaken yet unhurt officers to move to the unit's relatively safer ravine-side camp. Night guard duty required sharp attention for enemy activity, including rumored breakout attempts, men bringing in percussion caps to the besieged city, and Confederate deserters, who increased in greater numbers as the siege wore on. Facing the constant threat of death, the Lead Mine men and their comrades grew indifferent to and unruffled by the killing and wounding of their comrades, with a comrade's death often eliciting nothing more than a dispassionate and fatalistic comment such as "I wonder who will be the next one?" The toughened Lead Mine men, along with the war's other combatants, had likely steeled themselves to "endure the vast physical, psychological, intellectual, emotional, and moral challenges" and "insulate themselves from the horrors of the war." The sweltering heat and humidity and tormenting mosquitoes added to their discomfort, and the resulting sickness and heatstroke reduced the rolls of both armies.[15]

The Confederate soldiers experienced a far harsher and more dangerous siege. The constant Federal artillery and sharpshooter fire and the threat of another Union attack kept them from getting much rest. Before long, limited ammunition prevented Confederate snipers from answering Union fire, which lowered morale. By June food shortages forced the issuance of bread made from peas and rice, a recipe the men found inedible, and soon the rebels received only two meals a day; their enslaved people working on the fortifications received even less. With a lack of good drinking water and little cover, the men suffered from sunburn, dysentery, malaria, and fevers. Nights brought greater freedom and less danger from Union fire, but also more work for the tired, weakened men, who had to repair fortifications damaged by Union cannons and bring up new artillery pieces to replace those destroyed. It is little wonder that desertions from Pemberton's army increased during the siege. One ingenious Confederate sniper who found cover in the thick foliage of a tall tree caused Union casualties near the Shirley House. The distinctive sound of his rifle gave away his position, however, and a well-placed cannon shot likely killed him. During the siege, the Federals' advantage in sharpshooters, artillery, and plentiful ammunition resulted in over 3,176 Confederate casualties to just 600 Union casualties.[16]

Despite the relative scarcity of Confederate munitions, Union sharpshooters still died. Enemy fire killed Pvt. John Battle Harrison and Pvt. William Eddy of the 45th. Harrison, wounded at Shiloh and Champion Hill and taken prisoner at Medon Station, refused to go to the hospital after being wounded on May 22; he died on June 4 during a sharpshooter duel. Drunkenness was fatal for Private Eddy, who obtained whiskey from an unknown source, escaped a watch meant to keep him safe, and somehow reached the 3rd Louisiana Redan during daylight, where a Confederate shot and killed him.[17]

To keep up his soldiers' morale and check on the progress of the saps, General Grant often fraternized with the men, including those of the 45th. On a particularly hot day in June, Grant, "perspiring and puffing greatly," visited the sharpshooter trenches when Sergeant Crummer was on duty. Grant asked Crummer, his Galena neighbor, if he had any water. The sergeant replied that he had only the warm water in his canteen. Grant offered the water to a staff member, who refused, but the general took a "hearty drink" and gave it back to Crummer, then thanked him before leaving. Another day, Grant visited the sharpshooter trenches where a Lead Mine man, Pvt. Frank Wells, was on duty. The general proceeded to stick his head above the head log to survey a Confederate position. This led a shocked Lead Mine man to yell out, "Get down from there, old fool you, you will get your head shot off," to which Grant replied, "I guess not." These acts bonded Grant with the 45th, whose comrades at Vicksburg shared this "familiar reverence" for their commanding general. The regiment lost its connection with their former colonel on June 3, when the army promoted Brig. Gen. John E. Smith to division command in the 17th Corps; Brig. Gen. Mortimer D. Leggett replaced Smith.[18]

On the morning of June 22, the siege's daily drudgery ended for Logan's soldiers when his approach, now 1,500 feet long, reached the 25-foot-high embankment of the 3rd Louisiana Redan. The general's men had won the race against those building the other Union saps, making it Grant's best chance for a breakthrough. After a call went out to Logan's troops for men who had "practical knowledge of coal-mining," Captain Hickenlooper selected the "strongest and most experienced" men to dig the mine: thirty-five Lead Mine men, some coal miners from the 124th Illinois, and men from other units. Several sources noted that the 45th was "largely instrumental" in digging the mine and tamping the charges of gunpowder. Three parties worked in one-hour shifts, and by the morning of June 25 they had dug a 45-foot-long, 4-foot-wide, and 5-foot-high tunnel that went straight under the fort, as well as two smaller, 15-foot-long tunnels at forty-five-degree angles. The area's "loess soil" consisted of "peculiarly tenacious clay," which made for tough digging but also eliminated much of the need for bracing. By 9 A.M. the miners had deposited 2,200 pounds of gunpowder—800 in the main gallery and 700 in each smaller gallery. The men timed the movement of the gunpowder into the mine between the explosions of Confederate hand grenades and artillery shells, which were intended to collapse the mine's mouth. As the Union men finished their work, they could hear the voices of enemy soldiers who were digging countermines to collapse Hickenlooper's mine. This created the urgency to explode the mine that day. Sergeant Crummer called the Confederate bastion the "key to Vicksburg," and now it was time to "try the burglar's plan, and with the aid of powder blow up the lock to 'smithereens.'"[19]

General Logan, however, needed a regiment to lead the attack. After his old regiment, the 31st Illinois, had declined the job the night before, Logan conferred with Colonel Maltby. Thus on the morning of June 25, the general asked the 45th Illinois to lead the attack after the mine's detonation. According to Corporal Bellingall, Logan stepped in front of the regiment and said, "Now . . . I come to the 45th, who, I am satisfied, never refused anything that I asked them. All the boys who are willing to go hold up your hand." At that all in the unit raised their hands. Colonel Maltby picked a lead echelon of the ten best men from each company to charge the fort. The young Bellingall accepted his selection; despite being afraid, he feared looking like a coward even more, as did others in the Union army, and wrote that this would hurt his mother more than if he died during the attack. The Lead Mine men's willingness to be the first to attack is clear evidence that despite their hardships since leaving Milliken's Bend in April, with the hot conditions, periodic hunger, tormenting insects, and risk and randomness of death during the siege, their patriotism for their republic had not diminished.[20]

General Grant ordered the mine's detonation to happen at 3 P.M. One hour before, the 45th and the rest of General Leggett's 1st Brigade moved up to the parallel trenches that were closest to the Confederate redan. Leggett ordered the regiment to charge into the breach from the mine's explosion. If practical, they were to "charge over and drive the enemy from their works"; if not, they needed to hold the breach "at all hazards" to enable the brigade to move in and exploit it. The 23rd Indiana was to charge up the left-hand slope of the fort to divert enemy fire away from the 45th. As the clock neared 3 P.M. the Union artillery and musket fire ceased, a rare moment of silence, the first since the May 25 truce. Captain Hickenlooper called the lack of sound "deathlike and oppressive." Up and down the Union lines, troops moved into their trenches; Grant had ordered that upon the mine's detonation, they were to unleash their entire arsenal to prevent Confederate commanders from reinforcing the men at and near the fort. The general, his staff, and Generals McPherson and Logan watched from Battery Hickenlooper, the closest artillery to the 3rd Louisiana Redan. The 45th, about twenty-five feet from the fort, held "firm and steady" with "breathless suspense"; while some were excited, others dreaded the mine's explosion. Their strained nerves matched those of the Confederates in the redan.[21]

At about 3:15 P.M. a cannon fired near General Logan's command post, signaling the lighting of the mine's fuses. The mine exploded about fifteen minutes later, the first successful detonation of a mine in the Union's military history. To one soldier, the explosion was louder than thunder and "felt for miles." Captain Hickenlooper wrote, "The whole fort and connecting outworks commenced an upward movement, gradually breaking into fragments . . . until it looked like an immense fountain of finely pulverized earth, mingled with flashes of fire and clouds of smoke." Through the smoke, he could see "men, gun-carriages, shelters, etc." thrown high into the air. A few lucky Confederates landed alive in the Union lines, but the blast tore apart at least six brave enemy counterminers. One Federal saw "heads, legs, arms and all parts of the bodies of the rebels go up in the air." Sergeant Crummer recalled that the mine sent "huge masses of earth" up into the air and the ground shook like an earthquake, followed by a bright glare of fire that quickly died out. Before the dust had settled and the smoke had cleared, the 45th's lead echelon, led by Hickenlooper and ten of his pioneer troops, charged into the breach and "great saucer-shaped crater" rent by the mine where the fort had once stood. And so began a twenty-six-hour battle, a fight that earned the 45th lasting recognition.[22]

As the men entered the crater, the Union lines covered them with fire from 150 cannons and 50,000 muskets along the length of the rebels' fortifications. Despite this fire, the deafening explosion of the mine, and the Confederate casualties, enemy fire quickly met the Union charge. Hickenlooper had not dug the mine farther west for fear that the explosion might not destroy the eastern portion of the fort, a requirement for success in the attack. As a result, the mine failed to take out a second line of Confederate entrenchments built in case the mine's explosion succeeded in demolishing the entire redan. Crummer recalled that the Confederate soldiers met the Lead Mine men's charge with a "terrible volley" of musket fire and that their cannons "belched forth their death-dealing missiles" from the west end of the hole. Capt. John Adair wrote that the enemy's fire "flashed in their faces like the wind-driven rain." Nevertheless, the 45th's soldiers reached the west wall of the crater, but they could not break through. As Colonel Maltby led the 45th Illinois into the crater, three bullets struck Maj. Leander B. Fisk, recently promoted to replace Major Cowan; one pierced his heart and killed him nearly instantly. Also early in the attack, three enemy bullets struck Lt. Col. Melancthon Smith in the head, where one lodged in his brain, a mortal wound.[23]

Instead of the expected "very large breach," the explosion had created a saucer-shaped hole with a diameter of only fifty feet at most. This small size meant that only two companies, about sixty to eighty men, could fight in it at one time. Therefore, Colonel Maltby rotated two companies into the breach at a time and ordered the rest of the regiment to stay out. With the crater sloping sharply upward fifteen feet from east to west, the Lead Mine men had to charge uphill. Making this more difficult, the soil had been "pulverized . . . into fine sand" by the mine's detonation. As the battle progressed, the ground became "slippery with blood." At the crater's far west end stood an eight-foot-high embankment with an opening, through which the Confederates fired their rifles and cannons. Some, like Sergeants Crummer and Axel Esping, reached the northwest corner of the crater, where they poured effective fire on the enemy. Their position was dangerous, however, as it exposed the two men to fire from three directions. Esping ignored Crummer's warning to not show his head too long, and he almost immediately fell on his friend, dead with a "ball through his brain." Thus Esping, wounded at both Fort Donelson and Shiloh, did not survive the desperate fight in the crater. The unit's color guard, Color Sgt. Henry H. Taylor, guided his comrades to the western wall of the crater, where, despite the danger, he planted the regimental colors at the top of the fort after playing "tug-of-war" with an enemy soldier, who was able to tear off a piece of a flag. For placing Old Glory closer to Vicksburg than it had been for over two years, Congress awarded Taylor the regiment's only Medal of Honor in 1893.[24]

The hole in the crater's west wall enabled the Confederates to assault the men of the 45th with bayonets as well as rifle and cannon fire, so Captain Hickenlooper directed the 20th Illinois pioneer troops and some Lead Mine men to bring up pre-staged timbers to fill in the opening. To enable the Federals to fire in relative safety, the top logs had holes bored in them. Colonel Maltby, though weak from three wounds suffered already, pitched in and used his shoulder to help hold up one of the last beams. Just after he moved away, a Confederate gunner fired a thirty-pounder howitzer at the beam, shattering it and "mutilating a lot of the men," including the colonel. The solid shot broke the beam "into kindling" and drove "great sharp pieces of wood" with a "terrific force" into Maltby's side and head. The blow knocked him to the ground, bruised him internally, and burned his arm and shoulder. He was rushed to a hospital, where a surgeon said "it would be hard work to count" the colonel's many wounds. After the fight, Logan said of Maltby, "He is the bravest man I ever saw on the field of battle." With Adj. James Clifford severely wounded in the arm, the battle had either killed or severely or mortally wounded all the 45th's senior commanders.[25]

With the opening in the crater's back wall now filled, the fight devolved into men on both sides blindly firing their rifles and throwing lighted shells and cannonballs over the wall. Lieutenant Rollins wrote that men in both armies "fought with a desperation amounting almost to madness," but that the Confederates had the advantage of fighting downhill. He and his comrades were "covered with blood and blackened with powder, maniacally fighting amid the smoke of battle, bursting of shells, and roar of artillery and musketry"; it was the "most desperate" fighting the private had experienced, the memories of which stayed with Rollins for the rest of his life. The soldiers' rifle fire resulted in few casualties, but the lighted shells, according to Hickenlooper, did "fearful destruction" in both armies, "horribly mangling" the soldiers—with one Confederate shell causing a dozen casualties. Brave men on both sides grabbed the shells and grenades before they exploded and threw them back over the wall to explode among their senders. The 45th's Lt. Leander Bander saw that the enemy's six-pounder shells had fuses that were too long, so they did not explode until hitting the ground. Thus he caught six of the shells and threw them all back to explode within the Confederate ranks. Lieutenant Jones said that few others matched Bander's heroism that day. Sergeant Crummer wondered years later how anyone was able to walk out of "Fort Hell," or the "Death Hole," as the men soon called the crater, where one-third fired their rifles up near the wall, while others either threw lighted shells or loaded rifles and passed them to the front. The first echelon of men fought in the crater for one hour, then were replaced by other companies. Others also took the place of those who grew too exhausted or whose rifles became too hot to handle.[26]

The men of the 45th held the crater until 6 p.m., when General Leggett substituted the 20th Illinois. The 31st Illinois fought next, followed by the 56th Illinois, whose bad ammunition led to their quick replacement by the 23rd Indiana. The 17th Iowa followed and fought until the 31st Illinois again entered the fight. The combat continued through the night, and the next morning saw the 45th Illinois return to the crater, fighting until 10 a.m., after which the 124th Illinois held the crater until 5 p.m. Leggett then ordered the men back behind a parapet built by Hickenlooper's pioneers, where the enemy shells could not reach them. Historian Justin Solonick conceded the inexact science on the matter but contended that the Union attack failed because of Hickenlooper's inexperience (he had not studied engineering at West Point), which resulted in his not using a big enough charge of explosives. Solonick, however, gave credit to Maj. Samuel Lockett, Pemberton's chief engineer, for his "ingenuity and foresight" when, as the Union mine neared completion, he had a second line of entrenchments built behind the 3rd Louisiana Redan.[27]

Sergeant Crummer recalled a notable exchange between General Logan and his staff that he overheard as the men of the 45th retired to rest in the trenches after their first tour in the crater. As the men carried their wounded by the general, they heard him exclaim "in great agitation" to his staff, "My God! They are killing my bravest men in that hole." A staff member suggested ordering a retreat, but the exasperated Logan replied that he could not, as Grant had commanded him to "hold every inch of ground." Logan's respect for the 45th's fighting ability and concern for their lives was evident in his exclamation. After the war, Crummer and Captain Adair blamed Grant and McPherson for their "serious" and "fearful costly mistake" that led to the "terrible sacrifice" and "losses" in the Union ranks in holding "that little piece of ground."[28]

For the Confederate soldiers, the fight at the crater was equally harrowing. The brave counterminers who died in the explosion had kept digging, knowing the mine could explode at any minute. Col. Eugene Erwin had his 6th Missouri stationed on the hill leading down away from the redan and rushed them to the second line of entrenchments behind the fort. Despite Union artillery and rifle fire causing casualties in his troops, Erwin urged them on, and they responded with the "yip-yip of the Rebel Yell." But as they reached the western wall of the crater, Erwin died, felled by several Union bullets.

Estimates of the Confederates' casualties during the fight range from 88 to 134 soldiers killed, wounded, or missing.[29]

Of the units that fought in the crater, the 45th Illinois suffered the most casualties, 61 of 219; of these, 7 men were either killed in action or died later from their wounds and 54 were wounded. Dead were two of the unit's senior commanders, Lieutenant Colonel Smith and Major Fisk, and Colonel Maltby and Adjutant Clifford lay in a hospital recovering from their severe wounds. Two other officers were wounded: along with Sergeant Esping, Sgt. Isaac Sines died during the battle, and Sgt. Louis Breezier also received a mortal wound. The wounded included 8 other sergeants, 3 corporals, and 41 privates, and 6 of the wounded were discharged. Newspapers back north touted the regiment's bravery. The *Belvidere Standard* in Illinois said of the "noble Lead Mine regiment" that its "conduct . . . was grand in the extreme." The *Western Reserve Chronicle* in Warren, Ohio, called the fighting by all of Logan's men "very brilliant," while the *Galena Daily Advertiser* wrote of the 45th's fighting in an article titled "Brave Deeds of Noble Men."[30]

A newspaper back in Illinois noted, however, that it was "painful duty" to arrange the eulogy for Maj. Leander B. Fisk. Captain Adair loved Fisk like a brother, and the major's death caused him "deep sorrow." Adair and Fisk had made a pact that if one died, the other was to have his friend buried back home. Adair honored the agreement and buried Fisk in Mount Carroll, Illinois; he visited his friend's grave often after the war. Lt. Col. Melancthon Smith, after being struck in the head by three bullets, lingered for three days in a "state of half-consciousness" and little pain, during which time he repeatedly spoke of his "satisfaction . . . and his entire willingness to die for his country." He died on Sunday morning, June 28, 1863, at the age of thirty-five after uttering, "I die as a true soldier and as I would wish to die," and thus joined other soldiers during the war who were resigned to their fate after suffering a mortal wound. Smith perished after having just returned to the unit from a three-month term as Memphis provost marshal. A group of Memphis merchants appreciated Smith's work so much that they came to Vicksburg and petitioned General Grant for the colonel's return to their city. Grant approved their request, but Smith was permitted to stay with the unit until Vicksburg fell. The regiment sent Colonel Smith's body back to Rockford for his funeral; the reverend's eulogy described Smith's "devotion to his duties, his zeal in the cause of his country and his true soldierly bearing."[31]

Captain Hickenlooper began another mine under the 3rd Louisiana Redan, but no Union attack followed the mine's detonation at 1 P.M. on July 1; the losses sustained on June 25–26 and the failure to break through persuaded General Grant not to order an attack. Perhaps Grant believed as Lieutenant Rollins did that "it was not possible for mortal man" to break through the enemy's fortifications. The "massive explosion" of the second mine caused 68 Confederate casualties, with some 20 soldiers buried in their "permanent tomb" of the wrecked fort. For one lucky young slave working on the rebel redan, the explosion did not kill him but instead threw him into a Union trench "somewhat bruised and badly shaken," "smeared with mud," and with an "ugly cut in his head" that trickled blood down his forehead, after which he "trembled violently." When asked how high he thought the explosion had sent him, the boy replied, "Don't know massa, guess two or dree miles, ole massa went up furder'n I did, when I was coming down, me ol' mass going up." Once he had recovered from his injuries, the boy became a paid servant in General Logan's headquarters.[32]

General Leggett's brigade continued fighting from the new parapet until June 28. The fatigued members of the decimated 45th Illinois then passed the last days of the siege uneventfully—that is, all except Sergeant Crummer. On July 2, as first sergeant of Company A, Crummer was working in the back of the Shirley House completing paperwork when a Confederate bullet came through the wall and "went crashing through" his right lung. Blood poured from Crummer's wound and "gushed from his mouth," and his comrades took him to a surgeon, who declared the wound mortal. Many years later, he wrote that he saw pass before his eyes "the good deeds and the evil of his life," and thinking he was dying, he prayed, "O, Lord, spare my life and I will serve thee all my days."[33]

Men loaded the twenty-year-old Crummer into an ambulance. He said goodbye to the men and rode to a hospital a few miles back from the lines. As the sun sank, the ambulance reached the hospital, where a surgeon inspected his wound and predicted that Crummer had just hours to live. Thus he had Crummer's friend Sgt. Louis LaBrush, who had ridden to the hospital with his comrade, put the wounded sergeant under a tree, as the hospital had no room for someone expected to die. As July 3 dawned, despite the dire prediction, Crummer was still alive. This prompted the surgeon to make a rather painful examination of the sergeant's wounds, causing LaBrush to scream at the doctor to let Crummer "die in peace!" Though at least one rib had been splintered by the enemy bullet, the next morning he was still alive. The doctor examined Crummer again, then had him moved into the hospital, had his wound dressed, and had orderlies attire the fortunate sergeant in clean clothes.

Years later, Crummer attributed his survival to the "tender care" provided by LaBrush and Pvt. Henry Winters, another comrade in the 45th, who had been captured at Champion Hill and worked at the hospital after his parole. The wound forced Crummer's discharge.[34]

At 10 A.M. on July 3 white flags appeared over the Confederate works across from the Shirley House. With half his men hospitalized, the rest growing weaker from the poor food and water, and some having threatened mutiny days earlier, General Pemberton requested a meeting with Grant. The two generals soon met under a flag of truce 100 yards south of the 3rd Louisiana Redan. After agreeing to terms, Pemberton surrendered his army early on July 4, 1863—a surrender that saved the Union soldiers from attacking a third time, as Grant had planned on July 6. On Pemberton's surrender, General McPherson wrote to Colonel Rawlins, asking that the 45th Illinois lead the Union army into Vicksburg to "take possession" of the city's courthouse, stating that the regiment had "borne the brunt of the battle oftener than any other in my command, and always behaved nobly." Rawlins replied with an order from Grant, leaving the decision as to which regiment led the troops into the captured city up to McPherson's discretion. McPherson then ordered General Logan to have his 3rd Division ready to march into the city, with the 45th Illinois in the lead, followed by the rest of the 1st Brigade and division. To Lieutenant Rollins, this was "the most welcome order" the regiment had ever received. The *Chicago Tribune* called the honor just because the unit's conduct on June 25 and 26 was "grand in the extreme." That Grant acceded to McPherson's request is not surprising, given his history and interaction with members of the 45th before and during the war.[35]

The Union soldiers began their march into the surrendered city at 10 A.M. on July 4. To one man, the "stillness was oppressive," with no "bullets whistling, nor roar of artillery." Grant led the column with his staff and corps commanders, followed by what remained of the 45th Illinois, and then the 3rd Division. Capt. Robert P. Sealy, the senior captain, led the unit, as Colonel Maltby's wounds forced him to travel in an ambulance. When the procession reached the city's courthouse, Col. William E. Strong of McPherson's staff raised the 45th's "battle-torn" colors to the top of the courthouse steeple. Some of Vicksburg's residents watched with stunned and dour faces, while several formerly enslaved people smiled as they watched the Union flags go up, the first to fly over Vicksburg since Mississippi had seceded two and a half years earlier. On seeing the 45th's flags over the courthouse, the 1st Brigade let out a "loud burst of cheers," which violated Grant's orders for no cheering, "no shouts of triumph," and no music by the bands—nothing that his men's now "vanquished but gallant foe" might find rude. The Lead Mine men had mixed feelings about the day's events. One man believed it was "the most glorious Fourth of July we ever spent, and the proudest day of our lives," and Lt. John P. Jones wrote to his wife, "Quite an honor wasn't it? . . . Didn't I strut? I guess I did." Private Corbin's thoughts, however, dwelled on those who had died, suffered wounds, or lost limbs during the campaign, and a comrade similarly wrote, "We could not help but drop a tear of sorrow for the many brave comrades we left sleeping on the battle-field, beneath the little mounds that mark their honored graves." Vicksburg had fallen, and when Port Hudson fell to Union soldiers five days later, President Abraham Lincoln expressed understated joy: "Thank God . . . the Father of Waters again goes unvexed to the sea." Lincoln rightly recognized the significance of these victories to the Union winning the war. Back home, a paper described the 45th's battle flags flying over Vicksburg as the regiment's "crowning glory."[36]

After the flag raising, the Union soldiers learned of the civilians' experiences during the siege and fed the "downcast" Confederates "bacon, hard tack, and coffee" to get them to talk about what they had gone through. In firing on the Union men, enemy sharpshooters had risked a "reply in the shape of a shell" from their Union counterparts, along with "a score of musket shot," and Confederate artillery fire usually resulted in accurate Union return fire damaging or destroyed their guns. During the final days, the men in gray had existed on quarter rations, surviving on mule and rat meat, which horrified the Union soldiers. Union artillery fire even made the Confederates' trek to get water dangerous. The poor health of General Pemberton's soldiers forced their parole to take several days. The Union food improved the health of many, but despite leaving Vicksburg with five days' rations, a good number left "silently and sadly" on their paroles, with some telling the Federals that they would not fight again afterward. On July 4 General Logan named the 45th and 20th Illinois regiments Vicksburg's provost guard. While serving here, the Lead Mine men learned of the excitement the capture of Vicksburg had created back home, and that because of their stalwart service to date, the people of Galena planned to purchase new regimental banners to replace the 45th's tattered original colors.[37]

The Vicksburg Campaign had finally ended. According to historian Timothy Smith, Grant's campaign to take the city compared "with some of the greatest in all of history," and historian Charles D. Grear, among others, considered it a "greater milestone on the road to final Union victory" than the more celebrated Union triumph at Gettysburg. The 45th Illinois had gained great honors, but at a terrible price. The regiment had started the campaign with fewer than 400 members and sustained 133 casualties—14 killed, 116 wounded, and 3 missing or captured—or 33 percent of the unit. Of these, 40 men never returned to the ranks, most because their wounds forced their discharge. While their brigade mates, the 20th Illinois, had a higher number of casualties during the campaign, only four of the fifty-four Illinois regiments in Grant's army exceeded the 45th's casualty total. It was the losses to its command staff, however, that made the regiment singular: Lieutenant Colonel Smith was mortally wounded, Majors Cowan and Fisk were killed in action, and Colonel Maltby and Adjutant Clifford suffered severe wounds. No other Illinois regiment had more than one casualty in their command staff. The unit's senior leadership's willingness to command from the lead, as it had in previous battles, and share in their soldiers' sacrifice likely endeared them to their men and strengthened their men's respect, loyalty, and obedience. Despite the terrible cost paid by the Lead Mine men and their comrades, their fighting on the campaign had achieved a great victory for their country.[38]

Over the next several months, the depleted 45th Illinois received a well-earned rest as the Lead Mine men camped in or near Vicksburg while tasked with mostly tedious duty. July 4, 1863, marked roughly the halfway point in the regiment's service during the war. The men had endured the tribulations of Civil War combat and the vicissitudes of life in uniform, while suffering from intense cold, heat, and gnawing hunger. Lieutenant Rollins reflected, "Notwithstanding the exposure and hardships of the campaign, I have enjoyed the best of health, and by the protecting care of a kind Providence have thus far been impervious to rebel steel and bullets, I trust for some good purpose." He shared with other Lead Mine men the belief that Providence had enabled them to survive the long, eight-month campaign to take Vicksburg. Their faith and their patriotism, extensive training, and experience gained at Donelson and Shiloh, along with their officers' excellent leadership, had sustained them through the campaign's rigors and extensive fighting, especially in the harrowing fight in the crater. During the second half of their service to the Union, they would face new tests of their patriotic resolve and commitment to their country as they walked thousands of miles in implementing the Union's hard war on the Confederacy.[39]

8. ❧ The Meridian Raid and Atlanta Campaign

On February 29, 1864, Pvt. William Williams of the 45th, a farmer from Jo Daviess County, died in the brutal Confederate prisoner-of-war camp in Andersonville, Georgia. Three other Lead Mine men and hundreds of their comrades suffered the same fate at Andersonville after being captured while serving in Gen. William T. Sherman's early 1864 Meridian raid, the trial run of his implementation of the Union leaders' new hard war policy toward the Confederacy and its citizens. During the expedition, the regiment's first significant service since the Vicksburg Campaign ended in early July 1863, the 45th's patriotism, its members' character, and the unit's capable new leadership—former junior officers who had been promoted to take the place of the many lost senior officers—led to commendations from their brigade commander. The unit reenlisted before the raid, another demonstration of the 45th's continued commitment to the Union, and the men enjoyed a well-earned furlough home before serving faithfully in Sherman's Atlanta Campaign.

For about eight and a half months, from July 4, 1863, until March 17, 1864, the battered 45th received much-needed rest after the long Vicksburg Campaign. Some, including Colonel Maltby, returned home to recuperate from their wounds. Maltby reached Galena on July 14, 1863, receiving a hero's welcome from a throng of citizens, along with a band, waving banners, and lighted torches. The colonel visited other recuperating members, and on August 4 General Grant promoted him to brigadier general, saying of Maltby, "No man has won greater distinction throughout the entire campaign than he" and "there is no more gallant and deserving officer." Maltby returned to the regiment in mid-August.[1]

To the people of Galena, the recuperating soldiers' "bronzed and sunburnt appearance" was evidence of their tough service. Pvt. Charles Evans recuperated from the effects of the shell that had sent him through the pilot house of the *Anglo Saxon* in April 1863. Capt. Henry Boyce's right hip finally healed after a doctor removed a half-inch-long piece of wood from the wound he had suffered eighteen months earlier at Fort Donelson. The captain was one of just thirteen men left of the forty from Lake County, Illinois, who had enlisted in 1861. On July 19 over 1,500 people attended the funeral of Maj. Leander B. Fisk in Mount Carroll, Illinois. The simple epitaph to honor Fisk's service was "He died for his country." In September patriotic women in Galena raised money and purchased new regimental colors to replace the unit's tattered ones. Home on furlough, 1st Lt. Otto C. Hager, 1st Lt. Joseph Vincent, and Adj. James Clifford brought the "worn and faded" old colors back to Galena. After a speech by a Galena woman, Capt. James Rouse, also on furlough, gratefully received the new colors.[2]

Those who remained in Vicksburg were no longer threatened by Confederate bullets, but men still died, some from malaria carried by the abundant mosquitoes. Other diseases also caused deaths, like that of Pvt. Abner Dalby, who died of chronic diarrhea on November 12, 1863. During this time, "tens of thousands" of formerly enslaved people poured into the Union lines. Some came on wagons filled with goods or rode on horses and mules taken from their former enslavers' plantations. Many of the men joined the nearby Black cavalry units that protected the camps of formerly enslaved people on the Louisiana side of the Mississippi River. One Lead Mine man believed these troops proved "to be excellent scouts, successfully engaging bands of the enemy on many occasions." According to this member, most of the Illinois soldiers had a favorable view of the Black soldiers because of their fine drilling, clean camps, and adaptation to military discipline, as well as the fact that they relieved the white soldiers of tedious garrison duty.[3]

On October 14 the regiment left on Gen. James McPherson's sixty-mile reconnaissance northeast to Canton, Mississippi. With Brigadier General Maltby's promotion to command the 3rd Division's 3rd Brigade, the recently promoted Lt. Col. Robert Sealy led the 45th. The men regretted losing Maltby, whom they considered an "efficient commander, a brave man and a true friend." McPherson's men moved out to prevent Confederate general Joseph E. Johnston from moving north to attack General Sherman's troops. The Federals reached the Big Black River at dusk on October 14, and the next day Brig. Gen. Mortimer Leggett's 1st Brigade and Maltby's 3rd Brigade skirmished heavily with the enemy and forced their retreat. The fighting continued over the next two days, with the fiercest action at Bogue Chitto Creek, where the Lead Mine men killed and wounded several rebels and captured twenty. The Federals then turned back, reaching Vicksburg on October 20. The soldiers enjoyed good weather, but a member of the 45th noted that the mission only accomplished the removal of the civilians' livestock, food, and tobacco and the devastation of their fences, cotton gins, some houses, and a steam grist-mill. Some pitied the noncombatants, but most in the regiment supported the pillaging and destruction as a way to end the war quicker.[4]

Other than a move to a camp on the Big Black River, the rest of 1863 passed uneventfully for the regiment. Like other veteran units who returned to drill during the war, the Lead Mine men spent much of their time in what Capt. John Adair wrote was "long neglected" company and battalion drill. Drilling helped the men maintain their proficiency in battle and stay competent and disciplined, knowing the value of this work in future combat. Adair believed the men favored the tighter discipline, as it reminded them of their time back in Illinois. Overall, their duties were light, and they enjoyed plenty of food. Meanwhile, recruiting by members back in Galena added fourteen new enlistees, who would receive $700 and an honorable discharge if they stayed in the army for nine months.[5]

In November a Copperhead meeting in Warren, Illinois, angered a man in the regiment, who voiced his displeasure in a letter to the *Warren Independent*. He was amazed that "a foulmouthed traitor had been allowed to belch forth a tirade of slander and abuse against the Government and the President" and said that the meeting dishonored both those who had died during the war and the soldiers who had suffered. He urged the paper's editor and its readers to remember the "widows and orphans" made by the "cursed rebellion" before letting another "black-hearted traitor" denounce the war. Another member believed Providence would defeat the "traitorous bands" of Copperheads.[6]

Lt. John P. Jones wrote home to his wife, telling her how much he missed her and that he and many others attended church services on Sundays and on weekdays; he believed that some attended services to avoid losing money gambling. As the unit's quartermaster, Jones had the important job of signing discharge certificates so that his comrades could receive government pensions. On December 31, 1863, he summed up the "eventful year," with the periods of "hardships, fierce conflicts, and pleasure" in the bloody battlefields near Vicksburg, the 45th's deadly service on the siege lines, and the unit's glorious entry into the captured city. The May 22 attack and the unit's desperate fight in the crater were "stamped indelibly" on his mind, memories he expected to have until he died. Jones looked forward to 1864, as it meant he was closer to reuniting with his wife.[7]

The Lead Mine men and their comrades in 3rd Division celebrated Christmas 1863 with whiskey liberally supplied by General Leggett. The next day

Leggett, with some officers and soldiers, attended the wedding of two formerly enslaved people, the bride an army hospital cook and the groom a member of the 12th Louisiana (African Descent). From October 22, 1863, to January 1, 1864, seven freedmen joined the regiment as undercooks, after the army authorized the enlistment of two Black undercooks per cook at a salary of $10 per month each. Of the seven undercooks, five deserted from the 45th, some as soon as five weeks after enlisting. Only Charley Grigsby mustered out with the unit in 1865, while Hosea R. Simmons received an honorable discharge on April 16, 1865, to join the 4th Mississippi Regiment of Black soldiers.[8]

The 45th Illinois became a veteran regiment on January 11, 1864, when over 75 percent of the unit reenlisted. The army had launched a preemptive reenlistment program in late 1863 to maintain the army's strength and avoid losing the experience of the veterans who had enlisted for three years in 1861. Units that had at least 75 percent of their members reenlist for three additional years got to keep their names, earned the veteran designation, and received a thirty-day furlough home and a $400 bounty. Historians have cited propaganda, peer pressure, the soldiers' patriotism, the furlough, and the bounty as reasons soldiers reenlisted. Bell I. Wiley stated that 200,000 Union men reenlisted, but James McPherson put the number at 136,000, or 65 percent of those eligible. Jonathan White questioned these numbers, maintaining that only 15 percent of eligible soldiers reenlisted. White, however, overestimated the number of men eligible to reenlist in late 1863 and early 1864. With most 1861 regiments having a strength of only 300 to 400 men after a few years in service, Zachery Fry's 33 percent reenlistment rate is more accurate. Lieutenant Jones boasted that those in the 45th who reenlisted did so out of patriotism, for they could not be "outdone" by the other regiments from Illinois, "nor any other state." He said that by enlisting, they hoped to demoralize their enemy and defeat the spineless Copperheads. Captain Adair believed the soldiers' reenlistment was a moral victory over the Confederates, who had hoped for a reduction in the Union army. Cpl. Peter Bellingall wrote that he signed on for three more years out of peer pressure, and though he expected his poor health to invalidate his reenlistment, the inspecting doctor found his health satisfactory. After their reenlistment, the 45th and two other veteran units in their brigade celebrated loudly with the brigade's band.[9]

The regiment used the rest of January to prepare for General Sherman's Meridian raid. Union soldiers, as demonstrated here and by Joan Cashin, had brought a hard war to Confederate civilians since the first Federals entered Confederate territory, but historian Mark Grimsley contended that this expedition marked the official beginning of the Union's hard war phase; for the first time, the army committed considerable military assets to go beyond the destruction of private property and taking of civilian foodstuffs to devastate Southern public property and ruin the Confederacy's economy by laying waste to its industry and transportation network. Previous actions by individual soldiers targeted civilian property randomly, but this raid included ordered demolition at the army level. The 20,000 men of the 16th and 17th Army Corps and 7,000 cavalrymen took just their weapons, ammunition, rations, blankets but no tents, and only enough wagons to carry extra ammunition, meat, bread for ten days, salt, sugar, and coffee. While Sherman had a herd of cattle brought along, he wanted his men to travel light so they could wreck twelve miles of railroad per day. His primary objective was the rail junction at Meridian, Mississippi, so that Confederate cavalry and guerrillas could no longer use it as a refuge and to prevent the gray horsemen from raiding along the Mississippi River. To oppose Sherman, there were just 12,000 Confederate soldiers in Mississippi. Before leaving, Sherman's men wrote home to tell loved ones that they would not hear from the soldiers for some time.[10]

Sherman's army moved out on February 3. With Lt. Col. Robert Sealy in Illinois recruiting, Maj. John O. Duer, promoted to replace the late Major Fisk, led the 45th. The 17th Corps first skirmished with enemy cavalry twenty-five miles east of Vicksburg, with the Confederates easily driven back eighteen miles to Clinton (see Map 8.1). At dawn on February 5 the 3rd Division, with General Leggett newly in command, moved forward under the cover of Union artillery to attack a now larger group of Confederate dismounted cavalry with artillery in a "strong position" east of Clinton. The 45th and 124th Illinois regiments led the division and fought with the enemy for eleven miles to Jackson, where Union cavalry chased the retreating rebels so

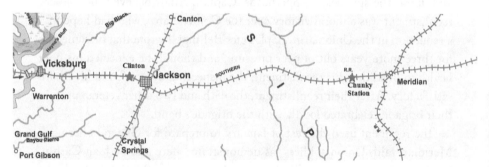

Map 8.1. Meridian Raid, February 3–March 6, 1864. *Source: Map created by Hal Jespersen, https://www.cwmaps.com* (changes made to the original).

closely that they could not re-form in their trenches outside of the city. The heavily outnumbered Confederates retreated over the Pearl River on a pontoon bridge, which they partially detached to delay the Federals from following. The heavy skirmishing resulted in only two wounded Union soldiers, none in the 45th.[11]

The next day Sherman had his men repair the bridge, forage for food, and burn any building in Jackson of military value. As the Union troops renewed their eastward march on February 7, one Lead Mine man wrote that Jackson looked completely ruined. Sherman's advance slowed over the next several days, as pioneers had to corduroy the poor roads and repair bridges left in ruins by the retreating Confederates. Meanwhile, the Union soldiers damaged many miles of the Southern Railroad and its depots, while the cavalry skirmished with lurking gray horsemen who had captured some Union stragglers and foragers.[12]

On the morning of February 14 the 1st Brigade, newly commanded by Brig. Gen. Manning F. Force, moved out south with a battery of artillery and two companies of cavalry, bound for Chunky's Station with orders to destroy the railroad there. After marching six miles, still two miles from the station, the men picked up the trail of Maj. Gen. Stephen D. Lee's 1,400 Confederate cavalrymen. The Federals moved out quietly and quickly, reaching the station at 9 A.M. Force ordered Major Duer to throw out skirmishers, with the rest of the regiment following. The skirmishers, Company F, quickly came under fire, prompting the general to order the 45th to attack. After a "sharp skirmish," the enemy retreated across the railroad trestle over Chunky Creek. The 45th then deployed as sharpshooters to protect the 124th Illinois, whose men worked to tear down the stout bridge. The rest of the brigade wrecked the town's water tanks, enemy headquarters, half a mile of railroad, and several buildings.[13]

Despite the sharp fight, Force's brigade suffered just eight casualties, half of them men from the 45th, including three skirmishers in Company F. Pvt. Peter Griffin's wounds caused his discharge in January 1865. Pvt. Charles Collar, shot in the left forearm and the right leg above the knee, had his forearm amputated successfully but died on May 9 while surgeons amputated part of his leg. The total number of Confederate casualties is unknown, but General Force reported that the enemy "left blood on both sides" of Chunky Creek. The general noted that the 45th "behaved handsomely" in the fight and that, overall, the brigade fought well with little direction. Given the terrible loss of leadership during the Vicksburg Campaign, the 45th's performance here reflected on Duer's capable leadership and the work of the regiment's veterans.

The Lead Mine men ate breakfast left by the Confederates and then moved out toward Meridian, which they reached on February 18.[14]

Most of Sherman's army had reached Meridian four days earlier. After skirmishing with the Confederates and chasing them out of the city, the general's men laid waste to much of the town in and around the railroad station and the rail lines of the Southern and the Mobile and Ohio Railroads to the west, south, east, and north. Sherman said his men "made the most complete destruction of railroads ever beheld" and had obliterated many warehouses filled with corn and bacon; much of Meridian no longer existed. The Federals also foraged liberally on civilians' food.[15]

On February 20 Sherman's men started their return march to Vicksburg. With them were several white families and many formerly enslaved people. After marching sixty-nine miles, the 17th Corps reached Canton on February 26. They spent four days tearing up the railroad lines near the town, getting their food from a supply train and foraging. They took wagons, horses, mules, and cattle from "disloyal men" to carry the food. Foraging did not always produce enough sustenance, and on some days the men had only hardtack or parched corn to eat. On February 29 General Leggett ordered General Force to send men out to forage, cautioning them to be wary of Confederate cavalry. The fifty mounted soldiers and four officers included Adj. James Clifford and ten other Lead Mine men. The soldiers had completed their foraging when, still six miles from Canton, they encountered a larger force of Confederate horsemen. After a sharp skirmish, the Union men abandoned their horses and their foraged food, and retreated. Half of the men made it to a swamp, sidestepped a Confederate camp, and reached Canton safely on March 1. The rebel cavalry captured the rest, including Privates William Williams, John Rolfe, Henry C. Errett, and Alfred B. Ramsey of the 45th. With the two armies no longer paroling prisoners, Privates Rolfe, Ramsey, and Williams died at the notorious Andersonville prison camp before the war ended, as did many of Sherman's soldiers captured during the raid. Errett, however, escaped his captors on December 8, 1864, and returned to the 45th. Before leaving Canton, the 45th and their comrades demolished more of the rail line, a trestlework, all railroad-related buildings, and the locomotives and cars. They then marched fifty-two miles over four days and reached their camp on the Big Black River on March 4, after skirmishing the day before with Confederate cavalry near Bogue Chitto Creek.[16]

The Federal army brought ruination throughout the raid. This included over 100 miles of rail lines, railroad bridges, trestleworks, many train cars and locomotives, steam mills, and wagons. One source estimated the destruction at Meridian alone came to $2 million. Lieutenant Jones believed his comrades had made the Mississippi countryside barren out to Meridian. The raid cost Sherman 729 casualties, of which 383, or 53 percent, were captured by the Confederates or missing, including the 4 in the 45th. In comparison, with a 50 percent larger army than Sherman, General Grant on his final campaign to capture Vicksburg (from Port Gibson to July 4 and Vicksburg's surrender) had only 453 soldiers go missing or captured, or just 5 percent of the total casualties. Sherman's implementation of the Union's escalated hard war devastated the Confederates' war-making machinery and likely inflicted greater hardship on its people but also brought more misery to Union soldiers, with a larger number captured. As there was no chance for parole at this time, capture meant worse suffering and a higher probability of dying in the horrid conditions of a Confederate prison camp.[17]

Despite the lost men, General Sherman congratulated his soldiers for rendering Meridian "useless" as a supply depot for the Confederates. A paper back in Waukegan called the raid the Union's "great achievement," saying it would shorten the war. Sherman boasted that even with a 360-mile march, most of his men returned in "better health and condition than when [they] started." A Lead Mine man, Pvt. William Williamson, likewise wrote that the men "all stood the march pretty well." Notwithstanding Sherman's optimistic long-term assessment of his raid, Confederates used enslaved laborers to get the rail line operational again by April 1, and their cavalry continued to use Mississippi as a base to hit Union supply lines in Tennessee, Alabama, and Georgia.[18]

Not all of the 45th took part in the Meridian expedition. Company D started on its furlough early and arrived in Galena on Sunday, February 7, 1864. A newspaper reported that these "invincible heroes" drilled on February 22 before an exuberant crowd, then enjoyed a free dinner. Also at home, Capt. James Rouse of Company C successfully recruited fifty-eight new members in the first four months of 1864. The men's time at home was not without tragedy, as Sgt. George Dye perished while riding a horse to see his sick father. When his frightened animal threw him off, Dye's foot caught in the stirrup, and the horse dragged him for more than 100 feet, during which his head hit the hard, frozen ground several times. The unconscious sergeant died just minutes later. Dye's father passed away a few days afterward, which left the family without support. The church overflowed with 300 people, including Company D, for the joint father-son service. Two weeks later the men of the company with the furloughed 12th Illinois enjoyed a ball in their honor before the Lead Mine men took a train on March 13 to Freeport, Illinois, fifty-five miles southeast of Galena in Stephenson County, where they stayed until the unit's furlough ended in late April.[19]

As soon as Sherman's force returned to Vicksburg, the reenlisted regiments started home for their furloughs, with instructions to be prompt in their return so that they would be available on May 1 for the start of the general's planned spring offensive to take Atlanta. Before leaving, the 45th's enlisted men and their comrades received welcome news—the army had increased their monthly pay to $16. On March 17 the men boarded a transport and began their journey north. Six days later they reached Cairo, where the regiment dispersed. The new recruits unhappily stayed in Cairo, while the veterans and those who had not reenlisted boarded a train for Freeport, reaching their destination on March 26.[20]

With advance notice, some in the 45th came home to a hero's welcome, as did many of their comrades in the Army of the Tennessee. Warren threw a grand dinner for about eighty men; the tables "fairly groaned" with the weight of the food, and many rousing toasts thanked the soldiers for their service. Some men attended the funeral service for Major Cowan on March 30. Pvt. John T. Venable got married on April 21, but sadly, he never returned to his bride; he died of consumption on June 18, 1865, less than a month before the unit mustered out of service.[21]

Pvt. Nathan Corbin decided to spend his furlough in Kansas with his family. At Cairo he boarded a ship for East St. Louis. After a short ride on a wagon, Corbin took a train 160 miles west, and then walked 30 miles to Tipton, Missouri. Here, although Corbin was wearing his blue uniform, a Confederate cavalryman gave the surprised private a ride across a ford of the Grand River and fed Corbin dinner in his house—likely a rare act of kindness, given the ferocity of the conflict in Missouri. The private then walked 30 miles to Warrensburg and took a train to his parents' home in Leavenworth, Kansas, where he arrived sick from his twenty-three-day journey. Corbin made no mention of the cost of his travels. His mother's help quickly returned Corbin to health, but before long he had to leave to rejoin the regiment. The private walked 40 miles north to St. Joseph, Missouri, and then rode by rail 330 miles northeast to Wataga, Illinois, but his health again worsened. Corbin believed he may have died without the care provided by a friend and a doctor. Once healthy, he traveled to Freeport by train, arriving on April 25, just three days before the regiment was to leave for Cairo. He reported to his surprised yet grateful lieutenant, who said, "Why, Corbin, is that you? We all thought you dead . . . But we're glad you're back, and with us again, for we need everyone, to the last man."[22]

The Lead Mine men began to reassemble in Freeport on April 24. One new recruit, Thomas Comstock of Winnebago County, apparently had reservations about his recent enlistment; a sentry, likely Pvt. Michael Murphy, shot and killed Comstock as he tried to desert the unit. On April 28 the soldiers boarded a train and began their journey to Cairo. Cpl. John Marquis wrote of the women who waved at the men, "God bless the patriotic women of the North!" The men reached still-muddy Cairo on April 29 and quickly worked to make it clean and livable. The rough conditions and deep mud shocked new recruit Pvt. George C. Lawson, who had just enlisted despite having a wife and four children, the youngest just eight weeks old.[23]

The Lead Mine men's stay in muddy Cairo lasted just two days; they and other elements of the 3rd and 4th Divisions of the 17th Corps boarded ships on May 1 as part of the efforts of their new commander, Maj. Gen. Francis P. Blair Jr., to get his widely scattered corps moving toward Georgia to join Sherman's Atlanta Campaign, which had started that day. The thirteen transports left Cairo on May 4, and two days later, after a 200-mile journey up the Ohio and Tennessee Rivers, they reached Clifton, Tennessee, where the 45th spent eight days guarding cattle and on picket duty.[24]

General Blair arrived on May 14 with the rest of his corps, which now totaled 8,000 soldiers. The next day the men, with thirty pieces of artillery, 400 wagons, and thousands of cattle, marched for Huntsville, Alabama, 115 miles to the southeast. The Federals reached Pulaski, in south-central Tennessee, on May 19. Private Lawson wrote to his wife that several hundred soldiers fell out of the hard march. Some, like new recruit Pvt. Daniel Fish of the 45th, became sick after crossing the frigid Pulaski River. An ambulance took Fish to Huntsville, where he stayed a week recuperating from a "raging fever" and "aching bones."[25]

Blair's divisions reached Huntsville on May 23 after marching through barren country and towns containing only men with missing limbs, a few women, and ruined buildings. Private Lawson wrote that although he was new to soldiering, he "travelled like a brick" on the tough march. At each stop on the movement, the soldiers stole the civilians' food and used their fences for cooking fires. The men much appreciated Huntsville's spring water after their "rapid and fatiguing march" over the rugged terrain. The 45th made no mention of resistance or even defiant language and insults from the civilians in Huntsville—evidence of the impact of their comrades' hard war in northern Alabama in 1863–64.[26]

The southwesterly movement resumed early on May 25, and two days later the soldiers crossed the Tennessee River at Decatur, Alabama. They then made a nine-day, 130-mile march east to Rome, Georgia. A Lead Mine man, Corporal Marquis, said the tough march took them over the tallest mountains he had ever seen. Private Corbin wrote that the muddy southern Appalachian mountain trails were "very hard to gain" and the "swollen streams" were difficult to cross. Despite their toils, Blair believed his men reached Rome on June 5 in "good health, spirits, and condition."[27]

The 45th Illinois and their comrades had marched about 275 miles in twenty-three days over difficult terrain. They expected to rest for a few days in Rome, but General Blair had other ideas; the weary soldiers marched 26 miles on June 5 before reaching the Etowah River bridge the next day. The bridge, a few miles south of Cartersville on the Western and Atlantic Railroad, was a key link in Sherman's only supply line back to Chattanooga. When Blair's divisions marched off on June 7 to reach Sherman at Acworth, the 45th Illinois and 3rd Iowa stayed to guard the damaged bridge, some pontoon bridges, and the rail line.[28]

General Sherman began his Atlanta Campaign on May 1 as part of General Grant's spring 1864 five-pronged strategy (see Map 8.2). Grant wanted Sherman to attack and break up Confederate general Joseph E. Johnston's Army of Tennessee, then enter the countryside to destroy the enemy's war-making ability and resources. Since May 1 Sherman had used his three armies to flank Johnston out of several strong defensive positions. The battles fought between the two armies resulted in Johnston's retreat of over seventy miles from Dalton to just north of Marietta. On June 8 the Confederates were in strong positions twenty-three miles north of Atlanta at Kennesaw, Pine, and Lost Mountains, about twelve miles southeast of Sherman at Acworth.[29]

Sherman had waited there for the arrival of General Blair's 17th Corps, men he needed to replace his campaign casualties and units detached to guard his supply line. He also needed the Etowah bridge repaired to feed and supply his troops as they drove on to Atlanta, after retreating Confederates had partially damaged it on May 19. Over three days, Union engineers and the 600 skilled members of Sherman's Railroad Construction and Repair Corps worked on the sturdy 75-foot-high and over 300-foot-long bridge. Despite Confederate fire, the first train went over the restored bridge on June 11, and soon five trains per day passed over it.[30]

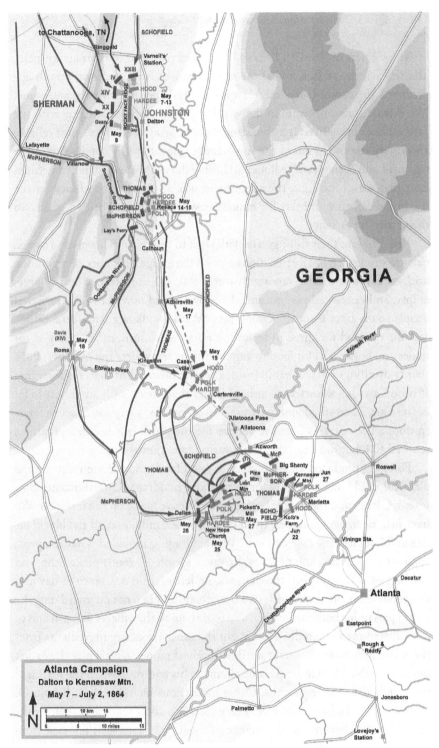

Map 8.2. Atlanta Campaign, May 7–July 2, 1864. *Source: Map created by Hal Jespersen on September 25, 2011, https://www.cwmaps.com* (changes made to the original).

The soldiers of the 45th Illinois had mixed reactions to their assignment. The few who were sick and those with sore feet from the long march appreciated the camp. Corporal Marquis enjoyed the river's water, and some, like Private Lawson, swam in it every day. Many of those unhappy with the assignment rationalized it by boasting that the army needed its "most reliable and trusty troops" to guard the important bridge, but to Captain Adair, the regiment had been given "tedious and insipid duty." Private Fish noted decades later that with hindsight, the assignment was a "streak of good luck" given the brutal fighting and terrible casualties suffered by their brigade mates in the battles for Atlanta.[31]

Regardless of their feelings, the 45th went to work using shovels and cotton bales to strengthen the fortifications around the bridge, redoubts, and pontoon bridges. The cotton bales, reportedly worth $50,000, came from a nearby large, empty, and ransacked plantation, whose owner had moved his 200 enslaved people south away from the Union men. While soldiers guarded the bridge and the railroad for three miles to the north and south, others foraged for mules and horses and for food to augment their army diet. The members built shanty dwellings in their camp inside the earthworks. Through his foraging, Private Lawson's shanty was perhaps better than most, with a window to let in fresh air, a bed stand and mattress, plates, spoons, a cupboard, and a fancy spittoon. The shanties failed to relieve the men in July, when temperatures reached 104, but did keep them dry during June rains.[32]

Foraging produced an abundance of good food, and the men also ate the plentiful wild blueberries raw or in pies and puddings. Quartermaster Sgt. Joseph Glenat told the people back home, "We are living on the top shelf. We have fish, beef, new potatoes, fresh bread, butter, milk, and all the blackberries and huckleberries we can eat." While foraging provided potatoes, peas, apples, plums, pears, and peaches, Private Lawson diligently picked the wild blueberries. Disregarding the dangers, he left early at 3 A.M. each day and returned before breakfast with two buckets full. When not on guard duty, he baked pies in his homemade oven and sold them to the officers for cash and to the enlisted men on credit. He bought the other necessary ingredients from the regiment's sutler on credit until he received money for his pies. Lawson's business enabled him to send money home to his wife even when the regiment went unpaid for some months. Other industrious men, like Sgt. Edwin O. Hammond, baked and sold blackberry pies, and still others sold their fresh-baked bread. Despite the abundance of fresh fruit, men still fell sick from diarrhea and other diseases.[33]

Although close to the front, the regiment received little news of the campaign. In early June they could still hear thunderous cannonading, but by July 4 they could no longer hear the sounds of fighting. The supply trains returning north loaded with wounded men, however, were evidence of heavy fighting to the south. New to war, Private Lawson believed the wounded an "awful sight." The 45th's sick lived in a frame house and in a tent attached to it. Later in August, while the Lead Mine men were stationed at Marietta, Georgia, a school housed the sick men, who told Dr. James R. M. Gaskill, the regiment's new assistant surgeon, that it was the best field hospital to date. The doctor himself suffered severely from diarrhea and spent time in Chattanooga healing before reaching Etowah on June 10.[34]

On July 4 the 45th Illinois enjoyed a dinner of normal army food and, for some, alcohol. They were entertained by speeches, including one from a Missouri colonel on his time in and escape from a Confederate prison. That night, rumors spread that the army might consolidate the unit with the 40th Illinois. Quartermaster Glenat wrote that the men were against the move because "the northern boys don't like to associate with the Egyptians," a term used for people living in southern Illinois. These negative views likely stemmed from the regiment's pro-Republican leanings as opposed to the southern Illinois soldiers' pro-Democrat leanings, or perhaps the 45th's members had read of the Copperhead antiwar activity in southern Illinois. These traitors worked to protect and hide Union deserters, hindered pro-Union men from voting, prevented enlistments into the army, clashed with Union soldiers in pitched battles, and helped raiding Confederate cavalry from Missouri and Kentucky.[35]

The dangers for the Lead Mine men at Etowah were certainly much less than for the 1st Brigade at the front. Yet service in an isolated outpost, with units of Confederate cavalry roaming throughout the countryside, was not without its perils. Early in June, after capturing an enemy courier, the men learned that General Johnston had ordered his cavalry commander, Maj. Gen. Joseph Wheeler, to destroy the Etowah bridge. This news added to the rumors that thousands of Confederate horsemen would soon attack the squads of men guarding the span. Guard duty was a nerve-racking affair for Private Corbin, who thought for sure a rebel had shot him when a bird smacked his leg. On June 18 the danger of attack became real when fifteen enemy horsemen shot and killed Pvt. Richard Grening and Pvt. Theodore Hildebrand while they patrolled the railroad three miles south of the bridge. The Confederates then wrecked sections of the rail line. Ordinary activities could also be dangerous, as Pvt. Jacob Bruce drowned on June 21 while bathing in the Etowah River. No general attack occurred at the bridge while the 45th guarded it, but Wheeler did attack the rail line in force farther north at Resaca.[36]

The 45th Illinois left the Etowah bridge on July 10 to guard the railroad pass at Kennesaw Mountain, twenty-one miles southeast. While the weather varied between cool and hot days there, Dr. Gaskill wrote to his wife about another insect tormentor: "But oh! The flies—horse flies, dog flies, or ox flies or whatever they should be called." During the two weeks at the railroad pass, the men visited the location of the recent battle there. Gaskill toured the enemy's strong fortifications, while the decayed bodies of both armies appalled Private Corbin. The men also turned out in good numbers for church services—the first held since they came to Georgia. At Kennesaw, the men traded food with local destitute women, both Black and white, swapping their army fare for the women's berries, butter, and buttermilk. The civilians only wanted to trade for food, as the local markets had none to purchase. The 45th found that the civilians had no more fight or resistance to the Union soldiers.[37]

During the Atlanta Campaign, the Lead Mine men's faith in Providence continued, and more men attended religious services, as did their comrades across the Confederacy. Lieutenant Jones wrote in June to his wife that he hoped God would spare him until his expiration of service late in 1864. In another letter, he told her that he "ought to be able to thank in Providence" for keeping him safe during his years of service and that the soldiers trusted only "in God and Gen. Sherman." Dr. Gaskill reminded his wife that Providence would help them survive their separation until he came home. Private Lawson twice noted his good health to his wife and twice thanked "God for his protective care." On September 14 Rev. William D. Atchison became the 45th's first chaplain in fourteen months. Atchison's arrival led to greater attendance at services by the unit, which previously had only infrequent services or visited those of other units or perhaps, as Lawson once did, a freedmen's church. Twice the regiment repurposed buildings for their services.[38]

While on guard duty or in camp at Kennesaw, the Lead Mine men heard the sound of the fighting near Atlanta and learned how their mates in the 1st Brigade had distinguished themselves at Bald Hill on July 21 and 22. Just four days earlier, President Jefferson Davis had removed General Johnston for his failure to prevent Sherman's advance and promoted Lt. Gen. John Bell Hood to command the Army of Tennessee. Hood quickly attacked part of Sherman's army on July 20 at the Battle of Peachtree Creek. In the Battle of Atlanta two days later, on July 22, the 1st Brigade and the rest of the 3rd Division held Bald Hill, a critical point in the Union lines despite many Confederate assaults to retake it. The knoll soon became known as Leggett's Hill because of the division's bloody fighting there, and Generals Leggett and Force and their soldiers received great praise. The 1st Brigade lost nearly 350 men, or 10 percent of the total Union casualties, losses that made the Lead Mine men feel fortunate for their tedious yet relatively safe assignments at Etowah and Kennesaw. In his address over forty years later at a reunion in 1905, Daniel Fish believed that had the 45th been there, the reunion "would hardly have been possible."[39]

From July 26 to October 3 the 45th Illinois guarded the railroad bridge over the Chattahoochee River at Roswell and served as provost guard in Marietta, thirteen miles to the southwest. The inexperienced Dr. Gaskill ended the sixteen-mile march to Roswell with sore feet. The doctor summed up his views after two months in uniform: "Sick is war." The unit's detached service made mail duty dangerous for Corporal Marquis, who was captured by Confederates on his return to Marietta with the 45th's mail. After Marquis and a captured Union captain had been taken south, the two got the better of their captors and used the rebels' horses to return safely to Marietta. On September 1 the soldiers heard from Atlanta the explosions of the munitions that General Hood could not take with his retreating army. Private Corbin wrote, "The whole sky above was lighted by the flames." Hood evacuated Atlanta after Sherman's men had cut his last remaining supply line, the Macon and Western Railroad, with their victory at the Battle of Jonesboro south of Atlanta. On September 2 the Union soldiers moved into Atlanta, and Sherman thanked all his troops for their efforts. Private Lawson wrote to his wife, "Atlanta is ours! Thank God!" Optimistic members believed the war's end was near and that they would soon receive their back pay, rest, and new clothes. Some hoped the victory silenced the Copperheads, whom Gaskill considered "the government's worst enemies." The regiment sustained just four casualties, with only two killed in action during the Atlanta Campaign. Their foraging and trading army salt, coffee, and sugar for civilians' butter, fresh bread, cucumbers, and onions meant they likely ate much better than their brigade mates. On September 8, to add to their diet, 500 soldiers including Lead Mine men foraged in force and captured a Confederate foraging train of wagons. Despite the good food and mostly restful service, the 45th still had to contend with the tormenting mosquitoes and lice.[40]

With General Wheeler's Confederate cavalry in the area, the Lead Mine men on guard duty and especially those out foraging had to keep a sharp watch for Wheeler's men, who routinely caught Union foragers. Wheeler's cavalry worried Private Lawson because the unit numbered less than 400 men and had replaced three regiments guarding the Chattahoochee bridge. At Marietta, 1st Lt. Louis G. Trimble of Company I died of chronic diarrhea. The lieutenant had received two promotions after enlisting as a private. In a tribute to Trimble, Capt. James Palmer of Company F and the unit's officers passed a resolution, which was published by papers in Waukegan and Keithsburg, Illinois. It said the lieutenant had been an "efficient and faithful solder," who, because of his "meritorious conduct, in the faithful discharge of his duty . . . [had] endeared himself to our memories, and caused us deep sorrow as his early death." According to Captain Adair, Trimble was the only man in the unit ever escorted to his grave by his comrades.[41]

While at Roswell and Marietta, the soldiers again saw many poor women, children, and elderly people, both white and Black, who struggled to survive without their men. Dr. Gaskill had a low impression of the white civilians, as expressed in a letter to his wife. He particularly disliked the women, mainly because they chewed tobacco, but he still provided medical care to them, even to one woman he referred to as an "opium eater." However, Gaskill worried that the poor women and children had no protection and were sickly, and Lawson once bought gingerbread for some children because all they had to eat was hard biscuits. Despite the good food and good weather, Dr. Gaskill's sick list totaled not quite 10 percent of the unit. Private Fish's severe sickness caused his move to an Atlanta hospital to fully recuperate. As he recovered, he became a surgeon's assistant and formed a friendship with the famous Mother Mary Bickerdyke, whom he also met after the war and personally thanked for her service. Late in September the mustering out of forty soldiers who had not reenlisted in January further reduced the regiment's rolls.[42]

After a short stay in Acworth, the 45th Illinois moved to Kennesaw Mountain on October 4 with other units of General Sherman's army. The general moved out to confront General Hood, who had marched his men west around Atlanta, torn up the Western and Atlantic Railroad, and waited there to ambush Sherman. Members of the 45th went to the top of Kennesaw Mountain to observe Sherman directing his troops, the fighting between the two armies, and the miles of burning rail line. The Union soldiers successfully forced Hood to move west into Alabama in search of food, while Sherman had the railroad repaired. The regiment also bade farewell to Capt. James Rouse and Capt. John Adair, whose service had expired. Adair later wrote that he regretted resigning, but with his poor health and the loss of his hearing from the fight in the Fort Hill crater, he knew he would not have been able to endure the exertions of Sherman's upcoming campaign. Thus Adair joined other Union soldiers who did not reenlist because of health concerns.[43]

After General Hood moved west, Sherman feared that by chasing him, he would lose the "moral and political effect" of his capture of Atlanta. Thus he pressed General Grant and received approval for his Savannah Campaign. He would detach his army from his Chattanooga supply line and destroy Georgia's war-making ability, factories, railroads, and mills; the campaign would be Sherman's full implementation, at the army level, of the Union's hard war policy. This would weaken the civilians' morale and resolve by showing them the "terribleness of war," how vulnerable they were to ruination, and that their government could "no longer provide them with protection from the invader." In other words, he wanted to make "Georgia Howl!" Grant approved the campaign only after Sherman agreed to send two corps to Maj. Gen. George Thomas in Nashville to defeat Hood's army. Sherman's remaining four corps then spent ten frantic days preparing for the campaign. Trains poured into Atlanta with ammunition and food and returned north with surplus artillery, wounded men, and those too sick or weak for the campaign.[44]

On November 9 the army paid the 45th for the first time in 1864. The unit also marched to East Point, just south of Atlanta. After seeing some comrades lose their pay gambling, Private Lawson wrote, "May God pity the wife and children of the gambling soldier." The private sent his wife $192—all his pay and most of the money he made selling pies. While Dr. Gaskill received his requisitioned medical supplies, the Lead Mine men, like their comrades, disposed of items unneeded on the campaign. Some members entered Atlanta in the final days before the army left the city. The metropolis was in a state of confusion, as per Sherman's orders; civilians streamed out of Atlanta, while the Federals demolished items of military value, such as the 200-foot-tall chimney of the city's gas house, which crashed to the ground amid hurrahs from onlooking Union troops. Estimates of the damage done by Sherman's veterans reached into the millions, and as the army left Atlanta, his chief engineer, Capt. Orlando M. Poe, wrote that "for military purposes the city of Atlanta has ceased to exist." This saddened Private Lawson, who noted in his diary, "My heart aches for the women and children. May God care for the destitute and starving families."[45]

The men of the 45th, like their Illinois comrades, did not vote in the monumental presidential election of 1864; the state's Democrat-controlled state legislature in 1863 refused to draft and pass a law pushed by Republican governor Richard Yates to allow the soldiers to vote in absentia. The regiment did, however, continue with their commitment to the citizen-soldier ethos and took a straw vote in early October. Major Duer reported to a paper back home that over 95 percent of the 45th voted for Lincoln. This exceeded the support for Lincoln in the Army of the Tennessee and the Union army as a whole, an unsurprising result given the Republican dominance in the unit's home counties. James McPherson stated that 80 percent of the soldiers who could vote voted for Lincoln. However, Jonathan White found that McPherson did not include the 20 percent of eligible soldiers who chose not to vote in the election. White also took issue with McPherson's contention that Lincoln won the soldiers' vote because they had adopted the Republicans' ideology and emancipation as a war goal. According to White, Lincoln won their vote because of the Democrats' peace platform and the Copperheads' antiwar efforts, as well as intimidation by pro-Republican soldiers of pro-Democrat soldiers to either vote for Lincoln or choose not to vote. Zachery Fry agreed with White's numbers but sided with McPherson over White as to why Lincoln won the soldiers' vote. Finally, Gary Gallagher asserted that because of the Democrats' peace platform and the Copperheads' antiwar work, the soldiers saw that a vote for Lincoln meant a vote to save the Union. On November 11, upon hearing of President Lincoln's reelection, the men rejoiced, and Private Lawson wrote, "Glory Hallelujah!"[46]

Not all the Lead Mine men went on Sherman's Savannah Campaign. At least seventeen soldiers left for home when their enlistments expired. Before he had the rail line destroyed, Sherman also sent north 3,000 soldiers—men too sick or weak to handle the campaign's rigors. On returning from a furlough, Private Fish of the 45th reached Chattanooga, where he learned of Atlanta's devastation and that Sherman's army had already left for Savannah. In Chattanooga, Fish joined the 3,000 men of the Provisional Division of the Army of the Tennessee, or PDs. The army moved the PDs to Nashville, where Fish, now a sergeant, met about 39 Lead Mine recruits who joined the PDs. This force fought in the Battle of Nashville on December 15 and 16, Fish's first battle. In the victory, the Lead Mine men survived unharmed. The PDs, with General Thomas's army, chased Hood's army into Alabama and eventually reunited with the 45th in North Carolina.[47]

On the eve of Sherman's Savannah Campaign, the tough, pragmatic hard war veterans of the 45th Illinois confidently prepared for their general's full implementation of his war against the Confederacy and its citizenry. They had overcome their initial disappointment with their guard duty assignment in June and defended sections of Sherman's supply line faithfully and successfully to the campaign's end.

9. ❦ The End of a Hard War

The hardy, resilient, and capable Lead Mine men lost few members as they and their comrades successfully implemented General Sherman's final phase of the Union's hard war from November 1864 to April 1865 during his Savannah and Carolinas Campaigns. The Federals laid waste through 250 miles of Georgia and caused even more destruction in South Carolina before they ended the war with their final combat while in North Carolina. The 45th ended its service in a triumphant postwar celebration in Washington, D.C.

On November 15, 1864, Sherman's army plunged into the interior of Georgia. Maj. Gen. Henry W. Slocum commanded the troops of Sherman's left wing, the Army of Georgia's 14th and 20th Corps, while Maj. Gen. Oliver O. Howard commanded the army's right wing, the Army of the Tennessee's 15th and 17th Corps. Sherman's army totaled 55,000 infantrymen, 5,000 cavalrymen, and 2,000 artillerymen. Only the 15,000 Confederates of General Wheeler's cavalry, some militia units, and some units at Macon, Augusta, and Savannah opposed Sherman.[1]

The Federals traveled light, with only one artillery field piece per 1,000 men, one ambulance per regiment, and one wagon to carry each unit's extra ammunition. The army's wagon train contained twenty days' worth of bread, forty days' worth of sugar and coffee, double the normal amount of salt for forty days, and 5,000 cattle. This was not enough to feed the men, and thus Sherman ordered his officers to send out foraging details as soon as the army left Atlanta. The general aimed one wing at Macon and the other at Augusta so the Confederates would be unsure of his intentions, thus forcing them to divide their forces (see Map 9.1).[2]

With Lt. Col. Robert Sealy on detached service, Maj. John O. Duer again commanded the 45th. The first sixteen days on the campaign were uneventful except for November 15, when the army provided whiskey rations to the men, which led to drunkenness, fighting, and swearing. Sherman's soldiers marched out of Atlanta "full of confidence," and General Leggett wrote that the 3rd

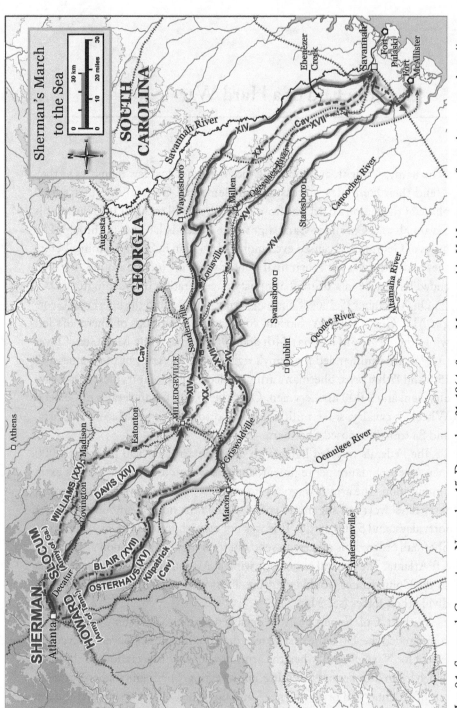

Map 9.1. Savannah Campaign, November 15–December 21, 1864. *Source: Map created by Hal Jespersen on September 25, 2013, https://www. cwmaps.com* (changes made to the original).

Division remained exuberant throughout the campaign. The men enjoyed mostly pleasant weather while en route to Savannah other than November 19–22, when they suffered from winter winds, snow, cold rain, and freezing temperatures. The November 20 movement of thirteen miles in seventeen hours stood out as particularly bad to the unit's veterans. It was made in a rainy downpour in deep mud, and the men told Lawson "they had never had such a time in three years of service." The Federals marched about 165 miles from November 15 to December 1, 1864, through several towns, where the 3rd Division skirmished lightly with overmatched enemy units before reaching the Confederate defenses at Savannah. The 17th Corps destroyed 113 miles of railroads on the way to Savannah, and according to Gen. Manning Force, the 1st Brigade enthusiastically went about this destruction. The men also burned cotton and cotton gins and used "houses, fences, woods and everything combustible" to fuel their fires each night.³

On December 2 the 45th Illinois, with the rest of the corps, reached Millen, eighty miles northwest of Savannah. General Sherman had pushed his men to reach the prisoner-of-war camp there to rescue Union prisoners, but no prisoners were found; the Confederates had already moved a reported 7,000 prisoners to other camps. The horrendous conditions of the camp and the graves of 750 of their comrades sickened the men, increased their bitterness and hatred toward the Confederacy, motivated them to cause greater destruction to civilian property, and led Sherman to ignore this destruction. The 17th Corps then moved out for Savannah and destroyed the Georgia Central Railroad along the way.⁴

On the way to Savannah, foraging amply fed Sherman's soldiers, who experienced only a few days of hunger. Usually they ate well, their diet including corn, hogs, geese, turkeys, chickens, poultry, honey, molasses, and sweet potatoes. General Leggett organized foraging parties in his division with twenty soldiers and one officer per regiment. He chose brave men who could strictly adhere to orders and had the physical makeup to withstand the rigors of the work. Leggett's campaign report noted only one known instance of misconduct by his foragers. Selected for this work, Pvt. George Lawson saw few fit men working the farms, where only women, children, and "worn out negroes" remained. The private, like others in Sherman's army, described the results of the army's destruction using biblical terms: it caused the civilians to suffer as if from the "hands of an avenging God." and some nights the "whole heavens" were "lit up by the burning railroads and soldiers' campfires." General Kilpatrick reported that the army had "gutted this part of the confederacy."

The men arrived at Savannah sore and tired from the miles they had walked while foraging for food in addition to the daily ten-mile marches.[5]

The corps reached the Confederates' strong entrenchments around Savannah on December 10 after heavy skirmishing with some of Confederate Lieutenant General William J. Hardee's 13,000 soldiers. As the skirmishing ended, Sherman's troops had pushed Hardee's men into their final fortifications closest to the city. The 17th then moved south and to the right on December 14, with the 3rd Division placed just left of the Plank Road. The men marched in icy cold, knee-deep water through swamps and rice fields, the latter flooded by the rebels to make a Federal assault more difficult. With no protection from enemy artillery and rifle fire, General Leggett ordered some men to fire on the Confederates, while others built fortifications, constructed artillery batteries, and dug trenches. Hardee had the Plank Road and the four other causeways into Savannah heavily defended with infantry and heavy artillery, guns too powerful for Sherman's lighter field cannons. In need of heavier artillery guns and food for his men, Maj. Gen. Oliver Howard, via an order from Sherman, sent a scout in a canoe down the Ogeechee River and out to the Union navy ships blockading the city to open communications with the commander of the navy flotilla, Rear Adm. John A. Dahlgren.[6]

The siege lines at Savannah were the first for the Lead Mine men in nearly eighteen months. The veterans considered the sniper fire as dangerous as it had been at Vicksburg, where a quick death awaited anyone who raised his head above the trenches. The Confederate artillery at Savannah, though, was more abundant and deadly than at Vicksburg, killing and wounding many Federals. The enemy cannon fire made picket duty hazardous, but Private Lawson's faith in God abated his fears while picketing. During the siege, the weather turned so cold it froze the water in the soldiers' canteens. At Savannah, the men grew tired of the abundant rice, and with foraging now turning up little food, one man refused an offer of $5 for his hardtack. One night Lawson and a comrade found a bag of beans, which the two cooked and ate only after removing the rat and mouse dung.[7]

On December 12 the 15th Corps moved to the regiment's right to attack Fort McAllister—the key bastion in General Hardee's southern defenses and the barrier preventing Union supplies and larger siege guns from reaching Sherman. The next day, during an artillery duel, the 15th Corps attacked and captured the fort, leading Private Lawson to write, "Thank God!" During their time on the siege lines, the men of the 45th Illinois encountered hundreds of formerly enslaved people and poor white women and children. The freedmen helped the men mill corn and shell rice and spoke in their own language. After Fort McAllister's capture, Sherman quickly messaged the navy, and soon ships brought food to his men, allowing them to eat well again. After the arrival of the army food, poor civilians and freedmen begged for hardtack. Lawson wrote that the "suffering of the negroes is terrible," and he and another man sympathized with the formerly enslaved people. Many of the white civilians, broken in spirit, admitted their cause seemed hopeless and preferred peace under the "Yankee heel" rather than continued conflict. McAllister's capture also enabled the men to receive and send letters home for the first time since Atlanta.[8]

The 45th went to sleep on December 20 expecting to attack Savannah's fortifications the next day with their comrades. Unbeknownst to them, to avoid losing his entire force, General Hardee evacuated his men northward overnight along the only causeway the Union soldiers could not block. Sherman's men quickly entered the city and captured 800 of Hardee's rear guard, over 100 artillery pieces, 12,000 bales of cotton, 190 train cars, and 13 railway vehicles.[9]

With the campaign over, one happy Lead Mine man reported home on the campaign's success, writing that it had proved wrong the Confederate and Copperhead newspapers, which had called Sherman's campaign foolish and predicted his army would be "cut to pieces" and "demoralized and melt away into nothingness" before it reached Savannah. In his campaign report, Sherman boasted that his men had done $100 million in damage and his soldiers' hard war had brought "the sad realities of war home" to those who were "directly or indirectly instrumental in involving us [in] its attendant calamities." He also commended his generals' and soldiers' self-confidence in the campaign. As historian Brooks Simpson put it, "Sherman's march across Georgia had confounded the Confederacy, destroying property and devastating morale—as evidenced in increased desertion from Lee's army," which occurred after the men read letters from family members telling of their suffering from the destruction caused by Sherman's army.[10]

Confederate calvary captured or killed a greater percentage of men in Sherman's army than during his Meridian raid; having to travel farther to find food likely was one reason. The number of missing and captured, 1,597, made up 83 percent of Sherman's 1,905 casualties. Enemy horsemen killed an unknown number of the missing and captured in retaliation for the Union's foraging and destruction. The 3rd Division had five men captured, but none were Lead Mine men, perhaps as a result of their discipline, resilience, learned service, and experience foraging on the Vicksburg Campaign and Meridian raid. Sherman ordered his men to forage liberally but not to enter private homes or destroy private property, and they were to leave the civilians some food. While he admitted that men disobeyed these orders and "did some things they ought not to have done," Sherman punished only a few violators. Skirmishes occurred between the Confederate cavalry and Union foraging teams and between the enemy and Sherman's "bummers," men who, without permission, worked ahead of the army's advance to forage for food and rob civilians of their valuables. The bummers likely committed most of the violations of Sherman's orders, but by working ahead of the Union columns, they often secured towns ahead of the soldiers' arrival.[11]

In addition to the destruction of nearly 200 miles of rail line, the Army of the Tennessee captured 9 million pounds of corn and fodder, more than 9,000 cattle, and nearly 1,000 horses and 2,000 mules; the foraging by the Army of Georgia far exceeded these figures. The amount of food the men found led some in the 45th to doubt their foraging could force a starved Confederacy into surrendering, as one man estimated that enough food existed in just the counties the army passed through to feed an enemy army of 50,000 for a year.[12]

While at Savannah, sixty-eight men who had not reenlisted and whose three-year enlistments had expired mustered out of the 45th, further reducing the small regiment. Lt. John P. Jones and the other mustered-out men traveled by ship in early January 1865 to New York, where they stayed in the Astor House for free. Jones and the other soldiers were "regarded almost as curiosities by the New Yorkers" because of their toughened appearance. Traveling by riverboat and train, the soldiers arrived home in late January. Those in Savannah celebrated Christmas and New Year's Day 1865 with pork, beef, and the ubiquitous rice, and some, like Private Lawson, attended church services.[13]

Dr. Gaskill's monthly medical reports for the last three months of 1864 provide a glimpse into the health of the 45th while near Atlanta and during the Savannah Campaign. The regiment averaged 349 members—21 officers and 328 enlisted men—while its sick list averaged 51 men; this was near the average, percentage-wise, for the Army of the Tennessee. Pvt. Albert Wilder died of dysentery back at Kennesaw Mountain; the same ailment also killed Pvt. John Wolfe as a prisoner at Andersonville. Of the 104 sick cases during those three months of 1864, nearly 40 percent suffered from acute and chronic diarrhea and fever. The unit had one deserter, Pvt. Henry Beales, who had deserted and returned to the unit many times, either voluntarily or after being arrested. Beales deserted for good on December 17 in Savannah.[14]

The Lead Mine men, with others in General Sherman's army, started on the general's Carolinas Campaign on January 6, 1865, after receiving new clothes and taking a transport from Savannah to Beaufort, South Carolina, seventy-five miles northeast (see Map 9.2). They waited in Beaufort for seven days until enough ships could transport the rest of the Army of the Tennessee. During the wait, Private Lawson visited the nearby forts manned by Black soldiers, who impressed him, but he wrote of hearing other Union soldiers who "hated the negro soldiers worse than . . . the rebels." Lawson did not

Map 9.2. Carolinas Campaign, February–April 1865. *Source: Map created by Hal Jespersen, https://www.cwmaps.com* (changes made to the original).

mention whether those with this sentiment were in the 45th. Historian Chandra Manning found that in 1864 and 1865, bigotry kept many in the Union army from accepting their Black comrades.[15]

The Lead Mine men ate well while at Beaufort, with food from the U.S. Sanitary Commission augmented by foraging. Finally, with the 17th Corps having arrived, the Federals moved out on January 13 and marched twenty miles north that day. The 3rd Division forced the retreat of Confederate units that guarded two bridges, and after skirmishing with the enemy, on January 14 they reached the Pocotaligo Fort—the point where Sherman planned to reunite his army and take control of the Charleston and Savannah Railroad. The fort, surrounded by swamps, was south of town on the opposite side of a creek and had strong earthworks. This left a road and bridge as the only avenue of attack. At about 4 P.M. the Lead Mine men moved out as skirmishers, the advance guard for the corps. About forty-five minutes later they entered an open field, and when they were still 200 to 400 yards from the fort, a "perfect shower of grape, canister, shrapnel and musketry" met the 45th. Officers ordered the men to drop to the ground. Private Lawson, after his first battle, wrote that he had never lain closer to "mother earth," and Sgt. Edwin Hammond and others "hugged the ground for a while for dear life." The men hid behind their haversacks and dug holes with their bayonets, knives, and forks. Cpl. Nathan Corbin's small earthwork and a spent bullet likely saved him; the bullet went through the dirt but only burned a hole in his clothes. Many men had "knapsacks completely riddled with bullets."[16]

With its captain serving on detached duty and its lieutenant recuperating from a wound, Sgt. Peter Bellingall commanded Company D. Lieutenant Colonel Duer, recently promoted after Colonel Sealy's discharge, again commanded the regiment. Duer ordered Bellingall that night to make sure two privates, George Chapman and John Edwards, got into the battle the next day; these men had always skulked back and had yet to fight in a battle. Bellingall recalled that Chapman "couldn't stand fire." When night fell, Duer ordered the sergeant to take the major's horse and a squad of men to get spades and picks. On Bellingall's return, Chapman and Edwards were gone. The two did, however, return to the unit before the end of the war and received honorable discharges when the regiment mustered out of service. It is unknown whether they returned to the unit by May 10, 1865, and were pardoned under the stipulations of President Lincoln's March 11, 1865, Proclamation 124.[17]

At 2 A.M. on January 15 Duer woke up Bellingall. General Leggett had heard sounds from the fort and wanted to know if the enemy had evacuated, so he ordered Duer to send someone to see. The colonel told Bellingall why he had selected him: "No one that I feel as sure of as I do of you, Billy." The two men went to Leggett, who asked the sergeant, "Well, my boy, do you think you can go in there and find out if they are evacuating or not?" The general told Bellingall that his only path was the road to the bridge and to be watchful for enemy guards. Chosen again for a dangerous mission, the sergeant first moved in a stooped, quick walk, then crawled to within 100 yards of the fort, where he saw an enemy guard near its gate. When the Confederate moved to the other side of the gate, Bellingall bravely made a "bold dash" toward the fort. With no guards in sight, the sergeant crept into the bastion and saw the enemy guard walking northward out of the fort. After alerting a comrade that the fort was empty, the relieved and very fortunate Bellingall took a Confederate flag and presented it to Leggett and Duer. Leggett then moved his division through the fort and into Pocotaligo.[18]

The 3rd Division suffered fifteen casualties on January 14, of which all but one were in the 1st Brigade. As at Chunky Station, the 45th's assignment as the lead unit caused the regiment to have the most casualties, with eight wounded. The 12th Wisconsin had one killed and five men wounded. One Lead Mine man, Pvt. John Miller, was wounded in the thigh and later died of disease in Louisville, Kentucky, on March 27, 1865; the wounds of two others in the regiment forced their discharge. Pvt. George Holyoke and Pvt. George Lawson believed it was God's mercy that spared more from wounds or death. The Army of the Tennessee's commander, General Howard, reported the loss of "service of several valuable men." Once again a general officer had chosen the 45th to lead an attack, with no apparent resistance or complaining from the men; the reason was likely the unit's esprit de corps, confidence because of so many victories in battle, and patriotism.[19]

The 45th Illinois and the 17th Corps stayed encamped near Pocotaligo for the rest of January. Private Holyoke wrote home that he always thought that "South Carolina must feel the effect of secession most bitterly before the war is over" and that the soldiers were ready to "burn and destroy everything before them." Many in Sherman's army shared Holyoke's sentiments. Over the next two weeks, the Union men built breastworks to protect the camp, foraged for food, destroyed the nearby Charleston and Savannah rail line, reconnoitered, and skirmished with Confederates. They enjoyed the mostly good weather, and besides the food found foraging, they ate fish, salted pork, and hardtack provided by the army and enjoyed "canned milk, tomatoes, [and] soda crackers," among other provisions provided by the U.S. Christian

Commission. In a letter to his mother, Sergeant Hammond wrote that the men were doing well, with new clothes and tents, which protected them from the cold and rainy weather that had started on January 18. He also disabused her of a rumor that Confederates had captured the regiment.[20]

Early on January 30 the 17th Corps moved out north with the goal of getting beyond the Salkehatchie River. Over the two-day movement, the Lead Mine men crossed many ice-cold, hip-deep swamps and streams swollen with winter rains. The men told Dr. Gaskill that it had been their most "*disagreeable*" march in the war. Despite the tough, cold day, Lawson pitied two boys he passed who stood beside their burned-out house—the work of Federals earlier that day.[21]

In February 1865 the 45th Illinois marched nearly 300 miles. According to Dr. Gaskill, the state burned "in consternation," and its people were "fleeing from the 'wrath to come.'" The men crossed over many icy swamps and streams, ate well at times from foraging, destroyed "most of the railroads" near their marches, skirmished with overmatched Confederates, and suffered only two casualties. Just General Hardee's 13,000 soldiers and Lt. Gen. Wade Hampton's 7,000 cavalrymen faced Sherman. The Confederates contested the Federals' movement at most of the river crossings, but Sherman simply used one unit to demonstrate in front of the rebels, while other units went up- or downriver, crossing over frigid waters on pontoon bridges, to flank their enemy. On February 12 the Army of the Tennessee was at Orangeburg, sixty-five miles north of Pocotaligo. As one division confronted the Confederates in their fortifications at a bridge across the North Edisto River, the 3rd and another division moved downriver two miles and crossed over a quickly deployed pontoon bridge; after crossing a deep swamp, they attacked the enemy's left flank, compelling the rebels to retreat. The Union men then destroyed the rail line for twelve miles north of the town, which, according to Gaskill, felt the "iron heel of war." Sergeant Hammond bragged in a letter home that the 45th had captured "beautiful" Orangeburg, which was "committed to the flame." Hammond also commented on the passage of the Thirteenth Amendment by Congress: "While the war was terrible, it happened because of God's providence," and the "people no longer deny the oppressed their rights." Clearly, the sergeant had adopted the Radical Republicans' message of equal rights and joined others in the Union in believing God's hand had brought the war as punishment for the national stain of slavery.[22]

The 17th Corps arrived before Columbia on February 16. Elements of both the 15th and 17th Corps then entered the city on February 17, with

Sherman's orders to spare private property but to destroy all items of military value, including railroads, depots, and machinery. After fire destroyed much of Columbia, the general contended that the wind and Confederate general Hampton's orders for "all cotton, public and private" to be "moved into the streets and fired" had caused the inferno. Sherman reported that after his men had partially put out the fires, but before they "fired" any public buildings, the wind revived the flames, which consumed most of the city. Dr. Gaskill's, Sergeant Bellingall's, and Corporal Corbin's accounts of Columbia's burning matched Sherman's—before leaving, the Confederates "set fire to some cotton and buildings containing commissary stores." The smoke from the conflagration was so thick that some Lead Mine men fainted from suffocation. Corbin considered the burning city a "wonderful sight," and a comrade commented, "I guess the boys wanted to 'teach her a lesson'"—that is, teach South Carolina a lesson for starting the war.[23]

The 45th Illinois and the rest of the 17th Corps marched through burned-out Columbia on February 18. They exited the city and then proceeded to destroy miles of railroad over the next ten days. Corporal Corbin recalled that the constant cold, rainy, and raw weather made it the worst winter he ever experienced; the soldiers' boots never dried out because of the many icy swamps and cold streams crossed, and their clothing was "very, very scant." They marched in the rain over several days, and at least one night they went to sleep with no tents or cover from the nightlong downpour. The soldiers' intermittent success with foraging meant that on some days they had nothing to eat but hardtack crackers and peas infested with bugs, and some mornings coffee equaled breakfast. Sergeant Bellingall said it was the "old story" of "feast or famine," as during the Vicksburg Campaign and Meridian raid. The 45th's foraging in South Carolina resulted in the loss of two members. Confederates captured Pvt. Peter Axen near Robertsville on January 31 and, luckily for Axen, sent him to a prisoner-of-war camp in Jacksonville, Florida, and not to the horrific prison at Andersonville, Georgia. Paroled on April 28, the private mustered out of service on May 23. On February 18 Confederates captured Pvt. Edward Jordan, a cook, as he foraged; sadly, the private died while a prisoner of war.[24]

The Lead Mine men with their comrades burned thousands of bales of cotton in South Carolina, destroyed many locomotives and train cars, captured significant war ordnance, and set fire to many buildings, public and private. They also tore apart buildings to construct bridges along the march and captured many "demoralized and disheartened" Confederates. The burning railroads, houses, buildings, and cotton gins made the air smoky during most of their movement through South Carolina. Private Lawson pitied the women and children because the Union soldiers left little food, with many Federals not caring "who they plunder and rob." The private attempted to assuage his conscience by going to church. The 45th's willingness to serve their country remained strong, even though the hard war policies meant a greater chance of dying while foraging in frigid conditions in inadequate clothing, and with the uneven results of their foraging leaving them in hunger at times.[25]

On February 26, three Union foragers were found with their throats cut. During February, at least thirty-seven Union soldiers were found with throats cut or heads beaten in, and some had papers pinned to their chests saying, "Death to Foragers." This led Sherman to order the execution of one Confederate prisoner for every murdered Union man, and he sent Hampton a copy of his order. On March 2 Sherman's men found two comrades shot outright and Pvt. Robert M. Woodruff of the 30th Illinois with his head bashed to pieces by a wooden club. At this, General Blair followed Sherman's order and had prisoners draw papers out of a hat to determine the man to be executed that day. A married, forty-year-old preacher, father of nine, pulled the marked paper. After praying with a Union chaplain, the prisoner spoke: "I was forced into the army, never was in a battle, never wished the Yankees any harm. I have a large family, all girls." The man then cried, as did some of the thousands of onlooking Federals. Lawson spoke to the doomed man but could not watch his execution. Although he pitied the man, Lawson expressed his willingness to execute other prisoners he believed were guilty of "treason through and through." The doomed man was taken to a tree, and after he again prayed with the chaplain, the Union soldiers blindfolded him. A major in the 30th Illinois gave the twelve-man firing squad the command to fire, and the man fell dead, shot six times (half of the firing squad was given blanks), which brought more tears from some of the Union troops. Corporal Corbin wrote, "And the pity of it was enough to make the stoutest heart break down." The other four prisoners executed that day were just some of the twenty-three retaliatory executions carried out by Sherman's army.[26]

The Army of the Tennessee resumed its northward movement on March 3, and five days later the men were in Floral College, North Carolina, about fifteen miles into the state. On March 11 bummers in the Army of the Tennessee, after skirmishing with General Hampton's cavalry, captured Fayetteville, with Pvt. William C. Taylor of the 45th Illinois receiving the mayor's surrender. The regiment constituted the 3rd Division's rear guard that day, and thus it is probable that Taylor was a bummer.[27]

Sherman then moved his army toward Goldsboro on March 13, some sixty miles northeast of Fayetteville, to join up with the 40,000 men in Maj. Gen. John Schofield's 10th and 23rd Corps, who had landed on the coast. Sherman acted here because Confederate Lieutenant General Joseph E. Johnston had finally concentrated substantial forces against him. From March 19 to 21, with his two wings twenty miles south of Goldsboro at Mill Creek, near Bentonville, Sherman clashed with Johnston's soldiers. In its last battle, the 45th had three soldiers wounded, including 1st Sgt. William Kinkade, whose wounded foot forced his discharge. Sergeant Hammond wrote, "The Rebels lost heavily as they played their old game of charging our breastworks," which the Union men had just completed, according to Dr. Gaskill, before the Confederates' last charge. The next morning Johnston retreated northwest toward Raleigh. By March 23 Sherman reached Goldsboro and linked up with General Schofield's men. The Union troops stayed encamped around Goldsboro until April 10.[28]

The arrival of Schofield's corps united the 45th Illinois with Pvt. Daniel Fish and the rest of the unit's Provisional Division of the Army of the Tennessee members. After helping chase General Hood's Army of Tennessee into Alabama, the PDs went by foot, rail, and steamship to Washington, D.C., before marching to Annapolis, Maryland. A ship took the men, many of whom became seasick, to New Bern, North Carolina, where Schofield's corps began a sixty-mile inland march, which included a running three-day fight with General Johnston's soldiers. Private Fish believed the PDs had behaved like "true Army of the Tennessee men." Their commander, Maj. Gen. Jacob D. Cox, reported that these men acted "in the most soldierly manner" and fought well during the clashes, where one Lead Mine man received a slight head wound.[29]

At Goldsboro, General Sherman used the time to resupply and refit his army. The 45th gratefully rested in the warm weather after three weeks of marching in mostly rainy conditions on muddy and slow roads and across many cold swamps in hip-deep water. Foraging provided uneven results, and some days the men had only parched corn to eat. The destruction of Confederate rail lines continued, but the devastation of private property ceased when Sherman's army entered North Carolina, except for that by the bummers, who persisted in searching for and taking valuables buried by civilians.[30]

During this time, Hammond and others in the 45th became the mounted provost guards for General Leggett's 3rd Division, which pleased Hammond, for it meant no marching. The 45th and their comrades gratefully received new clothes and shoes, as most were "clad in rags" or wore "rebel clothing." The new clothes also meant ridding themselves of their eternal enemy, the "grayback" lice. The thankful soldiers could again send and receive letters to and from home for the first time since leaving Savannah.[31]

On April 6, 1865, General Sherman received news that Gen. Robert E. Lee had pulled his army out of his Petersburg, Virginia, siege lines and that General Grant's army had given chase. Grant ordered Sherman to destroy Johnston's army so that he could not link up with Lee. The news of Lee's movement away from Petersburg brought jubilation in Sherman's army. The next day the men moved out northwesterly to confront Johnston, who retreated in front of the larger Union host. The first Federals reached Raleigh, North Carolina's capital, on April 13. While in the capital, Sherman's soldiers celebrated greatly on learning that Lee had surrendered to Grant on April 9. On April 17, however, the men heard the news of President Lincoln's assassination. Dr. Gaskill said this caused a "deep solemnity" to pervade the Union camp, with the men "more angry with the South than ever," while Private Fish noted that the men "mingled grief and rage." Corporal Corbin wrote that many wept, and the sorrow ran "very deep" in the army. The "death of our beloved President" saddened Hammond's heart. On hearing of Lincoln's death, some in the army, including Lead Mine men, were so angry that they vowed that if more fighting awaited them, they would take no prisoners. Men in the 15th Corps attempted to destroy Raleigh before their commander, General Logan, turned them back.[32]

The Lead Mine men's belief in Providence remained strong on Sherman's two campaigns, and they regularly attended religious services. At Savannah, Private Lawson saw the hand of Providence in the capture of Fort McAllister, Sherman's work opening the supply line, and the food they received from the Sanitary Commission. Also at Savannah, Private Holyoke said he left it up to God as to whether the war would end in 1865, and Sergeant Hammond at Pocotaligo echoed other Union men on why they served: "Our cause is holy." The sergeant believed it was Providence that enabled him to survive his wounding at Pocotaligo. After seeing Columbia's devastation, Dr. Gaskill prayed that Providence would never bring such destruction to the country again. Later in March, Lawson wrote that it was God's hand that had spared his loved ones from the rampant sickness at home, protected him during the battle at Mill Creek, and safeguarded the men on their long journey. As to why the war had lasted so long, Lawson thought it was because "God disapproved events." Finally, on hearing of Lee's surrender, men in the unit held a prayer meeting, where in song, they attributed his capitulation to Providence. Reverend Atchison continued to hold services throughout both campaigns, while the devout Lawson also attended services in a freedmen's church, where a Black minister gave "one of the sweetest sermons" he had ever heard.[33]

Sherman first met with Johnston on April 17 to discuss the surrender of the Confederate general's army. The terms reached the next day allowed the Confederates to march home with their arms after simply promising not to wage war on the country again. Secretary of War Edwin Stanton rejected the treaty, considering the terms excessively lenient, and in a rage, he sent Grant to arrest Sherman as a traitor and take over the surrender talks. Grant instead told Sherman to renegotiate the terms. Stanton found the new set of terms acceptable, though barely, and Johnston signed them on April 26. For the Lead Mine men and their comrades, the news of Johnston's surrender alleviated their apprehension, and thus with lighter hearts they celebrated: the war was over![34]

The ever-industrious Private Lawson penned two songs while at Goldsboro and Raleigh, the first being twenty-two verses about the Savannah and Carolinas Campaigns. He used the printing press in Sherman's headquarters to print copies of the song and sold thousands to everyone from generals down to privates at one for 15 cents or two for 25 cents. By the end of April he had made hundreds of dollars on his songs. The last verse of his campaign song is not surprising, coming from the faithful and patriotic Lawson:

> Sherman he was sent by God
> (and it was God's decree)
> To lead the Yankees through the South,
> And set the negro free,
> And trample down the bastard flag,
> The hated stars and bars
> And hoist the flag of liberty,
> The glorious stripes and stars.[35]

On April 27 General Sherman issued orders for his army to march for Richmond and then Washington, D.C. Before the march, the 45th and their comrades attended to the final "settlement of difficulties" by accepting rifles and other war equipment and munitions from Johnston's soldiers, while peacefully conversing with their former enemies. The march north began on April 29 in the direction of Richmond, about 160 miles northeast of Raleigh. The 45th happily moved out because they were one step closer to going home. The soldiers had nice weather, cool nights, and plenty of good water along the route. For Hammond and the other mounted Lead Mine men, it "was the most pleasant and agreeable march" during the war. Those walking, however, considered it their hardest march of the war. Generals Logan and Blair had made a bet as to which corps would reach Washington first, so they pushed their soldiers hard despite Sherman's order to move slowly, with no marching before sunrise or after sunset, and some days the men marched over twenty-five miles. According to Sergeant Bellingall, Sherman was furious with his subordinates when he heard of the bet and its impact on the men. While the pace caused deaths in some regiments, no one in the 45th died during the race to Washington. Sherman's army reached Richmond on May 12 and Alexandria on May 19, where the men rested for four days. According to the Illinois adjutant general's report, the Lead Mine men had walked 1,750 miles from May 14, 1864, to May 23, 1865, through six states.[36]

On May 23 General Leggett marched his division into Washington to watch the Army of the Potomac participate in the Grand Review of the Armies. The eastern soldiers' new uniforms, with polished black boots or shoes, white gloves, gleaming brass, and brightly shining guns, impressed Sergeant Bellingall and others. Back at camp, the men of Sherman's army worked to improve their appearance. Bellingall wrote that some formed their blue shirts to look like jackets, and others received new pants. The sergeant boasted that although the Lead Mine men knew their uniforms would never look as good as those of their eastern comrades, they prepared for the review "guiltless" because they were proud of their service since leaving Atlanta. The sergeant joked that other than their worn boots, the only "blackening" in their appearance was their wind- and sunburned hands and faces, which had gone unwashed for some time.[37]

At 6 A.M. on May 24 the Lead Mine men and their comrades marched into the capital, and by 9 A.M. they were in position. Sherman headed the Army of the Tennessee, with the 15th Corps in the lead, followed by the 17th Corps and then the Army of Georgia. Corporal Corbin wrote that while marching on the cobblestones of Pennsylvania Avenue, "'twas hard to step without a groan." With their tattered, wind- and battle-torn banners flying, the Lead Mine men, like their comrades, marched with pride. Sergeant

Bellingall wrote that he was "proud as the proverbial peacock" and boasted of his impeccably straight company, saying the regiment "marched perfectly" as the 45th Illinois paraded down Pennsylvania Avenue on the second day of the Union's postwar celebration. Bellingall, Company D's twenty-one-year-old sergeant, had commanded the company since the unit left Atlanta seven months earlier. Corbin said that as the Lead Mine men received welcome cheers from civilians, they simply marched like soldiers. Recently promoted Second Lieutenant Hammond wrote that the men "took on the appearance of glory and holiness" and marched like they never had before.[38]

The men in the Armies of Tennessee and Georgia marched for six hours, and a paper back home proclaimed the civilians' love for Sherman's soldiers; they had strewn the street with "roses and evergreens," and ladies almost buried some men "under the abundance of bouquets and wreaths bestowed upon them." President Andrew Johnson, General Grant, and others watched from a viewing stand. Sherman joined them on reaching the stand, where the 45th passed with their rifles at "shoulder arms." Although the men had eaten only coffee and hardtack, their "hearts throbbed," and Hammond wrote that the people "cheered so loudly they deafened" the men's ears. Private Fish called Sherman's army "the best that ever assembled on Earth," and Sherman said it was "the most magnificent army in existence." To anyone who believed his men "little more than an armed mob bereft of true discipline," the general wrote that they were "an army in the proper sense, well organized, well commanded and disciplined; and there was no wonder that it had swept through the South like a tornado." An Ohio reporter wrote that most thought "the West overtopped the East in the physical appearance of her troops, and their fine, soldiery bearing."[39]

On May 30 General Sherman issued special field orders in which he thanked the soldiers of the Armies of the Tennessee and Georgia for their service and recounted their "bold" deeds during the recent campaigns. He noted that the men had "contributed to the final overthrow of the Confederacy" and had done everything they could to defend the government of the United States. The general attributed the soldiers' success to their hard work and discipline, which would make them as good citizens as they were soldiers, saying that if war again came to the country, he was sure "Sherman's Army" would be the first to defend the nation.[40]

The Army of the Tennessee remained in camp near Washington until June 7. On June 3 the army mustered out men who had been mustered into service for one year before September 30, 1864. Corporal Corbin did not meet these requirements—he had enlisted for three years in 1862 and had reenlisted—yet the army mustered him out. He "bid the boys good-bye" and left Washington on June 6. Corbin reached Springfield, Illinois, by rail on June 12 and then walked 124 miles northwest to Galesburg, where he spent two weeks visiting friends. He left Galesburg on June 26 and joyfully reached home in Leavenworth, Kansas, on July 14. Corbin carried on his journey his overcoat with brass buttons and his haversack. Like other returning men who brought mementos home, he also had with him his "color-bearer's gift"—the last star on the regiment's flag. During the rest of the regiment's stay in the capital, Lieutenant Hammond claimed that "society is much disturbed" and that "Washington is in more danger today than when defended by McClellan's troops." Hammond was likely referring to soldiers who were setting off ammunition or engaging in pretend battles.[41]

The rest of the 45th Illinois and the 3rd Division left Washington on June 7 by train and traveled 330 miles west, reaching Parkersburg, West Virginia, on June 9. The next day the regiment embarked on a steamboat; the men made a 570-mile trip down the Ohio River and reached Louisville, Kentucky, on June 12. At Louisville, the soldiers were unhappy to learn that they would not have a short stay there. Disappointment and melancholy permeated the regiment because of the delay in their mustering out and because they had not received news on when they would head home. Some, like Lieutenant Hammond, "hardly knew how to endure the disappointment." Private Lawson voiced his vexations with the army and the government in a letter to the *Louisville Daily Journal*, complaining about the poor drinking water near the camp, the swarming mosquitoes, and the soldiers' biggest gripe—that the army had not told them when they would be going home. The soldiers' frustrations also stemmed from having seen comrades already go home—men who had enlisted in 1864, fought little, and made hundreds of dollars in enlistment bonuses, money the 1861 men had not received. The army had also failed to pay the men since November 1864. Lawson signed his letter "Noswal First Brigade, 3d Div. 17th Corp," but this clever backward spelling of his last name did not fool General Leggett, who arrested him for writing the letter. Leggett, while still angry, released Lawson after learning he "had the good will of whole army" in mind when he wrote the letter. The Lead Mine men were not alone in their anger and frustration over the delay in being sent home.[42]

Several sources provide a picture of the unit's health from January through July 12, 1865. The regiment's strength averaged 306 members, with 16 officers and 290 enlisted men. During January and February, an average of only 251 members could report for duty, with 100 unable to report because of sickness or wounds. In total, the regiment's ranks were thinned by 17 men during this time, with 7 expired enlistments, 3 discharges for various reasons, 4 deaths from disease, 2 captures (who remained prisoners at the end of the war), and 1 resignation by an officer. The unit's strength reached 395 in May after adding the PD men and 24 new recruits to its rolls.[43]

Finally, on July 4 orders reached the 1st Brigade that July 12 was their muster-out date. To celebrate the unit's mustering out, on July 11 the Lead Mine men enjoyed a feast courtesy of the regiment's sutler, A. H. Davis. The next day 368 members of the 45th Illinois mustered out of service, including 210 original members. Although the army had promoted Lieutenant Colonel Duer to colonel in May, at the mustering out the army promoted him to brevet brigadier general, likely in recognition of his services in command of the unit for the last seventeen months. This made Duer the ninth Galena man to reach the rank of general during the war. The men stacked their guns and left their cartridge boxes, canteens, knapsacks, and haversacks, then boarded a train for Chicago, 300 miles northwest. They reached the city on July 15 and again stayed at Camp Douglas, this time to await their pay and discharge. Meanwhile, Galena and other towns prepared to welcome home their fathers, brothers, and sons with much fanfare and celebration. Ahead of the main contingent, a few "somewhat bronzed" members arrived in Galena on Tuesday, July 18. The *Galena Daily Gazette*, in a patriotic ode to the regiment, boasted that the soldiers had enlisted out of "pure patriotism."[44]

On Friday, July 21, the people of Rock Island, Illinois, welcomed home members of Company H and some from Company I. Of the original 89 members of Company H, only 18 remained, while Company I had only 17 of the original 49 men from Henry, Mercer, and Rock Island Counties. A band and many citizens feted the veterans, who had a "sumptuous breakfast," while speeches recounted the soldiers' service, hardships, and "daring deeds and acts of valor." That same day, Galena welcomed home the rest of 45th's members from Jo Daviess County. The *Galena Daily Gazette* reported the Germania band played music while thousands hailed the soldiers, and some men fired a cannon in their honor. The paper noted that the men had survived their "fiery trial" and described them as "erect in person, bronzed in countenance, and with the cool and quiet port of men who have done their whole duty." The soldiers and citizens proceeded along flag-lined streets to the DeSoto House, where a man gave a speech recounting the regiment's deeds, including a "graphic and stirring sketch of the assault on Ft. Hill at the siege of Vicksburg" and the unit's colors waving over the captured city's courthouse. After thanking everyone for the welcome and the "flattering words," Brigadier General Duer humbly stated that the men had served out of a "single purpose of doing [their] duty" for their country. The soldiers gave three cheers for the people of Galena and then enjoyed a first-rate supper.[45]

Most of the Lead Mine men reached home having held to their oaths to serve their Union honorably to the end. At Pocotaligo, one of their final battles, the 45th had again been chosen to lead an attack—this time with their entire corps—and the regiment had served well. Their wartime service had helped end the rebellion, restore their republic, and abolish slavery. In doing so, many members had died for their country, while others were maimed or debilitated by disease. The survivors now began an uncharted journey to transition from soldier back to civilian. They also began a new war—this one a war of words with fellow veterans and civilians to protect their service record and their achievements bought by suffering and sacrifice.

10. ❧ Postwar Lives and Fighting with Words

The members of the 45th returned home as heroes. Many went back to their hometowns and picked up their past occupations, while others moved off to begin anew elsewhere. With little guidance on how to become civilians again, some Lead Mine men smoothly reentered their civilian lives and led a normal existence, while others, who found the war to be a "profoundly disorienting experience" that they could not simply forget, did not. The veterans of the unit did not allow "their 'martial past' to simply fade away," as some historians have contended; rather, they fought for their legacy, especially that at Vicksburg. Daniel Fish, who began the war as a sixteen-year-old private, and others, notably Wilbur Crummer, fought for the glory the regiment was "fairly entitled" to have. The Lead Mine Regiment's veterans held reunions periodically after the war and worked to memorialize their service at Vicksburg. Many were active in the Grand Army of the Republic (GAR) and met in Galena's E. D. Kittoe GAR Post, named in honor of the 45th's venerable first head surgeon, among other locations. As they entered their postwar lives, these veterans worked to receive government pensions, money they believed their republic owed them for their sacrifice and achievements while in uniform.[1]

Not long after the end of the war, the regiment's veterans joined with other Union veterans in writing as means to fight some Northern civilians—those who called for reconciliation; those who believed the ex-Confederate officers' Lost Cause history of the war, which held that the war was about "arcane constitutional issues," or a history that ignored the soldiers' suffering and sacrifices; and those willing to let ex-Confederates waste the Union soldiers' sacrifices, which had reunited the county and achieved freedom for those who were formerly enslaved, by implementing a near-slavery existence for the emancipated Black people. The 45th's veterans followed their former commander, John Logan, who reminded Northerners that the Union men "had fought, suffered, and died to secure the nation and enabled the perpetuation of their liberties."[2]

Former captain John Adair wrote a history of the 45th for the regiment's second reunion on September 28, 1869, at Freeport, Illinois. He told of visiting Medon, Tennessee, where the holes made by Confederate bullets were still visible in the train station. The Confederates had fired the bullets "with the hope of letting out the life blood of one of my comrades and friends," and thus he could not forgive his former enemies. To those who pushed for reconciliation with the ex-Confederates, Adair could not "let by-gones be by-gones." In recalling the Union soldiers' achievement, their defeat of "the greatest, the wickedest and most unholy rebellion, ever inaugurated and against the best government," he called on his comrades to share in the happiness of re-uniting with their former brothers and reliving the regiment's history, while remembering that their achievements had come at the cost of their "dead comrades who lie scattered" across the country. The former captain appealed to his comrades to protect the unit's "brilliant record," which was "an heirloom of honor to be handed down from generation to generation, with pride and satisfaction," for the unit was "conspicuous upon every battlefield [and in] camp . . . and on the march." The men owed it to their comrades who had died, their "weeping widows, and the fatherless children," and the parents who had lost their sons not to let the nation forget.[3]

Former lieutenant John P. Jones, writing in the years after the war on his service, also countered the Lost Cause history of the war. Jones wrote that while "volumes have been written, and however men may differ as to minor and indirect causes, there can be no doubt that the great overwhelming cause was human slavery." He and others in 1861 had believed the war would be a "desperate struggle, and that it would end only with the extinction of slavery," and had he not thought this, he would not have "volunteered in defense of the Government." Jones called Southerners' accusations "that the war was waged by the Yankees for the abolition of slavery" untrue—the Union men had served to defend their nation and government from the war "forced by the South." When he enlisted, he believed the war "would also be the end of the great National iniquity." Jones and others from the 45th, with thousands of their army comrades, were "abolitionized" and could not let the proponents of the Lost Cause deny the true causes of the war.[4]

The first soldiers' home for Union veterans opened in New Jersey just fifteen months after the war, on July 4, 1866. While it is probable that some 45th Illinois veterans became residents at the national homes in Milwaukee and Chicago, a fire in the National Archives destroyed most of the homes' records. The first Lead Mine man known to be admitted into a veterans' home was

David Cline, who entered the Illinois state home at Quincy on July 2, 1887, just four months after it opened. Cline suffered from a gunshot wound to his left breast, deafness, and a cold. At least forty-seven members of the regiment spent time at this home, with some entering through 1915 and perhaps even later. Some, like former private John Glattaar, entered and left the home several times. The most common reasons the unit's veterans noted for admittance were rheumatism and general debility or disability. John Baker, wounded at Shiloh, entered the home on April 10, 1891, with rheumatism and alcoholism, the latter an affliction he shared with many veterans. James Borland stayed for only seven months in 1896 and 1897, but others, like Andrew Blair, never left; some twenty months after he entered with a general disability, Blair died on April 22, 1894. For those admitted in 1892 and thereafter, administrators recorded whether the veteran currently received a government pension and, if so, how much. It is likely that this home, like other state homes, required the veterans to turn over their monthly pensions to help defray costs. It is unknown whether any 45th veterans chose not to enter the home rather than surrender their pensions.[5]

As with most Union veterans, the Lead Mine men and their families worked to obtain federal pensions, both during and after the war. To the veterans, the pensions were not something they should have to beg for, but rather a "sacred debt" or "debt of honor" the country owed them for their service and suffering in the war. Initially, for a member to receive a pension, he had to show that his service caused a disability. Family members, typically a soldier's wife, children, or parents, had to prove the veteran had died in or after the war and that his service in the war had caused his death. For Union soldiers, pensions were first issued in 1862 for family members whose son, husband, or father had died while in uniform. In 1866 Congress passed an act granting children of a fallen soldier who were under age sixteen $2 per month. In 1890 the Dependent Pension Act extended eligibility for pensions to veterans who had disabilities not caused by their service in the war and could not provide for their families. Of the 1,269 Lead Mine men, just over two-thirds, 850, received pensions, as did 508 wives; 55 parents, mostly mothers; and the children of 54 members. Parents had to prove that their sons had supported them financially before the war and that they could no longer support themselves. For 53 members, their or their families' applications were denied for various reasons: for example, the veteran could not prove that his service in the war had caused his disability, family members could not prove their loved one had died during or after the war from a wound suffered in uniform, or the veteran applied for a pension in more than one unit he had served in. Pensions for enlisted men started at $8 a month and increased over the years into the early twentieth century. Officers received more, up to $40 per month.[6]

For the government to approve a pension application, some men or their families had to submit many affidavits, sometimes dozens, to substantiate their claims. Sgt. Hollis M. Hurd's wife, Lovina, may have been one of the earliest of the regiment's loved ones to get a pension, receiving it less than one year after her husband's death on April 6, 1862, during the Battle of Shiloh. For some, like Wilbur Crummer, it was relatively easy to get his application approved. The Pension Bureau denied William Dougherty's application, however, because a postwar inspecting surgeon reported that the former corporal's condition had not disabled him, even though Dougherty's wound forced his transfer to the Veteran Reserve Corps. Like Dougherty, many others, despite a war wound, were denied a pension because of no visible disability.[7]

Pvt. Thomas Morehead's enlistment expired in late November 1864, but he fell sick on the way home and died in a Louisville hospital. It took many affidavits, letters, and documents to convince the Pension Bureau that Morehead had died while still in uniform so that each of the private's two daughters would receive a monthly $2 pension. Pvt. Lewis Franklin Myers's parents were unable to secure a pension. Myers went missing after the regiment's May 22, 1863, attack on the Confederate fortifications at Vicksburg. The Pension Bureau denied his parents' applications even though they never saw or heard from their son again and despite many affidavits from his comrades that Confederates had either captured or killed Myers.[8]

The men of the 45th Illinois led varied postwar lives. The first to die after the war was likely 2nd Lt. Ephraim Graham, who was killed just two weeks after the men returned to Galena. Graham, promoted twice in the war, survived wounds suffered at Shiloh and Champion Hill, only to die when a runaway wagon ran over him. Matthew M. Miller left the regiment in April 1863 for a commission in the 9th Louisiana Infantry (African Descent) and eventually commanded a regiment as a colonel. He and his wife moved to Kansas, where Miller practiced law and the couple adopted three foster children. The colonel died at age seventy-eight on November 30, 1918. Peter Bellingall, who had enlisted as a sixteen-year-old store clerk and rose to command Company D from Atlanta to Washington as its first sergeant, went to California soon after the war to be with his mother and sister, who had moved there early in the war. Here he married and had a family. With General Grant's and Congressman Washburne's help, he became the night watchman at San Francisco's customs house. In 1872 he started the P. W. Bellingall Customs Brokerage, which, remarkably, is still in business today. Nathan Corbin returned home to Kansas and eventually owned a farm of 840 acres. He and his second wife had a daughter, Nathana, who, after her father's death on January 23, 1914, typed out his wartime memoirs in poem form.[9]

Henry Winters survived a serious head wound he sustained at Fort Donelson. He returned to the unit after a six-month stay at Union hospitals, but constant headaches from the bullet's shards still in his head forced Winters to leave his bugler and sharpshooter positions to become a drummer, He was captured at Champion Hill, and once paroled, he worked in a Union hospital near Vicksburg, luckily for Wilbur Crummer. Crummer sent him letters of gratitude throughout the years, for he believed the care provided by Winters and Louis LaBrush had saved his life. Eventually, with his head wound still causing pain, Winters transferred to the Veteran Reserve Corps in May 1864. After the war, Winters returned home and operated general stores, a post office as postmaster, and a jewelry store. He married and had eleven children. Winters suffered from his wound for the rest of his life, dying on December 19, 1919, at the age of seventy-eight. Erhart Dittmar survived a serious wound to his leg, which he nearly lost, at Shiloh. He came home in 1865, bought farmland, and married. The couple had eight children, and Dittmar began receiving a government pension in 1878. Like many veterans, Dittmar could not readjust to civilian life, and he committed suicide on September 18, 1888, perhaps believing it was his only means of escaping his memories of the war's terrors or his suffering from his wound.[10]

Pvt. Henry H. Taylor mustered out of the 45th when his enlistment expired on September 8, 1864. He died on May 3, 1909, in Leavenworth, Kansas, and was survived by his wife and five children. For his bravery in planting the regiment's banners on the 3rd Louisiana Redan's ramparts on June 25, 1863, during the fight in the crater, Congress awarded Taylor the Medal of Honor in 1893; he was the only man in the regiment to receive the award. On hearing the news, a throng of people and a band came to Taylor's house and celebrated. After the war, officials had the U.S. flag Taylor had carried placed on display in the state capitol building in Springfield, Illinois, and his medal of honor now resides in Vicksburg National Military Park's museum. In an 1885 letter to his old colonel, John E Smith, Taylor wrote that he believed Providence had saved him: "I have never been able to fully understand why I was always so fortunate but always have and always expect to believe that *God* the ruler of all things *Cared for Even Me.*"[11]

Former captain John Adair, after his resignation in late 1864, went back to his hometown, where he ran the *Mount Carroll Mirror* newspaper. He married in November 1869, and three years later the couple moved to Springfield, where Adair worked in the state government. His hearing, damaged during the fight in the Fort Hill crater, never returned, and after being in poor health and diagnosed with "consumption," Adair died at age fifty-seven on February 15, 1887. The regiment's connection to Grant did not end with the general's death in 1885, as former captain Henry Boyce acted as one of Julia Grant's escorts at the dedication of Grant's tomb on April 27, 1897. Boyce died on October 14, 1903, in New York City after being struck by a cable car.[12]

After the war, Daniel Fish, who had joined the 45th in February 1864 at the age of sixteen, became a teacher, studied law, passed the bar exam, and moved to Minnesota, where he practiced law and held several judgeships. He married in 1873 and had five children. He later became active in the GAR and became its youngest adjutant general in 1887. Fish died on February 9, 1924, at seventy-six. Former lieutenant John P. Jones returned home to Boone County, Illinois, to his wife and young son after his enlistment expired on December 31, 1864. The family moved to Sheldon, Missouri, in 1865 and later settled in McAlester, Oklahoma, where Jones died on November 22, 1911. Dr. James Gaskill continued to practice medicine but died on May 7, 1894, at a boardinghouse after drinking coffee laced with "great quantities" of arsenic. The other eight boarders also drank the coffee but only got sick.[13]

Capt. Henry O. Harkness was one of the last Lead Mine men wounded in the war. A Confederate bullet hit the captain in his testicles during the fight at Fort Pocotaligo. Despite the wound, Harkness served six more months until the regiment's mustering out on July 12, 1865. The famous brigadier general Joshua Chamberlain suffered a similar wound, and both he and Harkness received government pensions. Luckily for Harkness, the wound did not impair his reproductive functioning as it did Chamberlain's. After the death of his first wife, the still-virile former captain remarried at the age of sixty-seven, and the couple had four children, the last in 1909, just two years before his death at age seventy-seven in 1911.[14]

Dr. Edward D. Kittoe mustered out of service on October 31, 1865, returned to Galena, and restarted his medical practice. Over the next decade, he became "one of the oldest and most prominent medical practitioners in Illinois." Kittoe, whom Lt. John P. Jones called "a rough austere man apparently, but with a heart as big as an ox," died of heart disease on September 30, 1877, at age seventy-three. Kittoe was mourned by Galena's people, and a tribute said he was an "honest, brave, true man, an affectionate husband and kind and indulgent father."[15]

John E. Smith, the 45th's original commander, became a major general and eventually commanded a division in the 15th Corps of the Army of the Tennessee. Grant commended Smith's leadership of his division, which contributed to victory in the Battle of Chattanooga in December 1863. As opposed to most of the other veterans of the 45th, who gladly set aside their uniforms to become citizens again, Smith joined other volunteers and stayed in uniform. After his mustering out on April 30, 1866, he received a colonelship of the 27th U.S. Infantry and served in the West during the Indian Wars, commanding two other regiments before retiring on May 19, 1881, as a brevetted major general. In retirement, Smith traveled to Galena for the celebration of Grant's seventy-fourth birthday in April 1896 but returned home to Chicago in worse health. His health deteriorated over the next several months, and he died on January 29, 1897, at the age of eighty and was buried in Galena.[16]

Brig. Gen. Jasper A. Maltby, the unit's second commander, remained in Vicksburg after the 45th and other units went on furlough in March 1864. He returned home to Galena in June and stayed there for a year, recuperating from his wounds suffered in the fight in the crater on June 25, 1863. Later, after Maltby had spent three months in command at Jackson, Mississippi, the army sent him home again to await orders; with none coming, Maltby retired on January 15, 1866. The general then returned to Vicksburg and worked in a mercantile business before his appointment as military mayor. Maltby later resigned because of continued sickness and died on December 12, 1867; he was buried back in Galena. Initially, doctors attributed Maltby's death to yellow fever, but the diagnosis was later changed to internal injuries, bleeding in his lungs from the wounds he had received in the Fort Hill crater fight over four years earlier. Maltby joined Charles Evans, who died a few years after the war from internal injuries sustained on the *Anglo Saxon* in 1863, as just two of the deaths from the Civil War not normally included in its death toll.[17]

The army honorably discharged the 45th's third commander, Lt. Col. Robert P. Sealy, on January 10, 1865. He returned home to Rockford, Illinois, and in 1868 moved to Council Bluffs, Iowa, where he lived until his death in 1888 at the age of fifty-three. The unit's final commander, Brig. Gen. John Duer, started the war as a second lieutenant and was just twenty-eight years old in 1865 when he returned to Galena. He then moved to Monticello, Iowa, fifty miles southwest of Galena. He married a year later, and the couple had five children. As a leading businessman in Monticello, Duer ran two mercantile businesses and became a city councilman. Later, as Monticello's treasurer and school director, he was elected the town's mayor. While still serving as mayor, treasurer and school director, the former general, though in apparent good health, fell ill and died of a hemorrhaging lung, possibly pneumonia, on December 11, 1880, at age forty-three. Over 100 people attended his funeral, with all businesses closed for the service.[18]

While the 45th's veterans undoubtedly held reunions in the years since 1869, the next recorded reunion occurred on August 29, 1900, when seventy-nine members met in Chicago. The next year, the regiment met in Cleveland at the national encampment of the Grand Army of the Republic on September 12–13, 1901, joining over 269,000 of their former brothers in blue. Four years later, on May 24, 1905, the unit's veterans met in the Memorial Hall in Rockford, Illinois, for the fortieth anniversary of the regiment's march in the Washington Grand Review. Judge Daniel Fish spoke to the sixty members in attendance of his gratefulness—that so many had survived the past forty years, for the soldiers' government postwar pensions, and for the work of many to recover the fallen soldiers' bodies and place them in the national cemeteries. Fish did not boast of the 45th, calling it an average, typical regiment whose history equaled "that of a hundred others, a simple tale of duty faithfully performed, of patient endurance, of unflinching courage." The judge also used information from the *Official Records* and other sources to defend the 45th's service record—that it had been the first to attack once the mine exploded under the 3rd Louisiana Redan on June 25, 1863, and that it had led Grant's troops into the captured city of Vicksburg on July 4. Fish did so to counter veterans who wrote in the *National Tribune* to challenge the unit's record. In noting that the regiment was "fairly entitled" to the honors received at Vicksburg, he added that there was "glory enough for all" who served.[19]

Many veterans published histories of their service to ensure that their sacrifices and achievements in uniform were not forgotten. In 1915 former first sergeant Wilbur Crummer published a book on his two years of service in the 45th. Crummer wrote of his and the unit's experiences and sacrifices to inform the current generation on the war, defend the regiment's triumphs and honors against those wanted to take them away, demonstrate reconciliation with his former enemies, and defend Ulysses S. Grant's record. Crummer believed that his work, an enlisted man's perspective on the battles in which his unit fought, countered the histories that told of the battles only from the generals' point of view. He told of a postwar conversation with his old colonel, John E. Smith, who sarcastically said that the histories of Shiloh caused him to wonder if he had been in the battle at all. Regarding the attack on the 3rd Louisiana Redan on June 25, 1863, Crummer used official reports and other sources from the *Official Records* to show that the 45th was the first to enter the crater and had led Grant's army into Vicksburg. The former sergeant was proud that the 45th had helped "perpetuate but one flag, the Stars and Stripes."[20]

Given his age when he wrote his book (he was seventy-two when it was published), it is not surprising that Crummer wrote on his reconciliation with his former foes. The former first sergeant joined other elderly veterans from both armies, who met in reunions on battlefields across the country in the early twentieth century. Crummer wrote of his trip in 1909 to an annual reunion held at Shiloh on the anniversary of the battle by the National Association of Battle of Shiloh Survivors. Crummer included his and two ex-Confederates' pro-reconciliation speeches, as well as a statement from a Confederate veteran who believed that the years since the war had proved the Union men correct in fighting to restore their republic. He also wrote of the fine dinner given to the Union veterans by their Confederate counterparts at the Shiloh church.[21]

Crummer used several pages to defend the reputation of his former general and president, Ulysses S. Grant. After the war, Crummer worked as a clerk for his former lieutenant and Grant's staffer, Brig. Gen. William Rowley, who was now the judge of Jo Daviess County court. Rowley routinely called the Lost Cause men's contentions that Grant was a drunk "all a d——d lie." Crummer's connection to Grant continued when, during the Republican presidential convention in 1880, he, Rowley, and President Grant spent several nights reminiscing about the war and discussing the events of the convention and whether the Republicans would nominate Grant for a third term. Five years later in Galena, Crummer spoke at the memorial held for Grant after the general's death. He recounted Grant's victories and urged, "We cannot forget" the war or the actions of the Union soldiers. Reminding his listeners how the general and the Union soldiers had "stood in trying places against evil treason," he told them that their tears were the best and loudest way that Grant could be "honored and extolled as one of the greatest of all the nations."[22]

After Crummer was discharged in 1863 because of his lung wound at Vicksburg, it took him five years, with the help of his parents, to fully heal. He married and had a daughter. In the late 1880s, after his clerkship in Galena, he moved his family to Oak Park in Cook County, Illinois, where he worked for the Chicago Title and Trust Company, a position he held until his death. Crummer became the chairman of the 45th's Grand Army of the Republic veterans' organization, and no member did more than he to memorialize the unit at Vicksburg National Military Park. Crummer wrote often to the park's commissioner, Capt. W. T. Rigby, and in August 1902 he visited the park, where he helped place markers on the locations of the 45th's camp, the trenches where they had served as sharpshooters, the spot where Major Cowan died, the route of Logan's approach, and the 3rd Louisiana Redan. Crummer also visited the Shirley House, where his emotions nearly overwhelmed him when he stood in the exact spot where a Confederate bullet had gone through his right lung thirty-nine years earlier. In his final years, he authored lectures on the war. Crummer died on February 17, 1920, at the age of seventy-seven, after two strokes over the previous four days.[23]

In addition to joining with Crummer to work with Rigby to memorialize the 45th at Vicksburg, several of the unit's veterans joined their fellow Union veterans in having their letters published in the *National Tribune*, from 1883 to at least 1915. The most common topics were the Union attack on the 3rd Louisiana Redan on May 22, 1863, and the fighting in the crater on June 25–26, 1863. The 45th's veterans wrote to ensure that their role in the May attack was accurately reported, but they most vehemently defended the regiment's record as the first to attack after the mine had exploded under the redan on June 25, 1863. Here they argued with a veteran of the 23rd Indiana, who contended his unit had been the first to enter the crater, and with another from the 4th Minnesota, who claimed his unit had been the first to enter Vicksburg on July 4, 1863. Notably, Wilbur Crummer relied on the same sources that he later used in his book—official reports and other memoranda from the *Official Records*—to convincingly prove that the 45th Illinois had been the first regiment to enter the crater on June 25, 1863, and the first to enter Vicksburg on July 4.[24]

In 1917 sixteen surviving members met at the Shirley House in Vicksburg National Military Park for a reunion as part of the Peace Jubilee celebrating the fiftieth anniversary of the city's surrender to Union forces. The 45th's veterans also came for the dedication of a bronze portrait tablet in honor of Lt. Col. Melancthon Smith, who had died from a mortal wound suffered fifty-four years earlier during the attack in the Fort Hill crater. Like veterans across the country who raised memorials so that Americans would not forget the veterans' sacrifices, Wilbur Crummer had organized the reunion and led the effort to raise the money for the tablet, for which he received heartfelt gratitude from Smith's widow. The now elderly veterans noted during the reunion their hope to get tablets put up for Majors Cowan and Fisk in the future. Besides the tablet for Smith and the park's markers located by Crummer, other memorials include the unit's plaque in the Illinois Memorial near the Shirley House, a monument for the 45th that stands in front of the house, and another that marks the trenches the unit held during the siege. Finally, the name of Lead Mine man Joel G. Childs is on the Niagara, New York, memorial to its fallen soldiers. Childs, a private in the regiment, died on May 9, 1862, from his wound sustained at Shiloh.[25]

The toll on the 45th from its service in the war was not extreme for a Civil War regiment (see Appendix A), although 6.7 percent of its members died from combat, 2 percent more than for the Union army as a whole. Despite their hardships while in uniform, as they suffered from the heat, cold, hunger, and other afflictions, most of the unit's members served honorably during the war. As with all units in the war, however, some men shirked, refused to fight, got drunk, fought with other soldiers, spent time in jail for various transgressions, gambled, or deserted. Notably, just 34 Lead Mine men deserted during the war. This equaled just 2.7 percent of the 1,269 men who served in the 45th, far lower than the 8.6 to 14.3 percent that historians have found deserted from the Union army.[26]

Patriotism, the desire to defend their republic and protect their liberties, was the prime reason for the Lead Mine men's honored service and why they never broke and ran during combat, valiantly answering every call. The members' six months of training, which many other regiments failed to receive, stood them well when they entered battle for the first time. Their generally high character, with their faith in Providence and consistent, capable, and committed officers, also contributed to the unit's exceptional war record despite a disastrous casualty rate. The Lead Mine men's esprit de corps and their unblemished battle record likely led to their volunteering for the dangerous attack on June 25, 1863. Elsewhere—at Corinth, Port Gibson, Chunky Station, and Pocotaligo—general officers selected the 45th to lead attacks, a clear indication of the regiment's excellence. The men's patriotism and pragmatic nature led the majority to support President Lincoln's emancipation of their enemy's enslaved people and his creation of the Black regiments, knowing that these measures hurt the Confederacy and helped shorten the war. Likewise, the men supported the Union leadership's hard war on the Confederacy and its citizenry, even though it caused them much hunger and increased the probability of death in a prison camp. The Copperhead antiwar campaign was responsible for many desertions in other units, but for the 45th, it stiffened resolve and led to few desertions. The farming background of many of its members and the generally younger age of the unit's enlisted men likely gave the unit the stamina to endure the war's tough campaigns. These hardy midwesterners were dependable and self-assured, just some of General Sherman's veterans on his final two campaigns. Perhaps two former commanders best summed up the 45th's excellence: Gen. John E. Smith noted, "The 45th can be relied on" and went "wherever I ordered," and Gen. John A Logan said of the men, "I am satisfied, [they] never refused anything that I asked them."[27]

William A. Balfour died on April 4, 1935, just hours before his ninetieth birthday and seventy years after his father had died of the wound received at Shiloh. Balfour suffered two strokes in 1930 before moving to his son's house to live out the rest of his days. John Mingle, a private in the regiment who sustained a wound to his breast at Shiloh, married in 1880 and had seven children. Amazingly, he survived until August 30, 1935, when he died at ninety-one in Chariton, Iowa, his home for sixty-three years. Balfour and Mingle likely were the last Lead Mine men to pass away. The dutiful, honor-bound, and exceptional men of the 45th Illinois infantry, the Washburne Lead Mine Regiment, with their comrades in Union blue, had saved their republic and extinguished slavery. The impacts of these patriotic citizen-soldiers' efforts and sacrifices are still felt to this day.[28]

Appendixes
Notes
Bibliography
Index

Appendix A

The War's Toll and Soldiers' Misbehavior

The war took a toll on the 45th, like all Civil War units, and the regiment's rolls were reduced for many reasons: men were killed in action; died or were discharged because of wounds, disease, or sickness; were transferred to other units; or deserted (see Table A.1). Overall, 213 Lead Mine men died during the war; this was 16.8 percent of the unit, 1.4 percent higher than the rate in the Union army as a whole. Not unsurprisingly, as with both armies in the war, disease or sickness caused the most deaths in the 45th, 115 men, or 9 percent of the unit—slightly higher than the Union army's 8.6 percent. Of these, typhoid fever took the most members' lives, with other top killers including diarrhea and scarlet, yellow, or other fevers. The unit's 6.7 percent killed in battle or suffering mortal wounds was 2 percent more than for the Union army. Accidents caused another 6 men to die, and 4 men died in Confederate prisoner-of-war camps.[1]

During the Civil War, the army discharged soldiers for a variety of reasons, the great majority for disability. The 45th Illinois lost 274 men, 21.6 percent, to discharges. Disease or sickness caused the most discharges, 101, with diarrhea the most common reason, followed by rheumatism, tuberculosis, typhoid fever, syphilis, diphtheria, and measles. Battlefield wounds were responsible for another 68 men leaving the unit, typically because their wounds resulted in a limb's amputation. General disability caused another 67 men to leave the unit, while unspecified reasons removed 25 additional men. Accidents, unsoundness, or exposure to the elements removed another 8 from the unit's rolls. Finally, 3 members were dishonorably discharged and 2 others received honorable discharges.[2]

Another 134 soldiers left the unit before the end of war because their enlistments expired. All but one left the 45th between late September 1864 and late January 1865. These men had enlisted in 1861 and early 1862 but had not reenlisted in early 1864. Transfer to another unit cost the regiment 79 men, or 6.2 percent of its strength during the war. The largest number, 33 soldiers, transferred to the Veteran Reserve Corps, formerly known as the Invalid

Table A.1. Losses suffered by the 45th Illinois

Reason		Number
Discharged		274
	Disease/sickness	101
	Wounds	68
	Disability	67
	No reason provided	25
	Accident/unsoundness/exposure	8
	Dishonorably	3
	Honorably	2
Died		213
	Disease/sickness	115
	Killed in action	42
	Wounds	43
	Accident	6
	Prisoner of war	4
	No cause provided	3
Expiration of service		134
Moved to other regiment		79
	Veteran Reserve Corps	33
	Discharged/transferred/mustered out	27
	U.S. Colored Troops	11
	Promoted	4
	U.S. Navy	2
	Resigned and transferred to other unit	1
	Returned to original unit	1
Deserted		34
Resigned commission		23
Dropped from rolls		8
Missing in action		3
Military prison		3
Absent/sick		2
Detached service		1
Drummed out for stealing		1
Prisoner of war		1
N/A		14
Total		790

Sources: Regimental Service, Medical Records, and Regimental Pension Records, National Archives; Office of the Illinois Secretary of State, Muster and Descriptive Rolls.

Corps. The War Department created the corps for men who still wanted to serve but whose wounds or illness prevented their service in the field. These soldiers had varied roles; notably, some helped defend Washington, D.C., from Confederate marauders, while others served as the honor guard at President Lincoln's funeral in Springfield, Illinois. Importantly, these men enabled more able-bodied soldiers to serve in the field. Wounded at both Shiloh and Vicksburg, Pvt. Freeman Shores choose to serve in the corps. No records exist of whether Shores or the other 32 men liked the work in the corps, resented their lessened status, reacted to taunts and disrespect from soldiers in regular army units, took pride in bolstering the army's strength, or saw the corps as a means of recovering their self-esteem after leaving the 45th. It is likely some joined the corps to keep earning their army pay.[3]

Another 27 members transferred to other units or service. The lure of a higher rank and more money caused 11 men to transfer to Black regiments. Of these, Capt. William T. Frohock, promoted twice already and wounded severely in the crater fight on June 25, 1863, received a promotion to colonel and command of the 4th Mississippi Infantry (African Descent). Pvt. Matthew M. Miller accepted a captaincy in the 9th Louisiana Infantry (African Descent), which fought in the violent Battle of Milliken's Bend on June 7, 1863.

Members recuperating from disease, sickness, or wounds reduced the strength of the 45th throughout the war. In total, the unit's members spent 53,678 days, or 147 man-years, away from the regiment in hospitals. Recovery from battlefield wounds was responsible for 23 percent of this time, or 12,580 days missed. The standard army fare of salted pork, coffee, and hardtack, along with bad drinking water, caused men to miss nearly 9,000 days because of diarrhea. Some members spent many more days in the hospitals. Pvt. Alexander Boyd mustered into service on December 31, 1863. He first got sick in mid-March 1864 with diarrhea and then spent another 155 days recovering from various maladies. Pvt. Charles H. Haveland served through the entire history of the 45th Illinois but missed 366 days because of "debilitas" (general lameness or weakness), diarrhea, pneumonia, and other ailments. All told, 962 members out of 1,269 men, or 75.8 percent, spent at least one day in a hospital.[4]

Disease, sickness, and the rigors of service in uniform affected the younger and older members differently during the war. Of the 33 soldiers under eighteen years of age, 21.2 percent either died or were discharged. The 92 soldiers age forty and older fared worse—55.5 percent, or 51 men, died, were discharged, or transferred to the Veteran Reserve Corps.[5]

While the 45th Illinois ended the war with an exemplary record, not all in the regiment acted patriotically. By the war's end, a total of 34 members had either deserted or were absent without leave—a significantly lower number than the average for all other regiments in the army. Another soldier was drummed out for stealing, and 3 others ended the war in a Union military prison. Of these, Pvt. John Haley received the harshest punishment: one year of hard labor and one year of lost wages for unstated offenses. Pvt. Henry J. Beales's service was perhaps unique. Beales first deserted on March 16, 1862, at Savannah, Tennessee, but returned over two years later on May 6, 1864, only to spend time in a hospital sick, before his arrest again in July. The army confined Beales in a military jail until returning him to the unit. Beales deserted for a final time on December 27, 1864, in Savannah. The 34 members who deserted equaled just 2.7 percent of the regiment, a much lower percentage than the Union army suffered—the number of deserters equaled 8.6 to 14.3 percent of the army. The reasons for the 45th's much lower percentage of deserters were likely the Lead Mine men's patriotism, the character of most in the unit, and the esprit de corps that developed from the regiment's unblemished battle record.[6]

The Lead Mine men were not saints in uniform, however. Some 20 members contracted gonorrhea and syphilis during their service, which meant they, like others in the army, had sex with prostitutes. The men also gambled, sometimes with their officers, which led Colonel Maltby to issue orders forbidding gambling, as did officers in other units; yet the men continued to gamble, typically when they received their wages. The men cussed, drank alcohol, and stole. Stealing from the unit's sutler cost Pvt. Samuel Boyd $5 and his extra pay for being a teamster, and his diet was reduced to bread and water for five days. Another member, Pvt. George Matterson, had to serve thirty days of hard labor, working ten hours a day, for stealing government books. Yet Boyd and Matterson served until the end of their enlistments. The army dishonorably discharged Pvt. Thomas Murphy for stealing and two other members for unstated reasons. Although Pvt. James Sullivan was punished for fighting, there is no evidence of "roughs" in the unit, as historian Lorien Foote found in many Union regiments. The low number of disciplinary actions taken by officers suggests that the 45th Illinois was similar to some of Foote's units, whose members kept their honor throughout the war and upheld the ideals of manhood in the Union.[7]

Finally, drinking alcohol likely caused the most misbehavior. This includes those in Chicago who sneaked out of camp to drink and those who stole the whiskey in Kentucky. On several occasions the army supplied the alcohol, such as to help the men finish the macabre work of burying the dead at Shiloh. Luther Cowan loathed those who got drunk but also understood why they did so—the men drank and gambled "to keep from thinking too much about the things which corrode on their minds," to forget the horrors of war.[8]

Appendix B

Regimental Demographic Statistics

Table B.1. Age statistics of the 45th Illinois compared with the Union army

	45th Illinois		Union army	
	Officers	*Enlisted*	*Officers*	*Enlisted*
Mean	31.6	24.9	29.9	25.8

Sources: Office of the Illinois Secretary of State, Muster and Descriptive Rolls; Gould, *Investigations*, 35, 58.

Table B.2. Age statistics of enlisted Union soldiers

Age	*45th Illinois (%)*	*Illinois (%)*	*Union army (%)*
13–19	29.2	20.1	23.1
20–29	48.2	58.1	53.1
30–39	14.6	16.1	16.8
40–49	6.3	5.5	6.8
50 & older	0.7	0.2	0.2
N/A	1.1	0	0

Sources: Office of the Illinois Secretary of State, Muster and Descriptive Rolls; Gould, *Investigations*, 38, 50.

Table B.3. Occupations of 45th Illinois soldiers, Illinois men, and Union soldiers

Occupation	45th Illinois	Illinois men	Union army from Illinois	Union army	Union army (Wiley in McPherson)	All Union males (1860 census)
Agriculture	65.7	50.9	66.9	48.7	47.8	42.9
Skilled labor	12.4	19.5	16.3	25.2	25.2	24.9
Unskilled labor	10.2	17.5	5.3	16.3	15.1	16.7
White collar and commercial	5.8	8.1	3.4	3.5	7.8	10.0
Professional	3.2	3.6	3.0	2.2	2.9	3.5
Miscellaneous/ unknown	2.6	0.5	5.0	4.1	1.2	2.0

Sources: Office of the Illinois Secretary of State, Muster and Descriptive Rolls; Kennedy, *Population*, 104–5; Gould, *Investigations*, 201, 212; McPherson, *Battle Cry*, 607–8.

Table B.4. Occupations of 45th Illinois soldiers, other Union soldiers, and Confederates

Occupation	45th Illinois	20th Maine	Walker's division	Stonewall brigade	Confederate army	White males in 7 CSA states
Agriculture	65.7	32.0	78.1	31.1	61.5	57.5
Skilled labor	12.4	29.0	5.8	28.7	14.1	15.7
Unskilled labor	10.2	24.0	7.9	19.4	8.5	12.7
White collar and commercial	5.8	2.0	3.9	10.5	7.0	8.3
Professional	3.2	2.0	2.8	4.9	5.2	5.0
Miscellaneous/ unknown	2.6	11.0	1.5	5.4	3.7	0.8

Sources: Office of the Illinois Secretary of State, Muster and Descriptive Rolls; McPherson, *Ordeal*, 387; Lowe, *Walker's Texas Division*, 22; Pullen, *Twentieth Maine*, 13; Simpson, *Hood's Texas Brigade*, 15–16.

Table B.5. Nativity of the 45th Illinois

Place of birth	#	%	Nativity details
Illinois	212	16.7	
U.S. East	474	37.4	Connecticut, Maine, Maryland, Massachusetts, New Hampshire, New Jersey, New York, Pennsylvania, Rhode Island, Vermont
U.S. Midwest	183	14.4	Indiana, Iowa, Michigan, Missouri, Ohio, Wisconsin
U.S. South	35	2.8	Kentucky, Louisiana, Mississippi, North Carolina, Tennessee, Virginia
Ireland	105	8.3	
Germany	88	6.9	Germany, Bavaria, Hanover, Hesse-Darmstadt, Prussia, Wurtemburg
Great Britain	79	6.2	England, Scotland, Wales
Canada	32	2.5	
Other European countries	29	2.3	Austria, Belgium, Europe, France, Holland, Norway, Sweden, Switzerland
N/A	32	2.5	
Total	1,269		

Source: Office of the Illinois Secretary of State, Muster and Descriptive Rolls.

Table B.6. Prewar county residencies of the 45th Illinois

County	#	%
Jo Daviess	393	31.0
Winnebago	149	11.7
Carroll	117	9.2
Rock Island	88	6.9
Knox	82	6.5
Mercer	61	4.8
Lake	50	3.9
Stephenson	40	3.2
Boone	38	3.0
Henry	23	1.8
Cook	17	1.3
Other Illinois county	85	6.7
Other outside of Illinois	60	4.7
N/A	66	5.2
Total #	1,269	
Total % from top 11 counties		83.3

Sources: Office of the Illinois Secretary of State, Muster and Descriptive Rolls.

Table B.7. Familial and marital statistics of the 45th Illinois

	#	%	% fathers
Married	271	21.4	66.4
Single	867	68.3	1.0
N/A	131	10.3	—
	1,269		14.9

Sources: Office of the Illinois Secretary of State, Muster and Descriptive Rolls; U.S. Census Bureau, 1860 Census.

Notes

Introduction

1. Adair, *Historical*, 11. *Note*: All quoted material appears as it did in the original, including any errors in spelling, grammar, or punctuation.
2. Winschel, *Triumph*, 143.
3. Grimsley, *Hard*, 4.
4. Phillips, "Battling," 1408–10, 1416–20; Carmichael, *War*, 7–10.
5. Bledsoe, *Citizen-Officers*, 87, 101–2, 112–13, 133–34, 160, 220.
6. Gordon, *Broken Regiment*, 1, 34; Hess, *Civil War*, 63.
7. For a discussion of the progress of military history over the last forty years, see Biddle and Citino, "Role"; Dyer, *Compendium*, vol. 3; Vinovskis. "Have Social Historians," 1; Dunkelman, *Brothers*; Gordon, *Broken Regiment*; Egerton, *Thunder*; Mezurek, *For Their Own Cause*; Ural, *Hood's Texas Brigade*; Mellott and Snell, *Seventh West Virginia Infantry*; Rein, *Second Colorado Cavalry*; Glatthaar, *March*, i–ii, xiii–xiv; Smith, *Union Assaults*, 180.

1. From Citizen to Soldier

1. Chetlain, *Recollections*, 69–73; Simon, *From Galena*, 165; Simpson, *Ulysses S. Grant*, 75–79.
2. Federal Writers' Project, *Galena*, 9, 13, 17–18, 20, 22, 25, 35, 46; Owens, *Galena*, ii–iii, 2, 6–7, 17, 19, 23–32; McPherson, *Battle Cry*, 31.
3. *Galena Daily Advertiser*, April 30, May 2, 9, 11, 16, 29, 1861; Duerkes, *I for One Am Ready*, 316.
4. *Wichita Daily Eagle*, January 30, 1897; Chernow, *Grant*, 115, 129–130, 363; Hobbs; *Glamorous*, 51; Adair, *Historical*, 2.
5. Bellingall, "Autobiography," 8; Shaw, "Johnny Has Gone," 423; Billings, *Hardtack*, 28, 198.
6. McPherson, *Battle Cry*, 45–50; Catton, *Coming Fury*, 469–73; Woodworth, *Nothing*, 8; Washburne to Smith, July 23, 1861, GPL; Adair, *Historical*, 2; *Galena Daily Advertiser*, July 24, 25, 1861.
7. *Galena Daily Advertiser*, July 26, 29, 31, August 9, 1861; Barnet, *Martyrs*, 47; *Chicago Daily Tribune*, April 2, 1861; Adair, *Historical*, 2.

8. Adair, *Historical*, 2; *Warren Independent*, August 13, 1861; *Galena Daily Advertiser*, August 10, 14–15, 26–27, 29, 1861; *Rockford Republican*, August 8, 29, 31, 1861; Cowan Diary, August 30, 1861, *GPL*.

9. *Warren Independent*, August 20, 27, September 3, 10, 1861; Bledsoe, *Citizen-Officers*, 13, 30, 39–40, 61; Billings, *Hardtack*, 30; Office of the Illinois Secretary of State, Muster and Descriptive Rolls; Regimental Medical Records, *NA*.

10. Washburne to Smith, September 2, 1861, *GPL*; Owens, *Galena*, 40; Morris, Hartwell, and Kuykendall, *History 31st*, 19; *Galena Daily Advertiser*, August 31, 1861; Reese, *Report of the Adjutant General*, 360; *Warren Independent*, November 19, 1861; Woodworth, *Nothing*, 19.

11. Office of the Illinois Secretary of State, Muster and Descriptive Rolls; Adair, *Historical*, 2; *Warren Independent*, September 10, November 26, 1861; Cowan Papers, *GPL*; Robertson, *Soldiers*, 122–34; Woodworth, *Victory*, 27–28; Billings, *Hardtack*, 213; Simpson, *Ulysses S. Grant*, 83; *Carroll County Weekly Mirror*, September 9, 1861; *Galena Daily Advertiser*, August 20, September 4, 5, 9, 10, 1861; Foote, *Gentlemen*, 10; Hess, *Civil War*, xiii, 34–38, 60, 226.

12. *Rockford Register*, September 6, 1861; *Rockford Republican*, September 12, 1861; Manning, *What This Cruel War*, 4–5, 11; Barnet, *Martyrs*, 47; *Waukegan Weekly Gazette*, September 14, 1868.

13. *Galena Daily Advertiser*, September 17, 19–21, 23, 1861; *Galena Weekly Northwestern Gazette*, September 17, 24, 1861; Chernow, *Grant*, 148; Grant, *Civil War* Memoirs, 40; Simon, *From Galena*, 173; Simpson, *Ulysses S. Grant*, 89; Office of the Illinois Secretary of State, Muster and Descriptive Rolls; Regimental Medical Records, *NA*; Compiled Military Service Records, *NA*.

14. *Galena Daily Advertiser*, September 24, 25, 28, 1861; Woodworth, *Nothing*, 12.

15. *Galena Daily Advertiser*, October 8, 1861; *Carroll County Weekly Mirror*, October 8, 1861; Chernow, *Grant*, 150; *Freeport Bulletin*, October 10, 12, 14, 17, 1861; Robertson, *Soldiers*, 155; Office of the Illinois Secretary of State, Muster and Descriptive Rolls; *Warren Independent*, Cowan Diary, November 19, 1861, *GPL*.

16. *Galena Daily Advertiser*, October 19, 1861; Washburne to Maltby, October 20, 26, 29, 1861, Smith Papers, *GPL*; *Warren Independent*, October 29, 1861; *Waukegan Weekly Gazette*, November 2, 1861.

17. *Galena Daily Advertiser*, November 1, 2, 5, 11–13, 18, 1861; Office of the Illinois Secretary of State, Muster and Descriptive Rolls; Eddy, *Patriotism*,

223; *Warren Independent*, November 12–13, 1861; *Chicago Daily Tribune*, November 15–16, 21, 1861.

18. *Galena Daily Advertiser*, November 15–16, 1861; Adair, *Historical*, 2–3; *Galena Weekly Northwestern Gazette*, November 12, 1861; Wiley, *Life of Billy Yank*, 28–29; Woodworth, *Nothing*, 13–14.

19. *Galena Daily Advertiser*, November 19, 20, 23, December 9, 1861; *Chicago Daily Tribune*, November 21, 1861; *Warren Independent*, November 19, 1861.

20. *Galena Daily Advertiser*, November 21–23, 1861; Washburne to Smith, November 20, 1861, *GPL*; Owens, *Galena*, 40.

21. Adair, *Historical*, 3; *Galena Daily Advertiser*, November 23, 24, 1861; *Warren Independent*, November 26, 1861; Reese, *Report of the Adjutant General*, 360; *Chicago Daily Tribune*, February 28, 1862; Lowe, *Walker's Texas Division*, 29; McPherson, *Battle Cry*, 332; Wiley, *Life of Billy Yank*, 30–31; Woodworth, *Nothing*, 14–15.

22. *Galena Daily Advertiser*, November 25, December 6, 1861; *Chicago Journal*, November 26, 1861; *Warren Independent*, November 26, 1861; Eisendrath, "Chicago's Camp Douglas," 38, 41–42.

23. *Warren Independent*, November 26, 1861; Adair, *Historical*, 3; Office of the Illinois Secretary of State, Muster and Descriptive Rolls; Logue, *To Appomattox*, 34; Wiley, *Life of Billy Yank*, 114; Linderman, *Embattled*, 115, McPherson, *Battle Cry*, 487; Mitchell, *Civil War*, 60; Lowe, *Walker's Texas Division*, 27–28, 36–38.

24. Bellingall, "Autobiography", 8; Tebbetts to parents, December 5, 1861, *ALPL*; Eisendrath, "Chicago's Camp Douglas," 41; McPherson, *Ordeal*, 417.

25. Kittoe to Smith, December 7, 1861, and Smith to wife, January 4, 1862, *GPL*; *Warren Independent*, November 26, 1861; Regimental Medical Records, *NA*.

26. *Waukegan Weekly Gazette*, January 4, 1862; *Galena Daily Advertiser*, December 3, 5–6, 1861; Office of the Illinois Secretary of State, Muster and Descriptive Rolls; Adair, *Historical*, 2; *Chicago Daily Tribune*, November 25, 28, December 19, 1861.

27. *Galena Daily Advertiser*, December 6, 1861; *Chicago Daily Tribune*, November 27, 1861.

28. *Galena Daily Advertiser*, December 6, 1861; Bridgford to wife, December 1, 1861, *SNMP*; *Chicago Daily Tribune*, February 28, 1862.

29. *Galena Daily Advertiser*, December 7, 1861; *Waukegan Weekly Gazette*, December 7, 1861; *Chicago Daily Tribune*, November 25, 1861; Woodworth, *Nothing*, 8.

30. *Galena Daily Advertiser*, December 7, 23, 1861; *Chicago Daily Tribune*, December 6, 24–25, 1861, January 14, 16, 1862.

31. Cowan to wife, December 9, 1861, *GPL*; Boatner, *Civil War Dictionary*, 624; Pelka, *Civil War Letters*, 45–47.

32. *Galena Daily Advertiser*, December 16, 23, 1861.

33. *Galena Daily Advertiser*, December 23, 30, 1861; *Chicago Daily Tribune*, December 30, February 28, 1862; Regimental Order Book 3, *NA*. The Mechanic Fusileers were likely the original incarnation of 56th Illinois Infantry. The Fusileers were fully mustered out and discharged by February 5, 1862, refusing to be mustered in because their pay for building Camp Douglas was less than they had been promised. See Jennifer, "Topics in Research: The Veteran Who Never Served," Rainy Day Genealogy Readings (blog), May 23, 2010, https://rainydayreadings.blogspot.com/2010/05/topics-in-research-veteran-who-never.html, which cites several primary sources. This is consistent with the newspapers cited here about why the Fusileers had rioted. State of Illinois, *Illinois Military Units in the Civil War*, 26, notes that the second incarnation of the 56th Illinois was mustered in on February 27, 1862. This same source, 47, also mentions a group of soldiers with the popular name "Indiana Company, Mechanics' Fusillers," whose official name was 56th Regiment Infantry—old (Company C). In Reese, *Report of the Adjutant General*, 181, the 56th was mustered in Shantytown, at the southern tip of Illinois. Finally, Reese and the State of Illinois nearly match regarding the Illinois counties that this second incarnation of the 56th hailed from. Thus both the Mechanic Fusileers and the southern Illinois men were in the 56th Illinois but were different incarnations of the regiment.

34. U.S. War Department, *War of the Rebellion: Official Records* (hereafter cited as *OR*), ser. 1, vol. 7, 507.

35. Reese, *Report of the Adjutant General*, 360; Office of the Illinois Secretary of State, Muster and Descriptive Rolls; Compiled Military Service Records, *NA*; Regimental Medical Records, *NA*; Billings, *Hardtack*, 44; Grant to D. C. Fuller, December 26, 1861, *WSS*; Smith to wife, December 27, 1861, *GPL*; *Warren Independent*, December 31, 1861.

36. Rable, *God's*, 1, 2, 5, 8; *Warren Independent*, November 26, 1861, January 21, 1862; *Freeport Bulletin*, Thursday, January 16, 1862; Tebbetts to parents, December 5, 1861, *ALPL*; *Galena Daily Advertiser*, January 23, 1862.

37. Duerkes, *I for One Am Ready*, 313–14, 317–18, 321, 323; Bellingall, "Autobiography," 8; Tebbetts to parents, October 4, December 5, 1861, *ALPL*; Gallagher, *Union*, 62–63, 65–69; Cowan to wife, January 21, 1861, March 8, 1862, *GPL*; Cowan Diary, February 6, 1862, *GPL*; Bledsoe, *Citizen-Officers*,

3, 5–6, 23; Carmichael, *War,* 7–9; Crummer, *With Grant,* 17, 19; Manning, *What This Cruel War,* 70–71; Phillips, "Battling," 1411.

38. Jones, "Father's Personal History," 56–57, *FHS*; Carmichael, *War,* 257; Gallagher, *Union,* 62, 68, 80, 108–9; Fry, *Republic,* 1.

39. Wiley, *Life of Billy Yank,* 37–40; Mitchell, *Civil War,* 1–3, 12–15, 17–18; Jimerson, *Private,* 1, 11, 27, 29–31, 35–36, 41; Logue, *To Appomattox,* 9, 13–17; Robertson, *Soldiers,* 3, 6–8, 10; Linderman, *Embattled,* 8–11; Hess, *Liberty,* viii, ix, 1, 3–5, 12, 20, 28, 30; McPherson, *For Cause,* 5–6, 8, 17, 19, 25–28; McPherson, *Ordeal,* 184–87; McPherson, *Battle Cry,* 309; Manning, *What This Cruel War,* 6, 26, 39–43, 70–71; Duerkes, *I for One Am Ready,* 314; Gallagher, *Union,* 7, 34, 56; Fry, *Republic,* 3, 17.

40. Foote, *Gentlemen,* 1; Hess, *Civil War,* xiv, xx, 69.

2. The Men of the 45th

1. Demographic information in this chapter for the regiment came from Office of the Illinois Secretary of State, Muster and Descriptive Rolls; U.S. Census Bureau, 1860 Census.

2. Office of the Illinois Secretary of State, Muster and Descriptive Rolls.

3. Gould, *Investigations,* 2:50, 171.

4. Gould, *Investigations,* 2:58.

5. Wiley, *Life of Billy Yank,* 299–302; Shaw, "Johnny Has Gone," 423–24; U.S. Census Bureau, 1860 Census; Office of the Illinois Secretary of State, Muster and Descriptive Rolls; Regimental Medical Records, *NA*; Compiled Military Service Records, *NA*; Gould, *Investigations,* 2:94–95.

6. McPherson, *Battle Cry,* 602–11; Marvel, *Lincoln's Mercenaries,* xi–xii, 6.

7. Marvel, *Lincoln's Mercenaries,* 3, 5–6, 24–25; Office of the Illinois Secretary of State, Muster and Descriptive Rolls; U.S. Census Bureau, 1860 Census; Cowan to wife, July 10, 1862, and to a friend, February 25, 1863, *GPL*.

8. Office of the Illinois Secretary of State, Muster and Descriptive Rolls; Kennedy, *Population,* 104–5; Gould, *Investigations,* 201, 212; McPherson, *Battle Cry,* 607–8; McPherson, *Ordeal,* 387; Lowe, *Walker's Texas Division,* 22; Pullen, *Twentieth Maine,* 13; Simpson, *Hood's Texas Brigade,* 15–16.

9. Office of the Illinois Secretary of State, Muster and Descriptive Rolls; Kennedy, *Population,* xxvii, 103; Lonn, *Foreigners,* 106, 668; Gould, *Investigations,* 2:27; Wiley, *Life of Billy Yank,* 307–9.

10. Office of the Illinois Secretary of State, Muster and Descriptive Rolls; U.S. Census Bureau, 1860 Census.

11. Office of the Illinois Secretary of State, Muster and Descriptive Rolls; U.S. Census Bureau, 1860 Census.

12. Office of the Illinois Secretary of State, Muster and Descriptive Rolls; Murdock, *Patriotism*, 7, 10, 12, 14–16, 18, 27, 31, 81–82, 84, 91, 93, 97–98; Lonn, *Desertion*, 7, 138, 220; Long, *Wages*, 39–49; Billings, *Hardtack*, 214–15; McPherson, *Battle Cry*, 601; Geary, *We Need Men*, 13.

13. Office of the Illinois Secretary of State, Muster and Descriptive Rolls; Murdock, *Patriotism*, 103; Lonn, *Desertion*, 138; Gould, *Investigation*, 210–12; McPherson, *Battle Cry*, 607–8; U.S. Census Bureau, 1860 Census.

14. Owens, *Galena*, 10; Federal Writers' Project, *Galena*, 35; Office of the Illinois Secretary of State, Muster and Descriptive Rolls; Allen and Lacey, *Illinois Elections*, 9–11, 135–43.

15. Allen and Lacey, *Illinois Elections*, 11–12, 144–49, 12, 150–52; McPherson, *Battle Cry*, 560–61.

16. Allen and Lacey, *Illinois Elections*, 12, 150–52; Gallagher, *Union*, 2–3, 52–53, 92, 102, 106–7; White, *Emancipation*, 4–5, 10, 100, 102, 104, 106–7, 109–10, 127, 160; Fry, *Republic*, 2, 8, 69, 102.

17. Foner, *Free Soil*, 9, 316; Maizlish, *Triumph*, xii–xiii, 234, 236–37; Baum, *Civil War*, 7; Gienapp, *Origins*, viii, 10, 103, 125, 175, 286, 295, 414, 417, 443, 444, 447.

18. *Galena Weekly Northwestern Gazette*, January 1, 12, 29, February 19, March 11, 18, May 20, 27, June 3, August 19, 25, September 8, 9, 1856, March 31, April 21, July 9, August 11, November 17, 23, December 1, 22, 1857, January 5, 19, February 10, March 9, April 6, 20, June 29, September 7, October 12, 26, November 18, December 21, 1858, October 25, November 8, 29, December 13, 20, 1859; *Freeport Journal*, March 13, June 19, 1856; *Freeport Daily Journal*, May 23, June 12, November 5, 1856, March 26, 1857; *Rock Island Weekly Advertiser*, June 19, May 24, June 4, 19, November 19, 1856; *Carroll County Republican*, April 4, June 13, October 31, 1856; *Rock Islander*, May 21, June 4, 11, November 12, 1856, March 18, April 1, 1857; *Rockford Republican*, May 28, 1856, November 26, December 31, 1857, April 8, October 28, 1858, October 29, November 3, December 3, 6; 1859; *Rockford Democrat*, June 8, 1856, November 17, 1857, November 2, 9, 1858; *Rock Island Daily Argus*, May 30, November 5, 1856, March 10, September 12, December 1, 24, 1857, February 9, 1858; *Galena Daily Advertiser*, August 13, November 5, 22, 1856, April 4, July 9, August 20, November 23, 1857. *Warren Independent*, January 6, April 11, 16, 1858; *Freeport Weekly Bulletin*, March 18, July 23, September 9, October 21, November 4, 1858, October 27, November 10, 17, 1859; *Galena Daily Courier*, July 8, 17, 22, 28, November 2, 3, 1858; *Rock Island Weekly Register*, October 26, 1859; *Carroll County Home Intelligencer*, November 18, December 30, 1859.

19. *Galena Weekly Northwestern Gazette*, January 3, February 28, May 8, 15, 22, July 31, August 14, October 16, 23, November 20, December 4, 18, 1860; *Carroll County Home Intelligencer*, March 20, May 4, June 26, 1860; *Rock River Democrat*, July 31, August 21, 1860; *Rock Island Weekly Register*, May 23, October 17, 24, November 7, 24, December 5, 19, 1860; *Galena Daily Courier*, May 18, 22, 26, June 4, 25, 27, October 15, November 2, 3, 11, 17, 19, December 26, 1860; *Freeport Weekly Bulletin*, May 10, June 7, December 27, 1860; *Rockford Republican*, May 3, November 6, 1860; *Freeport Wide Awake*, November 6, 1860; *Rockford Democrat*, December 19, 1860.

20. *Galena Daily Courier*, January 9, 15, 31, February 14, 18, 26, March 7, 26, April 9, 13, 17, 22, 27, May 9 14, 1861; *Galena Weekly Northwestern Gazette*, January 29, February 5, March 12, 19, April 9, 16, 23, 30, May 7, 1861; *Warren Independent*, February 5, 19, March 12, 16, April 16, 23, May 28, 1861; *Freeport Weekly Bulletin*, January 24, March 6, April 3, 17, May 8, 13, 1861; *Rockford Democrat*, February 26, 1861; *Rockford Republican*, April 11, 1861.

3. Down among the Secesh

1. Tebbetts to parents, January 4, 1862, *ALPL*; *Galena Daily Advertiser*, January 1, 1862; Cowan to wife, January 4, 1862, and n.d., *GPL*; *Galena Daily Advertiser*, January 23, 1862; *Freeport Bulletin*, January 16, 1862.

2. Tebbetts to parents, January 4, 1862, *ALPL*.

3. Hewett et al., *Supplement*, pt. 2, vol. 11, 398; Smith to wife, January 16, 1862, *GPL*; Adair, *Historical*, 3; *Chicago Tribune*, January 16, 1862; *Galena Daily Advertiser*, January 17, 23, 1862; Cowan Diary, Cowan Papers, *GPL*. Hewett et al., *Supplement*, has the regiment leaving on January 15, 1862, whereas Dyer, *Compendium*, 1066, and Reese, *Report of the Adjutant General*, 360, have the regiment leaving Chicago on January 12.

4. *Chicago Tribune*, January 15, 1862; Jones, "Father's Personal History," 58–59, *FHS*; Linderman, *Embattled*, 130–31; McPherson, *Battle Cry*, 486; Mitchell, *Civil War*, 60–61, 223n.

5. Hewett et al., *Supplement*, pt. 2, vol. 11, 398; Cowan to wife, January 18, 1861, Cowan to daughter, January 18, 1861, *GPL*; Miller, *Vicksburg*, 3; *Warren Independent*, August 13, 1861; Hunt Diary, January 16, 17, 1862, *VHS*. Hewett et al., *Supplement*, has the regiment arriving on January 16, 1862, whereas Dyer, *Compendium*, 1066, and Reese, *Report of the Adjutant General*, 360, have the regiment arriving in Cairo on January 15.

6. Cowan to daughter, January 21, 1862, *GPL*; Adair, *Historical*, 2; Smith to wife, January 19, 1862, *GPL*; January 22, 1863, entry, Regimental Book 4;

Hess, *Civil War*, 63; Crummer, *With Grant*, 11–12; Taylor to father, January 19, 1862, *WSS*.

7. *Daily Green Mountain*, January 15, 1862; *Freeport Bulletin*, January 16, 1862; Woodworth, *Nothing*, 67; Smith to wife, January 19, 23 1862, *GPL*; Taylor to father, January 19, 1862, *WSS*; Special Order No. 321, McClernand to Smith, January 30, 1862, *ALPL*.

8. Smith to wife, January 4, 19, 1862, *GPL*; Cowan to wife, January 21, 1861, *GPL*; Balfour to wife, January 28, 1862, *ALPL*; Foote, *Gentlemen*, 38.

9. Cowan to wife, January 21, 1861, *GPL*; Balfour to wife, January 28, 1862, *ALPL*; Woodworth, *Nothing*, 68–70; *Galena Daily Advertiser*, January 23, 1862; Mitchell, *Civil War*, 39; Cowan to wife, January 21, 29, 1861, *GPL*; Crummer, *With Grant*, 12–13; Dunlop to McClernand, February 1, 1860, *ALPL*

10. Reese, *Report of the Adjutant General*, 360; Wallace to wife, February 1, 1862, *ALPL*; Woodworth, *Nothing*, 68–70; Chernow, *Grant*, 169; Miller, *Vicksburg*, 37; Simpson, *Ulysses* 109–10; Grant to McClernand, February 1, 1862, *ALPL*.

11. Hewett et al., *Supplement*, pt. 2, vol. 11, 398; Bellingall, "Autobiography," 8, *GPL*; Bridgford to wife, February 3, 1862, *SNMP*; Cowan to wife, January 29, 1862, *GPL*; Consolidated Morning Report for Friday, January 31, 1862, *ALPL*; Wallace to Brayman, February 3, 1862, *ALPL*; Logue, *To Appomattox*, 34; Linderman, *Embattled*, 116–17; Robertson, *Soldiers*, 147–49; McPherson, *Battle Cry*, 326, 487; McPherson, *Ordeal*, 416–17; Lowe, *Walker's Texas Division*, 27–28, 36–38; Wiley, *Life of Billy Yank*, 23.

12. Office of the Illinois Secretary of State, Muster and Descriptive Rolls; Regimental Medical Records, *NA*; Compiled Military Service Records, *NA*; Regimental Book 4, *NA*.

13. Reese, *Report of the Adjutant General*, 360; Order, Grant to McClernand, February 2, 1862, *ALPL*; Chernow, *Grant*, 170; Bridgford to wife, February 4, 1862, *SNMP*; *Freeport Bulletin*, February 20, 1862; Cowan to wife, February 4, 1862, *GPL*; Wallace to wife, February 4, 1862, *ALPL*.

14. Bridgford to wife, February 4, 1862, *SNMP*; Crummer, *With Grant*, 13–16; Grant, General Order No. 7, Regimental Order Book 3, *NA*; Woodworth, *Nothing*, 73; Morris, Hartwell, and Kuykendall, *History 31st*, 30; Grimsley, *Hard Hand*, 2–3.

15. Hewett et al., *Supplement*, pt. 2, vol. 11, 398; Adair, *Historical*, 3; Bridgford to wife, February 4, 1862, 45th Illinois Folder, *SNMP*; Drawing of Camp Halleck, Feb. 4, 1862, McClernand Papers, *ALPL*; Woodworth, *Nothing*, 74; Bellingall, "Autobiography," 8; Wallace to wife, February 4, 1862, *ALPL*:

Order No. 8, McClernand to brigade commanders, February 4, 1862, *ALPL*; Crummer, *With Grant*, 16–18; Cowan Diary, February 6, 1862, *GPL*; Fry, *Republic*, 2; Danielson, *War's Desolating Scourge*, 45–46; Manning, *What This Cruel War* 76; Bledsoe, *Citizen-Officers*, 62.

16. Waukegan Weekly Gazette, February 15, 1862; *Carroll County Mirror*, February 19, 1862; Hunt Diary, February 6, 1862, *VHS*; Wiley, *Life of Billy Yank*, 66–67; Robertson, *Soldiers*, 215–16; Grant, Field Order No. 1, *ALPL*; McClernand to Grant, February 6, 1862, *ALPL*; Woodworth, *Nothing*, 75–76; Adair, *Historical*, 3; Crummer, *With Grant*, 19; Morris, Hartwell, and Kuykendall, *History 31st*, 31–32; *Galena Daily Advertiser*, February 13, 1862; Smith to wife, February 8, 1862, *GPL*.

17. Smith to wife, February 8, 1862, *GPL*; McClernand to Grant, February 6, 1862, *ALPL*; Woodworth, *Nothing*, 77; *Carroll County Mirror*, February 19, 1862; Crummer, *With Grant*, 19, 21; Adair, *Historical*, 3; *Chicago Tribune*, February 12, 1861; Cowan Diary, February 6, 1862, *GPL*; Smith, *Grant Invades*, 119.

18. Crummer, *With Grant*, 22–23; *Carroll County Mirror*, February 19, 1862; Adair, *Historical*, 3; *Galena Daily Advertiser*, February 13, 1862; *Chicago Tribune*, February 8, 1862; Woodworth, *Nothing*, 78; Miller, *Vicksburg*, 39; Morris, Hartwell, and Kuykendall, *History 31st*, 33; Smith, *Grant Invades*, 113.

19. Goodbrake to Sterns, February 9, 10, 11, 1862, Wallace to Brayman, February 12, 1862, Grant to McClernand, and McClernand to Grant, February 7, 1862, *ALPL*; *Galena Daily Advertiser*, February 13, 1862; Woodworth, *Nothing*, 82–83; Chernow, *Grant*, 176; Miller, *Vicksburg*, 40; Wallace to wife, February 8, 1862, *ALPL*; Consolidated Morning Reports for Sunday, February 9 to Wednesday 12, 1862, *ALPL*.

20. Grant General Orders No. 7, 9, and 12, February 10, 11, 1862, *ALPL*; Brayman to Wallace, February 10, 1862, and McClernand to Wallace, February 11, 1862, *ALPL*.

21. Reese, *Report of the Adjutant General*, 360; *OR*, ser. 1, vol. 7, 161, 168, 192; Miller, *Vicksburg*, 42; Woodworth, *Nothing*, 85; *Warren Independent*, March 4, 1862, Crummer, *With Grant*, 25–26; Adair, *Historical*, 4; *Galena Daily Advertiser*, February 28, 1862.

22. *OR*, ser. 1, vol. 7, 171, 193; Smith to friend, March 6, 1862, *GPL*.

23. Woodworth, *Nothing*, 24–26, 87–88, 248–51, 430–34; *Galena Daily Advertiser*, February 28, 1862; *Chicago Tribune*, February 28, 1862; *OR*, ser. 1, vol. 7, 172–73, 194; Miller, *Vicksburg*, 43; Smith to friend, March 6, 1862, *GPL*; Reese, *Report of the Adjutant General*, 147; Hewett et al., *Supplement*, pt. 2, vol. 11, 398.

24. Crummer, *With Grant*, 27–28, 37; *Galena Daily Advertiser*, March 5, 1862; Taylor to Smith, December 28, 1885, *VNMP*; *Warren Independent*, March 4, 1862; Adair, *Historical*, 4.

25. *Galena Daily Advertiser*, March 5, 1862; *Warren Independent*, March 4, 1862; Adair, *Historical*, 4; OR, ser. 1, vol. 7, 202, 206; Foote, *Gentlemen*, 57–59; Cowan to wife, February 19, 1862, *GPL*; Smith to friend, March 6, 1862, *GPL*.

26. *OR*, ser. 1, vol. 7, 174–75, 194, 202; Warrant Independent, March 4, 1862: Adair, *Historical*, 4; Woodworth, *Nothing*, 89–90; Simpson, *Ulysses S. Grant*, 114; Compiled Military Service Records, *NA*; Crummer, *With Grant*, 30–31; Miller, *Vicksburg*, 46–47.

27. Crummer, *With Grant*, 32; *OR*, ser. 1, vol. 7, 163, 175; Woodworth, *Nothing*, 95, 111; *Warren Independent*, March 4, 1862; Adair, *Historical*, 4.

28. *OR*, ser. 1, vol. 7, 176, 178, 195–96, 202; Hess, *Civil War*, 47–48, 105, 145, 148–49; Stevens to uncle, February 28, 1862, *VNMP*; Woodworth, *Nothing*, 98, 102; Crummer, *With Grant*, 33; *Galena Daily Advertiser*, March 5, 1862; Miller, *Vicksburg*, 48.

29. Woodworth, *Nothing*, 99; Rable, *God's*, 115–16.

30. *OR*, ser. 1, vol. 7, 159–60, 180; Simpson, *Ulysses S. Grant*, 116; Woodworth, *Nothing*, 111–13, Crummer, *With Grant*, 38; Hunt Diary, February 15, 16, 1862, *VHS*.

31. Adair, *Historical*, 4; Crummer, *With Grant*, 42–43; Hunt Diary, February 16, 1862, *VHS*; Woodworth, *Nothing*, 118.

32. Grant, *Civil War*, 72; *OR*, ser. 1, vol. 7, 179, 197–98, 202; Adair, *Historical*, 4; *Galena Daily Advertiser*, February 28, 1862; Warrant Independent, March 4, 1862; Cowan to a friend, March 6, 1862, *GPL*; *Rockford Republican*, March 18, 1862; *Galena Daily Advertiser*, March 7, 10, 1862.

33. Wallace to wife, February 17, 1862, *ALPL*; Warrant Independent, March 4, 1862; *Galena Daily Advertiser*, February 19, 1862; Woodworth, *Nothing*, 113; Adair, *Historical*, 5; Smith, *Grant Invades*, 374; Crummer, *With Grant*, 37–38; Cowan to wife, February 19, 1862, *GPL*; Smith to friend, March 6, 1862, *GPL*; Carmichael, *War*, 110.

34. Cowan to wife, February 19, 1862, *GPL*; Crummer, *With Grant*, 34–35; Tebbetts to sister, March 2, 1862, *ALPL*.

35. *Galena Daily Advertiser*, March 4, 1862; McGinty, "Civil War"; Office of the Illinois Secretary of State, Muster and Descriptive Rolls.

36. Cowan Diary, December 10, 1862, *GPL*.

37. Bridgford to wife, February 21, 1862, *SNMP*; Bellingall, "Autobiography," 8–12.

38. *OR*, ser. 1, vol. 7, 168–69, 202; Casualty Listing for the First Division, February 15, 1862, *ALPL*; *Galena Daily Advertiser*, February 19, March 5, 13, 24–25, 1862; *Chicago Tribune*, March 11, 1862; Regimental Medical Records, *NA*; Compiled Military Service Records, *NA*; Hess, *Civil War*, 59; Cowan to wife, February 19, 1862, *GPL*; *Freeport Bulletin*, March 20, 1862.

39. *Rockford Republican*, February 20, March 20, 1862; Office of the Illinois Secretary of State, Muster and Descriptive Rolls.

40. Crummer, *With Grant*, 47; Balfour to wife, before March 1, 1862, *ALPL*; Grant, *Civil War*, 72–73; Cowan to wife, February 19, 1862, *GPL*; Woodworth, *Nothing*, 122–23; *Rock River Times*, November 15, 2016.

41. Bridgford to wife, February 21, 24, March 9, 1862, *SNMP*; *Galena Daily Advertiser*, February 19, 28, March 5, 13, 1862; Smith to friend, March 6, 1862, *GPL*; Balfour to wife, before March 1, 1862, *ALPL*; Cowan to wife, March 1, 1862, *GPL*; Woodworth, *Nothing*, 121–22; Crummer, *With Grant*, 49.

42. Bridgford to wife, February 24, 1862, *SNMP*; Order No. 3, Grant, February 18, 1862, *ALPL*; Orders No. 196 and 199, McClernand, February 26, 1862, *ALPL*; Miller, *Vicksburg*, 52; Simpson, *Let Us Have Peace*, 20–21.

43. Chernow, *Grant*, 120–21, 126, 128; *Galena Daily Advertiser*, March 4, 1862.

44. Order No. 17, March 1, 1862, Grant, *ALPL*; Order No. 210, March 2, 1862, McClernand, *ALPL*; Simon, From Galena, 176; Crummer, *With Grant*, 50; *Galena Daily Advertiser*, March 5, 1862.

4. Bloodied yet Unbroken

1. Adair, *Historical*, 5; Bellingall, "Autobiography," 12; Cowan to wife, March 7, 1862, *GPL*; Bledsoe, *Citizen-Soldiers*, 73; Cousins, *Bodies*, 41; Woodworth, *Nothing*, 131; Hunt Diary, March, 6, 1862, *VHS*; Bridgford to wife, March 9, 1862, *SNMP*; 1862; *Galena Daily Advertiser*, March 20, 1862; Reese, *Report of the Adjutant General*, 360; Hewett et al., *Supplement*, pt. 2, vol. 11, 399.

2. Cowan to wife March 7, 1862, *GPL*; Bridgford to wife, March 9, 1862, *SNMP*; Cashin, *War Stuff*, 7–8, 58, 60; *Galena Daily Advertiser*, March 20, 1862; Danielson, *War's Desolating Scourge*, 37–40, 69–70, 75–76; Fry, *Republic*, 2, 38, 39, 45.

3. Cashin, *War Stuff*, 3–7, 31, 54, 58, 82–92, 108, 110; Grimsley, *Hard*, 2–5; Catton, *Grant Moves*, 294; *OR*, ser. 1, vol. 10, pt. 1, 150; Ballard, *Vicksburg*, xii.

4. Reese, *Report of the Adjutant General*, 360; Miller, *Vicksburg*, 62; Simpson, *Ulysses S. Grant*, 127; Cowan to wife, March 1, 7, 8, 23, 1862, *GPL*; Bridgford to wife, March 9, 15, 1862, *SNMP*; Woodworth, *Nothing*, 131.

5. *Galena Daily Advertiser*, March 20, 1862; Bridgford to wife, March 15, 1862, *SNMP*.

6. Bridgford to wife, March 25, 1862, *SNMP*; Smith to wife, March 13, 1862, *GPL*; Manning, *What This Cruel War* 47; McClernand to Smith, March 14, 1862, *ALPL*; Order No. 255, McClernand, March 14, 1862, *ALPL*; Wallace to McClernand, March 17, 1862, *ALPL*; Hewett et al., *Supplement*, pt. 2, vol. 11, 399.

7. Requisition, Cowan, March 21, 1862, *ALPL*; McClernand to Smith, March 14, 1862, *ALPL*; Kittoe to division surgeon of 2nd Division, March 14, 1862, *ALPL*; Robertson, *Soldiers*, 70–71; Wiley, *Life of Billy Yank*, 127–28; Sword, *Shiloh*, 14.

8. Reese, *Report of the Adjutant General*, 360; *OR*, ser. 1, vol. 10, pt. 1, 63–64; *Galena Daily Advertiser*, March 31, 1862; *Cleveland Morning Leader*, March 29, 1862; Hewett et al., *Supplement*, pt. 2, vol. 11, 399. Cowan to wife and children, March 30, 1862, *GPL*; Sword, *Shiloh*, 40; *Cleveland Morning Leader*, March 29, 1862.

9. Cowan to wife and children, March 30, 1862, *GPL*; *Waukegan Weekly Gazette*, April 12, 1862; Chernow, *Grant*, 184; McPherson, *Battle Cry*, 353; Office of the Illinois Secretary of State, Muster and Descriptive Rolls.

10. Grimsley, *Hard*, 101; Sword, *Shiloh*, 40; Danielson, *War's Desolating Scourge*, 37–40, 45–50, 54–63, 65–80.

11. Hewett et al., *Supplement*, pt. 2, vol. 11, 399, and pt. 1, vol. 1, 631; Reese, *Report of the Adjutant General*, 360; Simpson, *Ulysses S. Grant*, 128; Balfour to wife, March 27, 1862, *ALPL*; Blanchard, *I Marched*, 52; Smith to wife, March 28, 1862, *GPL*; Woodworth, *Nothing*, 168; Sword, *Shiloh*, 11, 27, 311; Waterloo, *Illinois*, 139.

12. Balfour to wife, March 25, 27, 1862, and to son, April 4, 1862, *ALPL*; Bridgford to wife, March 25, 1862, *SNMP*; Miller, *Vicksburg*, 65; Cowan to wife and children, March 30, 1862, *GPL*; Mitchell, *Civil War*, 119; Teters, *Practical Liberators*, 8, 10–11, 18–26; *Galena Daily Advertiser*, April 10, 1862. Sword, *Shiloh*, 28.

13. Hewett et al., *Supplement*, pt. 1, vol. 1, 631; Cowan to wife and children, March 30, 1862, *GPL*; Sword, *Shiloh*, 28; Bridgford to wife, March 25, 1862, *SNMP*; Office of the Illinois Secretary of State, Muster and Descriptive Rolls; Balfour to wife, March 27, 1862, and to son, April 4, 1862, *ALPL*; Smith to wife; March 28, 1862, *GPL*; Regimental Medical Records, *NA*.

14. Cowan to wife and children, March 30, 1862, *GPL*; Balfour to son, April 4, 1862, *ALPL*; *Warren Independent*, May 17, 1862; *Chicago Tribune*, April

14, 1862. On enlisted men enforcing their society's concept of honor, see Foote, *Gentlemen*, 4–6, 19; Carmichael, *War*, 141.

15. Order No. 352, McClernand, April 4, 1862, *ALPL*; *Chicago Tribune*, April 14, 1862; Bellingall, "Autobiography," 12, *GPL*; Hewett et al., *Supplement*, pt. 1, vol. 1, 631; Crummer, *With Grant*, 51–53; Sword, *Shiloh*, 110–11, 122–24, 128; Blanchard, *I Marched*, 53; *Warren Independent*, May 17, 1862.

16. Hewett et al., *Supplement*, pt. 1, vol. 1, 631; Crummer, *With Grant*, 51–53; Sword, *Shiloh*, 32–33, 37–38, 106, 112–13; Daniels, *Shiloh*, 133; Cowan to wife, April 6, 1863, *GPL*.

17. Crummer, *With Grant*, 55, 76; Sword, *Shiloh*, 308; Woodworth, *Nothing*, 142–44, 199; Smith to wife, April 14, 1862, *GPL*; *Warren Independent*, May 17, 1862; Chernow, *Grant*, 199; Smith, Untold Story, 22–24; Catton, *Grant Moves*, 220; Waterloo, *Illinois*, 7; Miller, *Vicksburg*, 63; Simpson, *Ulysses S. Grant*, 129.

18. Sword, *Shiloh*, 142, 200; 203, 308; Woodworth, *Nothing*, 169, 172; Smith to wife, April 10, 1862, *GPL*; *OR*, ser. 1, vol. 10, pt. 1, 114–15, 133; *OR*, ser. 1, vol. 52, pt. 1, 21–22; Crummer, *With Grant*, 54, 56–58; Daniel, *Shiloh*, 177; Miller, *Vicksburg*, 63; Waterloo, *Illinois*, 5; *Warren Independent*, May 17, 1862; Frank and Reaves, *Seeing*, 88; *Waukegan Weekly Gazette*, April 19, 1862; Adair, *Historical*, 5; Reese, *Report of the Adjutant General*, 360; Hewett et al., *Supplement*, pt. 1, vol. 1, 631; *Chicago Tribune*, April 14, 1862.

19. Crummer, *With Grant*, 57–61, 63; *OR*, ser. 1, vol. 10, pt. 1, 114, 116, 133; Sword, *Shiloh*, 201–4, 207, 211, 310; 312–13; Daniel, *Shiloh*, 180; Bellingall, "Autobiography," 12, *GPL*; National Tribune, October 14, 1897; Adair, *Historical*, 5; *Rock River Democrat*, April 15, 1862; *Galena Daily Advertiser*, April 4, 1862; Woodworth, *Nothing*, 174; Waterloo, *Illinois*, 26.

20. Woodworth, *Nothing*, 176; Sword, *Shiloh*, 208, 318, 324–26; Daniel, *Shiloh*, 188; *Rock River Democrat*, April 15, 1862; *Galena Daily Advertiser*, April 4, 1862; *OR*, ser. 1, vol. 10, pt. 1, 117, 133–34; Dittmar, Autobiography, *SNMP*, 8; Crummer, *With Grant*, 63; Adair, *Historical*, 5; *Warren Independent*, May 17, 1862; Miller, *Vicksburg*, 78; Bellingall, "Autobiography," 13, *GPL*; *Chicago Tribune*, April 14, 1862.

21. *OR*, ser. 1, vol. 10, pt. 1, 100–108, 116–17, 134; Sword, *Shiloh*, 326–29; Daniel, *Shiloh*, 189; Hewett et al., *Supplement*, pt. 1, vol. 1, 631–32; *Warren Independent*, May 17, 1862; Bellingall, "Autobiography," 13, *GPL*; Crummer, *With Grant*, 63; Adair, *Historical*, 5; Bridgford to wife, April 8, 1862, *SNMP*.

22. *OR*, ser. 1, vol. 10, pt. 1, 117, 134; Hicken, *Illinois*, 59; Sword, *Shiloh*, 329–31, 335; Hewett et al., *Supplement*, pt. 1, vol. 1, 632.

23. *OR*, ser. 1, vol. 10, pt. 1, 117, 134; Sword, *Shiloh*, 204, 333, 353–55; Daniel, *Shiloh*, 239; Crummer, *With Grant*, 64–67; Adair, *Historical*, 6; Hewett et al., *Supplement*, pt. 1, vol. 1, 632–33; Miller, *Vicksburg*, 80.

24. Adair, *Historical*, 6; Waterloo, *Illinois*, 28; *OR*, ser. 1, vol. 10, pt. 1, 134; Crummer, *With Grant*, 68–72, 79; National Tribune, October 14, 1897; Hewett et al., *Supplement*, pt. 1, vol. 1, 633; Blanchard, *I Marched*, 57; *Warren Independent*, April 22, 1862; Sword, *Shiloh*, 371, 374; Chernow, *Grant*, 204; Daniel, *Shiloh*, 263, 265; Miller, *Vicksburg*, 82.

25. Woodworth, *Nothing*, 192, 194; *OR*, ser. 1, vol. 10, pt. 1, 134–35; *OR*, ser. 1, vol. 52, pt. 1, 16; Crummer, *With Grant*, 72; Reese, *Report of the Adjutant General*, 361; *Warren Independent*, April 22, 1862; Adair, *Historical*, 6; Hewett et al., *Supplement*, pt. 1, vol. 1, 633.

26. Adair, *Historical*, 6; Hewett et al., *Supplement*, pt. 1, vol. 1, 633–34; Daniel, *Shiloh*, 283; Crummer, *With Grant*, 72–74; Miller, *Vicksburg*, 83; Reese, *Report of the Adjutant General*, 361; Billings, *Hardtack*, 46; Chernow, *Grant*, 206; Force, *From Fort Henry*, 118–19; Sword, *Shiloh*, 29, 307–9, 312; Daniel, *Shiloh*, 110.

27. Crummer, *With Grant*, 73–74; Sword, *Shiloh*, 418; Cowan to wife, April 6, 1863, *GPL*; Woodworth, *Nothing*, 200; Hewett et al., *Supplement*, pt. 1, vol. 1, 633–34; *Warren Independent* April 22, 1862; Adair, *Historical*, 6.

28. Jones, "Father's Personal History," 59, *FHS*; Sword, *Shiloh*, 420.

29. Sword, *Shiloh*, 428–31; Crummer, *With Grant*, 74–75; Miller, *Vicksburg*, 84; Adair, *Historical*, 6; *OR*, ser. 1, vol. 10, pt. 1, 111; *Warren Independent* April 22, 1862; Chernow, *Grant*, 206–8; Linderman, *Embattled*, 125–27; Robertson, *Soldiers*, 225.

30. Cowan to wife April 16, 1862, and to daughter, April 16, 1862, *GPL*.

31. Dittmar, "Autobiography," 6–9.

32. Stanton to Grant, April 9, 1862, *ALPL*; General Order No. 16, Maj. Genl. Halleck, April 13, 1862, *ALPL*; Sword, *Shiloh*, 21; *OR*, ser.1, vol. 10, pt. 1, 99, 109, 111–12.

33. *OR*, ser. 1, vol. 10, pt. 1, 113, 136; *OR*, ser. 1, vol. 52, pt. 1, 21–22; Washburne to Smith, May 10, 1862, *GPL*; Crummer, *With Grant*, 53, 65; Taylor to Smith, December 28, 1885, *VNMP*; *Ottawa Free Trader*, April 19, 1862; *Galena Daily Advertiser*, April 16, 1862; Bledsoe, *Citizen-Officers*, 83–84, 128, 144, 147–48, 152–53.

34. *OR*, ser. 1, vol. 10, pt. 1, 100–108; Brayman to Rawlings, April 12, 1862, *ALPL*; Hicken, *Illinois*, 70; Fox, *Regimental Losses*, 428; *Galena Daily Advertiser*, April 16, 1862; Office of the Illinois Secretary of State, Muster and Descriptive Rolls; Regimental Medical Records, *NA*; Compiled Military

Service Records, *NA*; Smith to wife, April 14, 1862, *GPL*; *Keithsburg Observer*, May 1, 1863; *Ottawa Free Trader*, April 26, 1862.

35. *Galena Daily Advertiser*, April 19, 1862; *Warren Independent*, April 22, 1862; Cowan to daughter, April 16, 1862, *GPL*; Office of the Illinois Secretary of State, Muster and Descriptive Rolls; Hunt Diary, April 6, 7, 1862, *VHS*.

36. Bridgford to wife and children, April 20, 1862, *SNMP*; Office of the Illinois Secretary of State, Muster and Descriptive Rolls; *Waukegan Weekly Gazette*, April 19, 1862; Crummer, *With Grant*, 86; War Department to Grant, April 9, 1862; Regimental Order Book 3, *NA*; Dittmar to family, April 15, 1862, *SNMP*.

37. *Galena Daily Advertiser*, April 15–18, 21, 25, 28, 1862; Office of the Illinois Secretary of State, Muster and Descriptive Rolls.

38. Baugher to father, April 9, 1862, *GPL*; *Galena Daily Advertiser*, April 15, 16, 19, 21, 28–29, 1862; *Warren Independent*, April 22, 29, 1862.

39. *Galena Daily Advertiser*, May 8, 17, 24, 1862; *Warren Independent*, May 6, 1862.

40. *Warren Independent*, May 7, 17, 1862; *Galena Daily Advertiser*, May 17, June 6, 19, 1862.

41. *Warren Independent*, June 17, 1862.

42. Woodworth, *Nothing*, 205; *OR*, ser. 1, vol. 10, pt. 1, 100, 109; Order No. 39, Grant, April 17, 1862, *ALPL*; Order No. 21, Halleck, April 22, 1862, *ALPL*.

43. Smith, *Untold Story*, 27; Hess, *Civil War*, 25, 62–62, 64, 80, 229.

5. Pragmatic Emancipators

1. Miller, *Vicksburg*, 198.

2. Jones, "Father's Personal History," 60–61, *FHS*; *OR*, ser. 1, vol. 10, pt 1, p. 753; Adair, *Historical*, 6–7; Cowan to daughter, June 12, 1862, *GPL*; Woodworth, *Nothing*, 206–7; Catton, *Grant Moves*, 265, 268–70; Hewett et al., *Supplement*, pt. 1, vol. 1, 399; Smith to wife, April 27, 1862, *GPL*.

3. Hewett et al., *Supplement*, pt. 2, vol. 11, 399; Smith to wife, April 27, 1862, *GPL*; *Galena Daily Advertiser*, May 17, June 16, 1862; *OR*, ser. 1, vol. 10, pt. 1, 755; Office of the Illinois Secretary of State, Muster and Descriptive Rolls; Cowan to daughter, May 3, 6, 1862, and to wife, May 27, 1862.

4. Hunt Diary, May 9 and June 3, 1862, *VHS*; Office of the Illinois Secretary of State, Muster and Descriptive Rolls; Regimental Medical Records, *NA*; Bledsoe, *Citizen-Officers*, xii, 161–62, 183–84, 224–25, 231–38.

5. Hewett et al., *Supplement*, pt. 2, vol. 11, 399; *OR*, ser. 1, vol. 10, pt. 1, 666–67, 756–57; Woodworth, *Nothing*, 206–8; Barnet, *Martyrs*, 47; *Warren*

Independent, June 17, 1862; Cowan to daughter, June 12, 1862, *GPL*; Hunt Diary, May 28–29, 1862, *VHS*.

6. *Warren Independent*, Tuesday, June 17, 1862; Cowan to daughter, June 12, 1862, and to wife, June 4, 1862, *GPL*; McPherson, *Battle Cry*, 416; Jones, "Father's Personal History," 61, *FHS*; *Galena Daily Advertiser*, April 21, 29, June 6, 1862.

7. McPherson, *Battle Cry*, 512; Woodworth, *Nothing*, 210–11; Feis, "Developed by Circumstances," 155; Hewett et al., *Supplement*, pt. 2, vol. 11, 399–400; Reese, *Report of the Adjutant General*, 361; Cowan to wife, June 10, 1862, and to daughter, June 12, 1862, *GPL*; Adair, *Historical*, 7; Jones, "Father's Personal History," 61, *FHS*; *Galena Daily Advertiser*, June 4, 18, 27, 1862; Regimental Order Book 3, July 5, August 17, 30, 1862, *NA*; Bledsoe, *Citizen-Officers*, 78.

8. *Galena Daily Advertiser*, June 27, 1862; Jones, "Father's Personal History," 60–62, *FHS*; McPherson, *Battle Cry*, 497, 500; Woodworth, *Nothing*, 211–12; Catton; *Grant Moves*, 294–95, *OR*, ser. 1, vol. 17, pt. 2, 150; Chernow, *Grant*, 223; Simpson, *Ulysses S. Grant*, 147–48; Reid, Civil War, 118; Wiley, *Life of Billy Yank*, 115–16, 119; Danielson, *War's Desolating Scourge*, 99; Manning, *What This Cruel War* 21, 49, 71; Gallagher, *Union*, 80, 82.

9. Cowan to wife, June 10, Cowan to daughter, June 12, to Olds, July 15, 1862, *GPL*; Catton, *Grant Moves*, 293–94; Woodworth, *Nothing*, 211; Danielson, *War's Desolating Scourge*, 38–43; Pelka, *Civil War Letters*, 106; *Galena Daily Advertiser*, June 27, 1862; John P. Jones to wife, August 24, 1862, Benham Collection, *LOC*.

10. Cowan to daughter, June 28, 1862, and to wife, July 10, 12, August 27, 1862, *GPL*; Billings, *Hardtack*, 80–82; Bridgford to wife, June 29, July 27, 1862, and to wife and kids, July 7, 1862, *SNMP*; Office of the Illinois Secretary of State, Muster and Descriptive Rolls; *Freeport Bulletin*, July 24, 1862; April 7–8, Casualties, Battle of Shiloh, 2nd Brigade, 1st Division, McClernand Papers, *ALPL*.

11. Cowan to Olds, July 15, 1862, *GPL*; Boatner, *Civil War Dictionary*, 52, 260; Hewett et al., *Supplement*, pt. 2, vol. 11, 400–401; *Galena Daily Advertiser*, August 6, 1862; Office of the Illinois Secretary of State, Muster and Descriptive Rolls; Bellingall, "Autobiography," 12, *GPL*.

12. *Galena Daily Advertiser*, August 6, 22, 1862, 1862; *Warren Independent*, August 14, 31, 1862; Reid, Civil War, 119; Danielson, *War's Desolating Scourge*, 38–40, 100; Teters, *Practical Liberators*, 8, 10–11, 18–26; Carmichael, *War*, 94; Cowan to wife and daughter; July 24, 1862, *GPL*; Smith to Dickey, July 17, 1862, *ALPL*; Office of the Illinois Secretary of State, Muster and

Descriptive Rolls; Regimental Order Book 4, *NA*; Corbin, "Biography," 33, *ALPL*; Robertson, *Soldiers*, 38–39; Fry, *Republic*, 12, 40, 42.

13. *OR*, ser. 1, vol. 17, pt. 2, 155; Bellingall, "Autobiography," 13; Adair, *Historical*, 7; Teters, *Practical Liberators*, 8, 10–11, 18–26; *Galena Daily Advertiser*, August 22, 1862; McPherson, *Ordeal*, 380; Manning, *What This Cruel War*, 13; Gallagher, *Union*, 80; Fry, *Republic*, 8.

14. Adair, *Historical*, 7; Reese, *Report of the Adjutant General*, 361; *Galena Daily Advertiser*, September 9, 11, 18, 1862.

15. *Galena Daily Advertiser*, September 11, 18, 1862; *OR*, ser. 1, vol. 17, pt. 1, 44, 49; Crouch, Silencing, 19.

16. *Galena Daily Advertiser*, September 11, 18, 27, 1862; Adair, *Historical*, 7; *Cleveland Morning Leader*, September 26, 1862; Daily State Sentinel, September 26, 1862; National Tribune, November 1, 1883; *OR*, ser. 1, vol. 17, pt. 1, 44–45, 49–50; Hewett et al., *Supplement*, pt. 2, vol. 11, 400.

17. Bellingall, "Autobiography," 13–14.

18. Bellingall, "Autobiography," 14–17.

19. Jones, "Father's Personal History," 63, *FHS*; Cowan to wife, September 2, 1862, Cowan Papers, *GPL*.

20. *Galena Daily Advertiser*, September 18, 29, 1862; Adair, *Historical*, 7; Reese, *Report of the Adjutant General*, 361; Office of the Illinois Secretary of State, Muster and Descriptive Rolls; Compiled Military Service Records, *NA*; Duer to Maltby, September 3, 1862, *ALPL*; Bledsoe, *Citizen-Officers*, ix–xi, 67–69, 71–72, 85, 165; Feis, "Developed by Circumstances," 155.

21. Order No. 174, Grant, August 25, 1862, *ALPL*; *OR*, ser. 1 ,vol. 17, pt. 2, 212; Reese, *Report of the Adjutant General*, 361; Hewett et al., *Supplement*, pt. 2, vol. 11, 400; Cowan to wife, September 2, October 29, 1862, to children, October 1, 26, 1862, to daughter, October 5, 1862, to *Warren Independent*, October 5, 1862, to wife, October 5, 1862, and to daughter, November 18, 1862, *GPL*; Foote, *Gentlemen*, 12–13, 15; Regimental Order Book 3, *NA*; Woodworth, *Nothing*, 243; Rable, *God's*, 391.

22. Hewett et al., *Supplement*, pt. 2, vol. 11, 401; Woodworth, *Nothing*, 252; 265; Ballard, *Vicksburg*, 83; Welcher, *Union Army*, 2:220–22; Grimsley, *Hard*, 100–101; Chernow, *Grant*, 240; Simpson, *Let Us Have Peace*, xviii–xix; 25; 27; *Carroll County Mirror*, March 18, 1863; Adair, *Historical*, 7–8; Reese, *Report of the Adjutant General*, 361; *Galena Daily Advertiser*, 11/20/1862; *Memphis Daily Appeal*, November 24, 1862; Miller, *Vicksburg*, 195, 198–99, 205; Cashin, *War Stuff*, 57; Cowan Diary, November 8, 9, 10, 12, 1862, *GPL*; Cowan to wife, November 2, 12, 1862, to daughter, November 18, 21, 1862, to *Warren Independent*, November 23, 1862, *GPL*; Miller to Budlong,

November 7, 1862, *ALPL*; *OR*, ser. 1, vol. 17, pt. 2, 150, 338; *OR*, ser. 1, vol. 24, pt. 3, 2.

23. Cowan to daughter, November 21, 1862, *GPL*; Cowan to *Warren Independent* Editor, November 23, 1862, *GPL*; Carmichael, *War*, 247–48, 270.

24. Hewett et al., *Supplement*, pt. 2, vol. 11, 402; Adair, *Historical*, 7; *Warren Independent*, February 26, 1863; Cowan to wife, November 27, 30, December 7, 1862, *GPL*; Cowan Diary, November 28–30, December 1, 3–7, 1862, *GPL*; Miller, *Vicksburg*, 202, 205–6; Woodworth, *Nothing*, 243–44, 254, 256; Welcher, *Union Army*, 2:851.

25. Smith, *Union Assaults*, 193; *Galena Daily Advertiser*, December 8, 1862, and January 16, 1863; *Carroll County Mirror*, March 18, 1863; *Freeport Bulletin*, December 11, 1862. Cowan to Fuller, December 18, 1863, to children, January 4, 1863, *GPL*; *OR*, ser. 1, vol. 17, pt. 2, 492; *Galena Weekly Northwestern Gazette*, January 19, 1863; Adair, *Historical*, 7; Reese, *Report of the Adjutant General*, 361.

26. Woodworth, *Nothing*, 264–65; Miller, *Vicksburg*, 227; Smith, *Union Assaults*, 28; Welcher, *Union Army*, 2:851–52; Grant, *Civil War*, 135–37; Grimsley, *Hard*, 101; Miller, *Vicksburg*, 228; Simpson, *Ulysses S. Grant*, 167.

27. Blanchard, *I Marched*, 75; Adair, *Historical*, 7; Warrant Independent, February 26, 1863, Reese, *Report of the Adjutant General*, 361; Cowan Diary, December 22, 24–25, 1862, *GPL*; Jones, "Father's Personal History," 63, *FHS*; Ballard, *Vicksburg*, 126; Beck, "True Sketch," 3, *VNMP*.

28. Adair, *Historical*, 7; Jones, "Father's Personal History," 63, *FHS*; Reese, *Report of the Adjutant General*, 361; Cowan Diary, January 1–3, 5, 1863, to children, January 4, 1863, *GPL*; Morris, Hartwell, and Kuykendall, *History 31st*, 52; Warrant Independent, February 26, 1863.

29. Cowan to daughter, January 14, 1863, *GPL*; Cowan Diary, January 11, 15–21, 1863, *GPL*; Hewett et al., *Supplement*, pt. 2, vol. 11, 402; Woodworth, *Nothing*, 265; Ballard, *Vicksburg*, 83; Blanchard, *I Marched*, 75–78; Miller, *Vicksburg*, 231.

30. Corbin, "Biography," 36–39, *ALPL*; Office of the Illinois Secretary of State, Muster and Descriptive Rolls.

31. *OR* ser. 1, vol. 24, pt. 3, 20, 28; Welcher, *Union Army*, 2:860; Report, Inspector Gen., 17th Corps, for January 1863, *GPL*; Cowan to wife, February 7, 16, 1863, *GPL*; *Galena Daily Advertiser*, February 27, 1863; Foote, *Gentlemen*, 51–52.

32. Cowan to children, January 4, to wife, January 21, February 7, 1863, and to friends, February 25, April 21, 1863, *GPL*; *Warren Independent*, February 14, 1863; Gallagher, *Union*, 2, 76–77, 80; 93–101, 103–4; Fry, *Republic*, 2, 5, 8,

10, 83–85; Hicken, *Illinois*, 135–38, 141; Stabler and Hershock, "'Standing,'" 30.

33. Cowan to daughter, January 14, 1863, *GPL*; *Warren Independent*, February 14, 26, 1863; Towne, *Surveillance*, 3, 13–14, 16, 39–40, 66, 69, 72, 76, 94–103, 121, 127–31, 136, 139, 151, 158, 160–61, 166, 182, 189, 218, 226, 248, 252, 255, 257, 262, 277, 286, 289; Miller, *Vicksburg*, 183; *Galena Daily Advertiser*, February 21, 27, 1863; Wiley, *Life of Billy Yank*, 386–87; Jimerson, *Private*, 221–24; Mitchell, *Civil War*, 86–87; Logue, *To Appomattox*, 52; Hess, *Liberty*, 89–91; McPherson, *Cause*, 124, 142–45; Gallagher, *Union*, 129; Fry, *Republic*, 74, 79–83, 99.

34. Towne, *Surveillance*, 48–49, 55–57, 63; Miller, *Vicksburg*, 183; *Rock River Democrat*, February 11, 1863; Woodworth, *Nothing*, 295–97, 311–12; Ballard, *Vicksburg*, 84; Neely, *Union*, 42–43; Teters, *Practical Liberators*, 65–67; White, *Emancipation*, 69, 84, 108.

35. Wiley, *Life of Billy Yank*, 41–44; McPherson, *Ordeal*, 186; 321–22; McPherson, *Battle Cry*, 558–59; McPherson, *Cause*, 118, 121–26; Robertson, *Soldiers*, 10–11; Jimerson, *Private*, 42, 44, 46–47; Mitchell, *Civil War*, 42, 123, 126–27; Hess, *Liberty*, 97–100; Smith, *Black Soldiers*, 2, 4, 6; Manning, *What This Cruel War* 45, 47, 75, 123–24, 152; White, *Emancipation*, 8, 10, 39–40, 48, 96.

36. Wiley, *Life of Billy Yank*, 120–21; McPherson, *Cause*, 126–27; McPherson, *Ordeal*, 379–80; Robertson, *Soldiers*, 31–32, 34; Jimerson, *Private*, 47, 90, 92–93, 95–96, 102, 247–48; Mitchell, *Civil War*, 195, 197; Logue, *To Appomattox*, 15, 43–44, 57; Hess, *Liberty*, 100; Smith, *Black Soldiers*, 4–5, 39; Hewitt, "Ironic Route," 82, 98; Lowe, "Battle," 108, 110, 126–27; Robertson, "From the Crater," 175; Manning, *What This Cruel War*, 95–96; Stabler and Hershock, "'Standing,'" 31; Nofi, *Civil War Treasury*, 381; Gallagher, *Union*, 104–5.

37. Cowan to wife, February 18, 19, to daughter, February 25, 1863, *GPL*; Cowan Diary, February 20–22, 1863, *GPL*; *Galena Daily Advertiser*, February 27, 1863; Reese, *Report of the Adjutant General*, 361; Hewett et al., *Supplement*, pt. 2, vol. 11, 402; *OR*, ser. 1, vol. 24, pt. 1, 18; Woodworth, *Nothing*, 298–99.

6. On to Vicksburg

1. Reese, *Report of the Adjutant General*, 361; Woodworth, *Nothing*, 298; Cowan to daughter, February 25, 1863, *GPL*; *Galena Daily Advertiser*, March 11, 1863; Crummer, *With Grant*, 107.

2. Ballard, *Vicksburg*, 24–29, 53, 82; Smith, *Union Assaults*, 2; Chernow, *Grant*, 245.

3. Cowan to daughter, February 23, 1863, *GPL*; Cowan Diary, February 23, 1863, *GPL*; Hewett et al., *Supplements*, pt. 2, vol. 11, 402, 413; Crouch, Silencing, 43; Reese, *Report of the Adjutant General*, 361; Woodworth, *Nothing*, 298–99, 301; Welcher, *Union Army*, 2:860–61; *OR*, ser. 1, vol. 24, pt. 1, 15–16; *Galena Daily Advertiser*, March 11, 1863; Bonney to wife, March 12, 1863, Armstrong, "Civil War Letters of Bonney," *VNMP*; Scarborough, *Masters*, 299; Danielson, *War's Desolating Scourge*, 65–76.

4. Cowan Diary, February 23, to daughter, February 25, 1863, *GPL*; Jones, "Father's Personal History," 63, *FHS*; Crouch, Silencing, 43; Adair, *Historical*, 9; Woodworth, *Nothing*, 299–300; Bearss, *Campaign*, 1:470, 474–75; *Warren Independent*, March 26, 1863; *Galena Daily Advertiser*, March 11, 1863; Bonney to wife, March 12, 1863, Armstrong, "Civil War Letters of Bonney," *VNMP*; Miller, *Vicksburg*, 281; Simpson, *Let Us Have Peace*, 36–37; Gallagher, *Union*, 145,

5. *Galena Daily Advertiser*, March 11, 1863; Cowan to daughter, April 17, 1863, *GPL*; *Waukegan Weekly Gazette*, April 18, 1863; Crouch, Silencing, 43; Miller, *Vicksburg*, xvii, 264, 268, 309–12.

6. Cowan to Olds, February 25, 1863, *GPL*; *Galena Daily Advertiser*, March 11, 17, 21, 1863; *Warren Independent*, March 26, 1863; *Waukegan Weekly Gazette*, April 18, 1863; Teters, *Practical Liberators*, 65–67; Miller, *Vicksburg*, 312–14.

7. Cowan Diary, March 14–17, 1863, *GPL*; Cowan to wife, March 17, 1863, *GPL*; Woodworth, *Nothing*, 302; Bearss, *Campaign*, 1:477; Hewett et al., *Supplement*, pt. 2, vol. 11, 402, 413; Wesley, *Politics of Faith*, 2, 143–46, 151–52; Cashin, *War Stuff*, 7–8, 120.

8. Woodworth, *Nothing*, 302; Cowan Diary, March 17, 1863, *GPL*; Cowan to wife, March 17, 1863, *GPL*; Hewett et al., *Supplement*, pt. 2, vol. 11, 402, 413; Reese, *Report of the Adjutant General*, 361.

9. Cowan to daughter, March 20, 27, 1863, to Cain, March 21, 1863, *GPL*; Manning, *What This Cruel War*, 101.

10. Frohock to Fuller, December 18, 1862, *GPL*; Cowan to daughter, March 6, 1863, to Frohock, March 7, 1863, to wife, Harriet, March 12, 1863, to children, April 12, 1863, and to daughter, April 17, 1863, *GPL*; Cowan Diary, March 2, 28, April 12, 1863, *GPL*; Delaney, *Maltby Brothers' Civil War*, 117; Chernow, *Grant*, 307; Office of the Illinois Secretary of State, Muster and Descriptive Rolls.

11. Cowan to daughter, April 17, 1863, *GPL*; Hardee to Smith, April 1863, *GPL*; Ballard, *Vicksburg*, 192–94; *OR*, ser. 1, vol. 52, pt. 1, 354; Hewett et al., *Supplement*, pt. 2, vol. 11, 402, 413–14; Bearss, *Campaign*, 2:272; Simpson, *Ulysses S. Grant*, 182; MOLLUS, *Memorials*, 38–40.

12. *OR*, ser 1, vol. 24, pt. 1, 20–21, 24, 30, 73, 76–77; Miller, *Vicksburg*, 309–14, 316–17, 321–24, 327–32, 345–50; Welcher, *Union Army*, 2:861; Crouch, Silencing, 43; Joiner, "Running the Gauntlet," 11; Reese, *Report of the Adjutant General*, 361 Hewett et al., *Supplement*, pt. 2, vol. 11, 414; Woodworth, *Nothing*, 303–11; Cowan Diary, April 18–19, 1863, *GPL*; Smith, *Union Assaults*, 34–35.

13. Grant, *Civil War*, 156; *OR*, ser. 1, vol. 24, pt. 1, 47, 78; Joiner, "Running the Gauntlet," 15; Reese, *Report of the Adjutant General*, 361; Adair, *Historical*, 9–10; Miller, *Vicksburg*, 352; Groom, *Vicksburg*, 166; Crummer, *With Grant*, 93; Bearss, *Campaign*, 2:75–76; Reed, *Back-Bone*, 191–92; *Waukegan Weekly Gazette*, May 30, 1863; Cowan Diary, April 21–22, 1863, *GPL*; Cowan to wife, April 22, 1863, *GPL*; Woodworth, *Nothing*, 326; *Biographical Review*, 433; *Galena Daily Advertiser*, May 11, 1863; Illinois-Vicksburg Military Park Commission, *Illinois*, 191.

14. *OR*, ser. 1, vol. 24, pt. 1, 78, 567; Miller, *Vicksburg*, 352; *Waukegan Weekly Gazette*, May 30, 1863; Bearss, *Campaign*, 2:74,76; Ballard, *Vicksburg*, 200; Cowan to wife, April 22, 1863, *GPL*; *Phillipsburg Herald*, July 7, 1898; *Galena Daily Advertiser*, May 11, 1863; Woodworth, *Nothing*, 326, 328–29; Joiner, "Running the Gauntlet," 13.

15. *Waukegan Weekly Gazette*, May 30, 1863; Reese, *Report of the Adjutant General*, 361; Bearss, *Campaign*, 2:77–78; *OR*, ser. 1, vol. 24, pt. 1,79; Woodworth, *Nothing*, 330.

16. *OR*, ser. 1, vol. 24, pt. 1, 565, 567–69; *Galena Daily Advertiser*, May 11, 1863; Reese, *Report of the Adjutant General*, 361; Adair, *Historical*, 9–10; *Phillipsburg Herald*, July 7, 1898; Woodworth, *Nothing*, 328–30.

17. Reese, *Report of the Adjutant General*, 361; Adair, *Historical*, 9–10; *OR*, ser. 1, vol. 24, pt. 1,79; Reed, *Back-Bone*, 192; *Phillipsburg Herald*, July 7, 1898; Crummer, *With Grant*, 94; *Biographical Review*, 433; Bearss, *Campaign*, 2:79.

18. Crummer, *With Grant*, 91, 93; Adair, *Historical*, 10; *OR*, ser. 1, vol. 24, pt. 1, 5; Cowan to Rindlaub, April 21, 1863, *GPL*; Stabler and Hershock, "'Standing,'" 33; Wiley, *Life of Billy Yank*, 120–21; McPherson, *Cause*, 126–27; McPherson, *Ordeal*, 379–80; Jimerson, *Private*, 47, 90, 92–93, 95–96, 102, 247–48; Logue, *To Appomattox*, 15, 43–44, 57; Miller, *Vicksburg*, 323–24, 337–38; Teters, *Practical Liberators*, 77–78.

19. Hewett et al., *Supplement*, pt. 2, vol. 11, 402, 403, 414; *OR*, ser. 1, vol. 24, pt. 1, 31; *Waukegan Weekly Gazette*, June 20, 1863; Cowan to daughter, May 5, 1863, and to wife, May 6, 1863, *GPL*; Cowan Diary, April 25–27, 1863, *GPL*; Grant, *Civil War*, 155; Miller, *Vicksburg*, 355–57; Chernow, *Grant*, 257.

20. Hewett et al., *Supplement*, pt. 2, vol. 11, 414; Cowan Diary, April 27–28, 1863, *GPL*; Cowan to daughter, May 5, 1863, *GPL*; Chernow, *Grant*, 257; Miller, *Vicksburg*, 352; Bearss, *Campaign*, 2:300; Crouch, Silencing, 55; Post, *Soldiers' Letters*, 263.

21. Grant, *Civil War*, 157–58, 160–61; Cowan Diary, April 30, 1863, *GPL*; Hewett et al., *Supplement*, pt. 2, vol. 11, 403, 414; *OR*, ser. 1, vol. 24, pt. 1, 634, 642; *Galena Daily Advertiser*, June 6, 1863; Ballard, *Vicksburg*, 218–24; Bearss, *Campaign*, 2:305, 315; Woodworth, *Nothing*, 335–37; Miller, *Vicksburg*, 341; Joiner, "Running the Gauntlet," 17; Feis, "Developed by Circumstances," 162; Illinois-Vicksburg Military Park Commission, *Illinois*, 192. Generals McPherson and Logan, in their reports in the *OR*, stated that the 17th Corps and 3rd Division crossed over the Mississippi River at Hard Times Landing. However, Bearss, *Campaign*, 2:346, has the 17th Corps crossing at Disharoon's Plantation, where the 13th Corps crossed.

22. Cowan Diary, May 1, 1863, *GPL*; Cowan to daughter, May 5, 1863, *GPL*; *OR*, ser. 1, vol. 24, pt. 1, 3, 32; Adair, *Historical*, 10; Hewett et al., *Supplement*, pt. 2, vol. 11, 403, 414; Miller, *Vicksburg*, xvi, 364, 371; Grant, *Civil War*, 162.

23. Miller, *Vicksburg*, 373–74; Cowan Diary, May 1, 1863, *GPL*; Cowan to daughter, May 5, 1863, *GPL*; *OR*, ser. 1, vol. 24, pt. 1, 32, 49, 634, 643; *OR*, ser. 1, vol. 24, pt. 3, 262; Frawley, "In the Enemy's Country," 58–59; Welcher, *Union Army*, 2:866, 868; Bearss, *Campaign*, 2:366–67; Grant, *Civil War*, 162; Adair, *Historical*, 10; Hewett et al., *Supplement*, pt. 2, vol. 11, 403, 414; Smith to Townes, May 5, 1863, *ALPL*; Hess, *Civil War*, 93, 112; Post, *Soldiers' Letters*, 264.

24. Smith to Townes, May 5, 1863, *ALPL*; Bearss, *Campaign*, 2:400; Cowan Diary, May 1–2, 1863, *GPL*; Cowan to daughter, May 5, 1863, *GPL*; Miller, *Vicksburg*, 358–63, 372; Simpson, *Ulysses S. Grant*, 192; Joiner, "Running the Gauntlet," 17–19; Feis, "Developed by Circumstances," 154; *OR*, ser. 1, vol. 24, pt. 1, 35, 49, 634, 643; Post, *Soldiers' Letters*, 264; Hewett et al., *Supplement*, pt. 2, vol. 11, 403, 414; Adair, *Historical*, 10; Crummer, *With Grant*, 97–98; Smith to wife, May 5, 1863, *GPL*.

25. *Waukegan Weekly Gazette*, June 20, 1863; *Galena Daily Advertiser*, June 6, 1863; *OR*, ser. 1, vol. 24, pt. 1, 34, 582–85, 668; Smith to wife, May 5, 1863, *GPL*; Office of the Illinois Secretary of State, Muster and Descriptive Rolls.

26. Grant, *Civil War*, 163; Smith, *Union Assaults*, 36; Bearss, *Campaign*, 2:411–12; Miller, *Vicksburg*, 375–76; Cowan Diary, May 2, 1863, *GPL*; Post,

Soldiers' Letters, 264; *OR*, ser. 1, vol. 24, pt. 1, 32, 635, 644, 706–7; Hewett et al., *Supplement*, pt. 2, vol. 11, 403, 414; Simpson, *Ulysses S. Grant*, 192, 196.

27. Ballard, *Vicksburg*, 243–48, 253–55, 257; *OR*, ser. 1, vol. 24, pt. 1, 33, 636; Bearss, *Campaign*, 2:435–36, 443, 452; Smith, *Union Assaults*, 39; Dossman, "'Stealing Tour,'" 194, 197, 198–200; Miller, *Vicksburg*, 376–77, 379–80, 383–84; Simpson, *Ulysses S. Grant*, 193; Frawley, "In the Enemy's Country," 72; Hewett et al., *Supplement*, pt. 2, vol. 11, 403, 414; Crummer, *With Grant*, 99; Cowan Diary, May 7, 1863, *GPL*; Chernow, *Grant*, 260, 262.

28. Cowan Diary, May 12, 1863, *GPL*; Ballard, *Vicksburg*, 261; Bearss, *Campaign*, 2:489; *OR*, ser. 1, vol. 24, pt. 1, 3, 636–37, 645; Hewett et al., *Supplement*, pt. 2, vol. 11, 403, 414; Jones, "Father's Personal History," 63, *FHS*; Miller, *Vicksburg*, 385.

29. *OR*, ser. 1, vol. 24, pt. 1, 50, 636, 644–45; Hewett et al., *Supplement*, pt. 2, vol. 11, 403, 414–15; *Warren Independent*, June 4, 1863; Crummer, *With Grant*, 99.

30. *OR*, ser. 1, vol. 24, pt. 1, 644–46, 707–8, 711–12; *Carroll County Mirror*, June 17, 1863; Hewett et al., *Supplement*, pt. 2, vol. 11, 403, 414; *Galena Daily Advertiser*, June 6, 10, 1863; Hills, "Road to Raymond," 85–86; Hess, *Civil War*, 128; Adair, *Historical*, 10; Miller, *Vicksburg*, 385–86; Newsome, *Experience*, 45; Cowan Diary, May 12, 1863, *GPL*.

31. Hewett et al., *Supplement*, pt. 2, vol. 11, 415; Crummer, *With Grant*, 99; *OR*, ser. 1, vol. 24, pt. 1, 36, 50, 636, 646, 705–8, 739; Bearss, *Campaign*, 2:511; *Galena Daily Advertiser*, June 10, 1863; Miller, *Vicksburg*, 386; Cowan Diary, May 12, 1863, *GPL*; Adair, *Historical*, 10; *Waukegan Weekly Gazette*, June 20, 1863; *Warren Independent*, June 4, 1863; Office of the Illinois Secretary of State, Muster and Descriptive Rolls; Regimental Medical Records, *NA*; Rock Island Argus, August 26, 1909; *Galena Daily Advertiser*, June 6, 1863; Compiled Military Service Records, *NA*.

32. Cowan to daughter, May 5, 1863, and to wife, May 6, 1863, *GPL*; Crummer, *With Grant*, 100; Ballard, *Vicksburg*, 258; Dossman, "'Stealing Tour,'" 196, 202–3; *Waukegan Weekly Gazette*, June 20, 1863; Miller, *Vicksburg*, 386; Office of the Illinois Secretary of State, Muster and Descriptive Rolls; Regimental Medical Records, *NA*.

33. Ballard, *Vicksburg*, 254, 271; Miller, *Vicksburg*, 387; *Waukegan Weekly Gazette*, June 20, 1863; *OR*, ser. 1, vol. 24, pt. 1, 50; Simpson, *Ulysses S. Grant*, 196–97; Cowan Diary, May 13, 1863, *GPL*; Woodworth, "First Capture," 98; Post, *Soldiers' Letters*, 266.

34. *Galena Daily Advertiser,* June 6, 10, 1863; Cowan Diary, May 15, 1863, *GPL*; Ballard, *Vicksburg,* 275–78; Bearss, *Campaign,* 2:530–44; Woodworth, *Nothing,* 364–65; Woodworth, "First Capture," 100; Crummer, *With Grant,* 99–102; *OR,* ser. 1, vol. 24, pt. 1, 4, 36, 638; Billings, *Hardtack,* 246; Dossman, "'Stealing Tour,'" 204–8.

35. Crummer, *With Grant,* 100, 102; *OR,* ser. 1, vol. 24, pt. 1, 709; Cowan Diary, May 15, 1863, *GPL*; Miller, *Vicksburg,* 391–93; Post, *Soldiers' Letters,* 266.

36. Cowan Diary, May 15–16, 1863, *GPL*; Adair, *Historical,* 10; Miller, *Vicksburg,* 396; Simpson, *Ulysses S. Grant,* 199; Feis, "Developed by Circumstances," 167; *OR,* ser. 1, vol. 24, pt. 1, 50–51, 639, 646; *OR,* ser. 1, vol. 24, pt. 2, 3, 639, 646, 709; Hewett et al., *Supplement,* pt. 2, vol. 11, 403, 415; Smith, *Union Assaults,* 42; *Waukegan Weekly Gazette,* June 20, 1863; Bellingall, "Autobiography," 20, *GPL*; Crouch, Silencing, 81.

37. *OR,* ser. 1, vol. 24, pt. 1, 639–40, 646–48, 709, 712–13; *OR,* ser. 1, vol. 24, pt. 2, 116; Hewett et al., *Supplement,* pt. 2, vol. 11, 403, 415; Bellingall, "Autobiography," 20–21, *GPL*; Woodworth, "First Capture," 106–7; Miller, *Vicksburg,* 399–404; Woodworth, *Nothing,* 172; Post, *Soldiers' Letters,* 267; Crummer, *With Grant,* 103–4; *Waukegan Weekly Gazette,* June 20, 1863; Smith, *Union Assaults,* 42; Adair, *Historical,* 10; *Galena Daily Advertiser,* June 6, 1863; Simpson, *Ulysses S. Grant,* 200.

38. *OR,* ser. 1, vol. 24, pt. 2, 7–10; *OR,* ser. 1, vol. 24, pt. 1, 648; Hewett et al., *Supplement,* pt. 2, vol. 11, 403, 415; *Galena Daily Advertiser,* June 6, 1863; Crummer, *With Grant,* 104. Woodworth, *Nothing,* 387, says 15,500 Union soldiers took part in the battle while 17,500 were idle, for a total of 33,000. Smith, *Champion,* 372, and Miller, *Vicksburg,* 407, both state that a little more than 29,000 men were on the field. The former notes that only 15,380 actively took part in the fighting.

39. Jones, "Father's Personal History," 63–64, *FHS*; *Waukegan Weekly Gazette,* June 20, 1863; *OR,* ser. 1, vol. 24, pt. 1, 58; Crummer, *With Grant,* 104–7; Post, *Soldiers' Letters,* 267; Woodworth, *Nothing,* 388–89; Miller, *Vicksburg,* 407; *Galena Daily Advertiser,* June 22, 1863.

40. Bellingall, "Autobiography," 20–22, *GPL.*

41. *OR,* ser. 1, vol. 24, pt. 1, 640, 709; Bearss, *Campaign,* 3:751; Cowan Diary, May 17, 1863, *GPL*; Hess, *Storming,* 55, 110; Smith, *Union Assaults,* 21, 82–83, 91, 63, 65, 67; Simpson, *Ulysses S. Grant,* 202. Post, *Soldiers' Letters,* 267–68; Adair, *Historical,* 10; *Galena Daily Advertiser,* June 6, 22, 1863; Hewett et al., *Supplement,* pt. 2, vol. 11, 403, 415; Crummer, *With Grant,* 107; Reese, *Report of the Adjutant General,* 361.

42. *OR,* ser. 1, vol. 24, pt. 1, 641, 648.

7. Sacrifice in the "Death Hole"

1. Smith, *Siege*, xix.

2. Reese, *Report of the Adjutant General*, 361; Crummer, *With Grant*, 106–7, 110; Bearss, *Campaign*, 3:791–92; Smith, *Union Assaults*; 144: Grant, *Civil War*, 184–86; Woodworth, *Nothing*, 399, 406; Miller, *Vicksburg*, 414; Hess, *Storming*, 24, 65–66, 76–78; Dossman, "'Stealing Tour,'" 197–98, 209–10.

3. Crummer, *With Grant*, 132–34; *OR*, ser. 1, vol. 24, pt. 1, 87, 89 and ser. 1, vol. 24, pt. 2, 169–70; Hess, *Storming*, 17; Smith, *Union Assaults*, 22–23, 139–44; Bearss, *Campaign*, 3:795–96; Reese, *Report of the Adjutant General*, 361; *Galena Daily Advertiser*, June 22, 1863; *Waukegan Weekly Gazette*, June 20, 1863; Evening Statesman, July 7, 1905.

4. *OR*, ser. 1, vol. 24, pt. 1, 55; Grant, *Civil War*, 186; Simpson, *Ulysses S. Grant*, 203. Crummer, *With Grant*, 108; Hess, *Storming*, xiv, xvi, 43, 63, 295; Leggett to son, August 9, 1863, *VNMP*; Bearss, *Campaign*, 3:787; Woodworth and Grear, *Vicksburg Campaign*, 3; Smith, *Union Assaults*, 77, 131, 148–49, 153.

5. *Galena Daily Advertiser*, June 22, 1863; Simpson, *Ulysses S. Grant*, 203. Bearss, *Campaign*, 3:819–20, 846; Hess, *Storming*, 112; Crummer, *With Grant*, 110–11; Smith, *Union Assaults*, 24, 183–84, 193–97; *OR*, ser. 1, vol. 24, pt. 1, 170, 710.

6. Crummer, *With Grant*, 112–14; Smith, *Union Assaults*, 194, 271–73, 306; *OR*, ser. 1, vol. 24, pt. 1, 170, 710; Bellingall, "Autobiography," 19, *GPL*; Dan Cowan to Harriet Cowan, May 25, 1863, *GPL*; Adair, *Historical*, 11; Woodworth, *Nothing*, 422; Post, *Soldiers' Letters*, 269.

7. Crummer, *With Grant*, 112–14; *OR*, ser. 1, vol. 24, pt. 1, 37, 710; Hewett et al., *Supplement*, pt. 2, vol. 11, 403–4; Olds to father, May 25, 1863, *GPL*; Adair, *Historical*, 11; National Tribune, May 21, 1885, December 15, 1892; Hess, *Civil War*, 153–54; Smith, *Union Assaults*, 184–85, 306–8; Bearss, *Campaign*, 3:858.

8. *OR*, ser. 1, vol. 24, pt. 1, 89; Bearss, *Campaign*, 3: 860–61; Miller, *Vicksburg*, 430–31; Hess, *Storming*, 11–12, 261, 263–70, 291–92, 295; Smith, *Siege*, 82–85, 88; Smith, *Union Assaults*, 72, 186; Jones to wife, May 27, 1863, Jones Papers, *FHS*; Post, *Soldiers' Letters*, 268–69; *Galena Daily Advertiser*, June 22, 29, 1863; Williamson to sister, May 25, 1863, *WSS*.

9. *OR*, ser. 1, vol. 24, pt. 2, 160–65; Bearss, *Campaign*, 3:867; Hess, *Storming*, 68; Crummer, *With Grant*, 112; Office of the Illinois Secretary of State, Muster and Descriptive Rolls; Dan Cowan to Harriet Cowan, May 25, 1863, *GPL*; *Warren Independent*, June 18, 1863.

10. Olds to father, May 25, 1863, *GPL*; *Galena Daily Advertiser*, June 6, 22, 1863; Woodworth, *Nothing*, 428; Reese, *Report of the Adjutant General*, 361; Smith to wife, May 31, 1863, *GPL*; *Waukegan Weekly Gazette*, June 20, 1863; Adair, *Historical*, 11; *Warren Independent*, June 11, 1863, March 31, 1864.

11. *OR*, ser. 1, vol. 24, pt. 1, 37 and ser. 1, vol. 24, pt. 2, 293; Smith *Union*, 343, 351; Hickenlooper, "Vicksburg Mine," 539; Miller, *Vicksburg*, 433; Hewett et al., *Supplement*, pt. 2, vol. 11, 403–4, 415; Solonick, "Andrew Hickenlooper," 80; Crummer, *With Grant*, 109–10.

12. *OR*, ser. 1, vol. 24, pt. 1, 56; Williamson to sister, May 25, 1863, *WSS*; Hess, *Storming*, 240–41; Smith to wife, May 31, 1863, *GPL*; Crummer, *With Grant*, 144; *Galena Daily Advertiser*, June 12, 29, 1863; Beck, "True Sketch," 10, 12–13, *VNMP*; Hickenlooper, "Vicksburg Mine," 540; Bearss, *Campaign*, 3:907–8, 911; Steplyk, "Plying," 50, 53–54, 60; Hess, *Civil War*, 202–3.

13. Hickenlooper, "Vicksburg Mine," 539–40; Catton, *Grant Moves*, 469; *OR*, ser. 1, vol. 24, pt. 2, 171, 199; Beck, "True Sketch," 14, 18; Crummer, *With Grant*, 117; Miller, *Vicksburg*, 463; Bearss, *Campaign*, 3:907–8, 910, 912; Solonick, "Andrew Hickenlooper," 83; Hess, *Storming*, 168–69; Smith, *Siege*; 86, 314; Ernst, *Manual*, 64, 70; Steplyk, "Plying," 62.

14. Strong, "Campaign," 337–38; Bearss, *Campaign*, 3:908, 910, 912, 929–30; Gabel, *Staff Ride*, 172; *OR*, ser. 1, vol. 24, pt. 1, 88, 90–91, 99 and ser. 1, vol. 24, pt. 2, 173, 199–200, 293; Beck, "True Sketch," 10, 14, *VNMP*; Steplyk, "Plying," 52, 59; Hickenlooper, "Vicksburg Mine," 540; Smith, *Siege*, 66, 313; Woodworth and Grear, "Nights at Vicksburg," 69–70; Crummer, *With Grant*, 118–19.

15. Crummer, *With Grant*, 120–21, 124–26, 128–29; Beck, "True Sketch," 10, 12, *VNMP*; Miller, *Vicksburg*, 468; Adair, *Historical*, 12; Jones, "Father's Personal History," 65, *FHS*; *Galena Daily Advertiser*, June 10, 1863; *OR*, ser. 1, vol. 24, pt. 1, 39–40; *OR*, ser. 1, vol. 24, pt. 3, 352–53; Simms, "Louisiana," 374, 376; Bledsoe, *Citizen-Officers*, 146, 182; Carmichael, *War*, 203; Woodworth and Grear, "Nights at Vicksburg," 70–71, 73; Steplyk, "Plying," 49; Smith, *Siege*, 97, 131, 139–41, 155, 167, 189–90, 225, 231, 233–35, 297–98, 300–301.

16. Simms, "Louisiana," 373–76; Illinois-Vicksburg Military Park Commission, *Illinois*, 42; Smith, *Siege*, 129–30, 133–35, 146, 192, 196–97, 203–4, 213; Beck, "True Sketch," 13, GNP; Miller, *Vicksburg*, 435, 441.

17. Crummer, *With Grant*, 117; Office of the Illinois Secretary of State, Muster and Descriptive Rolls; Regimental Medical Records, *NA*; Steplyk, "Plying," 60–61.

18. Chernow, *Grant*, 278; Miller, *Vicksburg*, 432; Simpson, *Ulysses S. Grant*, 205, 209; Gallagher, *Union*, 133–34; Crummer, *With Grant*, 127–28, 155–56; National Tribune, July 1898; Office of the Illinois Secretary of State, Muster and Descriptive Rolls; Regimental Medical Records, *NA*; Smith to wife, June 7, 1863, *GPL*; *OR*, ser. 1, vol. 24, pt. 2, 155; Bearss, *Campaign*, 3:883; Smith, *Siege*, 258–59; *Galena Daily Advertiser*, July 1, 1863.

19. Adair, *Historical*, 11; *OR*, vol. 24, pt. 1, 99, 108; *OR*, ser. 1, vol. 24, pt. 2, 173, 202, 207, 293; Solonick, "Andrew Hickenlooper," 82–83, 85–86, 92; Solonick, Engineering Victory, 181, 187; Miller, *Vicksburg*, 462, 464; Bearss, *Campaign*, 3:913, 915; Illinois-Vicksburg Military Park Commission, *Illinois*, 192; Hickenlooper, "Vicksburg Mine," 540–42; Smith, *Siege*, 67, 366, 381; Crummer, *With Grant*, 123, 136; Reed, *Back-Bone*, 192; *Keithsburg Observer*, June 22, 1863.

20. Bellingall, "Autobiography," 24, *GPL*; National Tribune, February 9, 1893; Carmichael, *War*, 5, 133.

21. *OR*, ser. 1, vol. 24, pt. 1, 109; *OR*, ser. 1, vol. 24, pt. 2, 202, 294; *OR*, ser. 1, vol. 24, pt. 3, 440; Solonick, "Andrew Hickenlooper," 93; Miller, *Vicksburg*, 464; Hickenlooper, "Vicksburg Mine," 540; Bearss, *Campaign*, 3:915; Woodworth, *Nothing*, 441; Beck, "True Sketch," 14, *VNMP*; *Chicago Tribune*, July 6, 1863; Crummer to Rigby, October 21, 1902, *VNMP*; *Chicago Tribune*, July 6, 1863; Grant, *Civil War*, 196; Adair, *Historical*, 11; Bellingall, "Autobiography," 25; Corbin, "Biography," 44; Post, *Soldiers' Letters*, 270; Smith, *Siege*, 387.

22. *Galena Daily Advertiser*, July 3, 1863; Woodworth, *Nothing*, 442; Newsome, *Experience*, 19; Hickenlooper, "Vicksburg Mine," 540–42; Solonick, "Andrew Hickenlooper," 85, 94–95; Post, *Soldiers' Letters*, 270; Bearss, *Campaign*, 3:918; Bellingall, "Autobiography," 25, *GPL*; Crummer, *With Grant*, 136–37; Smith, *Siege*, 389; Miller, *Vicksburg*, 465.

23. Crummer, *With Grant*, 138, 140; Hickenlooper, "Vicksburg Mine," 542; *OR*, ser. 1, vol. 24, pt. 1, 109; *OR*, ser. 1, vol. 24, pt. 2, 294; Solonick, "Andrew Hickenlooper," 87, 95; Bearss, *Campaign*, 3:919; *Galena Daily Advertiser*, July 3, 1863; Strong, Campaign, 340–41; Corbin, "Biography," 44, *ALPL*; Reese, *Report of the Adjutant General*, 361; Tucker, *South's Finest*, 196; Adair, *Historical*, 11; Smith, *Siege*, 158, 386–87; Hewett et al., *Supplement*, pt. 2, vol. 11, 404, 415; *Galena Daily Advertiser*, July 3, 1863; *Chicago Tribune*, July 2, 1863; Barnet, *Martyrs*, 48; Nilsen, "Civil War Diary," 3.

24. *OR*, ser. 1, vol. 24, pt. 1, 99; Solonick, "Andrew Hickenlooper," 95, 97–98; Woodworth, *Nothing*, 443; Beck, "True Sketch," 14; Miller, *Vicksburg*, 465; Bassett to Edmiston, March 12, 1902, Beck to Rigby, March 12, 1902,

Bassett to Rigby, March 12, 1902, *VNMP*; Crummer, *With Grant*, 137, 167–68; Crummer to Rigby, October 21, 1902, *VNMP*; Hess, *Civil War*, 46; Office of the Illinois Secretary of State, Muster and Descriptive Rolls; *Clay Center Times*, September 7, 1893; Regimental Medical Records, *NA*.

25. *OR*, ser. 1, vol. 24, pt. 2, 207, 294; *OR*, ser. 1, vol. 24, pt. 3, 440; Solonick, "Andrew Hickenlooper," 96; Bearss, *Campaign*, 3:919; Crummer to Rigby, October 21, 1902, *VNMP*; Crummer, *With Grant*, 137, 140–41; Smith, *Siege*, 391; Corbin, "Biography," 41, *ALPL*; *Chicago Tribune*, July 14, 1863; Bellingall, "Autobiography," 25, *GPL*; *Wichita Daily Eagle*, January 9, 1902; *Colfax Chronicle*, December 23, 1911; *Freeport Bulletin*, July 16, 1863; Office of the Illinois Secretary of State, Muster and Descriptive Rolls; Regimental Medical Records, *NA*; Post, *Soldiers' Letters*, 270.

26. Beck, "True Sketch," 14–15, *VNMP*: *OR*, ser. 1, vol. 24, pt. 1, 109; *OR*, ser. 1, vol. 24, pt. 2, 173, 207, 294; Post, *Soldiers' Letters*, 270–71; Bearss, *Campaign*, 3:919–21, 925; Hickenlooper, "Vicksburg Mine," 542; Solonick, "Andrew Hickenlooper," 96–97; Smith, *Siege*, 393–395; Beck to Rigby, March 12, 1902, *VNMP*; Crummer to Rigby, October 21, 1902, *VNMP*; Crummer, *With Grant*, 138–39; Strong, Campaign, 342; Corbin, "Biography," 41–42, *ALPL*; *Galena Daily Advertiser*, August 8, 1863; Newsome, *Experience*, 19, 20; Jones, "Father's Personal History," 65, *FHS*; National Tribune, January 10, February 14, 1895.

27. Woodworth, *Nothing*, 441; Crummer to Rigby, October 21, 1902, *VNMP*; Crummer, *With Grant*, 141–42; *OR*, ser. 1, vol. 24, pt. 2, 173, 207, 294; Bearss, *Campaign*, 3:921, 924–25; Smith, *Siege*, 398; Hickenlooper, "Vicksburg Mine," 542; Bellingall, "Autobiography," 25, *GPL*; Western Reserve Chronicle, July 8, 1863; *Freeport Bulletin*, July 16, 1863; Nilsen, "Civil War Diary," 3; Strong, Campaign, 342. Crummer, *With Grant*, 137; Miller, *Vicksburg*, 466; Solonick, "Andrew Hickenlooper," 83–93, 99, 104.

28. Crummer, *With Grant*, 141–42; Adair, *Historical*, 11.

29. Tucker, *South's Finest*, 196, 198, 204; Hull Diary, June 25, 1863, *WSS*; Smith, *Siege*, 392; *Galena Daily Advertiser*, July 3, 1863, Bergeron, Jr., *Guide*, 78; Bearss, *Campaign*, 3:920.

30. *OR*, ser. 1, vol. 24, pt. 2, 167–68, 294–95, 373; Bearss, *Campaign*, 3:925; *Galena Daily Advertiser*, July 3, 1863; Reese, *Report of the Adjutant General*, 362; *Carroll County Weekly Mirror*, July 5, 1863; *Galena Daily Advertiser*, July 3, 21, 1863; *Keithsburg Observer*, July 16, 1863; *Belvidere Standard*, July 7, 21, 1863; *Daily Freeman*, July 3, 1863; Office of the Illinois Secretary of State, Muster and Descriptive Rolls; Regimental Medical Records, *NA*;

Compiled Military Service Records, *NA*; Western Reserve Chronicle, July 8, 1863.

31. *Carroll County Weekly Mirror*, July 5, 1863; Adair, *Historical*, 11; *Galena Daily Advertiser*, July 3, 1863; *Belvidere Standard*, July 7, 1863; Office of the Illinois Secretary of State, Muster and Descriptive Rolls; Barnet, *Martyrs*, 47–48; Rable, *God's*, 171, 175–76; *OR*, ser. 2, vol. 4, pt. 1, 476; *Rock River Democrat*, July 8, 15, 1863; Civil War Oath of Allegiance to U.S.A., Provost Marshal's Office, District of Memphis, Tenn. No. 1281, June 3, 1863; Regimental Medical Records, *NA*; Compiled Military Service Records, *NA*; *Galena Weekly Northwestern Gazette*, September 1, 1863; *Galena Daily Gazette*, April 9 1864.

32. Crummer, *With Grant*, 111–12, 137; Jones, "Father's Personal History," 65, *FHS*; Strong, Campaign, 341; Hewett et al., *Supplement*, pt. 2, vol. 11, 404, 415; Hickenlooper, "Vicksburg Mine," 542; *OR*, ser. 1, vol. 24, pt. 2, 173, 202–3; Bearss, *Campaign*, 3:927–28; Adair, *Historical*, 11; Grant, *Civil War*, 197; Post, *Soldiers' Letters*, 271; Bergeron, *Guide*, 78; Tucker, *South's Finest*, 200–201.

33. Smith, *Siege*, 409; Crummer, *With Grant*, 131, 150–51, 165.

34. Crummer, *With Grant*, 151–56.; McGinty, "Civil War"; Jim Flack, "Henry Winter" (memorial), Find a Grave, June 5, 2013, https://www.findagrave.com/memorial/111816510/henry-winter; Winter, *Baptism*, 220; Galena Weekly Gazette, March 2, 1916.

35. Miller, *Vicksburg*, 468, 471; Grant, *Civil War*, 200; Woodworth, *Nothing*, 449; Simpson, *Ulysses S. Grant*, 213; Smith, *Siege*, 401, 448, 475, 518; Crummer, *With Grant*, 114, 139–40, 158–59; Adair, *Historical*, 11–12; *OR*, ser. 1, vol. 24, pt. 2, 294; *OR*, ser. 1, vol. 24, pt. 3, 476; Post, *Soldiers' Letters*, 271; *Chicago Tribune*, July 14, 1863; Bellingall, "Autobiography," 25, *GPL*; Reese, *Report of the Adjutant General*, 362; Reed, *Back-Bone*, 192; *Galena Daily Advertiser*, August 8, 1863; *Clay Center Times*, September 7, 1893.

36. Crummer, *With Grant*, 140; Beck, "True Sketch," 16–17; Reed, *Back-Bone*, 7, 192; Bearss, *Campaign*, 3:1294–95; Miller, *Vicksburg*, 476–77; Jones, "Father's Personal History," 65, *FHS*; Jones to wife, July 4, 1863, Jones Papers, *GPL*; Post, *Soldiers' Letters*, 271–72; Strong, Campaign, 354; *Chicago Tribune*, July 14, 1863; Hewett et al., *Supplement*, pt. 2, vol. 11, 404; Illinois-Vicksburg Military Park Commission, *Illinois*, 49–50; Reese, *Report of the Adjutant General*, 362; Corbin, "Biography," 45–49, *ALPL*; *Waukegan Weekly Gazette*, July 18, 1863; *Galena Daily Advertiser*, August 8, 1863; Smith, *Siege*, 492–93; *Cleveland Morning Leader*, July 16, 1863; Woodworth, *Nothing*, 452–53, 455;

McPherson, *Battle Cry*, 638; Ballard, *Vicksburg*, 430; Coombe, *Thunder*, 232.

37. *Waukegan Weekly Gazette*, July 18, 1863; Crummer, *With Grant*, 123–24, 126, 143, 149, 157, 159–60; *Galena Daily Advertiser*, June 22, July 18, 21, August 8, 14, 17, 1863; *OR*, ser. 1, vol. 24, pt. 2, 175; *OR*, ser. 1, vol. 24, pt. 3, 477–79; Smith, *Siege*, 497–98, 510, 527; Miller, *Vicksburg*, 435; Simpson, *Ulysses S. Grant*, 212; *Belvidere Standard*, July 14, 1863; Bearss, *Campaign*, 3:1279, 1295; Jones, "Father's Personal History," 65, *FHS*; Stevens to Stevens, July 1863, *VNMP*; Hewett et al., *Supplement*, pt. 2, vol. 11, 404; Reese, *Report of the Adjutant General*, 362; *Warren Independent*, July 9, 1863.

38. Smith, *Union Assaults*, 26; Illinois-Vicksburg Military Park Commission, *Illinois*, 61–62, 66–68; Office of the Illinois Secretary of State, Muster and Descriptive Rolls; Grear, introduction to Vicksburg Besieged, 5; Bledsoe, *Citizen-Officers*, 88, 96–97, 100.

39. Post, *Soldiers' Letters*, 272; Carmichael, *War*, xv; Rable, *God's*, 1, 2,4, 5, 8, 9.

8. The Meridian Raid and Atlanta Campaign

1. *OR*, ser. 1, vol. 52, pt. 1, 435–36; *Cleveland Morning Leader*, July 16, 1863; *Chicago Tribune*, July 14, 1863; *Waukegan Weekly Gazette*, July 18, 1863; *Galena Daily Advertiser*, July 14, 15, August 8, 20, 1863; Office of the Illinois Secretary of State, Muster and Descriptive Rolls; *Warren Independent*, July 23, 1863; *Freeport Bulletin*, July 23, 1863; Adair, *Historical*, 12.

2. *Keithsburg Observer*, July 23, 1863; *Waukegan Weekly Gazette*, September 19, October 10, 1863; *Carroll County Weekly Mirror*, July 19, 1863; *Warren Independent*, July 30, 1863; Adair, *Historical*, 13; *Galena Daily Advertiser*, July 29, September 9, 22, 29, October 1, 1863.

3. Corbin, "Biography," 50, *ALPL*; Hewett et al., *Supplement*, pt. 2, vol. 11, 404; *Galena Daily Advertiser*, August 13, 20, September 3, 30, 1863; Adair, *Historical*, 12; *Galena Weekly Northwestern Gazette*, October 6, 1863.

4. *Galena Daily Advertiser*, October 6, 1863; Hewett et al., *Supplement*, pt. 2, vol. 11, 404, Reese, *Report of the Adjutant General*, 362; Roberts and Moneyhon, *Portraits*, 298; Jones to wife, October 20, 1863, *GPL*; Bellingall, "Autobiography," 25; *OR*, ser. 1, vol. 30, pt. 2, 802–5; *OR*, ser. 1, vol. 31, pt. 1, 822; Adair, *Historical*, 12–13; *Warren Independent*, November 12, 1863.

5. Reese, *Report of the Adjutant General*, 362; Adair, *Historical*, 13; Bledsoe, *Citizen-Officers*, 159, 219; Hewett et al., *Supplement*, pt. 2, vol. 11, 405, 416; Bellingall, "Autobiography," 25; Hess, *Civil War*, 72; *Galena Daily Advertiser*, December 2, 7, 1863; *Freeport Bulletin*, December 10, 1863; Office of

the Illinois Secretary of State, Muster and Descriptive Rolls; Regimental Order Book 4, *NA*.

6. Warrant Independent, November 12, 1863; *Galena Daily Advertiser*, October 12, 1863.

7. Jones to wife, November 1, 5, 20, December 31, 1863, *GPL*.

8. Nilsen, "Civil War Diary," 13; National Tribune, September 2, 1886; Billings, *Hardtack*, 70; *OR*, ser. 1, vol. 31, pt. 3, 564; General Orders No. 323, War Dept., Adjt. General's Office, September 28, 1863; Office of the Illinois Secretary of State, Muster and Descriptive Rolls.

9. Woodworth, *Nothing*, 488; Logue, *To Appomattox*, 55–56; Mitchell, *Civil War*, 182; Wiley, *Life of Billy Yank*, 342–43; McPherson, *Battle Cry*, 719–20; White, *Emancipation*, 89–90, 167–69; Fry, *Republic*, 129–31, 133; Hewett et al., *Supplement*, pt. 2, vol. 11, 405; Jones to wife, January 10, 1864, *GPL*; Adair, *Historical*, 13; Bellingall, "Autobiography," 25–26; Nilsen, "Civil War Diary," 15; *Galena Daily Advertiser*, February 5, 1864.

10. Reese, *Report of the Adjutant General*, 362; Grimsley, *Hard*, 4; Danielson, *War's Desolating Scourge*, 65–76; Hewett et al., *Supplement*, pt. 2, vol. 11, 405, 416; *OR*, ser. 1, vol. 32, pt. 1, 168, 172–73, 180, 182–86; Sherman, *Memoirs*, 1:394; Jones to wife, February 3, 1863, *GPL*; Marszalek, *Sherman's March*, 25; Foster, *Sherman's Mississippi Campaign*, 15, 38.

11. *OR*, ser. 1, vol. 32, pt. 1, 170, 174, 209, 225–26, 228; Compiled Military Service Records, *NA*; *Galena Daily Advertiser*, November 7, 1863; Nilsen, "Civil War Diary," 17–18.

12. *OR*, ser. 1, vol. 32, pt. 1, 173–74, 210–11, 226, 228, 235; Nilsen, "Civil War Diary," 18–19.

13. *OR*, ser. 1, vol. 32, pt. 1, 211, 226–28, 233–236, 362; Nilsen, "Civil War Diary," 19; Adair, *Historical*, 13; Hewett et al., *Supplement*, pt. 2, vol. 11, 405; Jones to wife, March 6, 1863, *GPL*; Foster, *Sherman's Mississippi Campaign*, 97.

14. Nilsen, "Civil War Diary," 19; *OR*, ser. 1, vol. 32, pt. 1, 211, 226–29, 233–34; Adair, *Historical*, 13; Reese, *Report of the Adjutant General*, 362; Hewett et al., *Supplement*, pt. 2, vol. 11, 405, 416; Office of the Illinois Secretary of State, Muster and Descriptive Rolls; Jones to wife, March 6, 1864, *GPL*.

15. *OR*, ser. 1, vol. 32, pt. 1, 173–74, 176, 211–13, 226; Smith, "Meridian," 1323–24.

16. *OR*, ser. 1, vol. 24, pt. 2, 167; *OR*, ser. 1, vol. 32, pt. 1, 187–88, 211–13, 226, 229, 231, 234; Nilsen, "Civil War Diary," 19–20; Hewett et al., *Supplement*, pt. 2, vol. 11, 405, 416; Williamson to brother, March 12, 1864, *WSS*; Foster, *Sherman's Mississippi Campaign*, 151, 164; Regimental Book 1; Nilsen, "Civil War Diary," 21–22.

17. *OR*, ser. 1, vol. 32, pt. 1, 177, 191–94, 212; *OR*, ser. 1, vol. 24, pt. 1, 6, 59; *Waukegan Weekly Gazette*, March 12, 1864; Jones to wife, March 6, 1863, *GPL*. Sherman lists in his report a direct loss of 170 soldiers, while the consolidated returns of casualties in the *OR* give a total of 729.

18. *OR*, ser. 1, vol. 32, pt. 1, 176, 178, 187, 212–13; *OR*, vol. 24, pt. 3, 249; *Waukegan Weekly Gazette*, March 12, 1864; Williamson to brother, March 12, 1864, *WSS*; Adair, *Historical*, 14; Smith, "Meridian Campaign," 1324; Foster, *Sherman's Mississippi Campaign*, 170–71.

19. *Galena Daily Advertiser*, February 8, 10–11, 1864; *Galena Daily Gazette*, February 16, 18–19, 24, March 1–4, 15, 1864; Office of the Illinois Secretary of State, Muster and Descriptive Rolls.

20. *OR*, ser. 1, vol. 32, pt. 1, 190, 607; Sherman, *Memoirs*, 1:405, vol. 2, 30; Robertson, *Soldiers*, 79; Williamson to brother, March 12, 1864, *WSS*; Jones to wife, March 6, 1863, *GPL*; *Galena Daily Gazette*, March 26, 1864; *Warren Independent*, May 19, 1864; Fish, *Forty-Fifth*, 5–6; Spirit of Democracy, March 30, 1864; Illinois-Vicksburg Military Park Commission, *Illinois*, 192; Nilsen, "Civil War Diary," 23; Adair, *Historical*, 13; Reese, *Report of the Adjutant General*, 362; Hewett et al., *Supplement*, pt. 2, vol. 11, 405, 416; *Cleveland Morning Leader*, March 24, 1864; Jones, "Father's Personal History," 65–66, *FHS*.

21. *Rock Island Daily Argus*, March 24, 1864; *Galena Daily Gazette*, March 26, 28, April 7, 27, 30, May 7, 1864; *Warren Independent*, March 31, 1864; Woodworth, *Nothing*, 489; Regimental Pension Records, *NA*.

22. Corbin, "Biography," 50–57, *ALPL*; Adair, *Historical*, 13.

23. Hewett et al., *Supplement*, pt. 2, vol. 11, 405, 416; Adair, *Historical*, 13; Reese, *Report of the Adjutant General*, 362; Jones, "Father's Personal History," 65, *FHS*; *Galena Daily Gazette*, May 7, 1864; *Keithsburg Observer*, May 12, 1864; Lawson to wife, April 29, 1864, *GPL*.

24. Hewett et al., *Supplement*, pt. 2, vol. 11, 416, 426; *OR*, ser. 1, vol. 32, pt. 3, 69, 519, 567; *OR*, ser. 1, vol. 38, pt. 3, 551; *OR*, ser. 1, vol. 39, pt. 2, 65; Corbin, "Biography," 57–58, *ALPL*; Adair, *Historical*, 14; Rock Island Argus, May 24, 1864; Jones to wife, May 14, 1864, Jones, "Father's Personal History," 66, *FHS*; Reese, *Report of the Adjutant General*, 362.

25. *OR*, ser. 1, vol. 38, pt. 3, 539, pt. 4, 131; Corbin, "Biography," 58–59, *ALPL*; Adair, *Historical*, 14; *Keithsburg Observer*, June 30, 1864; Lawson to wife, May 20, 1864, *GPL*; Fish, *Forty-Fifth*, 6; Hewett et al., *Supplement*, pt. 2, vol. 11, 416–17, 426; *Galena Daily Advertiser*, June 2, 1864.

26. Hewett et al., *Supplement*, 417; McDonald, *History*, 69; Adair, *Historical*, 14; Corbin, "Biography," 59, *ALPL*; Reese, *Report of the Adjutant General*, 362; *OR*, ser. 1, vol. 38, pt. 3, 539, 551 and ser. 1, vol. 32, pt. 3, 69; Lawson

to wife, May 20, 1864, *GPL*; *Galena Daily Advertiser*, June 2, 1864; *Keithsburg Observer*, June 30, 1864; Jones, "Father's Personal History," 66, *FHS*; Danielson, *War's Desolating Scourge*, 126–30.

27. Hewett et al., *Supplement*, pt. 2, vol. 11, 417, 426; *Galena Daily Advertiser*, June 2, 1864; *OR*, ser. 1, vol. 38, pt. 3, 540–41, 551–52; Corbin, "Biography," 59–60, *ALPL*; Adair, *Historical*, 14; Reese, *Report of the Adjutant General*, 362; McDonald, *History*, 69; *Keithsburg Observer*, June 30, 1864.

28. Hewett et al., *Supplement*, pt. 2, vol. 11, 416–17, 426; *Keithsburg Observer*, June 30, 1864; McDonald, *History*, 69; Adair, *Historical*, 14; Reese, *Report of the Adjutant General*, 362; Jones, "Father's Personal History," 66, *FHS*; Gaskill to wife, June 10, *ALPL*, *OR*, ser. 1, vol. 38, pt. 1, 61, 67; *OR*, ser. 1, vol. 38, pt. 3, 35, 570–71; Woodworth, *Nothing*, 517.

29. *OR*, ser. 1, vol. 38, pt. 1, 1, 3, 22, 59–60, 67; McPherson, *Ordeal*, 445–46.

30. Castel, *Decision*, 264, 266–67; *OR*, ser. 1, vol. 38, pt. 1, 61, 65, 67, 83, 110, 192; *OR*, ser. 1, vol. 38, pt. 3, 65, 558–59; Sherman, *Memoirs*, 2:46, 51; Corbin, "Biography," 65, 71, *ALPL*; Woodworth, *Nothing*, 517.

31. *Keithsburg Observer*, June 30, 1864; Lawson to wife, June 17, 1864, *GPL*; Gaskill to wife, June 10, 1864, *ALPL*; Adair, *Historical*, 14; *Galena Daily Gazette*, July 16, 1864; Fish, *Forty-Fifth*, 6.

32. Adair, *Historical*, 14; Gaskill to wife, June 10, July 4, 6, 1864, *ALPL*; Gaskill Diary, June 20, 1864, *ALPL*; Jones to wife, June 9, 13, 23, 1864, *GPL*; *Keithsburg Observer*, June 30, 1864; Lawson to wife, June 17, 1864, and to wife and children, July 3, 1864, *GPL*.

33. Adair, *Historical*, 14; Hammond to wife, July 7, 1864, 45th Illinois Folder, *WSS*; *Galena Daily Gazette*, July 16, 1864; Lawson to wife, June 17, July 3, October 26, 1864, *GPL*; Hammond to wife, July 7, 1864, *WSS*; Gaskill to wife, June 28, July 4, 1864, *ALPL*; Gaskill Diary, July 5, 1864, *ALPL*.

34. Jones to wife, June 9, 13, 23, July 6, 1864, *GPL*; Gaskill to wife, June 10, July 4, 6, August 21, September 22, 1864, *ALPL*; Billings, *Hardtack*, 300; Lawson to wife, June 17, 1864, and to wife and children, July 3, 1864, *GPL*; *Keithsburg Observer*, June 30, 1864.

35. Hammond to wife, July 7, 1864, *WSS*; *Galena Daily Gazette*, July 20, 1864; Adair, *Historical*, 14; Office of the Illinois Secretary of State, Muster and Descriptive Rolls; Gaskill to wife, July 4, 1864, *ALPL*; Gaskill Diary, July 4, 1864, *ALPL*; Towne, *Surveillance*, 13–14, 16, 39, 63–64, 66, 69, 72, 94–97, 99–103, 121, 128–30, 139, 151, 158, 166, 239, 250–51, 255–57, 262, 266, 271–76, 286, 289–90, 294–301, 312.

36. Lawson to wife, June 17, 1864, *GPL*; *Galena Daily Gazette*, July 20, 1864; Corbin, "Biography," 61–62, *ALPL*; Adair, *Historical*, 14; Gaskill to wife,

June 19, 1864, *ALPL*; Gaskill Diary, June 18, 20, 26, 1864, *ALPL*; Office of the Illinois Secretary of State, Muster and Descriptive Rolls; Sherman, *Memoirs*, 2:103.

37. Hewett et al., *Supplement*, pt. 2, vol. 11, 417, 426; Corbin, "Biography," 61, 144–45, *ALPL*; *Galena Daily Gazette*, July 20, 1864; *OR*, ser. 1, vol. 38, pt. 5, 26; Gaskill to wife, July 11, 15, 21, 24, 1864, *ALPL*; Gaskill Diary, July 12–14, 1864, *ALPL*; Adair, *Historical*, 14; Danielson, *War's Desolating Scourge*, 126–130.

38. Jones to wife, June 9, October 11, 1864, *GPL*; Gaskill to wife, July 24, August 12, 14, September 22, 1864, *ALPL*; Gaskill Diary, September 14, 1865, *ALPL*; Lawson to wife, June 17, August 15, September 7, October 13, November 13, 1864; Rable, *God's*, 1, 2, 4–5, 8–9, 90, 127–28, 142, 304–5, 340; Carmichael, *War*, 72–74.

39. Gaskill to wife, July 24, 1864, *ALPL*; Castel, *Decision*, 361, 383–84, 402; *OR*, ser. 1, vol. 38, pt. 1, 66, 71–73, 109, 132; *OR*, ser. 1, pt. 2, 29; *OR*, ser. 1, pt. 3, 20–21, 25, 39, 48, 543–44, 548, 550, 564; *OR*, ser. 1, vol. 44, 21; Tuthill, Artilleryman's Recollections, 296; Fish, *Forty-Fifth*, 6, 28.

40. Hewett et al., *Supplement*, pt. 2, vol. 11, 417–18, 426; Corbin, "Biography," 265–67, *ALPL*; *OR*, ser. 1, vol. 38, pt. 1, 82, 86–89; Woodworth, *Nothing*, 579–82; Lawson to wife, July 31, September 7, 8, 1864, *GPL*; National Tribune, April 5, 1888; Hammond to wife, September 8, 1864, *WSS*; Gaskill to wife, July 28, 30, September 9, 1864, *ALPL*; Hammond to wife, September 8, 1864, *WSS*.

41. Hewett et al., *Supplement*, pt. 2, vol. 11, 417–18, 426; Adair, *Historical*, 14; Gaskill Diary, July 26, 30, August 6, 21, 23, 1864, *ALPL*; Gaskill to wife, August 21, 23, 1864, *ALPL*; Hammond to wife, September 8, 1864, *WSS*; Corbin, "Biography," 146–48, 376, *ALPL*; Jones to wife, August 1, 1864, *GPL*; Evening Star, August 23, 1864; Lawson to wife, July 31, October 2, 1864, *GPL*; Office of the Illinois Secretary of State, Muster and Descriptive Rolls; *Waukegan Weekly Gazette*, September 16, 1864; Adair, *Historical*, 14.

42. Gaskill to wife, July 28, August 12, 14, 23, September 9, 12, 17, 1864, *ALPL*; Gaskill Diary, September 10, 1864, *ALPL*; Lawson to wife, September 7, 20, 1864, *GPL*; Fish, *Forty-Fifth*, 6–8.

43. Hewett et al., *Supplement*, pt. 2, vol. 11, 418, 427; Woodworth, *Nothing*, 585–87; Adair, *Historical*, 14–15; Castel, *Decision*, 552–53; Gaskill to wife, October 9, 1864, *ALPL*; Gaskill Diary, October 4–5, 7, 14–15, 1864, *ALPL*; Jones to wife, October 9, 11, 18, 1864, *GPL*; Lawson to wife, October 2, 13, 1864, *GPL*; *Galena Daily Advertiser*, October 10, December 8, 10, 1864;

Office of the Illinois Secretary of State, 1929 Illinois Roll of Honor, 1:113; Fry, *Republic*, 130.

44. Sherman, *Memoirs*, 2:166, 177; Castel, *Decision*, 553; Woodworth, *Nothing*, 586–87; Simpson, *Let Us Have Peace*, 68; Glatthaar, *March*, 6–7, 101.

45. Hewett et al., *Supplement*, pt. 2, vol. 11, 418, 427; *OR*, ser. 1, vol. 44, 34, 56; Gaskill Diary, November 9, 1864, *ALPL*; Orders, Blair to Boucher, November 8, 1864, *ALPL*; Regimental Order Book 4, *NA*; Woodworth, *Nothing*, 589; Davis, *Sherman's March*, 8; Corbin, "Biography," 287, *ALPL*; Leekly Diary, November 11, 1864; Adair, *Historical*, 14; Lawson Diary, November 10–14, 1864, *GPL*.

46. Collins, "Absentee Soldier Voting," 397; *Galena Daily Advertiser*, October 12, 1864; Bledsoe, *Citizen-Officers*, 221; McPherson, *Battle Cry*, 804; Woodworth, *Nothing*, 587; Manning, *What This Cruel War*, 183–84; McPherson, *Cause*, 129; White, *Emancipation*, 1–2, 4–6, 9–11, 115, 117–25; Fry, *Republic*, 8, 13–14, 54, 178, 182–83; Gallagher, *Union*, 53, 106–7; Lawson Diary, November 11, 1864, *GPL*.

47. Fish, *Forty-Fifth*, 8; National Tribune, November 3, 1887; Sherman, *Memoirs*, 2:172; *OR*, ser. 1, vol. 45, pt. 1, 102; Woodworth, *Nothing*, 587; Glatthaar, *March*, 19; Davis, *Sherman's March*, 10; Corbin, "Biography," 288, *ALPL*; *Galena Daily Gazette*, September 28, October 12, 25, December 9, 12, 14, 21, 1864, January 11, 21, February 2, May 18, 1865; Office of the Illinois Secretary of State, Muster and Descriptive Rolls.

9. The End of a Hard War

1. Glatthaar, *March*, 7–9; Woodworth, *Nothing*, 589, 594; *OR*, ser. 1, vol. 44, 7–8; Trudeau, "Stumbling"; Corbin, "Biography," 289, *ALPL*; Reese, *Report of the Adjutant General*, 362.

2. Woodworth, *Nothing*, 589, 594; *OR*, ser. 1, vol. 44, 7–8, 152; Trudeau, "Stumbling"; Corbin, "Biography," 289, *ALPL*; Cashin, *War Stuff*, 137.

3. Compiled Military Service Records, *NA*; Hewett et al., *Supplement*, pt. 2, vol. 11, 418; Corbin, "Biography," 292, 302, *ALPL*; *OR*, ser. 1, vol. 44, 8, 21, 34, 147, 149, 152–53, 848, 850–51; Woodworth, *Nothing*, 595, 597; Glatthaar, *March*, 136–138; Marszalek, *Sherman's March*, 67–68; Lawson Diary, November 15–16, 18, 20, 1864, *GPL*; *Keithsburg Observer*, January 19, 1865.

4. *OR*, ser. 1, vol. 44, 9, 34, 68, 148; Sherman, *Memoirs*, 2:192; Hewett et al., *Supplement*, pt. 2, vol. 11, 418; Leekly Diary, November 19–22, 1864; Corbin, "Biography," 299–300, *ALPL*; Woodworth, *Nothing*, 601; McDonald, *History*,

96; Davis, *Sherman's March*, 87–88; Glatthaar, *March*, 77; Marszalek, *Sherman's March*, 88–89.

5. Leekly Diary November 22 and December 17, 1864; Hewett et al., *Supplement*, pt. 2, vol. 11, 418, 427, 455; *OR*, ser. 1, vol. 44, 44, 67, 148, 152; Sherman, *Memoirs*, 2:181–83; Chernow, *Grant*, 458; Woodworth, *Nothing*, 603; *Keithsburg Observer*, January 19, 1865; Lawson Diary, November 15–20, 23, 1864, *GPL*; Lawson to wife, December 17, 1864, *GPL*; Rable, *God's*, 351; Corbin, "Biography," 294, 303–4, *ALPL*; McDonald, *History*, 95, 97.

6. *OR*, ser. 1, vol. 44, 9–10, 34–35, 71, 148, 152; Hewett et al., *Supplement*, pt. 2, vol. 11, 418, 427; McDonald, *History*, 97; Reese, *Report of the Adjutant General*, 362; Corbin, "Biography," 303–4, 309, *ALPL*; *Keithsburg Observer*, January 19, 1865; Lawson Diary, December 10, 1864, *GPL*; Marszalek, *Sherman's*, 101–2, Woodworth, *Nothing*, 603.

7. Lawson Diary, December 11–12, 14–16, 18–20, 1864, *GPL*; Corbin, "Autobiography," Corbin, "Biography," 304, 308, *ALPL*.

8. Lawson Diary, December 12–13, January 2, 1864, *GPL*; Lawson to wife, December 17, 1864, *GPL*; Corbin, "Biography," 305, 312, *ALPL*; *Keithsburg Observer*, January 19, 1865; *OR*, ser. 1, vol. 44, 15; Billings, *Hardtack*, 406; *Waukegan Weekly Gazette*, January 21, 1865.

9. *Keithsburg Observer*, January 19, 1865, *OR*, ser. 1, vol. 44, 7, 12, 35, 44, 57, 73, 152–53, Hewett et al., *Supplement*, pt. 2, vol. 11, 418, 427; Glatthaar, *March*, 9; McPherson, *Battle Cry*, 811.

10. *Waukegan Weekly Gazette*, December 31, 1864; *OR*, ser. 1, vol. 44, 13–14; Simpson, *Let Us Have Peace*, 72.

11. Sherman, *Memoirs*, 2:221; *OR*, ser. 1, vol. 44, 7, 14–15, 152; Woodworth, *Nothing*, 589–91; McDonald, *History*, 94; Bledsoe, *Citizen-Officers*, 185, 190, 200–201; Glatthaar, *March*, 119–33.

12. *OR*, ser. 1, vol. 44, 68, 76, 152; Lawson Diary, November 20–21, 24, 1864, *GPL*; *Waukegan Weekly Gazette*, January 21, 1865.

13. *OR*, ser. 1, vol. 44, 35; Lawson Diary, December 22–25, 27–28, 31, January 1, 1864, *GPL*; Corbin, "Biography," 316, *ALPL*; Jones, "Father's Personal History," 66–67, *FHS*.

14. Gaskill Monthly Medical Reports, *ALPL*, *OR*, ser. 1, vol. 44, 79; Office of the Illinois Secretary of State, Muster and Descriptive Rolls; Regimental Descriptive Rolls; Regimental Medical Records, *NA*.

15. Hewett et al., *Supplement*, pt. 2, vol. 11, 418; *OR*, ser. 1, vol. 47, pt. 1, 374; Lawson Diary, January 4–6, 1865, *GPL*; Manning, *What This Cruel War* 78–79, 154.

16. Lawson Diary, January 5–6, 12–14, 1865, *GPL*; Corbin, "Biography," 316–17, 320–22, *ALPL*; Hewett et al., *Supplement*, pt. 2, vol. 11, 419, 428; *OR*, ser. 1, vol. 47, pt. 1, 90, 97, 177, 374–75; Sherman, *Memoirs*, 2:239–40; Reese, *Report of the Adjutant General*, 362; McDonald, *History*, 97; Adair, *Historical*, 15; *Galena Daily Gazette*, February 4, 1865; *Galesburg Democrat*, February 16, 1865; Woodworth, *Nothing*, 607–8; Hammond to cousin, January 18, 1865, *WSS*.

17. Bellingall, "Autobiography," 33–34, *GPL*; Office of the Illinois Secretary of State, Muster and Descriptive Rolls; Abraham Lincoln, Proclamation 124—Offering Pardon to Deserters, March 11, 1865, American Presidency Project, https://www.presidency.ucsb.edu/node/202866.

18. Bellingall, "Autobiography," 34–36, *GPL*; *Galena Daily Gazette*, February 4, 1865; *Galesburg Democrat*, February 16, 1865; Hewett et al., *Supplement*, pt. 2, vol. 11, 419, 428; Corbin, "Biography," 325, *ALPL*; *OR*, ser. 1, vol. 47, pt. 1, 192; Lawson Diary, January 13–15, 1865, *GPL*.

19. *Galena Daily Gazette*, February 4, 1865; *Galesburg Democrat*, February 16, 1865; *OR*, ser. 1, vol. 47, pt. 1. 192; Hewett et al., *Supplement*, pt. 2, vol. 11, 419, 428; Corbin, "Biography," 320, *ALPL*; Lawson Diary, January 14, 1865, *GPL*; Gaskill Diary, January 15–16, 1865, *ALPL*; Office of the Illinois Secretary of State, Muster and Descriptive rolls.

20. *OR*, ser. 1, vol. 47, pt. 1, 17–18, 90, 97; *Galesburg Democrat*, February 16, 1865; Lawson Diary, January 17–22, 29, 1865, *GPL*; Hewett et al., *Supplement*, pt. 2, vol. 11, 419, 428; Sherman, *Memoirs*, 2:227–28; Gaskill Diary, January 22–23, 27, 29, 1865, *ALPL*; Woodworth, *Nothing*, 607; Hammond to cousin, January 18, 1865, to parents, January 29, 1865, to father, January 29, 1865, and to parents, January 29, 1865, *WSS*.

21. Gaskill Diary, January 30–31, 1865, *ALPL*; Lawson Diary, January 30, 31, 1865, *GPL*; Hewett et al., *Supplement*, pt. 2, vol. 11. 419, 428; Glatthaar, *March*, 12; Manning, *What This Cruel War* 187; *OR*, ser. 1, vol. 47, pt. 1, 19, 97, 169; Reese, *Report of the Adjutant General*, 362; Adair, *Historical*, 15; McDonald, *History*, 97.

22. Sherman, *Memoirs*, 2:277, 280, 286–87; Hewett et al., *Supplement*, pt. 2, vol. 11, 419, 428; Reese, *Report of the Adjutant General*, 362; Adair, *Historical*, 15; *OR*, ser. 1, vol. 47, pt. 1, 19–20, 97–98, 170, 197, 375–78, 404, 408; Corbin, "Biography," 328, 331, *ALPL*; Cashin, *War Stuff*, 157; Gaskill Diary, February 7, 12, 1865, *ALPL*; Hammond to cousin, March 30, 1865, and to parents, April 4, 1865, *WSS*; Neely, *Union*, 190; Rable, *God's*, 155, 257, 391.

23. *OR*, ser. 1, vol. 47, pt. 21–22, 97; 170–71; Woodworth, *Nothing*, 616; Davis, *Sherman's*, 161–64; Gaskill Diary, February 16, 1865, *ALPL*; Bellingall,

"Autobiography," 37, *GPL*; Corbin, "Biography," 333, *ALPL*; Hewett et al., *Supplement*, pt. 2, vol. 11, 419, 428; McDonald, *History*, 97–98; Glatthaar, *March*, xiii, xiv.

24. Corbin, "Biography," 324, 330–31, 334–35, *ALPL*; McDonald, *History*, 98; *OR*, vol. 47, pt. 1, 97–98, 380, 409; Bellingall, "Autobiography," 36, *GPL*; Gaskill Diary, February 1–2, 4–5, 7–11, 14, 17–22, 24–26, 28, 1865, *ALPL*; Lawson Diary, February 1–7, 18, 20–26, 28, 1865, *GPL*; Woodworth, *Nothing*, 610; Compiled Military Service Records, *NA*; Regimental Pension Records, *NA*; Office of the Illinois Secretary of State, Muster and Descriptive Rolls.

25. *OR*, ser. 1, vol. 47, pt. 1, 381; Gaskill Diary, February 13, 18, 1865, *ALPL*; Lawson Diary, February 3–7, 20, 28, 1865, *GPL*; Woodworth, *Nothing*, 612–13.

26. Lawson Diary, February 26, March 2–3, 1865, *GPL*; Lawson to wife, March 12, 1865, *GPL*; Corbin, "Biography," 336–37, *ALPL*; McDonald, *History*, 99–101; Gaskill Diary, March 2, 1865, *ALPL*; Office of the Illinois Secretary of State, Muster and Descriptive Rolls; Woodward, Nothing, 625–27.

27. *OR*, ser. 1, vol. 47, pt. 1, 22–23, 98, 172, 382–83; Reese, *Report of the Adjutant General*, 362; Adair, *Historical*, 15; Adair, *Historical*, 15; Hewett et al., *Supplement*, pt. 2, vol. 11, 419, 428; Woodworth, *Nothing*, 628; Gaskill Diary, March 8, 11, 1865, *ALPL*; Lawson Diary, March 11, 1865, *GPL*.

28. Reese, *Report of the Adjutant General*, 362; *OR*, ser. 1, vol. 47, pt. 1, 23–27, 98, 383, 409; Glatthaar, *March*, 175; Woodworth, *Nothing*, 629–32; Hewett et al., *Supplement*, pt. 2, vol. 11, 419, 428; Adair, *Historical*, 15; McDonald, *A History*, 347; Gaskill Diary, March 20–22, 1865, *ALPL*; Hammond to parents, March 26, 1865, *WSS*.

29. Fish, *Forty-Fifth*, 8–10; *OR*, ser. 1, vol. 47, pt. 1, 979; *Galena Daily Gazette*, March 2, 20, 24, April 7, 1865.

30. Reese, *Report of the Adjutant General*, 362; *OR*, ser. 1, vol. 47, pt. 1, 25, 28–29; 98, 173, 381, 383, 409–10; Adair, *Historical*, 15; Hewett et al., *Supplement*, pt. 2, vol. 11, 419; Gaskill Diary, March 3–4, 6–8, 14–16, 25, 1865, *ALPL*; Lawson Diary, March 3–6, 8–11, 1865, *GPL*; Lawson to wife, March 26, 1865, *GPL*; Woodworth, *Nothing*, 627; Corbin, "Biography," 341, *ALPL*

31. Adair, *Historical*, 15; McDonald, *A History*, 347; *OR*, ser. 1, vol. 47, pt. 1, 173, 409; Gaskill Diary, March 18, 1865, *ALPL*; Hammond to wife, March 26, 1865, and to parents, March 29, April 4, 1865, *WSS*.

32. Adair, *Historical*, 15; Reese, *Report of the Adjutant General*, 362; Hewett et al., *Supplement*, pt. 2, vol. 11, 419–420, 429; *OR*, ser. 1, vol. 47, pt. 1, 30–35, 90, 98–99; Bellingall, "Autobiography," 38, *GPL*; Lawson to wife,

April 19, 1865, *GPL*; Gaskill Diary, April 17, 1865, *ALPL*; Gaskill to wife, April 30, 1865; *ALPL*; Corbin, "Biography," 358, *ALPL*; Fish, *Forty-Fifth*, 10; Hammond to parents, April 28, 1865, *WSS*; McDonald, *History*, 104; Woodworth, *Nothing*, 635–36; Manning, *What This Cruel War*, 215–16.

33. Lawson Diary, December 12–13, 28, 1864, January 1, 6, 29, 31, February 4, 5, March 4–5, 1865, *GPL*; Lawson to wife, December 17, 1864, March 12, 26, April 19, 1865, and to parents, March 26, 1865, *GPL*; Hammond to cousin, January 18, March 30, 1865, and to parents, January 29, 1865, *WSS*; *Galesburg Democrat*, February 16, 1865; Gaskill Diary, February 18, 1865, *ALPL*; Rable, *God's*, 1, 2, 4–5, 8–9, 90, 127–28, 142, 304–5, 340, 358; Carmichael, *War*, 72–74.

34. *OR*, ser. 1, vol. 47, pt. 1, 31, 34; Gaskill Diary, April 17, 25, 1865, *ALPL*; Woodworth, *Nothing*, 635–37; Corbin, "Biography," 353, *ALPL*.

35. Lawson to family, April 4, 1865, and to wife, April 6, 19, 28, 1865, *GPL*.

36. *OR*, ser. 1, vol. 47, pt. 1, 35, 90–99; Lawson to wife, April 19, 1865, to family, April 28, 1865, *GPL*; Gaskill Diary, April 25, 29–30, May 1–5, 1865, *ALPL*; Glatthaar, *March*, 177–79; Carmichael, *War*, 277, 287, 289; Hewett et al., *Supplement*, pt. 2, vol. 11, 420, 429; Adair, *Historical*, 15; Reese, *Report of the Adjutant General*, 362; Bellingall, "Autobiography," 38–39, *GPL*; Corbin, "Biography," 358–59, *ALPL*; Hammond to parents, April 28, May 1, 1865, *WSS*.

37. Levings to parents, May 29, 1865, *WSS*; Hammond to parents, April 29, 1865, *WSS*; Bellingall, "Autobiography," 39–40, *GPL*; McDonald, *History*, 109; Glatthaar, *March*, 180; Woodworth, *Nothing*, 638.

38. Adair, *Historical*, 15; McDonald, *History*, 107; *OR*, ser. 1, vol. 47, pt. 1, 90; Fish, *Forty-Fifth*, 10, Corbin, "Biography," 361, 364; Bellingall, "Autobiography," 39, *GPL*; Hammond to parents, May 29, 1865, *WSS*.

39. Adair, *Historical*, 15; McDonald, *History*, 107–8; *Lancaster Gazette*, June 1, 1865; Evening Star, May 24, 1865; Corbin, "Biography," 362, 366, *ALPL*; Bellingall, "Autobiography," 39, *GPL*; *Waukegan Weekly Gazette*, May 27, 1865; Fish, *Forty-Fifth*, 31; Hammond to parents, May 29, 1865, *WSS*; Woodworth, *Nothing*, 638–40, 650; Glatthaar, *March*, 180–82; Sherman, *Memoirs*, 2:377; Hess, *Civil War*, 79; *Lancaster Gazette*, June 1, 1865.

40. *OR*, ser. 1, vol. 47, pt. 1, 44–46.

41. Corbin, "Biography," 369–72, *ALPL*; Carmichael, *War*, 316; *Galena Daily Gazette*, June 13, 1865; Hammond to parents, May 29, 1865, *WSS*; Jordan, *Marching Home*, 21.

42. Hewett et al., *Supplement*, pt. 2, vol. 11, 407–8, 420; *OR*, ser. 1, vol. 47, pt. 1, 90, 99; Lawson Diary, June 13, 20, 1865, *GPL*; Lawson to wife, June 18,

July 9, 1865, *GPL*; *Louisville Daily Journal,* June 15, 1865, *GPL*; Hammond to cousin, June 20, 1865, *WSS*; Adair, *Historical,* 15; Jordan, *Marching Home,* 31–33.

43. Gaskill Monthly Medical Reports, *ALPL*; Regimental Medical Records, *NA*; Office of the Illinois Secretary of State, Muster and Descriptive Rolls.

44. McDonald, *History,* 110–12; *Galena Daily Gazette,* July 7, 10, 1865; Adair, *Historical,* 15; Reese, *Report of the Adjutant General,* 362; "John Oliver Duer" (biography), Galena and U.S. Grant Museum, accessed October 31, 2021, http://www.galenahistory.org/research/nine-generals/john-oliver-duer/; Illinois-Vicksburg Military Park Commission, *Illinois,* 194; *Galena Daily Gazette,* July 13–14, 17–19, 21, 1865; Office of the Illinois Secretary of State, Muster and Descriptive Rolls; National Tribune, May 29, 1884.

45. *Rock Island Daily Argus,* July 21, 1865; Rock Island Weekly Union, July 21, 1865; *Galena Daily Gazette,* July 22, 23, 28, 1865; Office of the Illinois Secretary of State, Muster and Descriptive Rolls.

10. Postwar Lives and Fighting with Words

1. Bledsoe, *Citizen-Soldiers,* 216; Jordan and Rothera, introduction to *War Went On,* 1–4; Jordan, *Marching Home,* 2, 65, 68–69, 86, 10, 236, 251, 260; "Historical Summary of Grand Army of the Republic (GAR) Posts by State: Illinois," National GAR Records Program, July 18, 2013, https://suvcw.org/garrecords/garposts/il.pdf.

2. Bledsoe, *Citizen-Officers,* 217; Jordan and Rothera, introduction to *War Went On,* 4, 7; Sodergren, "Exposing False History," 137–51; Jordan, "Veterans," 313–14; Jordan, *Marching Home,* 2, 67, 62–64, 68–69, 71, 74, 86, 104, 193–94, 196.

3. Adair, *Historical,* 7, 15–16; National Tribune, July 19, 1888; *St. Louis (MO) Republic,* August 29, 1900; Bassett to Rigby, May 26, 1902, *VNMP.*

4. Jones, "Father's Personal History," 56–57, *FHS*; Jordan, *Marching Home,* 3.

5. Jordan, *Marching Home,* 3–4, 37–38, 43–46, 48–50, 57, 59, 66, 70, 183–87, 229–30, 307; Mezurek, "Colored Veterans," 235; Volkel, *Illinois Soldiers',* 1–2, 11–12, 18, 26, 31, 33–34, 38, 41, 46, 54–55, 60, 63–64, 69, 73, 88; Regimental Illinois Soldiers' and Sailors' Home Residents Records; Office of the Illinois Secretary of State, Muster and Descriptive Rolls; Regimental Medical Records, *NA*; Compiled Military Service Records, *NA.*

6. Gorman, "Civil War Pensions," 1; Jordan and Rothera, introduction to *War Went On,* 3, Jordan, *Marching Home,* 149, 152–59, 162, 169; Regimental Pension Records, *NA.*

7. Regimental Pension Records, *NA*; Cousins, *Bodies,* 77, 87–88.

8. Regimental Pension Records, *NA.*

9. Old Country Roots, "Sgt. Ephram Graham" (memorial), Find a Grave, July 26, 2011, https://www.findagrave.com/memorial/73990481/ephram -graham; *Galena Daily Gazette,* June 22, 1865; Topeka Daily State Journal, November 30, 1918; Bellingall, "Autobiography," 40–41; American Blue Book, 192; John Jackson, "Nathan A. Corbin," Flickr, April 30, 2007, https:// www.flickr.com/photos/civilwar_veterans_tombstones/1999547119/.

10. McGinty, "Civil War"; Jim Flack, "Henry Winter" (memorial), Find a Grave, June 5, 2013, https://www.findagrave.com/memorial/111816510 /henry-winter; Galena Weekly Gazette, December 25, 1919; Winter, *Baptism,* 219; Dittmar, Autobiography, 9–10; Crummer, *With Grant,* 154, 163; Cousins, *Bodies in,* 5; Jordan and Rothera, introduction to *War Went On,* 4; Jordan, *Marching Home,* 4, 60, 172, 189.

11. Henry Harrison Taylor, Ancestry Institution, accessed March 20, 2013, AncestryInstitution.com; *Clay Center Times,* September 7, 1893; Taylor to Smith, December 28, 1885, *VNMP.*

12. Office of the Illinois Secretary of State, 1929 Illinois Roll of Honor, 1:113, Civil War Company E, 45th Illinois Infantry; Adair, *Historical,* 14; *New York Sun,* April 27, 1897; *Butte Inter Mountain,* October 15, 1903.

13. *Minneapolis Journal,* August 19, 1906; Fish, *Forty-Fifth,* 6, 7; Shutter and Mc-Lain, *Progressive Men,* 619–22; National Tribune, November 3, 1987; Martin W. Johnson, "Judge Daniel Worthy Fish" (memorial), Find a Grave, December 19, 2013, https://www.findagrave.com/memorial/121941562/daniel -worthy-fish; Crummer to Rigby, March 27, 1903, *VNMP*; MillieBelle, "John P. Jones" (memorial), Find a Grave, December 3, 2003, https://www. findagrave.com/memorial/8153069/john-p-jones; certificate of death for Clara E. Gaskill, August 16, 1926, *ALPL*; clipping from untitled newspaper, May 8 and 9, 1894, *ALPL.*

14. "Henry O. Harkness" (biography), FamilySearch, accessed January 25, 2022, https://ancestors.familysearch.org/en/K2J3-PCD/henry-orville-harkness -1834-1911; U.S. Census Bureau, 1900 Census; U.S. Census Bureau, 1910 Census.

15. New York Tribune, October 1, 1887; Daily Evening Bulletin, October 1, 1887; Jones, "Father's Personal History," 59, *FHS.*

16. Military Order, Memorials of Deceased, 305–8; Bledsoe, *Citizen-Officers,* 207; Jordan and Rothera, introduction to *War Went On,* 3, 5, 6; Jordan, *Marching Home,* 23; National Tribune, February 4, 1897.

17. Jasper Adelmon Maltby, Ancestry Institution, accessed March 20, 2013, AncestryInstitution.com; *Galena Daily Gazette,* May 16, 30, 1864; *Warren*

Independent, May 19, 1864; *Colfax Chronicle*, December 23, 1911; Delaney, *Maltby Brothers' Civil War*, 121, 173.

18. *Galena Daily Gazette*, July 24, 1865; Office of the Illinois Secretary of State, Muster and Descriptive Rolls; RPD2, "Robert Palmer Sealy" (memorial), Find a Grave, April 12, 2008, https://www.findagrave.com/memorial /25962044/robert-palmer-sealy; In Memoriam, 3–7, 10, 16.

19. Record of the August 29, 1900, Reunion, *VNMP*; Crummer to regiment, April 3, 1905, *VNMP*; *Minneapolis Journal*, August 19, 1906; Fish, *Forty-Fifth*, 5, 10–12, 26–27.

20. Jordan, *Marching Home*, 83–84, 91; Crummer, *With Grant*, 9, 51, 53–54, 78, 169–70.

21. Crummer, *With Grant*, 81–87; Jordan and Rothera, introduction to *War Went On*, 3, Jordan, *Marching Home*, 195.

22. Crummer, *With Grant*, 173–90.

23. Crummer, *With Grant*, 81, 163–68, 173–74, 181; *Galena Daily Gazette*, March 13, 1903; Illinois-Vicksburg Military Park Commission, *Illinois*, 194–96; C. E. Bassett to Capt. Wm. T. Rigby, June 12, 1902, Crummer to Capt. Wm. T. Rigby, August 20, September 2, October 21, 1902, March 27, 1903, January 16, May 26, 1905, Capt. Wm. T. Rigby to Crummer, November 6, 1917; Larry Crummer, "Maj. Wilbur Fisk Crummer" (memorial), Find a Grave, July 22, 2011, https://www.findagrave.com/memorial/73753075 /wilbur-fisk-crummer.

24. McAllen to Rigby, September 29, 1901, Erwin to Rigby, March 31, 1902, Basset to Rigby, May 21, 25, 1902, and Crummer to Rigby, April 9, 1903, 45th Illinois Folder, *VNMP*; National Tribune, December 15, 1892, February 9, 1893, February 14, May 16, 21, 1895, February 10, 1898, March 5, April 23, June 25, August 20, September 17, 1903, December 21, 1905, November 8, 1906, January 3, 1907, August 5, 1909, April 14, September 29, 1910.

25. Crummer to Rigby and to members of the National Military Commission, October 18, 1917, *VNMP*; Galena Weekly Gazette, March 2, 1916, September 20, 1917; Jordan and Rothera, introduction to *War Went On*, 2–3; Jordan, *Marching Home*, 99–100; Regimental Medical Records, *NA*; Office of the Illinois Secretary of State, Muster and Descriptive rolls; Anton Schwarzmueller, "Town of Niagara Civil War Memorial," Historical Marker Database, July 8, 2014, https://www.hmdb.org/m.asp?m=75180.

26. Office of the Illinois Secretary of State, Muster and Descriptive Rolls; Compiled Military Service Records, *NA*; Lowe, *Walker's Texas Division*, 39, 263; Robertson, *Soldiers*, 148–14.

27. *OR*, ser. 1, vol. 24, pt. 1, 710; Bellingall, "Autobiography," 24, *GPL*.

28. "William Henry Mingles" (biography), Ancestry.com, accessed January 5, 2022, https://www.ancestry.com/family-tree/person/tree/5766431/person/-1398942865/facts; Nebraska City News-Press, April 4, 1835.

Appendix A: The War's Toll and Soldiers' Misbehavior

1. Regimental Medical, Service, and Pension Records, NA; Office of the Illinois Secretary of State, Muster and Descriptive Rolls; Fox, Regimental Losses, 48–50.

2. Regimental Service, Medical, and Pension Records, NA; Office of the Illinois Secretary of State, Muster and Descriptive Rolls.

3. Regimental Medical, Service, and Pension Records, NA; Office of the Illinois Secretary of State, Muster and Descriptive Rolls; OR, ser. 3, vol. 3, 452–53; Cousins, Bodies, 20–22, 25, 27, 30; Pelka, Civil War Letters, 1, 13, 15, 30.

4. Regimental Medical, Service, and Pension Records, NA; Office of the Illinois Secretary of State, Muster and Descriptive Rolls.

5. Regimental Medical, Service, and Pension Records, NA; Office of the Illinois Secretary of State, Muster and Descriptive Rolls.

6. Regimental Medical, Service, and Pension Records, NA; Office of the Illinois Secretary of State, Muster and Descriptive Rolls; Fox, Regimental Losses, 48–50; Long and Long, Civil War, 714; McPherson, Ordeal, 504; Carmichael, War, 177.

7. Regimental Medical Records, NA; Rable, God's, 92, 93, 105; Foote, Gentlemen, 22–26, 28–31, 69–73, 76–79, 128–29, 167–69; 175; Regimental Books 3 and 4.

8. Cowan to daughter, August 12, 1862, and to children, October 1, 1862, GPL.

Bibliography

Manuscripts and Unpublished Sources

Abraham Lincoln Presidential Library (ALPL), Springfield, IL
Balfour, James. Letters. Folder SC2451.
Corbin, Ida. "Biography of Nathan Albert Corbin."
Gaskill, James R. M. Papers and Letters.
McClernand, John A. Papers.
Miller, J. W. Papers. Folder SC1047.
Smith, John Eugene. Letters. Folder SC771–45.
Tebbetts, William H. Letters. Folder SC1525.
Wallace–Dickey Family. Papers.

Filson Historical Society (FHS), Louisville, KY
Jones, John P. "Father's Personal History of the Civil War." Letters and
Personal Account of Service.

Galena Public Library (GPL), Galena, IL
Cowan, Luther H. Papers.
Jones, John P. Papers.
Lawson, George C. Diary and Letters.
Smith, John E. Letters.

Library of Congress (LOC)
Benham, Donald. Civil War Collection. Manuscript Division.

National Archives (NA), Washington, DC
Compiled Military Service Records of Union Soldiers, Record Group
(RG) 94.
Records of the Adjutant General, RG 94.
Regimental Medical Records, RG 94.
Regimental Pension Records, RG 15.
Regimental Service Order Books 1–4, RG 94.

Shiloh National Military Park (SNMP), Shiloh, TN
Bridgford, Oliver. Papers. 45th Illinois Infantry Folder.
Dittmar, George, Sr. Autobiography. 1896. 45th Illinois Folder.

Vermont Historical Society (VHS), Barre, VT
Hunt, Luther B. Diary.

Vicksburg National Military Park (VNMP), Vicksburg, MS
Armstrong, Winfred Keen, ed. "The Civil War Letters of Pvt. P. C. Bonney."
Bassett, C. E. Letters. 124th Illinois Infantry Folder.
Beck, Steven C. Letters. 124th Illinois Infantry Folder.
———. "A True Sketch of His Army Life." N.d. 124th Illinois Infantry Folder.
Bellingall, Peter. "Autobiography of P. W. Bellingall." 1920. 45th Illinois Infantry Folder.
Crummer, Wilbur F. Letters. 45th Illinois Infantry Folder.
Leggett, Mortimer D. Letters.
Nilsen, Karen Hitchcock. "Civil War Diary of Charles Henry Snedeker." 1966. 124th Illinois Infantry Folder.
Smith, John E. Letters. File 95.
Stevens, Victor H. Letters. 20th Illinois Infantry Folder.
William Sean Scott Private Collection (WSS), McAlester, OK
Hammond, Edwin O. Letters. 45th Illinois Folder.
Hull, B. G. Diary. 43rd Mississippi Infantry.
Levings, Edwin D. Letters. 12th Wisconsin Infantry Folder.
Love, J. M. Diary. March 5, 1862–March 16, 1865. Copied from the Jackson/Madison County Library Tennessee Room.
Taylor, William C. Letters. 45th Illinois Folder.
Williamson, William. Letters. 45th Illinois Folder.

Newspapers (Illinois unless otherwise noted)
Belvidere Standard, 1863.
Butte (MT) Inter Mountain, 1903.
Carroll County Home Intelligencer, 1859–60.
Carroll County Mirror, 1862–63.
Carroll County Republican, 1856.
Carroll County Weekly Mirror, 1861–63.
Chicago Journal, 1861.
Chicago Tribune, 1862–63.
Clay Center (KS) Times, 1893.
Cleveland (OH) Morning Leader, 1862–64.
Colfax (LA) Chronicle, 1911.
Daily Freeman (Montpelier, VT), 1863.
Daily Green Mountain (Montpelier, VT), 1862.
Daily State Sentinel (Indianapolis), 1862.

Evening Star (Washington, DC), 1864–65.
Evening Statesman (Walla Walla, WA), 1905.
Freeport Bulletin, 1862–63.
Freeport Daily Journal, 1856–57.
Freeport Journal, 1856.
Freeport Weekly Bulletin, 1858–61.
Freeport Wide Awake, 1860.
Galena Daily Advertiser, 1856–64.
Galena Daily Courier, 1858–61.
Galena Daily Gazette, 1864–65.
Galena Weekly Northwestern Gazette, 1856–63.
Galesburg Democrat, 1865.
Gettysburg (PA) Sentinel, 1862.
Gettysburg (PA) Star and Banner, 1862.
Jackson (TN) War Eagle, 1862.
Keithsburg Observer, 1863.
Lancaster (OH) Gazette, 1865.
Louisville (KY) Daily Journal, 1865.
Minneapolis (MN) Journal, 1906.
Memphis (TN) Daily Appeal, 1862.
National Tribune (Washington, DC), 1883–1910.
News-Press (Nebraska City, NE), 1935.
New York Sun, 1897.
Ottawa Free Trader, 1862.
Phillipsburg (KS) Herald, 1898.
Red Cloud (NE) Chief, 1911.
Rockford Democrat, 1856–61.
Rockford Register, 1861.
Rockford Republican, 1856–62.
Rock Island Daily Argus, 1856–65.
Rock Islander, 1856–57.
Rock Island Weekly Advertiser, 1856.
Rock Island Weekly Register, 1859–60.
Rock River Democrat, 1860–63.
Rock River Times, 2016.
Spirit of Democracy (Woodsfield, OH), 1864.
St. Louis (MO) Republic, 1900.
Warren Independent, 1858–64.
Waukegan Weekly Gazette, 1861–65.

Weekly Standard (Raleigh, NC), 1869.

Western Reserve Chronicle (Warren, OH), 1863.

Wichita (KS) Daily Eagle, 1902.

Other Primary Sources

Adair, John M. *Historical Sketch of the Forty-Fifth Illinois Regiment.* Lanark, IL: Carroll County Gazette Printers, 1869. https://archive.org/details /historicalsketch00adai.

Biographical Review of Cass, Schuyler and Brown Counties, Illinois. Chicago: Biographical Review, 1892. https://archive.org/details/biographical rev00illi.

Collins, David A. "Absentee Soldier Voting in Civil War Law and Politics." PhD diss., Wayne State University, 2014. https://digitalcommons.wayne .edu/cgi/viewcontent.cgi?article=2042&context=oa_dissertations.

Fox, William F. *Regimental Losses in the American Civil War, 1861–1865: A Treatise on the Extent and Nature of the Mortuary Losses in the Union Regiments, with Full and Exhaustive Statistics Compiled from the Official Records on File in the State Military Bureaus and at Washington.* Albany, NY: Albany Publishing, 1889.

Gould, Benjamin Apthorp. *Investigations in the Military and Anthropological Statistics of American Soldiers.* New York: Hurd and Houghton, 1869. https://archive.org/details/investigationsi00goulgoog.

Grant, Ulysses S. *The Civil War Memoirs of Ulysses S. Grant.* 1885. Reprint, New York: Tom Doherty Associates, 2002.

Hewett, Janet B., Noah Andre Trudeau, Bryce A. Suderow, and Gary Gallagher, eds. *Supplement to the Official Records of the Union and Confederate Armies.* Wilmington, NC: Broadfoot, 1994. https://catalog.hathitrust.org /Record/002912198.

In Memoriam [of Col. John O. Duer, 45th Illinois Veteran Volunteer Infantry]. Monticello, IA: Express Print, 1880.

Kennedy, Joseph C. G., ed. *Population of the United States in 1860: Compiled from the Original Returns of the Eighth Census.* Washington, DC: Bureau of the Census Library, 1864. https://archive.org/details/populationofusin 00kennrich/page/n4/mode/2up.

Leekly, John Thompson. *1864 Diary of John Thompson Leekly, 45th Illinois.* Spared and Shared 19. September 15, 2019. https://sparedandshared19.word press.com/2019/09/15/1864-diary-of-john-thompson-leekly-45th -illinois/.

Lincoln, Abraham. Proclamation 124—Offering Pardon to Deserters. March 11, 1865. https://www.presidency.ucsb.edu/documents/proclamation -124-offering-pardon-deserters.

Office of the Illinois Secretary of State. Illinois Civil War Muster and Descriptive Rolls for the 45th Illinois. Record Series 301.020, roll 30–3646. Illinois State Archives. https://www.ilsos.gov/departments /archives/databases/datcivil.html.

———. Illinois Soldiers' and Sailors' Home Residents (1887–1916). Records for the 45th Illinois. Record Series Veterans' Case Files, RS 259.002. Illinois State Archives. https://www.ilsos.gov/departments/archives /databases/quincyhome.html.

———. 1929 Illinois Roll of Honor. Records for the 45th Illinois, vols. 1 and 2. Illinois State Archives. https://www.ilsos.gov/departments/archives /databases/honorroll.html.

Provost Marshal's Office, District of Memphis, TN. Civil War Oath of Allegiance to U.S.A. No. 1281. June 3, 1863. https://www.flickr.com/ photos/51992558@N00/9382001535/in/photolist-4bx6Br-od34LK-owseT5- bk7qy5-bk7qzu-fi4dca-od556s-osvv5Q-ouxuMP-owiC2n-ovM5Jk-oux U1T.

Shutter, Marion D., and J. S. McLain, eds. *Progressive Men of Minnesota. Biographical Sketches and Portraits of the Leaders in Business, Politics and the Professions Together with an Historical and Descriptive Sketch of the State.* Minneapolis: *Minnesota Journal*, 1897. https://cdn.loc.gov/service/gdc /lhbum/19129/19129.pdf.

U.S. Census Bureau. 1860 Census. https://www.census.gov/library/publications /1864/dec/1860a.html.

———. 1900 Census. https://www.census.gov/programs-surveys/decennial -census/decade/decennial-publications.1900.html.

———. 1910 Census. https://www.census.gov/programs-surveys/decennial -census/decade/decennial-publications.1910.html.

U.S. War Department. *The War of the Rebellion: A Compilation of the Official Records of the Union and Confederate Armies.* 128 vols. Washington, DC: Government Printing Office, 1880–1901. http://cdl.library.cornell.edu /moa/browse.monographs/waro.html.

Volkel, Lowell M. *Illinois Soldier's and Sailor's Home at Quincy.* Vol. 1, *Admissions of Mexican War and Civil War Veterans, 1887–1898.* Thomson, IL: Heritage House, 1975. https://www.familysearch.org/library/books /records/item/283524-redirect.

Secondary Sources

Allen, Howard W., and Vincent A. Lacey, eds. *Illinois Elections, 1818–1900: Candidates and Country Returns for President, Governor, Senate and House of Representatives*. Carbondale: Southern Illinois University Press, 1992.

The American Blue Book of Biography: Men of 1912. Chicago: Men of Nineteen-Twelve 1913.

Armstrong, Winfred Keen, ed. *The Civil War Letters of Pvt. P. C. Bonney*. Lawrenceville, IL: Lawrenceville Publishing, 1963.

Ballard, Michael, B. *Vicksburg: The Campaign That Opened the Mississippi*. Chapel Hill: University of North Carolina Press, 2004.

Barnet, James. *The Martyrs and Heroes of Illinois: Biographical Sketches*. Chicago: J. Barnet, 1865.

Barrett, John G. *Sherman's March through the Carolinas*. Chapel Hill: University of North Carolina Press, 1956.

Baum, Dale. *The Civil War Party System: The Case of Massachusetts, 1848–1876*. Chapel Hill: University of North Carolina Press, 1984.

Bearss, Edwin Cole. *The Campaign for Vicksburg*. 3 vols. Dayton: Morningside House, 1985.

Bergeron, Arthur W., Jr. *Guide to Louisiana Confederate Military Units, 1861–1865*. Baton Rouge: Louisiana State University Press, 1996.

Biddle, Tami Davis, and Robert M. Citino. "The Role of Military History in the Contemporary Academy." Society for Military History. November 30, 2014. https://www.smh-hq.org/whitepaper.html.

Billings, John D. *Hardtack and Coffee*. 1887. Reprint, Old Saybrook, CT: Konecky and Konecky, 2004.

Blanchard, Ira. *I Marched with Sherman: Civil War Memoirs of the 20th Illinois Volunteer Infantry*. San Francisco: J. D. Huff, 1992.

Bledsoe, Andrew S. *Citizen-Officers: The Union and Confederate Volunteer Junior Officer Corps in the American Civil War*. Baton Rouge: Louisiana State University Press, 2015.

Boatner, Mark M. *The Civil War Dictionary*. New York: David McKay, 1988.

Carmichael, Peter S. *The War for the Common Soldiers: How Men Thought, Fought, and Survived in Civil War*. Chapel Hill: University of North Carolina Press, 2018.

Cashin, Joan E. *War Stuff: The Struggle for Human and Environmental Resources in the American Civil War*. Cambridge: Cambridge University Press, 2019.

Castel, Albert E. *Decision in the West: The Atlanta Campaign of 1864*. Lawrence: University Press of Kansas, 1992.

Catton, Bruce. *The Coming Fury*. Vol. 1 of *The Centennial History of the Civil War*. 1961. Reprint, London: Phoenix, 2001.

———. *Grant Moves South*. Boston: Little, Brown, 1990.

Chernow, Ron. *Grant*. New York: Penguin Press, 2017.

Chetlain, Augustus, L. *Recollections of Seventy Years*. Galena, IL: Gazette, 1899.

Coombe, Jack D. *Thunder along the Mississippi: The River Battles That Split the Confederacy*. New York: Sarpedon, 1996.

Cousins, Sarah Handley. *Bodies in Blue: Disability in the Civil War North*. Athens: University of Georgia Press, 2019.

Crouch, Jerry Evan. *Silencing the Vicksburg Guns: The Story of the 7th Missouri Infantry Regiment, as Experienced by John Davis Evans, Union Private and Mormon Pioneer*. Victoria, BC: Trafford, 2005.

Crummer, Wilbur F. *With Grant at Fort Donelson, Shiloh, and Vicksburg, and an Appreciation of General U. S. Grant*. Oak Park, IL: E. C. Crummer, 1915.

Daniel, Larry J. *Shiloh: The Battle That Changed the Civil War*. New York: Simon and Schuster, 1997.

Danielson, Joseph W. *War's Desolating Scourge: The Union's Occupation of North Alabama*. Lawrence: University Press of Kansas, 2012.

Davis, Burke. *Sherman's March*. New York: Random House, 1980.

Delaney, Norman C. *The Maltby Brothers' Civil War*. College Station: Texas A&M University Press, 213.

Dossman, Steven Nathaniel. "The 'Stealing Tour': Soldiers and Civilians in Grant's March to Vicksburg." In Woodworth and Grear, *The Vicksburg Campaign*, 194–213.

Duerkes, Wayne. "I for One Am Ready to Do My Part: The Initial Motivations That Inspired Men from Northern Illinois to Enlist in the U.S Army, 1861–1862." *Journal of the Illinois State Historical Society*, 105, no. 4 (Winter 2012): 313–332.

Dunkelman, Mark H. *Brothers One and All: Esprit de Corps in a Civil War Regiment*. Baton Rouge: Louisiana State University Press, 2004.

———. *Marching with Sherman: Through Georgia and the Carolinas with the 154th New York*. Baton Rouge: Louisiana State University Press, 2012.

Dyer, Frederick H. *A Compendium of the War of the Rebellion*. 3 vols. 1908. Reprint, New York: T. Yoseloff, 1959.

Eddy, T. M. *The Patriotism of Illinois: A Record of the Civil and Military History of the State in the War for the Union, with a History of the Campaigns in Which Illinois Soldiers Have Been Conspicuous, Sketches of Distinguished Officers, the Roll of the Illustrious Dead, Movements of the Sanitary and Christian Commissions*. Chicago: Clarke, 1886.

Egerton, Douglas R. *Thunder at the Gates: The Black Civil War Regiments That Redeemed America*. New York: Basic Books, 2016.

Eisendrath, Joseph L., Jr. "Chicago's Camp Douglas, 1861–1865." *Journal of the Illinois State Historical Society* 53, no. 1 (1960): 37–63.

Ernst, Oswald H. *A Manual of Practical Military Engineering Prepared for the Use of the Cadets of the U.S. Military Academy, and for Engineer Troops*. New York: D. Van Nostrand, 1873.

Federal Writers' Project (Illinois). *Galena, Illinois: A History*. Galena, IL: Jo Daviess County Historical Society, 1937.

Feis, William B. "Developed by Circumstances." In Woodworth and Grear, *The Vicksburg Campaign*, 153–72.

Fish, Daniel. *The Forty-Fifth Illinois: A Souvenir of the Re-union Held at Rockford on the Fortieth Anniversary of Its March in the Grand Review*. Minneapolis: Byron and Willard, 1905.

Foner, Eric. *Free Soil, Free Labor, Free Men: The Ideology of the Republican Party before the Civil War*. New York: Oxford University Press, 1970.

Foote, Lorien. *The Gentlemen and the Roughs: Violence, Honor, and Manhood in the Union Army*. New York: New York University Press, 2010.

Force, M. F. *From Fort Henry to Corinth*. New York: C. Scribner's Sons, 1881.

Foster, Buck T. *Sherman's Mississippi Campaign*. Tuscaloosa: University of Alabama Press, 2006.

Frank, Joseph Allan, and George A. Reaves. *Seeing the Elephant: Raw Recruits at the Battle of Shiloh*. Urbana: University of Illinois Press, 2003.

Frawley, Jason M. "In the Enemy's Country: Port Gibson and the Turning Point of the Vicksburg Campaign." In Woodworth and Grear, *The Vicksburg Campaign*, 43–64.

Freeman, Douglas S. *Lee*. New York: Touchstone Press, 1991.

Fry, Zachery A. *A Republic in the Ranks: Loyalty and Dissent in the Army of the Potomac*. Chapel Hill: University of North Carolina Press, 2020.

Gabel, Christopher R. *Staff Ride Handbook for the Vicksburg Campaign, December 1862–July 1863*. Fort Leavenworth, KS: U.S. Army Command and General Staff College, 2001.

Gallagher, Gary W. *The Union War*. Cambridge, MA: Harvard University Press, 2012.

Geary, James W. *We Need Men: The Union Draft in the Civil War*. DeKalb: Northern Illinois University Press, 1991.

Gienapp, William E. *The Origins of the Republican Party, 1852–1856*. New York: Oxford University Press, 2012.

Glatthaar, Joseph T. *The March to the Sea and Beyond: Sherman's Troops in the*

Savannah and Carolinas Campaigns. New York: New York University Press, 1985.

Gordon, Lesley J. *A Broken Regiment: The 16th Connecticut's Civil War.* Baton Rouge: Louisiana State University Press, 2014.

Gorman, Kathleen L. "Civil War Pensions." *Essential Civil War Curriculum.* May 2012. https://www.essentialcivilwarcurriculum.com/civil-war-pensions .html.

Grear, Charles D. Introduction to Woodworth and Grear, *Vicksburg Besieged*, 1–5.

Grimsley, Mark. *The Hard Hand of War: Union Military Policy toward Southern Civilians, 1861–1865.* New York: Cambridge University Press, 1995.

Groom, Winston. *Vicksburg, 1863.* New York: Alfred A. Knopf, 2009.

Hess, Earl J. *Civil War Infantry Tactics: Training, Combat, and Small-Unit Effectiveness.* Baton Rouge: Louisiana State University Press, 2015.

———. *Liberty, Virtue and Progress: Northerners and Their War for the Union.* New York: Fordham University Press, 1997.

———. *Storming Vicksburg.* Chapel Hill: University of North Carolina Press, 2020.

Hewitt, Lawrence L. "An Ironic Route to Glory: Louisiana's Native Guards at Port Hudson." In Smith, *Black Soldiers in Blue*, 78–106.

Hicken, Victor. *Illinois in the Civil War.* Urbana: University of Illinois Press, 1991.

Hickenlooper, Andrew. "The Vicksburg Mine." In *Battles and Leaders of the Civil War*, edited by Robert U. Johnson and Clarence C. Buel, 3:539–42. 1887. Reprint, New York: Thomas Yoseloff, 1956.

Hills, J. Parker. "Roads to Raymond." In Woodworth and Grear, *The Vicksburg Campaign*, 65–95.

Hobbs, Richard Gear. *Glamorous Galena and Jo Daviess County: Little Switzerland of Illinois.* Galena, IL: Gazette, 1939.

Illinois-Vicksburg Military Park Commission. *Illinois at Vicksburg; Published under Authority of an Act of the Forty-Fifth General Assembly.* Chicago: Blakely, 1907.

Jimerson, Randall C. *The Private Civil War: Popular Thought during the Sectional Conflict.* Baton Rouge: Louisiana State University Press, 1988.

Joiner, Gary D. "Running the Gauntlet: The Effectiveness of Combined Forces in the Vicksburg Campaign." In Woodworth and Grear, *The Vicksburg Campaign*, 8–23.

Jordan, Brian Matthew. *Marching Home: Union Veterans and Their Unending Civil War.* New York: Liveright, 2014.

———. "Veterans in New Fields: Directions for Future Scholarship on Civil War Veterans." In Jordan and Rothera, *The War Went On*, 307–19.

Jordan, Brian Matthew, and Evan C. Rothera. *The War Went On: Reconsidering the Lives of Civil War Veterans*. Baton Rouge: Louisiana State University Press, 2020.

Linderman, Gerald F. *Embattled Courage: The Experience of Combat in the American Civil War*. New York: Free Press, 1987.

Logue, Larry M. *To Appomattox and Beyond: The Civil War Soldier in War and Peace*. Chicago: Ivan R. Dee, 1996.

Long, Clarence D. *Wages and Earnings in the United States, 1860–1890*. Princeton, NJ: Princeton University Press, 1960.

Long, E. B., and Barbara Long. *The Civil War Day by Day: An Almanac, 1861–1865*. 1971. Reprint, New York: Da Capo, 1985.

Lonn, Ella. *Desertion during the Civil War*. New York: Century, 1928.

———. *Foreigners in the Union Army and Navy*. Baton Rouge: Louisiana State University Press, 1951. https://babel.hathitrust.org/cgi/pt?id=uc1.c041792918 &view=1up&seq=1.

Lowe, Richard G. "Battle on the Levee: The Fight at Milliken's Bend." In Smith, *Black Soldiers in Blue*, 107–35.

———. *Walker's Texas Division, C.S.A: Greyhounds of the Trans-Mississippi*. Baton Rouge: Louisiana State University Press, 2004.

Lucas, Marion B. *Sherman and the Burning of Columbia*. Columbia: University of South Carolina Press, 2000.

Maizlish, Stephen E. *The Triumph of Sectionalism: The Transformation of Ohio Politics, 1844–1856*. Kent, OH: Kent State University Press, 1983.

Manning, Chandra. *What This Cruel War Was Over: Soldiers, Slavery, and the Civil War*. New York: Alfred A. Knopf, 2007.

Marszalek, John F. *Sherman's March to the Sea*. Abilene, TX: McWhiney Foundation, 2005.

Marvel, William. *Lincoln's Mercenaries: Economic Motivation among Union Soldiers during the Civil War*. Baton Rouge: Louisiana State University Press, 2018.

McDonald, Granville B. *A History of the 30th Illinois Veterans Volunteer Regiment of Infantry*. Sparta, IL: Sparta News, 1916.

McDonough, James Lee. *Shiloh: In Hell before Night*. Knoxville: University of Tennessee Press, 1983.

McGinty, Jon. "The Civil War: When They Marched to the Sound of the Guns." *Old Northwest Quarterly*, July 15, 2011. http://oldnorthwestterritory .northwestquarterly.com/2011/07/15/the-civil-war-when-they-marched-to -the-sound-of-the-guns/.

McPherson, James M. *Battle Cry of Freedom: The Civil War Era*. New York: Oxford Press, 1988.

———. *For Cause and Comrades: Why Men Fought in the Civil War*. New York: Oxford University Press, 1997.

———. *Ordeal by Fire: The Civil War and Reconstruction*. Boston: McGraw Hill, 2001.

Mellott, David W., and Mark A. Snell. *The Seventh West Virginia Infantry: An Embattled Union Regiment from the Civil War's Most Divided State*. Lawrence: University Press of Kansas, 2019.

Mezurek, Kelly D. "'The Colored Veterans Should Receive the Same Tender Care': Soldiers' Homes, Race, and the Post–Civil War Midwest." In Jordan and Rothera, *The War Went On*, 230–62.

———. *For Their Own Cause: The 27th United States Colored Troops*. Kent, OH: Kent State University Press, 2016.

Miller, Donald L. *Vicksburg: Grant's Campaign That Broke the Confederacy*. New York: Simon and Schuster, 2019.

Mitchell, Reid. *Civil War Soldiers*. New York: Penguin Books, 1988.

MOLLUS (Military Order of the Loyal Legion of the United States). *Memorials of Deceased Companions of the Commandery of the State of Illinois, Military Order of the Loyal Legion of the United States: From May 8, 1879, When the Commandery Was Instituted, to July 1, 1901*. 1923. Reprint, Wilmington, NC: Broadfoot, 1993.

Morris, W. S., L. D. Hartwell, and J. B. Kuykendall. *History 31st Regiment Illinois Volunteers: Organized by John A. Logan*. New ed. Carbondale: Southern Illinois University Press, 1998. First published 1902 by Keller.

Murdock, Eugene C. *Patriotism Limited, 1862–1865: The Civil War Draft and the Bounty System*. Kent, OH: Kent State University Press, 1967.

Neely, Mark E., Jr. *The Union Divided: Party Conflict in the Civil War North*. Cambridge, MA: Harvard University Press, 2002.

Newsome, Edmund. *Experience in the War of the Great Rebellion: By a Soldier of the Eighty-First Regiment Illinois Volunteer Infantry, from August 1862 to August 1865; Including Nearly Nine Months of Life in Southern Prisons, at Macon, Savannah, Charleston, Columbia and Other Places*. Carbondale, IL: Edmund Newsome, 1880.

Nofi, Albert A. *A Civil War Treasury: Being a Miscellany of Arms and Artillery, Facts and Figures, Legends and Lore, Muses and Minstrels, Personalities and People*. 1992. Reprint, New York: Da Capo, 1995.

Owens, Kenneth N. *Galena, Grant, and the Fortunes of War: A history of Galena, Illinois during the Civil War*. DeKalb: Northern Illinois University Press, 1963.

Pelka, Fred, ed. *The Civil War Letters of Colonel Charles F. Johnson, Invalid Corps.* Boston: University of Massachusetts, 2004.

Phillips, Jason. "Battling Stereotypes: A Taxonomy of Common Soldiers in Civil War History." *History Compass* 6, no. 6 (November 2008): 1407–25.

Post, Lydia M., ed. *Soldiers' Letters from Camp, Battlefield and Prison.* New York: Bunce and Huntington, 1865.

Proft, R. J., ed. *United States of America's Congressional Medal of Honor Recipients and Their Official Citations.* Columbia Heights, MN: Highland House II, 2006.

Pullen, John J. *The Twentieth Maine: A Volunteer Regiment in the Civil War.* Philadelphia: Lippincott, 1957.

Rable, George C. *God's Almost Chosen Peoples: A Religious History of the American Civil War.* Chapel Hill: University of North Carolina Press, 2010.

Reed, H. B. *The Back-Bone of Illinois in Front and Rear, from 1861 to 1865; and Memorial Hall, Springfield, Illinois.* Springfield: H. W. Bokker, 1886.

Reese, J. N. *Report of the Adjutant General of the State of Illinois.* Vol. 3, *Containing Reports for the Years 1861–1866.* Springfield, IL: Phillips Bros., 1900.

Rein, Christopher M. *The Second Colorado Cavalry: A Civil War Regiment on the Great Plains.* Norman: University of Oklahoma Press, 2020.

Roberts, Bobby L., and Carl H. Moneyhon. *Portraits of Conflict: A Photographic History of Mississippi in the Civil War.* Fayetteville: University of Arkansas Press, 1993.

Robertson, James I., Jr. *Soldiers Blue and Gray.* Columbia: University of South Carolina Press, 1988.

Robertson, William G. "From the Crater to New Market Heights: A Tale of Two Divisions." In Smith, *Black Soldiers in Blue,* 169–99.

Rothera, Evan C., and Brian Matthew Jordan. Introduction to Jordan and Rothera, *The War Went On,* 1–11.

Scarborough, William K. *Masters of the Big House: Elite Slaveholders of the Mid-Nineteenth-Century South.* Baton Rouge: Louisiana State University Press, 2006.

Shaw, Kathleen. "Johnny Has Gone for a Soldier: Your Enlistment in a Northern County." *Pennsylvania Magazine of History and Biography* 135, no. 4 (October 2011): 419–46. https://journals.psu.edu/pmhb/article/download/60388/60347.

Sherman, William T. *Memoirs of General William T. Sherman.* 1875. Reprint, New York: Da Capo Press, 1984.

Simms, L. Moody, Jr., ed. "A Louisiana Engineer at the Siege of Vicksburg: Letters of Henry Ginder." *Louisiana History* 8 (Autumn 1967): 371–78.

Simon, John Y. "From Galena to Appomattox: Grant and Washburne." *Journal of the Illinois State Historical Society* 58, no. 2 (Summer 1965): 165–89.

Simpson, Brooks D. *Let Us Have Peace: Ulysses S. Grant and the Politics of War and Reconstruction.* Chapel Hill: University of North Carolina, 1991.

———. *Ulysses S. Grant: Triumph over Adversity.* New York: Houghton Mifflin, 2000.

Simpson, Harold. *Hood's Texas Brigade: Lee's Grenadier Guard.* Waco: Texian Press, 1970.

Smith, John D., ed. *Black Soldiers in Blue: African American Troops in the Civil War Era.* Chapel Hill: University of North Carolina Press, 2002.

———. "Let Us All Be Grateful That We Have Colored Troops That Will Fight." In Smith, *Black Soldiers in Blue*, 1–77.

Smith, Timothy B. *Champion Hill: Decisive Battle for Vicksburg.* 2nd ed. New York: Savas Beatie, 2006.

———. *Grant Invades Tennessee: The 1862 Battles for Forts Henry and Donelson.* Lawrence: University Press of Kansas, 2016.

———. "Meridian Campaign." In *Encyclopedia of the American Civil War: A Political, Social, and Military History*, edited by David S. and Jeanne T. Heidler, 3:1323–24. Santa Barbara, CA: ABC-CLIO, 2000.

———. *The Siege of Vicksburg: Climax of the Campaign to Open the Mississippi River, May 23–July 4, 1863.* Lawrence: University Press of Kansas, 2021.

———. *The Union Assaults at Vicksburg: Grant Attacks Pemberton, May 17–22, 1863.* Lawrence: University Press of Kansas, 2020.

———. *The Untold Story of Shiloh: The Battle and the Battlefield.* Knoxville: University of Tennessee Press, 2006.

Sodergren, Steven E. "'Exposing False History': The Voice of the Union Veteran in the Pages of the *National Tribune*." In Jordan and Rothera, *The War Went On*, 137–56.

Solonick, Justin S. "Andrew Hickenlooper and the Vicksburg Mines." In Woodworth and Grear, *Vicksburg Besieged*, 80–110.

Stabler, Scott L., and Martin J. Hershock. "'Standing on the Banks': African American Troops in the Vicksburg Campaign." In Woodworth and Grear, *Vicksburg Besieged*, 27–48.

State of Illinois. *Illinois Military Units in the Civil War.* Springfield: Civil War Centennial Commission of Illinois, 1962.

Steplyk, Jonathan M. "Plying the Deadly Trade: The Sharpshooters' War at the Siege of Vicksburg." In Woodworth and Grear, *Vicksburg Besieged*, 49–68.

Strong, William E. "The Campaign against Vicksburg." In *Military Essays and*

Recollections: Papers Read before the Commanders of the State of Illinois, Military Order of the Loyal Legion of the Unites States, 2:313–54. 1894. Reprint, Wilmington, NC: Broadfoot, 1992.

Sword, Wiley. *Shiloh: Bloody April*. 1974. Reprint, Dayton: Morningside, 1988.

Teters, Kristopher A. *Practical Liberators: Union Officers in the Western Theater during the Civil War*. Chapel Hill: University of North Carolina Press, 2018.

Towne, Stephen E. *Surveillance and Spies in the Civil War: Exposing Confederate Conspiracies in America's Heartland*. Athens: Ohio University Press, 2015.

Trudeau, Noah Andre. "Stumbling in Sherman's Path." HistoryNet. Accessed August 16, 2021. http://www.historynet.com/shermans-march-to-the-sea.

Tucker, Phillip Thomas. *The South's Finest: The First Missouri Confederate Brigade from Pea Ridge to Vicksburg*. Shippensburg, PA: White Mane, 1991.

Tuthill, Richard S. "An Artilleryman's Recollections of the Battle of Atlanta." In *Military Essays and Recollections: Papers Read before the Commandery of the State of Illinois, Military Order of the Loyal Legion of the United States*, 1:293–310. 1891. Reprint, Wilmington, NC: Broadfoot, 1992.

Ural, Susannah. *Hood's Texas Brigade: The Soldiers and Families of the Confederacy's Most Celebrated Unit*. Baton Rouge: Louisiana State University Press, 2017.

Vinovskis, Maris A. "Have Social Historians Lost the Civil War? Some Preliminary Demographic Speculations." In *Towards a Social History of the American Civil War*, edited by Maris A. Vinovskis, 1–30. New York: Cambridge University Press, 1990.

Waterloo, Stanley. *Illinois at Shiloh; Report of the Shiloh Battlefield Commission and Ceremonies at the Dedication of the Monuments Erected to Mark the Positions of the Illinois Commands Engaged in the Battle; The Story of the Battle*. 1904. Reprint, London: Forgotten Books, 2018.

Welcher, Frank J. *The Union Army, 1861–1865: Organization and Operations*. 2 vols. Bloomington: Indiana University Press, 1993.

Wesley, Timothy W. *The Politics of Faith during the Civil War*. Baton Rouge: Louisiana State University Press, 2013

White, Jonathan W. *Emancipation, the Union Army, and the Reelection of Abraham Lincoln*. Baton Rouge: Louisiana State University Press, 2014.

Wiley, Bell I. *The Life of Billy Yank: The Common Soldier of the Union*. 1952. Reprint, Baton Rouge: Louisiana State University Press, 1994.

Winschel, Terrence J. *Triumph and Defeat: The Vicksburg Campaign*. New York: Savas Beatie, 2006.

Winter, James F. *Baptism by Toilet Water*. Maitland, FL: Xulon Press, 2019.

Woodworth, Steven E. "The First Capture and Occupation of Jackson, Mississippi." In Woodworth and Grear, *The Vicksburg Campaign*, 96–115.

———. "Nights at Vicksburg." In Woodworth and Grear, *Vicksburg Besieged*, 69–79.

———. *Nothing but Victory: The Army of the Tennessee, 1861–1865.* New York: Alfred A. Knopf, 2005.

Woodworth, Steven E., and Charles D. Grear, eds. *Vicksburg Besieged.* Carbondale: Southern Illinois University Press, 2020.

———. *The Vicksburg Campaign, March 29–May 18, 1863.* Carbondale: Southern Illinois University Press, 2013.

Index

Italicized page numbers indicate figures;
bold page numbers refer to tables.

Thomas B. Mack taught for several years at Dallas College at El Centro. His research focus is the Civil War soldier, whether Union or Confederate, and he explores soldiers' collective wartime and postwar experiences though writing modern regimental studies.

ENGAGING
the
CIVIL WAR

Engaging the Civil War, a series founded by the historians at the blog Emerging Civil War (www.emergingcivilwar.com), adopts the sensibility and accessibility of public history while adhering to the standards of academic scholarship. To engage readers and bring them to a new understanding of America's great story, series authors draw on insights they gained while working with the public—walking the ground where history happened at battlefields and historic sites, talking with visitors in museums, and educating students in classrooms. With fresh perspectives, field-tested ideas, and in-depth research, volumes in the series connect readers with the story of the Civil War in ways that make history meaningful to them while underscoring the continued relevance of the war, its causes, and its effects. All Americans can claim the Civil War as part of their history. This series, which was cofounded by Chris Mackowski and Kristopher D. White, helps them engage with it.

Chris Mackowski and Brian Matthew Jordan, Series Editors

emergingcivilwar@gmail.com

Other books in Engaging the Civil War

Imagining Wild Bill: James Butler Hickok in War, Media, and Memory
Paul Ashdown and Edward Caudill

*The Bonds of War: A Story of Immigrants and Esprit de
Corps in Company C, 96th Illinois Volunteer Infantry*
Diana L. Dretske

Matchless Organization: The Confederate Army Medical Department
Guy R. Hasegawa

*The Spirits of Bad Men Made Perfect: The Life and Diary
of Confederate Artillerist William Ellis Jones*
Constance Hall Jones

Entertaining History: The Civil War in Literature, Film, and Song
Edited by Chris Mackowski

Turning Points of the American Civil War
Edited by Chris Mackowski and Kristopher D. White

*Without Concealment, Without Compromise: The
Courageous Lives of Black Civil War Surgeons*
Jill L. Newmark

*Where Valor Proudly Sleeps: A History of Fredericksburg
National Cemetery, 1866–1933*
Donald C. Pfanz